John Pinkerton, William Musham Metcalfe

Ancient Lives of Scottish Saints

John Pinkerton, William Musham Metcalfe

Ancient Lives of Scottish Saints

ISBN/EAN: 9783744642170

Printed in Europe, USA, Canada, Australia, Japan

Cover: Foto ©ninafisch / pixelio.de

More available books at **www.hansebooks.com**

ANCIENT

Lives of Scottish Saints

TRANSLATED BY

W. M. METCALFE, D.D.

With an Introduction

PAISLEY:
ALEXANDER GARDNER
Publisher to Her Majesty the Queen

MDCCCXCV.

The Impression of this Edition consists of Sixty-five Copies, of which this is No.

CONTENTS.

	PAGE
INTRODUCTION,	ix.
S. NINIAN BY AILRED OF RIEVAUX,	1
S. COLUMBA BY CUIMINE THE FAIR,	29
S. COLUMBA BY ADAMNAN,	46
S. KENTIGERN BY JOCELIN, A MONK OF FURNESS,	175
S. SERVANUS,	281
S. MARGARET, QUEEN OF SCOTLAND, BY TURGOT,	295
S. MAGNUS,	323
INDEX,	367

ERRATA.

Page 51, line 11 from bottom, for "thing" read "things."
,, 142, ,, 6 ,, ,, "of hewn," etc., read "hewn out of pine and oak trees."
,, 161, ,, 9 from top, for "Vignous" read "Virgnous."
,, 161, ,, 14 ,, ,, "Vignous" read "Virgnous."
,, 251, ,, 22 ,, ,, "opprobium" read "opprobrium."
,, 283, ,, 20 ,, ,, "dragon" read "drake."

INTRODUCTION.

THE following pages contain a translation of the principal Lives in the new and enlarged edition of Pinkerton's *Vitæ Antiquæ Sanctorum Scotiæ*, which was issued some years ago.* Two of them—that of S. Columba by Cuimine the Fair, and the Life or Legend of S. Servanus—are, so far as I can make out, here published in English for the first time. The pieces in the collection just referred to which are not here translated are either passed over entirely or reserved for another possible volume in which may be included translations of Ancient Lives of other of the Scottish saints.

All through, my endeavour has been to keep as near to the original text as possible, and to make the translation as accurate a reflection of the different styles of the various authors as my own skill in translating and the idioms of modern English would allow. While making the translations I have consulted such other translations as were accessible to me, and have frequently been indebted to them for what has seemed to me a better rendering than my own. The translation of the Magnus Life was made during my summer vacation in 1890, but while the sheets were passing through the press, I have had the advantage of comparing them with Sir George Dasent's recently published translations of the Greater and Lesser Magnus Sagas. By altering the position of the chapters taken by Jonæus from the Lesser Saga, and by adding several paragraphs to them from the same source, I have tried to make this Life more full, continuous, and complete, and have included in it the narrative given in the Lesser Saga of the foundation of Kirkwall Cathedral by Rognvald Kali.

---

* Pinkerton's *Lives of the Scottish Saints*, 2 vols., 8vo. Paisley, 1889.

INTRODUCTION.

For an account of the Authors of the Lives I must refer the reader to the Introduction in the first volume of the Latin text.

All that has hitherto been said, or, as Dr. Whitely Stokes remarks, "one may almost say, all that *can* be said," as to the value of Lives of Saints for political and social history has been summed up in a remarkable passage by the late M. Fustel de Coulanges, in his volume entitled *La Monarchie Franque* (pp. 9-12). As he there points out, to a certain extent the Lives of the Saints are history. At the time many of them were written, the rules for canonisation had not been regularly determined ; the diocese canonised of its own accord its bishop, and the convent its abbot. To write the Lives of these was therefore a necessity. That they were not written as historical works is certain. Nor is it exactly correct to say that they were written merely for the edification of the faithful. They were composed rather for the purpose of demonstrating the sanctity of those whose lives they record, and of setting forth their worth as saints. Like the legend, the biography was explanatory of the relics which the convent possessed, and on account of which it derived a considerable revenue. To the biography was added a narrative of the miracles which the saint did both before and after his death. Generally speaking, the biography of a saint was written by one of his disciples or by one who had known him, or at least from the testimony of those who had been personally acquainted with him or with those who knew him. The cases in which these first or original biographies have come down to us are extremely few. As time went on they were copied and re-copied, additions and omissions were made, and a number of them were translated out of the vernacular into Latin, or from Latin into the vernacular. All this makes it extremely difficult, if not, in many instances, impossible to tell what was in the primitive text. Nevertheless, even as they have survived, they are of great value. The main object of the biographer was generally to pronounce a panegyric, still it is none the less true that he has described the life of an individual, and by comparing a number of these biographies one with the other, it is possible to tell with considerable certainty what the lives of these individuals were. That the author was not altogether an inventor is certain. If he added some virtues to the subject of his biography, he did not imagine the little details of his life. The habits and customs he describes were actually in vogue. In every miracle he narrates, that which interests us is not the miracle itself, but the details connected with it, the man for whom the miracle was wrought, his physiognomy, his civil state, his social condition, his conduct. It is evident, therefore, that these biographies are capable of furnishing more or less information not only as to the social condition of a people, but also as to their institutions. They may contain errors as to dates, proper names may be transposed, and even a number of facts may have been altered so as to suit the preconceptions of the authors, but this, though it would undoubtedly have been better had they been in all respects correct, is of small consequence. That for which the Lives of the Saints are valuable is the indications they contain of the life of the times to which they belong, and those general and permanent facts which the biographer had no interest in altering. He might invent a miracle, but not the circumstances connected with it. " I may doubt, for example," says M. Fustel de Coulanges, whose words I have been to some extent abridging, "that S. Amand wrought a miracle in order to save a criminal condemned to death, but I am assured by the narrative that sentence of death was pronounced, and I accept as correct the procedure which is there described. On these points the author was bound to be accurate, otherwise his contemporaries would not have believed his miracle. It is thus that the Lives of the Saints instruct us respecting the manners of men, the general character of the life of their times, the judicial practices, the administration and the government."

Of the seven Lives here translated, one—Turgot's Life of S. Margaret—is undoubtedly primitive. It is the only ancient Life of that Saint in existence, with the exception of a shorter one, printed by Surius (1618), which is evidently an abridgement of it. Cuimine's Life of S. Columba is the oldest Life of the Apostle of the Northern Picts which we possess, and must have been written within sixty years of his death (597), but whether it is the primitive Life is somewhat doubtful. Adamnan mentions other writings as among his sources of information, and cites an incident (Bk. III., c. 23, p. 170), which he says he found in a writing, and of which no mention is made by Cuimine (*ob.* 669). It may be, however, that these writings were not biographies, but such works as the Amhra, or panegyric, composed by a contemporary of S. Columba, or narratives of particular incidents in the life of the Saint. Adamnan's own Life of S. Columba consists of Cuimine's work, which he has incorporated almost verbatim, with very considerable additions. For these he was indebted to the traditions handed down by his predecessors in office as President of Iona (679-704), to various writings, and to the testimony of certain trustworthy witnesses who had been acquainted with the Saint, or had derived their information from those who were, or had been, his contemporaries. Three of the Lives are translations with additions. From the statements in the Prologues to the Lives of SS. Ninian and Kentigern, it is evident that both Ailred and Jocelin made use of older Lives, and the inference is that they were written in the Celtic tongue. These they seem to have translated and expanded with the help of the stories and traditions they found floating about among the people. The Life of S. Magnus, on the other hand, was originally written in Latin by a certain Master Robert, who seems to have been an Orkneyman. From Latin it was translated into Icelandic. Originally it would seem to have been used as a homily or sermon. The rhetorical and hortatory passages in the Greater Saga are evidently from the hand of Master Robert, but how much more, or who was the Icelandic editor, is unknown. Lastly, the Life of S. Servanus, though curious, is for the most part fiction, and was evidently written to extol the virtues and greatness of the Saint. If there is any truth in the narrative of his intercourse with Adamnan, he was evidently not the S. Servanus referred to in the Life of S. Kentigern, but must have lived at a later period. All the Lives with a single exception—that of S. Margaret—abound in miracles. For the most part they are miracles of healing, though a number of

INTRODUCTION. xiii.

them are miracles wrought on nature. The miracles themselves, as M. Fustel de Coulanges observes, may be nothing, but the details which surround them are authentic, and are therefore of value as to the social condition of the inhabitants of Great Britain and Ireland, and of their religious tenets and practices.

In the following notes, which do not profess to be exhaustive, I follow in a measure the arrangement adopted by Dr. Whitley Stokes in his *Tripartite Life of S. Patrick*, and in his *Lives of the Saints from the Book of Lismore*.

References to the phenomena of nature are fairly numerous. Most of them, however, are to storms and tempests, one of which is said to have lasted three days and three nights, 45, 171.* Mention is made of the whirlpool of Brecan, 63, 107; of a sudden and unexpected wave or commotion of the sea, 346; of certain strange phenomena witnessed by Cormac and his companions in the Northern Seas, 139; of a pillar of light which suddenly appeared during the night on which S. Columba died, 170; of a pestilential cloud, 100; of the Plague, 144; of rain and drought, 47, 141; of the destruction of a city in Italy and its inhabitants apparently by the eruption of a volcano, 77; of the tides, 197; and of a local storm, 116.

Among animals, birds, fishes, etc., the following are mentioned: oxen, 18, 200; cows, 46, 110, 113, 114, 187; sheep, 17, 88; lambs, 73; goats, 39; horse, 167, 217; dog (house), 39, 129; hounds, 46, 116, 257; deer, 129, etc.; wild boar, 119, (Skye), 229; wolf, 219, 362, 363; swine, 116, 291; crane, 93; redbreast, 189; crow, 39, 129; whale, 71; seal, 88; salmon, 39, 112, 129; aquatic monsters, 71, 119, 139; serpents, 120, 165; dragon, 292. Among animal products, we have hides, 21, 121, 186; venison, 38, 128; milk, 110, 111, 263; ivory (carved), 132; horn, 75; mare's flesh, 73.

The minerals referred to are: iron, 121, 152, 220; bronze, 94; silver, 305, 360; gold, 301, 305, 315; salt, 103; coal, 234.

Trees and plants:—oak, 142, 143; hazel, 192; apple, 99, 288; pine, 142; rushes, 136; mandrake, 283. The fruits and

---

* The numbers refer to the pages following.

cereals are:—apples, 99, 125; nuts, 125; mulberries, 261. Mention is made of wheat, 220, barley, 100, and reference is frequently made to them as corn. Table vegetables are spoken of and leeks are mentioned, 16. At the monastery in Iona there was a gardener, 70, as also at Whithorn, 16.

Turning now to man, his bodily needs and his means of supplying them—for food he had the flesh of oxen, 17, 86; sheep, 17, 72, 88, 291; deer, 39, 128; swine, 116, 291; also horse-flesh, 73; probably goats' flesh, 39; salmon, 39, 112; various other kinds of fish, 38, 112; game, 38; milk, 110, 206; butter, 206; cheese, 206, 263; pot herbs, 16; leeks, *ibid.*; also mulberries, 261; and bread, 88; made from wheat probably, 220, and barley, 88, 110. His drinks were besides water, milk, 110, 206; wine, 206, 289, though this is chiefly mentioned in connection with the celebration of the Mass, ale, 359.

Clothing:—tunic, 47, 119, 142; cowl, 117; cloak, 118; shoe, 108; kirtle, 350; and a coat with fringes, 47, are the only articles of clothing specifically mentioned. S. Kentigern's, however, are described, 207. Among them was a garment of rough hair-cloth worn next to the skin, and over this another of leather "tied on like a fisherman's." As a rule articles of clothing are referred to in the Lives in general terms. The clerical garb is mentioned, but not further described, 82.

Coal is mentioned as fuel, 234. Wood appears to have been generally used.

As shelters, or places for dwelling in, he had huts, 17, 81; houses, 32. Roofs are mentioned, 36, 42; also doors, 38, 81, 128, which were apparently made of wood, 28, and furnished with key-holes, 160, keys, 45, 128, and bolts, *ibid*. The huts and houses were made of planks, 75, 78, of wattles, 99, and were easily consumed, 82.

Furniture is mentioned generally, 92; specific articles are: bed (straw), 43, 103, 168, 289, 207; box, 104; cushion, 46, 56; pillow, 168, 207; ladle, 70; wooden griddle, 73; pail, 111; glass cup, 124; leathern milk-vessel, 130; water pot, 75; satchel for holding books, 104; spit, 116; lamps, 169, 191; axe, 113; knife, 93, 121; table, 186.

Connected with the farm we have sowing and reaping, 84;

INTRODUCTION. xv.

the threshing floor, 113 ; barn, 222 ; plough, 218 ; ploughing, *ibid.* ; cart, 165 ; fences, 52 ; hedges, 17 ; dykes, *ibid.* ; wheels, axle, linch-pin, 141 ; tools (iron), 121.

The following trades or occupations are mentioned : smith, 153, 263 ; gardener, 16 ; baker, 154 ; shepherd, 187 ; fisherman, *ibid.* ; cook, 194 ; rush-gatherer, 136 ; jester, 261. At Iona seals were reared, 88.

As beasts of burden, oxen, 200 ; and horses, 167, were used.

The usual mode of travelling by land was on foot, 217 ; but carts drawn by oxen or horses were employed, 140, 141, 165, 200 ; horses were also used for riding, 125. At sea various kinds of boats or vessels were in use. Some were made of wicker work covered with ox-hides, 121, 186 ; others were made of pinewood or oak, 142. The names for them were : *navis* (ship), 107 ; *barca* (bark), 77 ; *navicula* (boat), 81 ; *navis oneraria* (freight ship), 99 ; *alnus* (boat), 119 ; *caupallus* (coble), *ibid.* ; *cymba, symbulla* (vessel, skiff), 126, 127 ; *longa navis* (long boat), 140 ; *scaphis* (skiff), 143 ; *curuca* (curach), *ibid.* Some of the vessels were hollowed trunks of trees, 142. They were propelled by sails, *passim* in Adamnan ; and oars, 119, 143, 186.

The ailments from which men suffered were :—fevers, 254 ; ophthalmia, 103 ; blindness, 12, 27, 106, 243 ; deafness, 253 ; dumbness, 254 ; paralysis, *ibid.* ; bleeding at the nose, 112 ; scab, 26 ; closing of veins and arteries, *ibid.* ; insanity, 18, 243, 254 ; leprosy, 27, 106, 212, 243, 254, 358 ; twisted joints, 25, 359 ; swelling in the feet, 225 ; hereditary gout, *ibid.* ; incurable diseases, 243 ; plagues, 145 ; weariness, 84.

The means of healing were :—The prayers of Saints, which were sometimes efficacious to restore the dead, 18, 46, 103, 122 ; praying at the tombs of Saints, 27, 359 ; Saint's touch, 26, 103, 112, 358; washing in water consecrated by a Saint, 27, or in which a Saint had washed, 106, or washing, drinking, or being sprinkled with water in which something blessed by a Saint had been placed, as a white stone, 146, 55, bread, 110, a pinewood box, 112, a lump of salt, 103 ; mouthfuls of food or drink given or received, 254 ; touching the hem of a Saint's garment, 254 ; his shadow, *ibid.* ; a Saint's spiritual presence,

84; vows to Saints. S. Magnus in his apparitions to the diseased is represented as stroking or passing his hand over the part affected, 358.

Physicians are mentioned, 27, 181; the drugs named are litargion, 181; mandrake, 283.

At burial the corpse was wrapped in white linen cloths, 171, placed in a coffin, *ibid.*, and borne by men with singing to the grave, *ibid.*, or placed on a cart or bier drawn by two unbroken oxen, 200. The place of burial was near or in a church, before the altar, 24, 171, 321; where the oxen stopped, 200, or in a cemetery, 201. The corpse was sometimes placed in a stone coffin, 24. The lid of the coffin was sometimes inscribed, 196.

Obsequies were observed which lasted, in the case of S. Columba, three days and three nights, 171.

Turning now to the other side of human life, S. Ninian relieved the tedium of his journeys with reading, 20. S. Serf amused himself with a redbreast, 190; S. Columba apparently with writing, 47, 75; other modes of amusement mentioned are joking and jesting, 261; feasting, 353; gossiping and tale-telling, 19; gambling, 392. King Rederech maintained a jester, 261.

Hunting, 46, 116, 119, 257, and fishing by night as well as by day, 170, are mentioned, but these were prosecuted probably more from necessity than for amusement.

The literature referred to consists chiefly of portions of the Sacred Scriptures, the Psalter and the Four Gospels, 20, 75, 315; and Service Books, 149, 313. Songs composed in Irish in praise of S. Columba are mentioned, 57. The Psalter and Gospels were copied at Iona, 75. When the copyist had finished, his writing was examined and corrected by another, 75. Books were preserved in satchels of leather, which were secured with straps and hung upon the wall. Sometimes both the coverings and the books themselves were elaborately ornamented and adorned with jewels and gold, 315; see the description of the case of the Book of Armagh, Reeves' *Columba*, p. 115, note c., and Miss Stokes' *Early Christian Art in Ireland*.

The permanent arts mentioned or referred to, are writing,

carving, embroidery, jewel work, work in gold and silver, architecture, but very little light is thrown upon them. The art of the copyist was raised to a high pitch of excellence, among the Irish, and S. Columba is reckoned among the most expert. Nothing is said of this, however, in the Lives following. Embroidery was done under the direction of Queen Margaret, 302. Among the articles referred to are copes, chasubles, stoles, altar-cloths, and other priestly vestments, *ibid.* A cross with the image of the Saviour upon it covered with a vestment of purest gold and silver, and studded with gems, and other Church ornaments are spoken of, as well as vessels of solid and pure gold for the altar, *ibid.*, and vessels of gold or silver, or with gold and silver plated, 305. Precious stones are frequently mentioned, but not under specific names.

The notices of architecture are scanty. We read of a church built of stone, and described as the only stone church in Britain, 11. The workmen came from Tours, 10. For the rest, churches were built of wood and wattles, 143, 230, The cathedrals at Kirkwall and Dunfermline, however, which belong to a later date, were built of stone. Monasteries also were built of wood and wattles, 143, 230. Withes were gathered for building and repairing the guest chamber, 99. They were woven in between upright stakes, 104. The churches had side-chambers or side-chapels or oratories attached to them, 161. The church, president's hut, the huts of the monks, the refectory, kitchen, probably a chamber for preserving the books, tablets, styles, pens and inkhorns, the hospital, guest-house, workshop, and an open court, were surrounded by an enclosure, outside of which stood the barns, kiln, cow-houses, pond, and mill-stream.

Of the transitory arts, music is the only one referred to, and of that only the singing of songs, 57, and the chanting of the services of the church, 155, and the singing of the Angelic Choir, 187, are mentioned. No musical instrument is named, unless the bell be reckoned one.

The light thrown upon the religion of the period is not new, but a few points may be noted. The Trinity is spoken of, 258, 52; God is described as "our Redeemer and Creator," 325;

Christ as "the Only Begotten of the Eternal," 52; "our Nazarene Jesus Christ," 179, "the Brightness of the Eternal Light," "the Sun of Righteousness," 180; the Virgin Mary as "the Star of Virginity," "the Virgin Mother," 180. Prayers are offered to her, 185.

Angels are frequently mentioned, but none of them are named. They meet souls and carry them to heaven, 151. They haunt S. Columba, 157, and accompany him on his way, 32, 148. One flies from Iona to Ireland quicker than lightning to the help and deliverance of a monk who was falling from the roof of a house, 157. When in the island of Eilean-na-naoimh, S. Columba is visited by one who instructs him to ordain Aidan king, and when he refuses, smites him with a scourge, 149.

Demons or evil spirits occur frequently. They are seen carrying the souls of the wicked to hell, 56. They fight against S. Columba with iron darts, 152. The same Saint drives one away which is lurking in a milk-pail. People were believed to be possessed by them.

Antichrist and Doomsday, heaven and hell, are mentioned. There is no mention of Purgatory. The souls of men are carried or go straight to heaven or hell.

The Scriptures were studied by Ninian, 9, Columba, 75, Baithene, *ibid.*, Kentigern, 218, Margaret, 304, Magnus, 327. Adamnan, Ailred and Jocelin, and Master Robert show a very considerable acquaintance with the sacred writings.

The Religious Rites referred to are Baptism, the Eucharist, Ordination. Baptism was performed with water, 106, and was administered to adults, sometimes to a whole family, 123, 156, sometimes just before death, 156, 81, sometimes to children, 106, who were clad during the rite in white, 7. The Eucharist was celebrated with wine mixed with water, and bread, 91, on the Lord's day and on Saints' days, 144, 154, when all labour was suspended and the monks received some additions to their food, 155. The festivals began after sunset on the preceding day, 144, 154, 166, 359. By the time of Queen Margaret certain irregular practices had crept into the celebration of the rite, and the Lord's day was desecrated, 309. Ordination of

INTRODUCTION. xix.

deacons, presbyters, and bishops, is referred to; that of bishops is described, 9, 304. When the Angel instructed S. Columba to ordain Aidan king, he showed him a phantasm of the book of the ritual, 149.

In the earlier Lives matrimony is referred to, but not as a sacrament. Penance is there spoken of in the same way. The penitent was required to confess in the presence of all, and generally on bended knees, 79, 87, and to promise amendment, 96. A more or less extended period of discipline was sometimes enjoined, 74, 131.

Confirmation and Extreme Unction are not in the Earlier Lives referred to.

To the symbol of the Cross and to the signing of the Cross extraordinary efficacy was assigned. The sign of it was considered effectual to banish demons, 110, 111, to prostrate a wild beast, 119, to restrain a river monster, 120, to endow a pebble and other substances with healing virtue, 101, 103, 112, 124, to unlock doors, 127. It was customary before milking to make the sign of the Cross over the pail, 110, and to cross tools before using them, 121. At sea the cruciform arrangement of the mast and yards was regarded as conducive to a favourable voyage, 143. Numerous crosses were erected in various parts, 91, 167, 229, 269.

Prayer is continually mentioned, as also is fasting. The order of prayer is referred to, 155. Kentigern carried his Manual in his hand, 207. The references to the Service Books in the Life of S. Margaret are numerous. S. Columba was wont to retire into the Church, 161, or to some private place, 157, for prayer. S. Kentigern retired during Lent, 211. Instances of the miraculous effects of prayer are given, 18, 46, 103, 122.

Fasting is frequently mentioned. For the austerities of S. Columba see 54, of S. Kentigern, 206-8, of S. Margaret, 314, of S. Magnus, 338. In the Life of the last the practice of making religious vows or promises is frequently mentioned.

Pilgrimages were made to Iona, 80, 131, Rome, 8, 237, Jerusalem, 354, the Jordan, in which it was customary for the palmers to bathe, 354, St. Andrews, 312, and other sacred places, 342.

The Relics spoken of are those of SS. Ninian and Magnus. Mention is made of the Black Rood possessed by Queen Margaret, 319, and of the Staff of Kentigern, 268. The clothes of S. Columba and the books written with his own hand were regarded with extraordinary reverence, and on one occasion the exhibition of them was supposed to have had the effect of obtaining a copious rain, 142. For the miracles wrought at the shrines of SS. Ninian and Magnus, see 25, 28, and 358.

Idolatry or paganism is often referred to, but usually in the most general terms. For references to magic, sorcery and spaecraft, see 111, 126, 329-330. By making a circle with his staff S. Ninian is said to have confined a herd of cattle within it and to have rendered it impossible for men who had passed in to the circle to escape from it. The singing of songs in commemoration of S. Columba was supposed to have had the effect of protecting a number of men against the assaults of their enemies, 57.

Family Relations:—In the older Lives there are indications that marriage of some kind existed. Apparently it was regarded as dissoluble, 137. Concubinage was practised, 217. The practice of fosterage is referred to. Broichan, the Druid, is spoken of as the foster-father of King Brude, 125. Cruithnechan was the foster-father of S. Columba, 147. A man might bind himself to another as a slave for a certain period, 133, and captives taken in war were made slaves, 124. As a sign of their condition they wore a girdle, 133. This was unloosed on their being set free, *ibid.*, which they could be either with or without recompense, 124. Queen Margaret was in the habit of redeeming captives, 312.

Hospitality was freely given in the monasteries. Each had a guest-house. On the guest's arrival water was provided for the washing of his feet, 63, and special provision was made for his maintenance, *ibid*. He was admitted by or without the permission of the abbot, 59. The period of guesting seems to

INTRODUCTION.

have been three nights (*Revue Celtique*, ix. 495). Queen Margaret set up a guest-house on each side of the Forth, 312.

In the Civil State we have the following orders:—Bretwalda, King, Earl (Orkney and Wales), noble, franklin (Orkney), peasant, beggar, who carried a wallet, 113. The royal dignity in Dalriada descended according to the Irish law of Tanistry (Skene, *Celtic Scotland*, i. 230). The King and Earl were accompanied by their body-guard or retinue. Queen Margaret altered the Court arrangements and surrounded the King with greater state, 305.

Of social observances those only are indicated which were practised in the monasteries.

The crimes mentioned are arson, 82, and theft, 88 ; man-slaying, 89, murder, 68, incest, 74, fornication. For the law respecting the last see 182. Among vices, prostitution, 86, indolence and gossiping, 19, and hypocrisy, 214, are mentioned.

Military affairs do not, as might be expected, occupy much space in the Lives. Still, the following wars and battles are mentioned or referred to:—The battle of Cooldrevny, fought in 561, and said to have been one of the causes leading to S. Columba's withdrawal to Iona, 53 ; Hevenfeld, in which Oswald defeated and slew Cadwalla (634), and after which he was proclaimed Bretwalda, 57 ; Ondemone (563), between the Dalriadians and the Northern Hy Neill, 64 ; of the Miathi, which, according to Tighernach, was fought in 596 at Chircinn, probably the modern Kirkintilloch, 65 ; Arderydd ? (c. 573), 69 ; Roth (637), 150; the battle in which Malcolm Canmore was slain (Nov. 13, 1093), 319 ; Stamford Bridge, (1066), 328 ; Magnus Bareleg's expedition (1098).

Fortresses are mentioned, 85, 94, 125. The weapons spoken of are the spear, dart, sword, arrow. Echoid Laib, a Pictish King, is said to have escaped when vanquished in battle, riding in a chariot, 65. Nothing is said of the mode of fighting.

The kinds of ecclesiastics mentioned are the bishops, presbyter, deacon. The officers connected with monasteries were the Abbot or President, or *Patronus ;* the Superiors of daughter houses, who were called *praepositi*, Provosts, 79, and received their charge from the President, 91. They were either bishops or presbyters. Besides these there were the scribe, butler, 70; baker, 154; cook, 222; smith, 121; private attendant on the President or Superior, 154; the messenger, 70; gardener, *ibid.;* and the *legati*, expert seaman who had charge of the boats, and appear to have been employed as messengers, 79. The monks under S. Columba appear to have been divided into those who attended to the field work and those who worked within the monastery. On festivals all work was suspended. The monks were summoned by the sound of the bell to the church, where, clad in white, they celebrated the Eucharist. At his own will the abbot would sometimes insert the name of a friend among the names of the Saints. The chief festival was Easter.

The number of monks subject to S. Columba is not given. Its daughter houses were numerous both in Scotland and Ireland. At his monastery in Wales, S. Kentigern is said to have had no fewer than 965 living according to his monastic rule. They were divided into three companies, two of three hundreds each, and one containing the rest. To the three hundred who were illiterate was assigned the duty of tilling the ground and herding the cattle. The other three hundred were occupied within the walls of the monastery, preparing food and building offices. The remaining 365 kept up the services day and night in the Church, 233.

The vestments are alb, 207; cope, chasuble, stole, 302. At Iona the monks when engaged in divine worship were clad in white, 155. White also was the colour of S. Kentigern's alb, 207.

S. Columba, as well as the bishops, founded churches and preached. On two occasions he had to employ the services of an interpreter, 81, 123. SS. Ninian and Kentigern are said to have settled the bounds of parishes, but parochial divisions were not made till much later.

The monastic buildings have already been described. It has to be added that in the church there was an altar; and further that at Iona the monks were frequently summoned by the sound of the bell to services at midnight, at which times they carried lamps.

INTRODUCTION.

The Culdees are mentioned, 218, and perhaps referred to, 309.

In conclusion, I have to record my best thanks to my son, the Rev. W. Metcalfe, B.D., the translator of Paspates' *Great Palace of Constantinople*, for reading the proofs and comparing them with the Latin text; and also to Mr. W. A. Craigie, of St. Andrews University, for reading the proofs of the Magnus Life. To his accurate knowledge of Icelandic and Icelandic literature, I have been greatly indebted.

W. M. M.

March, 1895.

ANCIENT LIVES OF SCOTTISH SAINTS.

LIFE OF NINIAN.

BY

AILRED OF RIEVAUX.

ANCIENT LIVES OF SCOTTISH SAINTS.

LIFE OF NINIAN.

PROLOGUE.

MANY wise men of the past have endeavoured to commit to writing the words, manners, and lives of the Saints, more especially of those who were illustrious in their own day, in order to preserve the example of their more perfect life from oblivion, and perpetuate their memory for the edification of posterity. Those who were distinguished by their ability, copious diction and splendid eloquence did this the more profitably in proportion as they gratified the ears of their hearers with the charms of a graceful style. And even those from whom, by reason of the barbarism in which they lived, the faculty of writing in a graceful and elegant manner was withheld, did not fail, though in a more simple style, to communicate to posterity some account of those who ought to be imitated. Hence it is, that the life of the most holy Ninian, commended to us by the sanctity of his ways and his well-known miracles, was obscured by a barbarous language, and the less it pleased the reader the less it edified him. It has therefore pleased your reverence to lay upon me, insignificant though I am, the task of rescuing the life of this most renowned man, written truthfully enough by my predecessors, but in too barbarous a style, from a rustic dialect, as from darkness, and of bringing it forth into the clear light of the Latin tongue. I esteem your devotion, approve your desire, and applaud your zeal; but I am conscious of my inability, and fear I may only strip him of the coarse garment in which he has hitherto been hid, and not be able to array him in a more comely garb. But since I am unable to refuse that which you enjoin, I shall endeavour to obey your command, preferring that you should deem me incompetent rather than obstinate. For it may be that what incompetence denies, your faith will supply, your prayer obtain, your sanctity secure. He also, for whose honour and love you desire me to do this work, will himself assist your pious vows and aspirations, and aid me in my study and endeavour. Moreover, by his merits you trust that there may be given to me the tongue of the learned and facility of speech. To this must be added your assurance that the clergy and people of your holy Church, who are moved with great affection for this holy one of God, and live beneath his protection, will receive with the greatest reverence whatever I may write, because, as you say, they have unanimously desired that you should assign this work to me. Therefore that which you lay upon me, I undertake, moved indeed by your prayers, but animated by faith; and as far as He who maketh the the tongues of infants eloquent will deign to aid me, I shall endeavour so to temper my style that no offensive rudeness may obscure so high a theme, and that the simplicity of those who are unacquainted with the profuseness of rhetoric may not be defrauded of the desired fruit of my labour by a prolixity of speech more wearisome than eloquent. May the grace of the Saviour breathe upon the undertaking now begun; may He who bestows upon His Saint the virtues whereby he is deemed meet to be held in everlasting remembrance, make us who record them worthy; may He render unto us the reward of our labour, that in the way by which we hasten to our fatherland, his prayer may always be with us: and in the hour of our departure, when we look for the end of the way and the beginning of life, may his consolation be near us, and for the sake of his holy merits may we attain at last to the eternal reward of the good things in heaven.

PREFACE.

Testimony of Bede Concerning Ninian, with the Observations of Ailred.

THE glorious life of the most holy Ninian is commended to us by that same divine authority which from the beginning is acknowledged to have made the holy patriarch Abraham the father of many nations and a prince of the faith predestinated from of old by such an oracle as this: "Get thee out from thy country, and from thy kindred, and from thy father's house unto a land that I will show thee, and I will make of thee a great nation." In like manner the most blessed Ninian, having left the country and home of his father, learned in a foreign land that which he afterwards taught in his own, and was set by the Lord over nations and kingdoms, to overthrow and destroy, to plant and to build. Of this most blessed man, when commending to us in the fewest words the sacred beginnings of his life and the signs of his holiness, the dignity of his office and the fruit of his ministry, his most excellent end and the reward of his labour, the Venerable Bede, in his Ecclesiastical History of his own nation, writes as follows: "In the year of the Incarnation of our Lord, 565, at the time when Justin the Less had, after Justinian, received the government of the Roman Empire, there came to Britain from Ireland a presbyter and abbot, remarkable for his habit and rule, by name Columba, to preach the Word of God in the provinces of the Northern Picts; that is, to those who were separated from the Southern regions by lofty and rugged mountains. For the southern Picts, who have their dwellings among the same mountains, had long before abandoned the error of idolatry and received the faith in the truth at the preaching of the Word by Ninian, a most reverend bishop and a most holy man, of the nation of the Britons, who had been regularly instructed at Rome in the faith and mysteries of the truth, the seat of whose bishopric, dedicated to the Bishop S. Martin, and a remarkable church, where he rests in the body with many saints, is now in the possession of the nation of the Angles. That place which belongs to the province of the Bernicii, is commonly called Ad Candidam Casam (At the White House), because he there built a church of stone, a thing unusual among the Britons." What Bede here briefly narrates, I will now (God willing) more fully set forth.

On the trustworthy authority of so great a writer, we are informed : first, as to the origin of this man, inasmuch as he states that he was of the race of the Britons and was instructed in the rules of faith in the Holy Roman Church ; secondly, as to his office, because he declares that he was a bishop and a preacher of the Word of God ; thirdly, as to the fruit of his labours, because he proves that by his labours the Southern Picts were converted from idolatry to the true faith; and finally, as to his end, inasmuch as he testifies that he rests along with many saints in the Church of S. Martin. But what the Venerable Bede here, as the character of his History seemed to require, appears to have touched upon but briefly, a book of the Life and Miracles of S. Ninian, written in a barbarous tongue, sets forth in greater detail ; which book, never varying from the foundation of this testimony, has recorded after the manner of history, the way in which he made a beginning, how he merited such fruit, and how he attained so worthy an end.

CHAPTER I.

Birth and Education of Ninian.

BLESSED NINIAN was born in an island, which is said to have received its name of Britain from Brutus, among a people of the same name, and of a not ignoble family. The district in which he is supposed to have been born, is on the western side of the island, where the ocean, stretching out as an arm, and making, as it were, on either side two angles, divides the Kingdom of the Scots from the Kingdom of the Angles. This region, until the most recent times, belonged to the Angles, as is proved not only by the records of history but also by the actual memory of individuals, and had a King of its own. S. Ninian's father was a King and by religion a Christian. He was of such faith and merit towards God that he was deemed worthy to have an offspring by whom the things lacking in the faith of his people might be supplied, and by whom a nation of another race, who knew not the sacraments of the faith, might be imbued with the mysteries of our holy religion. Even in his infancy Ninian, being born again by the water of holy baptism, preserved the nuptial robe which he received when clad in white, immaculate, and a conqueror of vices presented it in the presence of Christ. That Holy Spirit whom he first received for his purification, he merited by his most holy life to retain as the enlightener of his holy heart. For while yet a boy, though not with the thoughts of a boy, whatever was contrary to religion, adverse to chastity, opposed to good manners, or at variance with the laws of truth, he, through His guidance, shunned. But whatsoever was of the law of grace, or of good report, whatsoever was of use to man, or acceptable before God, he did not cease to follow with a mind already matured. Happy was he whose delight was in the law of the Lord day and night, who, as a tree planted by rivers of water, brought forth his fruit in due season, when in the vigour of manhood, he strenuously fulfilled that which he had learned with the greatest zeal. His devotion towards the churches was wonderful; wonderful also was his love to the brethren. He was sparing in food, few in words, diligent in reading, and agreeable in manners; but jesting he avoided, and continually subjected the flesh to the spirit. Accordingly, directing his mind to the Holy Scriptures, when he had learned from certain of the more learned men of his own race the rules of Faith according to their way, the young man came, by reason of his quick intelligence, to understand, through the divine inspiration he had gathered from the Scriptures, that there were many things wanting to the perfection of these rules. At this his mind began to be troubled, and not enduring that he should be less than perfect, he was greatly afflicted and sighed; "his heart was hot within him, and while he mused the fire burned."

"And what," he said, "what shall I do? In mine own land I have sought Him whom my soul loveth, and have found Him not. I will arise and compass sea and land; I will seek the truth which my soul loveth. Surely it needeth such toil as this? Was it not said to Peter: 'Thou art Peter, and on this rock will I build my Church, and the gates of Hell shall not prevail against it?' Therefore, in the faith of Peter there is nothing wanting, nothing obscure, nothing imperfect, nothing against which false doctrine, nor perverse opinions, any more than the gates of Hell, can prevail. And where is the faith of Peter but in the See of Peter? Thither, thither must I go, that going out from my country, and from my kindred, and from my father's house, I may be deemed meet in the land of vision to behold the will of the Lord, and to be sheltered in His temple. The false prosperity of the age smiles upon me, the vanity of the world entices me, the love of kindred allures me, toil and the weariness of the flesh deter me. 'But he who loveth father and mother more than me,' saith the Lord, 'is not worthy of me.' 'And he who taketh not up his cross and followeth me is not worthy of me.' I have learned, moreover, that they who despise the royal court shall attain to the kingdom of heaven." Wherefore animated by the impulse of the Holy Spirit, spurning riches, and treading down all earthly affections, this noble youth set out on his pilgrimage, crossed the Britannic sea, and entering Italy by the Gallican Alps, arrived, after a prosperous journey, at the city of Rome.

CHAPTER II.

He arrives at Rome and is consecrated Bishop by the Pope. His Intercourse with S. Martin and his Return to his Native Land.

HAVING arrived at Rome, this most blessed young man, when he had shed tears, the signs of his devotion, before the sacred relics of the Apostles, and commended the desire of his heart with many prayers to their protection, presented himself before the Bishop of the Supreme See, by whom, when he had explained the reason of his journey, his devotion was accepted, and he himself received into the greatest affection and treated as a son. Soon the Pope placed him under teachers of the truth, to be instructed in the disciplines of the faith and in the sound doctrines of Scripture. But the young man, full of God, observed that he had not laboured in vain, nor to no purpose; he learnt, also, that he and many of his countrymen had been imbued by unskilful teachers with many things contrary to sound doctrine. Therefore with all eagerness, with open mouth, receiving the word of God, like a bee, he formed for himself the honeycombs of wisdom by arguments drawn from the opinions of different teachers, as from flowers of many kinds. And hiding them in the recesses of his heart, he preserved them to be inwardly digested, and afterwards brought forward for the instruction of his own inner man, and for the comfort of many others. Truly, it was a worthy recompense, that he who for love of truth despised country, wealth, and pleasures, brought, as I may say, into the secret chambers of the truth and admitted to the very treasuries of wisdom and knowledge, should receive for things carnal things spiritual, for things earthly things heavenly, and for benefits temporal eternal blessings. Meantime, being spoken of by all as chaste in body, prudent in mind, sagacious in counsel, and circumspect in every word and deed, it came to pass that he rose to the favour and friendship of the Supreme Pontiff himself.

Accordingly, having lived after a praiseworthy manner for many years in the City, and having been sufficiently instructed in the Sacred Scriptures, he attained to the height of virtue, and, borne on the wings of love, was raised to the contemplation of celestial things. Then the Roman Pontiff hearing that some in the western parts of Britain had not yet received the faith of our Saviour, and that others had heard the word of the Gospel either from heretics or from men insufficiently acquainted with the law of God, and moved by the Spirit of God, did, with his own hands, consecrate the said man of God to the Episcopate, and, having bestowed upon him his benediction, appointed him an Apostle to the promised people.

There flourished at this time the most blessed Martin Bishop of the city of Tours, whose life, resplendent with miracles, and already described by that most learned and holy man, Sulpicius, had illumined the whole world. When returning, therefore, from the city, Ninian, full of the Spirit of God, was touched with the desire of seeing him, and turned aside to the city of Tours. With what joy, devotion, and affection he was received, who shall easily tell? For verily by grace, as of prophetic illumination, the virtue of the new Bishop was not hid from the holy Bishop of Tours. God having revealed it to him, he knew that he was sanctified by the Spirit, and was about to be set forth for the salvation of many. These pillars in the tabernacle of the Lord are joined together, and the two cherubim, expanding their wings, touch each other; sometimes raised on the wings of virtue they soar to God; sometimes standing and folding their wings, they edify one another. But withdrawing from these exalted things to what is earthly, the blessed Ninian desired of the Saint masons, saying that, as in faith so also in the manner of constructing churches and in the ordering of ecclesiastical institutions, he proposed to himself to imitate the holy Roman Church. The most blessed man yielded to his request; and so, satisfied with their mutual intercourse as with heavenly feasts, after embraces and kisses, and tears shed by each, S. Martin remained in his own see, and Ninian hastened, with Christ as his leader, to the work whereto he was sent by the Spirit. On reaching his own country a great multitude of the people went out to meet him. Great was the joy of all, wonderful the devotion; everywhere resounded the praise of Christ, for all regarded him as a prophet. Straightway this diligent husbandman, having entered upon the field of his Lord, began to root out that which had been wrongly planted, to scatter that which had been wrongly collected, and to destroy that which had been wrongly built. Then, the minds of the faithful being purged of every error, he began to lay in them the foundations of the true faith, building thereon the gold of wisdom, and the silver of knowledge, and the stones of good works; and all the things requiring to be done by the faithful, he both taught by word and illustrated by examples, and likewise confirmed with many and great miracles.

CHAPTER III.
The Foundation of the Church of Whithorn.

HE chose a site for himself in the place which is now called Whithorn. This place is situated on the shore of the ocean, and, running far out into the sea, is enclosed by the sea itself on the east, west, and south, the way being open to those who would approach it only on the north. Here, therefore, by the command of the man of God, the masons, whom he had brought with him, built a church, before which, they say, no other had been built in Britain of stone. And, inasmuch as he learned that the most holy Martin, whom he always venerated with wondrous affection, had now passed away from the earth to the heavens, he was careful to dedicate it to his honour.

CHAPTER IV.
He Heals and Converts King Tudvallus.

THEREFORE this light set upon a candlestick began to shine forth with heavenly signs, and with the radiant flames of virtue, upon those who were in the house of God, to enlighten darkened minds with the clear and burning word of the Lord, and to kindle those who were cold in heart. There was a certain king in that region (for the whole island was divided and subject to divers kings) by name Tudvallus, whom riches, power and honour had excited to pride; for the lust of the flesh and the lust of the eyes, and the riches of the world, incite to pride and haughtiness, inasmuch as the more any-one has, the more he thinks he is able to do, and the more he believes is permitted to him. This man, despising the warnings of the man of God, both depreciated his doctrines and manners in secret and opposed his sound teaching to his face, so that the earth seemed rejected and nigh to being accursed, seeing that, though often drinking in the rain which came upon it, it brought forth thorns and thistles, and not wholesome herbs. But on a certain occasion when he had troubled the man of God more than usual, the Heavenly Judge suffered the injury of his servant to go unavenged no longer, but struck the haughty one on the head with an intolerable disease, and broke the crown of the head of him who was walking in his sins. And so much did his sickness increase that blindness suddenly darkened those proud eyes, and he who had fought against the light of truth, lost the light of the body; but not in vain nor to the increase of his folly. For as the wretched man lay oppressed with pain and deprived of sight, he was illumined within, though in darkness without, and when he came to himself, he confessed his sin, seeking a remedy from him alone whom he had always oppressed. At last, having summoned his kindred and taken their advice, since he was himself unable to go, being detained by his infirmity, he sent messengers to the man of God, beseeching him not to enter into judgment with his servant, neither to reward him according to his deeds, but, as an imitator of the Divine benignity, to return him good for evil, and love for hate. Hearing this, the most blessed man, not elated with human pride, but abounding, as always, in the bowels of compassion, having first prayed to God, went straight to the sick man with the greatest humility and devotion. At first he corrected him with gentle reproof, then he touched the head of the sick man with healing hand and impressed on the blind eyes the sign of saving life. What more shall I say? Pain fled, blindness was driven away by the incoming light. And so it came to pass that sickness of the body cured the sickness of the soul, and the sickness of the body was expelled by the virtue which proceeded from the man of God. Healed therefore in both, in body and soul, the king began with all affection to revere and venerate the man of God, knowing by experience both that the

Lord was with him, directing all his ways and giving him power over every one who exalted himself against the knowledge of Christ, and that He would speedily avenge every act of disobedience and every injury done to the servants of Christ. If, therefore, this contemptuous and proud man, by the grace of humility and penitence was deemed meet to be healed by the most holy man, who shall doubt that he who with an unfeigned faith and a sincere and humble heart, implores the aid of so great a man for the healing of the wounds of his spirit, shall not also receive a speedy remedy through his holy merits? But let us now pass to other matters, which seem to be so much the greater in proportion as they are proved to be contrary to nature.

CHAPTER V.

He Vindicates the Innocence of a Presbyter accused of Violation.

IN the service of one of the noblemen there was a certain girl, who according to the sinful flesh, was of a beautiful countenance and goodly to look upon. There was also an unchaste youth who, when he had cast his eyes upon hers, was seized with a blind passion of love; and, being unable to subdue the flame of the lust he had conceived, he began to urge her to consent to sin. At length, either by solicitation or gifts, he so wrought that she conceived sorrow and brought forth iniquity. The wretched woman yielded herself to the other's lust, little thinking of the judgment of God, though hoping to escape the eyes of men. But her crime was betrayed, and soon laughter was turned into weeping, joy into sorrow, pleasure into punishment. What could she do? Whither should she turn? The law, her parents, and her master were feared. Wherefore the unhappy woman made a covenant with death, and placed her hope in a lie, believing that she would appear less guilty if she said that she had been deceived or forced by some man of position. When therefore she was compelled by the elders to confess the name of her paramour, she laid the crime of her violation at the door of the presbyter to whom the bishop had entrusted the care of the parish. All who heard her confession were astonished to think that the crime should have been committed by a man in such a position, and absolved her. Accordingly the good were scandalized, the evil-disposed made merry, the common people laughed, the sacred order was scoffed at by the impious, and sorrow seized the presbyter, whose reputation was assailed. But the innocence of the priest was not hid from the beloved soldier of God, since it was revealed to him by the Spirit. Nevertheless he did not lightly bear the scandal which had befallen the Church and the injury done to holy religion. At length the days of the woman were accomplished that she should bring forth, and she brought forth a son, not, as was supposed, to the shame of the priest, but to that of the father and her shameless self. For when the bishop, having summoned the clergy and all the people to the church, had exhorted them in a sermon and laid his hands on those who had been baptized, this wanton woman, casting aside all shame, pushed herself forward along with those who belonged to her among the people, thrust the child into the face of the presbyter, and shouted in the ears of all the congregation, that he was the father of the child, her violator and deceiver. Clamour arose among the people; among the good, shame; among the wicked, laughter; but the Saint commanding the people to be silent, directed the child, which was then but one night old, to be brought to him; and being inspired by the Spirit of God, fixed his eyes upon him, and said: "Hearken, O child! in the name of Jesus Christ, say here, in the presence of the people, whether this presbyter begat thee." O marvel! O worthy of all admiration! O the marvellous clemency of God! O the ineffable power of the Christian faith! Verily, to him that believeth, all things are possible! But what do I say? To the faith of Ninian what was not possible? Truly, nature yieldeth to faith, and age to virtue. And why should not nature yield to the Lord of Nature? Age was not needed for an instrument, nor teaching for an office, nor time for practice, but by the effectual working of faith the Divine Power made the tongue of the infant eloquent, and out of the mouth of a babe and suckling confounded the guilty, convicted the liar, and absolved the innocent. Accordingly, out of the body of an infant there proceeded the voice of man; an untaught tongue framed intelligent words, and stretching forth his right hand, the child singled out among the people his real father, saying : " That is my father; he begat me; he committed the crime which is laid against the priest. Of a truth, O bishop, thy presbyter is innocent of this offence; between him and me there is naught save community in the same nature." This was enough. The child then became silent, to speak afterwards according to the law of nature and in the process of increasing years. Immediately there resound in the mouth of all thanksgiving and the voice of praise. All the people exulted with joy, seeing that a great prophet had arisen among them, and because God had visited his people.

CHAPTER VI.

He undertakes the Conversion of the Picts. He returns Home.

MEANWHILE the most blessed man, grieved that the devil, who had been driven out of the region beside the ocean, had found for himself a dwelling place in a corner of the island in the hearts of the Picts, girded himself as a strong wrestler to overthrow his kingdom, and put on, moreover, the shield of faith, the helmet of salvation, the breast-plate of charity, and the sword of the Spirit, which is the Word of God. Equipped with such arms and surrounded by a company of his holy brethren, as by a heavenly host, he invaded the empire of the strong man armed, to rescue from his power innumerable vessels of captivity. Wherefore going to the Southern Picts, among whom the error of the Gentiles still prevailed, compelling them to venerate and worship idols deaf and dumb, he preached the truth of the Gospel and the purity of the Christian Faith, the Lord working with him and confirming his word with signs following. The blind receive their sight, the lame walk, the lepers are cleansed, the deaf hear, the dead are raised, the oppressed of the devil are delivered. A door is opened for the Word of God; by the grace of the Holy Spirit faith is received, error abandoned, temples cast down, and churches built. To the font of the saving laver, rich and poor, young men and maidens, old and young, and mothers with their children hasten, and renouncing Satan with all his works and pomps, are joined to the body of the believers by faith, confession, and the sacraments. They give thanks to the most merciful God, that in the isles which are afar off he had revealed His name, sending to them a preacher of the truth, a lamp of salvation, and calling them His people which were not His people, and them beloved which were not beloved, and them as having obtained mercy which had not obtained mercy. Then the holy bishop began to ordain presbyters, to consecrate bishops, to distribute the other dignities of the ecclesiastical orders, and to divide the whole land into parishes with fixed bounds. Finally, having confirmed, in faith and good works, his children whom he had begotten in Christ, and having set in order all things which seemed to be necessary to the honour of God and for the salvation of souls, he bade farewell to the brethren, and returned to his own church, where in great tranquillity of soul, he spent a life perfect in all sanctity and glorious in miracles.

CHAPTER VII.

The Miracle among the Leeks.

IT happened on a certain day that the holy man went with his brethren into the refectory to dine, and seeing no pot-herbs or vegetables on the table, he called the brother who was entrusted with the care of the garden, and enquired why on that day no pot-herbs or vegetables were set before the brethren. He replied: "Truly, O Father, whatever remained of the leeks and such like, I to-day committed to the ground, and the garden has not yet produced anything fit for eating." Then said the

Saint: "Go, and whatever thy hand findeth, gather and bring to me." Amazed, he stood trembling, hesitating what to do. But knowing that Ninian could command nothing in vain, he went slowly to the garden. Then happened a marvellous thing, credible to those alone who think that nothing is impossible to him that believeth; for he saw leeks and other kinds of vegetables not only grown but bearing seed. He was astonished, and as if in a trance, thought he saw a vision. At length coming to himself and remembering the power of the holy man, he gave thanks to God, and gathering as many as seemed sufficient, he set them on the table before the bishop. The guests looked at each other, and with one heart and voice magnified God working in his saints, and so withdrew refreshed much more in mind than in body.

CHAPTER VIII.
Of the Animals and the Thieves.

IT sometimes pleased the most holy Ninian to visit his herds and the huts of his shepherds, desiring that the flocks which he had gathered together for the use of the brethren, and also for the poor and the pilgrims, should be partakers of the episcopal benediction. Therefore the animals being collected together into one place, when the servant of the Lord had looked upon them, he raised his hands and commended himself and all that he had to the Divine protection. Then going round, he marked off with the staff on which he was wont to lean, a little field in which he enclosed the cattle, and commanded that all within that circle should remain during the night under the Divine protection; and having done this, the man of God turned aside to rest for the night in the house of a certain honourable matron. But after they had refreshed their bodies with food and their minds with the Word of God, and all had given themselves to sleep, thieves came; and seeing that the cattle were neither enclosed by walls, nor protected by hedges, nor surrounded by a dyke, they searched about to see if there were any watchers, or anything to prevent them from carrying off the cattle. And when they found that everything was still, and that there was neither any sound nor motion, nor barking of which to be afraid, they crossed the bounds which had been set by the Saint, and rushing in among the cattle endeavoured to carry them all off. But the Divine power which was present, resisted the ungodly, and cast them down, using as an instrument against those who as brute beasts cared not for their minds but for their bellies, an irrational animal. For the bull of the herd, turning as in fury, rushed at them, and attacking the leader of the thieves, threw the wretched man down, and gored him in the belly with its horns, dashing out his entrails and his life together. Then digging up the ground with its hoofs, it struck a marvellous blow with its foot on a rock which it had found, and in a wonderful way, in testimony of so great a miracle, its foot sank into the stone, as into soft wax, leaving its print on the rock, and on account of the footmark giving the place its name ; for to this day the place is called in English, Farres Last, and in Latin, Tauri Vestigium, or the Footprint of the Bull. Meanwhile the most blessed father having finished the solemn service of prayer, went out, and seeing the man lying dead and disembowelled among the feet of the cattle, and the others rushing hither and thither, as if possessed by furies, was moved with pity, and turning earnestly to God, prayed that He would resuscitate the dead. Nor did he cease either from tears or prayers, until that same power by which the man had been slain had not only restored him to life, but had also made him sound and whole. For verily the power of Christ on account of the merit of the Saint smote him and healed him, slew him and restored him to life ; led him down to the grave and brought him back. Meanwhile the rest of the thieves, who had been running about the whole night, and whom a certain madness had shut up within the enclosure which the father had formed, when they saw the servant of God, cast themselves with fear and trembling at his feet, imploring pardon. Gently chiding them and impressing upon them, with salutary words, the fear of God and the punishment prepared for the rapacious, and having bestowed upon them his benediction, he gave them permission to depart.

CHAPTER IX.

Ailred Complains of the Manners of His Own Age. Ninian's Manner of Life. The Miraculous Shower.

WHEN I consider the devout walk and conversation of this man, I am ashamed of our negligence; I am ashamed of the sloth of this miserable age. Who of us, I ask, even among servants, does not more frequently in our mutual intercourse and conversation utter things jesting rather than serious, things idle rather than useful, and things carnal rather than things spiritual? Mouths which the Divine grace has consecrated for the praise of God and the celebration of the sacred mysteries, are day by day polluted with backbitings and worldly conversation. Weary of the Psalms and Gospels and Prophets of God, they busy themselves all the day long with the vain and unseemly works of men. How they conduct themselves on a journey! Is not the mind like the body, in motion all day long, and the tongue in idleness? Gossip and the ways of wicked men are in their mouths, religious gravity is dissipated by laughter and idle tales;[*] the affairs of kings, the duties of bishops, the ministeries of the clerics, the quarrels of princes, and above all the life and ways of all are discussed. We judge every thing save our own judgment, and what is more to be grieved at, we bite and devour one another that we be consumed one of another. Not so the most blessed Ninian; no crowd disturbed his tranquillity; no travelling hindered his meditations; nor did his prayers grow lukewarm through fatigue. Whithersoever he went he lifted up his soul to celestial things either in meditation or in prayer. Whenever he turned aside from his journey and indulged in rest, either for himself or the beast he rode, he brought out a book, which he carried with him for the purpose, and took pleasure in reading or chanting; for he felt as the prophet says: "O how sweet are thy words unto my taste, yea sweeter than honey to my mouth." Whence the Divine power conferred such grace upon

---

[*] Fabulis, B.M.

him that even when reclining in the open air and reading in the midst of the heaviest showers of rain no moisture ever touched the volume on which he was intent. But when every place around was wet with the water running upon it, he sat alone with his little book beneath the rain, as if protected by the roof of a house. And it came to pass that once while travelling with one of his brethren, by name Plebia, a man equally holy with himself, the most reverend man according to his wont, relieved the tedium of the journey with the Psalms of David, and that after a certain portion of the way had been accomplished, they turned aside from the public road, in order to rest a little, and their Psalters being opened they refreshed their souls by sacred reading. Presently the sweet serenity of the sky becoming obscured with black clouds, poured down upon the earth beneath the watery showers it had conceived by natural exhalation. What more shall I say? The thin air, arching itself like a chamber round the servants of God, stood like a wall impenetrable to the falling waters. During the singing, however, the most blessed Ninian turned away his eyes from the book, being somewhat affected by an unlawful thought, even tickled with a certain desire at the suggestion of the devil, when the shower bursting upon him and his book immediately proclaimed that which was hidden in his heart. Then the brother who was sitting by him, understanding what had happened, reminded him with a gentle reproof of his order and his age, and showed him how unbecoming such things were to such as he. Immediately coming to himself, the man of God blushed at having been overtaken by an unprofitable thought, and in one and the same moment of time, he both put away the thought and caused the rain to cease.

CHAPTER X.

The Miracles of Ninian's Staff on the Sea and on the Land.

MEANWHILE many, both nobles and persons of inferior rank, placed their sons with the blessed pontiff to be imbued with sacred learning. These he indoctrinated with knowledge and formed in manners; curbing with salutary discipline the vices by which their age is wont to be entangled, and instilling into their minds the virtues whereby they might live godly, righteous, and sober lives. On one occasion one of the young men committed a fault which it was impossible to hide from the saint of God; and because it was not right that the offender should be allowed to go unpunished, the rods, the severest torments of boys, were prepared. The lad fled in terror, and knowing the power of the man of God, was careful to carry with him the staff on which the Saint was in the habit of leaning, in the belief that he had obtained the best comfort for his journey if he did but bear anything with him which belonged to the Saint. Fleeing therefore from the face of the man, he sought diligently for a vessel to carry him over into Ireland. It is the custom in these regions to make a kind of boat by joining wands together in the shape of a cup, and of such a size as to be capable of holding three men sitting together. By stretching an ox-hide over it, they render it not only buoyant, but also impervious to water. Probably in the same way vessels of immense size were at that time built. One of these vessels, but without the covering of hide, the young man stumbled upon lying at the shore, and when he had incautiously entered it, by Divine Providence, (I know not whether on account of its own lightness, for with a slight touch these vessels float far out on the waves), it immediately shot out into the sea. As the waters poured in, the miserable sailor stood not knowing what to do, whither he should turn, or what it was requisite to do. If he abandoned the vessel, his life was in peril; if he remained, there was nothing before him but certain death. At last the unhappy youth, repenting of his flight, with pale face saw in the waves the avengers of the injury he had done to the father. Then coming to himself, and thinking that S. Ninian was present with him in his staff, as if at his feet he confessed his fault with tears, besought his pardon, entreated that by his most holy merits divine help might be vouchsafed to him. Then trusting in the known goodness as well as in the power of the Bishop, he fixed the staff in one of the holes, that it might not be hid from posterity what Ninian could do even in the sea. At the touch of the staff the element immediately trembled, and as if driven back by divine power, did not presume any longer to flow in at the open holes. These are Thy works, O Christ! who speaking to Thy disciples, hast endowed them with this promise: "He that believeth in me, the works that I do, shall he do also." Thou didst imprint Thy sacred footprints on the waves of the deep: the power of Ninian did restrain the natural powers of the sea. The disciple who was doubting, and therefore in peril among the waves, Thy holy hand sustained, lest he should sink: the staff of Ninian protected his fugitive disciple from being swallowed up by the waves. Thou didst command the wind and the waves that fear might be taken away from Thy disciples: the power of Ninian subdued the winds and the sea that the youth might be conveyed to the desired shores.

A wind, rising out of the east, bore the vessel gently along. The staff, instead of a sail, caught the wind; as a helm it directed the boat, as an anchor it stayed it. The people stood on the eastern shore, and seeing the little vessel resting on the waves like a bird, neither driven by sail, nor propelled with oar, nor steered with helm, awaited its approach, wondering what this miracle might mean. Meanwhile the young man landed, and in order that he might make the merits of the man of God more widely known, animated by faith, he fixed the staff in the shore, beseeching God, that in testimony of so great a miracle it might send forth roots, and contrary to its nature, receive moisture, and produce branches and leaves, and bring forth flowers and fruit. The Divine favour was not wanting to the prayer of the suppliant, and immediately the dry wood, sending forth roots and covering itself with new bark, produced branches and leaves, and afterwards growing into a no small tree, makes known even now to all who behold it the power of Ninian. Miracle is attributed to miracle. At the root of the tree a most limpid fountain springing up, sent forth a crystal stream, winding with gentle murmur and lengthened course, pleasant to the eye, and sweet to the taste, and on account of the merits of the Saint useful, and health-giving to the sick.

CHAPTER XI.

Declamation on the Death of Ninian. His burial at Whithorn.

THE most blessed Ninian, wondrously shining with such miracles as these, and excelling in the highest virtues, reached, after a prosperous course, the day of his summons. That day to the blessed man was a day of exultation and joy; but to the people over whom he ruled a day of tribulation and woe. He to whom heaven was opened rejoiced; the people who were bereaved of such a father mourned. He for whom an eternal crown was prepared rejoiced; they whose salvation was in danger sorrowed. But sorrow mingled with his joy; for to leave them seemed heavy to bear, but to be longer separated from Christ was intolerable. But Christ, consoling the soul thus hesitating, said: "Arise, hasten, my friend, my dove, and come." "Arise my friend," he said; "Arise my dove, rise by thought, hasten by desire, come by love." Truly, this voice pleased the most blessed man, as the friend of the Bridegroom, to whom that Heavenly Bridegroom had committed His Bride, revealed his secrets, and opened his treasures. Deservedly is that soul called "friend," to whom all was love, and nothing fear. "My friend," he says, "my dove." O dove! dove verily taught to mourn, who, ignorant of the gall of bitterness, weeps with them that weep, is weak with them that are weak, and burns with them that are offended. Arise, hasten, my friend, my dove, and come; for already the winter is passed, the rain is over and gone. Then verily O blessed man! the winter was passed to thee, when thou wast counted worthy to contemplate with joyful eye that heavenly country which the Sun of Righteousness illumines with the light of His glory, which love enkindles, and a wondrous calm, as of a sweet springtime, tempers with an indescribable evenness of seasons. Then to thee was passed and gone that wintry inclemency which unsettles all these earthly regions, and with the inroads of vice hardens the cold hearts of men, in which neither the truth shines fully nor charity burns; and from the showers of temptation and the hailstorms of persecutions, that holy soul, perfectly triumphant, escaped into the glory of a perpetual spring. "Flowers," he says, "have appeared on our earth." Verily, celestial odour from the flowers of Paradise was breathed upon thee, O blessed Ninian, when the crowd of purple-robed martyrs and white-robed confessors smiled to thee with placid countenance as to their most familiar friend, and welcomed thee whom chastity had made white, and love had made red as the rose, to their company. For although opportunity granted not the sign of bodily martyrdom here, it denied him not that without which martyrdom is nothing, the merit of martyrdom. For how often did he throw himself upon the swords of the perverse ! How often did he expose himself to the arms of tyrants in the cause of justice ! For truth he was ready to lay down his life: and for justice to die. Rightly therefore to the flowers of the roses and to the lilies of the valley is this empurpled and shining one summoned, ascending from Libanus that he may be crowned among the heavenly hosts. For the time of ingrafting was come ; for as a ripened cluster he must needs now be cut off from the stem of the body, or from the vine of the Church on earth, to be purified by love and laid up in heavenly cellars.

Wherefore the blessed Ninian, perfect in life and full of years, passed happily away from the world, and accompanied by angelic spirits was carried into heaven, to receive there an eternal reward. There, associated with the company of the Apostles, joined to the ranks of the martyrs, enlisted in the hosts of the holy confessors, adorned also with the flowers of the virgins, he fails not to succour those who hope in him, cry to him, and praise him. He was buried in the Church of the blessed Martin, which he had himself built from its foundations, and was placed in a stone sarcophagus beside the altar, the clergy and people being present, sounding forth with their voices celestial hymns, with their hearts, sighs and tears. There the power which shone in the living Saint, ceases not to manifest itself about the body of the departed one, that all the faithful may acknowledge that he who is known to work on earth, lives in heaven. For at his most sacred tomb the infirm are healed, lepers are cleansed, the wicked are terrified, and the blind receive their sight ; by all which things the faith of the believing is strengthened to the praise and glory of our Lord Jesus Christ, who liveth and reigneth with God the Father in the Unity of the Holy Spirit, world without end. Amen.

CHAPTER XII.

Miracles of the Relics of Ninian.

I.—ON A DEFORMED POOR MAN.

WHEREFORE, when the most blessed Ninian had been translated into heaven, the faithful people, who had loved him during his lifetime, frequented with the greatest reverence that which seemed to be left to them of him, namely, his most sacred relics. The Divine Power approving their reverence and faith, proved by many miracles that the Saint whom the common lot had taken away from the earth, was still living in the heavens. There was born to one of the people by his wife, a miserable son, who was the grief of both his parents, a gazing stock to the people, and a horror to those who saw him. Nature had formed him contrary to nature, all his members being turned the wrong way. The joints of his feet were twisted, his heels projected forward ; his back adhered to his face ; his breast was near the back of his head ; and his arms being twisted, his hands rested on his elbows. What more shall I say? There lay that black figure to whom members had been given without use, life without fruit, to whom among the wreck of other members the tongue alone remained, that he might bewail his misery and provoke his beholders to sorrow, and his hearers to tears. A continual grief to his parents, their sorrow grew daily. At length they thought of the power of the most holy Ninian which had so often proved efficacious ; and full of faith they caught up that wretched body and coming with it to the relics of the holy man, they offered the sacrifice of a contrite heart with shedding of tears, and continued instant in devout prayers until the hour of vespers. Then laying that body before the tomb of the Saint, they said: "Receive O blessed Ninian, that which we offer, a gift, hateful indeed, but well fitted to prove thy power. Wearied, worn out, oppressed with sadness, overcome with loathing, we present it to thy compassion. Truly, if it be a gift, favour is due to those who offer it ; if a burden, thou, whose power to aid is greater, art in every way better able to sustain it. Here, therefore, let him die or live, let him be healed or perish." These or similar things they urged with tears, and leaving the deformed child before the sacred relics, they departed. And behold in the stillness of the midnight the wretched child saw approaching him a man shining with celestial light, resplendent in the insignia of a bishop, who, touching him on the head, commanded him to rise up whole, and give thanks to God, his Healer. And when he was departed, the poor child awaking as from a deep sleep, twisted his members one by one by an easy motion into their natural position ; and having recovered the use of them all, he returned to his parents safe and sound. After this he gave himself wholly up to the Church and to ecclesiastical discipline, and after being first shorn for Holy Orders, and then ordained a presbyter, he ended his life in the service of the father.

II.—ON A POOR MAN AFFLICTED WITH SCABS.

The fame of this miracle being noised abroad, many ran together, each laying his own misfortune before the sacred relics. Among them came a certain simple man, poor indeed in fortune, but rich in faith and good will. A strange scab had attacked his whole body, and so laid hold upon his members that the skin strangely hardening was closing up the courses of the veins and everywhere contracting the arteries, and nothing but death awaited the sufferer. Accordingly, the unhappy man, drawing near to the body of the Saint, offered up the most devout prayers at the altar to the Lord of Faith. Tears flow, sighs heave forth, the breast is beaten, the very bowels tremble. To such faith and to such contrition neither the merit of the Saint was lacking nor the tenderness of Christ, who glorified his

Saint and mercifully healed the wretched suppliant. Why should I delay longer? The poor Adelfridus, for that was his name, ceased not from his prayers, and before many days were fulfilled he was restored to his former health.

III.—ON A BLIND GIRL.

Moreover, at that time there was among the people a certain girl, by name Deisuit, who was so afflicted with a pain in her eyes that the violence of the disease deprived her of all power of seeing, and the darkness resting upon all things, hid from her even the light of the sun. Painful to the sufferer, it was also a sorrow to her sympathising relatives. But what could they do? The efforts of the physicians gave place to despair, and Ninian, the only hope that remained, is sought. Led by the hand to that most sacred spot, she is left there weeping and wailing. She asks earnestly, seeks anxiously, knocks importunately, and the compassionate Jesus fails not of what he promised in his Gospel: "Ask, and ye shall receive; seek, and ye shall find; knock, and it shall be opened unto you." Therefore to the girl appeared the grace she sought. The door of pity at which she knocked was opened. The health she sought was given; for the darkness being taken away, the lost light was restored. All pain departed, and she who had come to the sacred tomb, led by another, returned home by the guidance of her own sight amid the great joy of her parents.

IV.—ON TWO LEPERS.

Further, there were seen to come into the city two lepers, who, deeming it presumptuous to touch holy things with the contagion of leprosy, implored, as it were, afar off the help of the Father. But coming to the fountain, and believing that whatever holy Ninian had touched was holy, they thought to wash themselves in that laver. O fresh miracle of Eliseus the prophet! O new cleansing, not of one but of two Naamans! Naaman came in the spirit of presumption; these in the spirit of lowliness; he came in doubt, these in faith. The King of Syria doubted; the King of Israel doubted; Naaman doubted. Doubted the King of Syria; he doubted and was proud, who imagined that his leper must be sent not to the prophet but to the King. Doubted also the King of Israel, who, having heard the letter of the King of Syria, rent his garments and said: "Am I God, that I am able to make alive and to kill?" Doubted Naaman, who, having heard the counsel of the prophet, went away angry. Naaman therefore stood in his chariot of pride at the gate of Eliseus. These in faith and lowliness of heart cried aloud to the mercy of Ninian. Rightly then is his fountain turned into a Jordan, and Ninian become a prophet. The lepers are cleansed at the touch of the laver, but by the merits of Ninian; and their flesh is restored as the flesh of a little child. They return to their friends healed, to the glory of Ninian, in praise of God, who worketh marvellously in his Saints.

But let this be the end of this book, though not the end of the miracles of S. Ninian. These do not cease to shine forth even now, to the praise and glory of our Lord Jesus Christ, who, with the Father and the Holy Spirit, liveth and reigneth for ever and ever. Amen.

LIFE OF COLUMBA.

BY

CUIMINE THE FAIR.

LIFE OF COLUMBA.

CHAPTER I.

The Nativity of Columba. An Angel appears to his Mother bearing a Mantle Adorned with Flowers.

THE nativity of Columba, sprung from a nation of saints for the salvation of many, is known to have had its beginning on this wise: One night between his conception and his birth, an angel of the Lord appeared to his mother in dreams, and standing beside her gave her a mantle of marvellous beauty, on which, sooth to say, the lovely colours of every flower seemed to be depicted. After a little, however, he demanded it back, took it from her hands, and raising it, spread it out, and sent it away through the empty air. But she, terrified at the mantle being taken from her, then addressed the man of venerable mien: "Why takest thou away from me the delightful mantle so soon?" He immediately replied: "Because this cloak is of such exceeding honour that it can no longer be kept with thee." At these words, the woman saw the aforesaid mantle recede further and further from her in its flight, and as it grew in size she beheld it exceed in breadth the plains, and surpass in extent the mountains and wooded valleys. At the same time she heard the following words: "O woman, be not grieved, for to the man to whom thou art bound in the bonds of wedlock, thou art about to bear a son of like beauty, who will be numbered among the prophets of the Lord as one of them; he is predestinated by God to be the leader of innumerable souls to the heavenly land." On hearing this the woman awoke.

CHAPTER II.

A Globe of Fire appears over the Face of Columba.

AFTER the birth of the child, a priest, a man of blameless life, to whose care the blessed youth had been confided, on returning home from church, after Mass, found his whole house lit up with a bright light, and saw a globe of fire resting over the face of the sleeping child. As soon as he beheld it he shook with fear, and lay prostrate on the ground in amazement, perceiving that the grace of the Holy Spirit was poured out upon the child from above.

CHAPTER III.

An Angel His Companion.

ON a certain occasion the Saint, while a young man, went to visit the holy Bishop Finnian, his master, who was then an old man. S. Finnian, when he saw him approaching, beheld likewise an angel of the Lord acting as his companion on the journey, and made known the fact to certain brethren who were standing by, saying: "Behold, see now S. Columba coming; he has been deemed worthy to have an angel of the Lord as the companion of his journey."

CHAPTER IV.

He Turns Water into Wine.

IN those days the Saint crossed over into Britain with twelve disciples and fellow soldiers. He arrived on a certain holy day, as his holy teacher and bishop Finnian was celebrating Mass, when it chanced that no wine could be found for the sacrificial mystery. On hearing the ministers at the altar complaining of this among themselves, he took a pitcher, and went to the fountain, in order that as a deacon he might draw spring water for the holy ministries of the Eucharist. The water being drawn, he said to the ministers: "You have now wine, which the Lord has sent for the celebration of his mysteries." On this being known, the holy Bishop with the ministers gave exceeding thanks to God. But the holy youth was wont to ascribe this miracle not to himself but to Bishop S. Finnian.

CHAPTER V.

He Consecrates Aidan King, and foretells future things concerning his Son.

AT another time the holy man, while staying in the Island of Hynba (Eilean-na-Naoimh), one night, when in an ecstacy of mind, saw an angel of the Lord sent unto him, who held in his hand the glass book of the ordination of kings. This book he received from the hand of the angel, and began to read. Refusing to ordain Aidan king as he was directed (for he loved his brother more), the angel suddenly stretched forth his hand and smote the Saint with a whip, the mark of the bruise whereof remained on his side all the days of his life. He also addressed to him this word : " Know for certain that I am sent by God, in order that thou mayest ordain Aidan king, which if thou wilt not do, I will smite thee again." The angel of the Lord giving him the same things in charge concerning the ordination of Aidan on three consecutive nights, the Saint sailed over to the Island of Iona, and Aidan coming thither, he ordained him king. Moreover, during the words of ordination, he foretold the future of his sons, and grandsons, and great-grandsons, and laying his hand upon his head, ordained and blessed him, and spake forth these words : " Believe unhesitatingly, O Aidan ; none of thine adversaries shall be able to resist thee, until thou first act unjustly towards me and my posterity. Tell these words to thy sons, lest they lose the kingdom. Because if they hearken not, the scourge which, because of thee I have endured from the angel of God, will be turned against them." And so it came to pass, for transgressing the commands of the man of God, they lost the kingdom.

CHAPTER VI.

He sees the soul of a monk received into Heaven.

ON another occasion, when staying in the island of Iona, the holy man saw a monk, who was fruitful in good works, reduced to the last extremity. When he visited him in the hour of his departure, the man of God, after standing for a little beside his couch, blessed him, and then quickly left the house, being unwilling to witness the death of him who at that moment was passing from among them. Then, indeed, the holy man, while walking in the court of his monastery, with his eyes fixed on heaven, was astonished and greatly amazed. One of the brethren, who at the time was alone with him, ventured to ask the cause of his amazement, when the Saint replied: "Just now I saw the holy angels warring against the opposing powers, and I give thanks to Christ, our Judge, because the victorious angels have received the soul of this pilgrim. But I beseech thee, that while I live, thou wilt reveal this secret to no one."

CHAPTER VII.

The Death of Saint Brendan revealed to him.

LIKEWISE on a certain day at the first dawn, the Saint called to him his servant, Diormit, and addressed him on this wise: "Let the services of the Holy Eucharist be at once prepared; for to-day is the natal day of the blessed Brendan." "Wherefore," said the servant, "orderest thou such things; for no messenger from Ireland has announced his death." "Go," replied the Saint, "obey my order; for during the night I saw the heavens suddenly open and choirs of angels, by whose bright and surpassing glory the whole world was in that moment illuminated, descend to meet the soul of S. Brendan.

CHAPTER VIII.

The Death of S. Columban, Bishop in Leinster, revealed.

ON another day, again, when the brethren were about to set out to their manual labour, the Saint, on the contrary, ordered the day to be spent in rest, the rites of the Holy Oblation to be prepared, and some addition to be made to their dinner. "I must needs celebrate," he said, "the mysteries of the Holy Eucharist for the holy soul which was last night carried among the angels." The brethren obeyed, spent the day in rest, and went with the holy Abbot to the Church as on a holy day. During the sacred mysteries of the Holy Sacrifice, the Saint said, "To-day prayer must be made for the holy Bishop Columban." Then understood the brethren who were standing by, that Columban, Bishop of the people in Leinster, the dear friend of Columba, had departed to the Lord. A short time after, some persons coming from the province of Leinster brought tidings that the Bishop died on the night the Saint said.

CHAPTER IX.

Columba fights with demons.

Now the Saint sought a place among the woods more remote from men and suitable for prayer. And there, when on a certain day he was praying, he suddenly saw before him an exceedingly black host of demons fighting with iron spits, who, as had been revealed to the holy man by the Spirit, were desirous of assailing his monastery and slaying many of the brethren with darts. But he fought against them, and so on both sides the battle was waged during the greater part of the day. But though innumerable, and he one, they were unable to overcome him, till at last the angels of God came to his aid, and through fear of them the demons fled from the place, as the Saint himself afterwards told the brethren.

CHAPTER X.

While staying in Iona he comes by the help of an Angel to the relief of a brother who is falling from the top of a house in Ireland.

AT another time, when the man of God was sitting in his hut writing, his countenance was suddenly changed, and he cried out from a pure heart, saying: "Help! help!" Two brethren, who were standing at the door, asked the reason for this sudden cry; and the man of God gave them the following answer: "I commanded the angel of the Lord, who was just now standing in our midst, to go quickly to the help of one of the brethren who was falling from the roof of a house which is being built." And the Saint immediately added: "Wonderful, indeed, and almost indescribable is the swiftness of the angelic flight; equal, I should think, to the speed of lightning. For that heavenly being who but now flew hence from us to that man as he was beginning to fall, came up, as if in the twinkling of an eye, and supported him before he touched the earth; nor did he feel any shock. How amazing, I say, and how timely the aid, which swifter than a word could be rendered so quickly over so many intervening lands and seas."

CHAPTER XI.

He converses with Angels.

ON a certain occasion, on one of the days when the brethren were assembled together, the Saint of God, Columba, said to them: "To-day I wish to go alone to the western plain of our island; but none of you follow me." They complied with his request, and he went out alone as he wished; but a certain brother, a crafty spy, following another path, hid himself on the top of a hill, anxious to spy out what he might and did see, but not without the permission of God, who was magnifying his Saint. For he saw him standing on a hill and praying with his hands opened out to heaven, and lifting up his eyes on high. Wonderful to say: lo! a marvellous sight suddenly appeared. Straightway holy angels, clothed in white raiment, flew towards the holy man with wondrous speed, and began to stand around him as he prayed, and joined in intercourse with the blessed Saint; but as if conscious of him who was spying them, they flew back on high. The blessed man, after the angelic meeting, betook himself to the monastery, and, the brethren being assembled, sought for him who was guilty of the transgression with a stern reproof. He, then, who knew within himself that he was the inexcusable transgressor, confessed his guilt and on bended knees prayed for pardon; and the Saint leading him aside, charged him, as he knelt, with a heavy threat to tell no man during his life-time what he had seen. For a time the brother obeyed, but after the Saint's death, he related with many protestations to the brethren what he had seen. Moreover the scene of this angelic assembly is called to this day the Mount of the Angels.

CHAPTER XII.

A ball of fire rises from his head.

MOREOVER, on another occasion, four brethren came from Ireland for the sake of visiting S. Columba, who was then residing in the Island of Hynba (Eilan-na-naoimh). With one consent they besought the Saint with prayers to celebrate the Sacred Mysteries; which also he did one Lord's Day. But after the reading of the Gospel they saw a certain ball fiery and very bright, blaze from the crown of the holy Columba's head, while he stood before the altar consecrating the Sacred Oblation, and beheld it rise upwards, in the form of a column, until the same Sacred Mysteries were ended.

CHAPTER XIII.
He enjoys celestial visions during three days.

LIKEWISE, on another occasion, when staying in the same island, the grace of the Holy Spirit was abundantly and incomparably poured out upon the holy man, and dwelt with him in a marvellous manner for the space of three days, so that for three days and three nights he neither ate nor drank, nor permitted any one to approach him, but remained in his house, which was shut up and filled with celestial brightness. At night rays of surpassing brilliancy were seen to burst from the house through the chinks in the doors and through the key-holes, and spiritual songs were heard being chanted by him, and songs before unheard. And as he afterwards openly confessed, he was deemed worthy to learn in that place many things, both obscure things of the Scriptures and mysteries unknown to men.

CHAPTER XIV.
He relieves the want of a poor man by a spit he blessed.

ON one occasion there came to the Saint a certain peasant who was very poor, complaining bitterly that he had not anything wherewith to feed his wife and little ones. Sympathizing with him, the merciful servant of God said: "Poor man! Take a stake from the neighbouring wood and bring it to me quickly." He obeyed, and went and brought one. And the Saint taking it, sharpened it into a spit, and with his own hand blessed it and gave it to him, saying: "Watch carefully over it, it will hurt neither man nor cattle, but only beasts and game and fish, and so long as thou keepest it, there will be no want whatever of venison in thy house." On hearing this the poor man returned to his home rejoicing; he also fixed the spit in remote parts of the country which the beasts of the forest were in the habit of frequenting, and when the night was passed, went with the first dawn of day to visit it, and found a stag impaled upon it. But why say more? Not a day passed but the stake caught a buck, a doe, or some other animal. His whole house, as it were, was overflowing with the flesh of wild animals. But not many days after, his foolish wife, overcome by the persuasion of the devil, spake thus to him : " Take the stake from the ground ; for if any of the men or domestic cattle should be killed upon it, thou and I with our children will be led captive or reduced to slavery." " It will not be so," replied the husband ; " for the Saint of God has interdicted it from hurting man or beast." Nevertheless, yielding to his wife, he took the stake out of the field, and placed it beside the wall of his house, when immediately his house dog, running against it, died. On this his wife again said : " One of thy sons will fall upon the stake and die." At this the husband removed it from beside the wall, and carrying it into the wood, placed it among thick bushes, so that it might hurt no one. But when he returned on the following day, he found that a goat had fallen upon it. Removing it thence, he hid and fixed it under water. But revisiting it another day, he found a huge salmon, which he was hardly able to carry alone, impaled upon it. Then he placed the stake upon the roof, when a crow flying by chance against it, was killed. Whereupon the poor man, who was now prosperous, led astray by the counsel of his wife, took the stake from the roof, seized his axe, cut it into many pieces, and threw it into the fire, and immediately became poor.

CHAPTER XV.

He is suffused with Heavenly Light in the Church.

ONE winter night S. Fernaus entered the Church alone to pray, and was devoutly praying at a certain seat. S. Columba, ignorant of this, entered the church a little after for the same purpose, and along with him there entered a golden light, which descended from heaven and filled the whole church. Moreover, the heavenly light filled also the chapel, though it was shut off, where Fernaus was lying hid in great alarm; and as no man can look at the summer sun at noontide with steady unblinking eyes, so also Fernaus could not endure that heavenly splendour. At length having seen the lightning brilliancy no strength remained in him. After a short prayer, however, S. Columba left the church, and on the morrow he called Fernaus to him and addressed him in these consoling words: " O my child, last night thou didst that which was pleasing in the sight of God in bending thine eyes down to the earth for fear of the light. For if thou hadst not so done, thine eyes would have been blinded ; but while I live, take care to keep this vision secret."

CHAPTER XVI.

The Life of Columba is prolonged in answer to the Prayers of the Church.

ON another occasion, also, when the man of God was staying in the Island of Iona, his face glowed with a sudden joyfulness, and lifting his eyes to heaven he rejoiced greatly ; but after a little he became sad. Two brethren, however, who were standing at the door inquired the reason of this sudden joy and the following grief. To whom the Saint replied : " Go in peace. I may not tell you." But when they were too troublesome to him concerning this occurrence, he said : " If you will keep it secret, I will tell you, for I love you." And when they gave their word, he spoke thus to them : " Up to the present day thrice ten years of my pilgrimage in Britain have been fulfilled. Moreover, I have asked from the Lord that in the end of this thirtieth year I might pass away and be with Him. And this was the cause of the joy concerning which ye trouble me. I also saw the holy angels coming to meet my soul as it was about to leave the body. But lo! they stand afar off, being suddenly held back and not suffered to approach nearer, because He who granted that what I besought should happen on this day, hearkening to the prayers of many churches concerning me, has changed more quickly than I can tell; for in answer to the prayers of the churches, it has been granted by the Lord that four years from this day shall be added to my continuance in the flesh. Now this delay was the cause of my grief. But when these four years are ended, I shall joyfully pass to the Lord by a sudden death."

CHAPTER XVII.

He predicts the Hour of his Death; and blesses Iona.

ACCORDING therefore to these words the man of God lived in the flesh for four years more, which being ended, one day in the month of May, infirm with age and conveyed in a waggon, he went to visit the brethren who were labouring in the fields and began to address them as follows: "During the Easter festival, in the month of April just past, I earnestly desired to pass away to Christ, but that the festival of joy might not be changed for you into sorrow, I preferred to delay the day of my departure longer." At these words the brethren were exceeding sorrowful. But the man of the Lord, as he sat in the vehicle, turned his face towards the East, and blessed the island with the islanders who dwelt therein, and from that day there was no viper in it hurtful to man or beast. At length after the words of benediction, the Saint was borne back to his monastery.

CHAPTER XVIII.

He sees an Angel.

BUT when a few days were passed, while the solemnities of the Mass were being celebrated according to custom on the Lord's Day, suddenly, his eyes being lifted up, the face of the blessed Columba was seen to be overspread with a bright glow. At the same moment he alone beheld an angel of the Lord hovering above within the walls of the oratory. For this was the cause of that sudden joy, concerning which when those present inquired, the Saint made to them this reply: "Wonderful and incomparable is the subtilty of the angelic nature! For lo! an angel of the Lord sent for the safe-keeping of some one dear to God, looking down upon us within the church and giving his benediction, has returned again through the roof of the church, and left no trace of such exit." These things the Saint said signifying them concerning himself; nevertheless at the time the brethren knew it not; but afterwards they understood.

CHAPTER XIX.

He indicates the Day of his Death to Diormit.

ACCORDINGLY the holy man at the end of the same week, that is on the Sabbath day (*i.e.*, our Saturday), privately called his servant Diormit to him, and thus spake: "In the Sacred Writings this day is called Sabbath, which, being interpreted, is Rest. And truly to me this day is a Sabbath, because to me it is the last day of life, in which, after the afflictions of my labours, I take my rest, and on the coming Lord's day night, shall go the way of my fathers. For already Christ invites me, and so it is revealed to me by Him." At this the servant was much grieved, but was consoled by the father. Thence going out and ascending to the summit of a hill overlooking his monastery, the Saint of God stood a little, and with uplifted hands blessed his community, and prophesied many things concerning the present and the future which the event afterwards confirmed.

CHAPTER XX.

When the Hour of Death is near, he makes a division of a Psalm.

AFTER these things, descending from the hill and being returned to the monastery, he was sitting in his cell writing a psalter. Coming at length to that verse of the thirty-third

Psalm, where it is written: "They that seek the Lord shall not want any good thing," he said: "Here I think I must stop. Baitheneus must write the words which follow." Now the verse which the Saint had just written applied very fitly to him to whom verily the good things of eternity will never be lacking. But to his successor, that is to the father of his spiritual sons, the following suited not less fitly; "Come my children, hearken unto me, I will teach you the fear of the Lord." For, as his predecessor enjoined, he continued, not only in writing but also in labouring in the rule of the monastery.

CHAPTER XXI.

The Last Words of Columba.

ACCORDINGLY, after he had finished writing this verse, which completed the page, he went into the holy church to celebrate the Mass of the Lord's Day night. Returning to his dwelling as soon as it was ended, he sat all night on his bed, where for straw he was wont to have the bare floor, for a pillow a stone, which even to this day remains beside his sepulchre, as it were the inscription on his monument. So then sitting there he commended his last words to his children, saying: "Among yourselves have always mutual and unfeigned charity with peace; but the Lord, the Comforter of the good, will be your aid, and I, abiding with Him, will intercede for you, that the good things of time and eternity may arise to you. After these words were said, S. Columba was silent for a little.

CHAPTER XXII.

Columba Dies in the Church.

THEN straightway at midnight, when the bell rang, rising hurriedly, he went to the church, and running more quickly than the rest, he entered alone, and fell down before the altar on bended knees in prayer. But Diormit, his servant, having followed more slowly, saw from afar at that moment the whole church filled from within with angelic light; as he drew near to the door the same light quickly vanished, but not before it had been seen by some of the brethren. But Diormit, entering the church, cried out repeatedly with tearful voice: "Where art thou, father?" And as lights had not yet been brought in by the brethren, he groped about in the darkness, and found the Saint lying upon his back before the altar. He raised him a little, and sitting beside him laid the holy head in his lap. But the other brethren running up and seeing that the father, whom they had loved while living, was dying, mourned exceedingly as he died. But the Saint, whose life had not yet passed away, raised his eyes to both sides, looked round with a joyful countenance, and saw the holy angels near. Diormit, having raised his right hand, signified that he should bless the brethren; but the holy father nodded to him and raised his hand himself as far as he could. And after his holy benediction thus signified, he straightway gave up the ghost. His face meanwhile remained ruddy, and in a wonderful degree enlivened by the angelic vision, so that it seemed to be the face not of the dead but of the sleeping.

CHAPTER XXIII.

His Burial.

MEANWHILE, after the departure of the holy soul, the hymns at Matins being finished, the sacred body was borne with the melodious singing of the brethren back from the church to his dwelling, where for three days and three nights his honourable obsequies were duly performed. When these were finished to the praise of God, the holy body, wrapped in clean linen cloths, was buried with due reverence, to be sometime raised in eternal glory.

CHAPTER XXIV.

A Storm occurs during the Days of his Obsequies as the Saint predicted.

FOR once one of the brethren said to the Saint: "All the people of the provinces will come after thy decease to thy obsequies." "No," said the Saint, "the event will not turn out as you say; for a mixed crowd will not be present at my obsequies; only my own monks with whom I have lived will fill my grave and honour my funeral with their attendance." And so it came to pass, for during those three days and nights of his obsequies, a great storm of wind without rain blew, so that no vessel was able to cross the sea to take part in the last rites of the man of God. At length, when the Saint was buried, the wind falling and the tempest being stilled, the waves of the sea became quiet. Glory to Thee O God. Amen.

CHAPTER XXV.

Eulogy of Columba. He raises the Dead. A Wonderful Stone. He Slays a Boar with a Word. He Blesses the Cows. He beholds souls received into Heaven. He appears to King Oswald. He predicts concerning King Aidan.

LET the reader therefore consider what and how great were the merits before God in the highest of him whom God so magnified by the prerogative of signs and the privilege of merits, and on whom, next to the Apostles, he bestowed the gift of his grace. For in the flesh, as an angel living, he stilled tempests, calmed seas, a Church not opened to him, he very often unlocked without a key, the bolt being uninjured, imprinting upon it only the sign of the Lord's cross. After kneeling some time, when he had poured himself out in prayer, rising from the ground, in the name of the Lord

he brings to life the dead son of some common man, and
after his obsequies are celebrated, he presents him alive to his
father and mother. Also a stone dipped by him in water, in a
wonderful way, contrary to its nature, floated upon the surface
of the water, nor could this which the holy man had blessed be
ever afterwards sunk. A sick man drank of the water in which
it was swimming and immediately returned from the brink of
death, and recovered soundness and health of body. Accordingly the same stone, afterwards preserved in the treasury of
the King, wrought many cures among the people by the finger
of God, by whom it had been blessed by the hand of Columba,
the man of God. Again, when he has entered a wood, a boar
of marvellous size, which the hounds chanced to be pursuing,
meets him. At the sight of it the Saint stopped, and having
raised his holy hand, said: " Come no further ; die where thou
art ; " and it died. He also blessed five cows belonging to a
poor man and commanded their number to increase to a hundred and five ; and this rich blessing was upon the man's sons
and grandsons. This Saint, too, very often beheld the souls of
just men carried by angels into heaven, and those of wicked
men taken down by demons to hell. Moreover, he spake to
King Oswald, who had marked out his camp, in preparation
for battle, and was sleeping in his tent on a cushion,
and commanded him to go forth to battle. He obeyed the
command and obtained the victory. Moreover, returning
afterwards he was ordained by God Emperor of all Britain,
and all the nation, who before that were unbelieving, were
baptized. He likewise examined the whole world, clearly
perceiving it as if collected under a single ray of the sun, its
bosom being wonderfully opened to his merits. One day,
also, the Saint of God instructed his servant to suddenly
toll the bell. Aroused by the sound, the brethren forthwith entered the Church. The Saint said to them : "Pour out
your prayers to the Lord for Aidan and his people." After a
time he went out, and looking to heaven, said : " Now the
barbarous host is turned to flight, and the victory is yielded to
Aidan." Also in the spirit of prophecy he told them of the
number of three hundred and three men of the army slain.

CHAPTER XXVI.

A Miracle Wrought by his Tunic.

AFTER the death of the man of God, a great drought occurred in the spring time. And the brethren fearing an approaching plague raised in the air the white tunic in which the blessed man was clad in the hour of death, and shook it thrice. They also read the books written by his own hand. When all these things were duly performed, wonderful to relate, on the same day a violent rain falling watered the thirsting land, and in the same year it produced rich crops.

CHAPTER XXVII.

AGAIN, once when the Saint was annoyed by a press of the brethren, a boy, very mean in countenance and dress, secretly drew near behind, that he might touch the fringe of the coat with which the Saint was clad without him knowing. But this was not hidden from the Saint; for reaching his hand behind him, he held the boy's neck. To whom, trembling, the Saint said: "Open thy mouth and put out thy tongue;" which doing, the Saint blessed him with outstretched hand, and said to those standing by: "This boy, now despicable to you, will from this hour be famous in all Ireland, and excel in wisdom, eloquence, in good manners, and in fruitfulness of virtues." Which, indeed, God fulfilled according to the prophecy of His Saint, to the praise and glory of His name, to whom is honour and glory for ever. Amen.

THE LIFE OF S. COLUMBA.

BY

ADAMNAN.

THE LIFE OF S. COLUMBA.

HERE BEGINS THE PREFACE TO THE LIFE OF S. COLUMBA, BISHOP.

WITH the aid of Christ I am about, in obedience to the urgent requests of the brethren, to write the life of our blessed Patron, and am anxious, in the first place, to warn those who may read, to pay heed to the facts recorded, and to weigh the things rather than the words, which, as I think, seem to be uncultivated and base. And remembering that the Kingdom of God is not in richness of eloquence but in fruitfulness of faith, let them not, on account of any names of men or tribes, or obscure places in the base Irish tongue, which, as I think, seem rude when compared with the different languages of foreign nations, despise a record of useful deeds which were not done without the help of God. Moreover, I think that the reader ought also to be warned that many things concerning this man of blessed memory, though worthy of remembrance, are here passed over for the sake of brevity, and that, as it were, only a few out of many are recorded, in order that the patience of the readers may not be wearied. And this, I think, every one who reads this work will probably observe that of the great actions of this same holy man, those which fame has published abroad among the nations are the least important, even when compared with the few which we shall now endeavour briefly to relate. After this first short preface, I shall now, with the help of God, proceed to explain in the beginning of the second the name of our President.

In the name of Jesus Christ the Second Preface is begun.

There was a man of venerable life and blessed memory, the father and founder of monasteries, who had the same name as Jonah the prophet; for though in the three languages the sound be different, in Hebrew Iona, in Greek Περιστερὰ, and in Latin Columba, the meaning in all is one and the same. Such and so great a name, it is believed, was not given to the man of God without divine guidance. For, according to the testimony of the Gospels, the Holy Ghost is shown to have descended upon the Only Begotten of the Eternal Father in the form of that little bird which is called the dove; and hence in the Sacred Books the dove is very frequently chosen to designate in a mystical sense the Holy Ghost. For this reason, also, our Saviour in His Gospel commanded the disciples to maintain the simplicity of doves engrafted in a pure heart; for the dove is a simple and innocent bird. With this name, therefore, it was meet that a man who was simple and innocent, and gave to the Holy Ghost a dwelling-place in his heart in dove-like ways, should be named; for to this name may not inaptly be applied that which is written in Proverbs: "A good name is better than many riches." Wherefore our President, not undeservedly adorned, was not only honoured with this special name from the days of his infancy, but was also so named as a child of promise many long years before in a wonderful prophecy by a certain soldier of Christ, unto whom it was revealed by the Holy Ghost. For a certain pilgrim from Britain, a holy man, a disciple of S. Patrick the Bishop, by name Maucta, thus prophesied concerning our Patron, as is known to us on the testimony of learned men of old: "In the last ages of the world shall be born a son, whose name, Columba, shall be spread abroad through all the provinces of the isles of the ocean; and he shall brilliantly illumine the last ages of the earth. The little farms of our two small monasteries, his and mine, shall be separated by the space of a little fence; he shall be very dear to God, and of great merit in His sight." Therefore, when describing the life and character of

this our Columba, I shall in the first place give, in the fewest
words I can, a general summary, and, at the same time, place
before the eyes of the reader his holy walk and conversation.
As a foretaste to those who eagerly read them, I shall also
briefly touch upon his miracles; these, however, will be more
fully related further on, and divided into three books. The First
of these books will contain his Prophetical Revelations; the
Second, the Divine Miracles which were wrought by him; the
Third, the Angelic Apparitions and certain manifestations of
the heavenly brightness upon the man of God. Let no one,
however, think of me either as saying anything false concerning
so great a man, or, as it were, about to write anything which
is doubtful or uncertain; but let him understand that I am
about to record without ambiguity, and to relate in a consis-
tent narrative the things which have been handed down from
my predecessors, who were learned and trustworthy men, and
that what I am about to write is taken either from the things
I have been able to find already recorded in books, or from
those which, on careful examination, I have myself ascertained
on the testimony of some trustworthy and learned ancients
who unhesitatingly bore witness to them, having themselves
diligently inquired into their truth.

S. Columba, then, was born of noble parents; his father was
Fedilmith, the son of Fergus, and his mother Aethne, whose
father may in Latin be called Filius Navis, but in the Irish
tongue is named Mac Nave. In the second year after the battle
of Cooldrevny (fought A.D. 561), when in the forty-second
year of his age, desiring to seek a foreign country for the sake
of Christ, he sailed from Ireland into Britain. From his boyhood he was brought up in the discipline of the Christian faith
and in the study of wisdom; and preserving, through the grace
of God, the integrity of his body and the purity of his soul,
though dwelling upon the earth, he proved himself fitted for
the heavenly life. For he was angelic in appearance, graceful
in speech, holy in deed, excellent in ability, great in counsel,
and for thirty-four years he lived upon an island as a soldier of
Christ. Not even the space of a single hour could he ever
spend without devoting himself either to prayer, reading,

or writing, or to some other similar work. He was so occupied day and night, without the slightest intermission in the unwearied exercise of fasting and watching, that the burden of each of these austerities seemed beyond the possibility of human endurance. And still in these he was beloved by all, always exhibiting in his countenance that holy cheerfulness with which the joy of the Holy Ghost was gladdening his inmost soul.

BOOK I.

OF HIS PROPHETIC REVELATIONS.

CHAPTER I.

A brief Narrative of his Miracles.

ACCORDING to the promise given above, the proofs which the venerable man gave of his power must here, in the beginning of this little book, be briefly set forth. By the virtue of his prayers and in the name of the Lord Jesus Christ, he healed men grievously afflicted with divers diseases; and alone, by the help of God, repelled innumerable hosts of malignant demons, which he saw with his bodily eyes warring against himself, and drove them away from this our chief island, when they were beginning to bring deadly distempers upon his monastic brotherhood. The furious rage of wild beasts, partly by mortification and partly by a bold resistance, he, with the help of Christ, subdued. Swelling seas also, which sometimes rose up in the greatness of the tempest like mountains, were quickly, at his prayers, brought low and stilled, and the ship in which he then chanced to be sailing, was driven in the calm which followed to the desired haven. When returning from the country of the Picts, where he had been staying some days, in order to confound the Druids, he hoisted his sail when the wind was against him, and his ship swept along with as much speed as if he had had the wind in his favour. At other times, also, winds contrary to those who were navigating were at his prayer changed into favourable. In the above mentioned country, he took a white stone from a river and blessed it for the working of certain cures; and the said stone when placed in water floated, contrary to nature, like an apple. This divine miracle was wrought in the presence of King Brude and his household. And what is a greater miracle, in the same country he raised the dead child of a humble believer to life, and restored him to his father and mother living and uninjured. At another time, while the blessed youth was a deacon, dwelling with the holy bishop Findbarr in Ireland, when the wine requisite for celebrating the holy mysteries was wanting, by the power of prayer he changed pure water into real wine. Moreover, an immense blaze of heavenly light on many and different occasions, appeared to certain of the brethren to be poured down upon him during the light of day, as well as in the darkness of the night. He so lived, also, as to enjoy bright hauntings, most sweet and pleasant, of the holy angels. Through the revelation of the Holy Spirit, he frequently saw the souls of just men carried by angels to the highest heavens, and the souls of the wicked borne down by demons into hell. Very often, too, he foretold the future deserts, sometimes joyful, sometimes sad, of many persons who were still living in mortal flesh. In the terrific onslaughts of battles, he obtained from God, by virtue of his prayers, that some kings should be vanquished, and that other rulers should come off victors. And this great privilege was granted unto him not only while he was here in this present life, but also after his departure from the flesh, as to a victorious and most valiant champion, by God, from whom all the saints derive their honour. I shall give one example of this great honour conferred by Almighty God upon this honourable man, which was made manifest to Oswald, the Saxon Ruler, the day before he engaged in battle against Catlon, a very brave king of the Britons. This same king Oswald, when he had pitched his camp in readiness for the battle, was one day sleeping in his tent upon a pillow, and saw S. Columba in a vision, shining in the form of an angel, and of figure so majestic that his head seemed to touch the clouds. The blessed man made his name known to the king, and, standing in the middle of the camp, covered the whole of it, except at one small extremity, with his glistening raiment, and addressed to him these cheering words, the same indeed as the Lord spake to Joshua, the son of Nun, before the passage of the Jordan, after the death of Moses, saying: "Be strong and of good courage; behold, I shall be with thee," etc.

Then S. Columba, having said these words in the vision to the king, added: "Go forth this night from the camp to battle; for on this occasion the Lord has granted unto me both that thy foes shall be put to flight, and that thine enemy, Catlon, shall be delivered into thy hands, and that after the battle thou shalt return in triumph and reign happily." After these words the king arose, and, having assembled his council, related the vision; and being encouraged by it, the whole people promised, that after their return from the battle they would believe and receive baptism; for up to that time all that Saxon land had been wrapped in the darkness of paganism and ignorance, except King Oswald himself and twelve men who were baptised with him during his exile among the Scots. What more need I say? The following night King Oswald, as he had been instructed in the vision, went forth from the camp to battle against many thousands with an army much smaller; and, according as it was promised, an easy and decisive victory was granted to him by the Lord, and King Catlon being slain, he returned from the war in triumph, and was afterwards ordained by God Bretwalda of all Britain. This narrative was unhesitatingly told to me, Adamnan, by my predecessor, our Abbot Failbhe, who solemnly declared that he heard it from the lips of King Oswald himself, when relating this same vision to the Abbot Seghine.

And this also, it seems, ought not to be omitted. By some songs composed in the Irish language in praise of this blessed man and by the commemoration of his name, certain wicked men, though of lewd conversation and stained with the blood of their fellowmen, the same night in which they sang these songs were delivered from the hands of their enemies, who had surrounded the house in which they were singing. From the flames and swords and spears they escaped unhurt, and strange to say, only a few, who had lightly esteemed these commemorations of the holy man, and had refused to join in the singing, perished in that assault of their enemies. The witnesses of this miracle are not two or three, as the law requires, but even hundreds and more can be brought forward to attest it. And this is known to have happened, not only in one place or on one occasion, but also at different times and in different places has it been proved beyond all measure of doubt to have happened in the same manner and by the same means, both in Ireland and in Britain. This I have learned for certain from well informed men of the very countries where the same thing has occurred through a similar miracle.

But to return to the matter in hand. Among the miracles which this same man of the Lord wrought by the gift of God while dwelling in mortal flesh, was that he began, even from his early years, to be able by the spirit of prophecy to predict things which were about to come to pass, and to make known to those who were with him things which were occurring in other places; for though absent in body, he was present in spirit, and could discern things which were done afar off. For, according to the words of S. Paul: "He that is joined to the Lord is one spirit." Whence also this same man of the Lord, S. Columba, as also, when a few of the brethren would sometimes inquire into this matter he did not deny, when the bosom of his mind was wonderfully enlarged, saw in many visions of the divine grace even the whole universe drawn together as into one ray of the sun and laid open to his sight.

These things are here narrated concerning the miracles of the holy man that the more eager reader may, in the things which are here briefly written, have a foretaste, as it were, of those richer banquets which lie before him in the fuller narratives to be given, with the help of the Lord, in the three following books. It seems to me not improper, though it may be out of the usual order, to speak now of some prophecies of the blessed man which he uttered at sundry times concerning certain holy and illustrious men.

CHAPTER II.

Of St. Fintan the Abbot, son of Tailchan.

S. FINTAN, who was afterwards well known through all the churches of the Scots, having by the help of God preserved from his boyhood purity of body and soul, and being devoted to the study of divine wisdom, held in his heart this one resolve, which he had nourished in the years of his youth, that leaving Ireland, he would make a pilgrimage in order to visit our S. Columba. Animated by this resolve he went to a certain friend older than himself, a venerable cleric, the most prudent in his own tribe, who, in the Irish tongue, was called Columb Crag, in order to obtain from him, as a prudent man, some advice. When he made known to him his thoughts, he received from him this reply: "Thy desire is devout, and is inspired, I believe, by God; who can therefore presume to say that thou oughtest not to cross the sea to S. Columba." By chance two of S. Columba's monks arrived at the very moment, who, being inquired of concerning their journey, said: "We have sailed lately over from Britain, and have come to-day from the Oakwood of Calgach." "Is your holy father, Columba, not well?" said Columb Crag. They wept sorely, and said with great sorrow: "Our Patron is well indeed, for a few days ago he departed to be with Christ." When they heard this, Fintan and Columb, and all who were there present, fell on their faces to the ground and wept bitterly. Fintan then inquired, saying: "Whom has he left as his successor?" "Baithene, his disciple," they said. And as they all cried out: "Meet and right," Columb said to Fintan: "What wilt thou do now, Fintan?" He replied: "If God permit, I will sail over to Baithene, that holy and wise man, and if he will receive me, I will have him for my abbot." Then kissing the aforementioned Columb, and bidding him farewell, he prepared for his voyage, and setting sail without the slightest delay came to the island of Iona. At that time his name was not known in these places. At first, therefore, he was received only with the hospitality given to every unknown guest. One day he sent a messenger to Baithene, saying that he desired to speak with him face to face; and he being always affable and pleasant to travellers, ordered him to be brought to him. Accordingly he was at once brought in, and at first, as seemed meet, he bowed down to the ground on bended knees, and when requested by the holy Abbot, he rose up, and, being seated, was questioned by

Baithene, to whom he was as yet unknown, respecting his race and province, name and manner of life, and for what cause he had undertaken his voyage. And being thus interrogated, he narrated all things in order, and humbly entreated that he might be admitted. The holy Abbot on hearing these things from his guest, and at the same time recognising that this was he of whom S. Columba had some time previously uttered a prophecy, said: "Verily, my son, I ought to give thanks to my God for thy arrival; but know of a certainty thou wilt not be our monk." Hearing this the guest was deeply grieved, and replied: "Perhaps I am unworthy, and do not deserve to become a monk." The Abbot immediately answered: "Not because, as thou sayest, thou art unworthy have I said what I have, but because, even though I would much rather have retained thee with me, I cannot desecrate the command of my predecessor, S. Columba, through whom the Holy Spirit prophesied of thee. For when alone with me one day, speaking with the mouth of prophecy, he said, among other things: 'These my words, O Baithene, thou must needs hearken unto very attentively; for immediately after my departure from this world to be with Christ, which I wait and earnestly desire, a certain brother from Ireland, Fintan by name, of the tribe of Mocumoie, whose father is called Tailchan, now carefully ordering his youth according to good morals, and well versed in sacred studies—he coming to thee, I say, will humbly entreat thee to receive and number him among thy other monks. But it has not been ordained for him in the foreknowledge of God that he should be the monk of any Abbot; but long since has he been chosen of God to be an Abbot of monks and a leader of souls to the heavenly kingdom. Detain not, therefore, that illustrious man with thee on these our islands, lest thou shouldst even seem to oppose the will of God; but make known these words to him, and send him back to Ireland, that he may found a monastery in the parts of the Leinstermen, near the sea, and there, feeding the flock of the sheep of Christ, lead innumerable souls to the heavenly land.'" Hearing these words the holy youth shed tears, and gave thanks to Christ, saying: "Be it unto me according to the prophetical and marvellous foreknowledge of the holy Columba." And obeying the words of the saint, and receiving a blessing from Baithene, he in the same days sailed back in peace to Ireland.

These things I have learned as unquestionably true from an aged pious presbyter, a soldier of Christ, Oissene by name, the son of Ernan, of the tribe of Mocu Neth Corb, who narrated them to me, and testified that he had himself heard the above recorded words from the mouth of S. Fintan, son of Tailchan, whose monk he himself had been.

CHAPTER III.

A Prophecy of S. Columba concerning Ernene, son of Crasen.

AT another time the blessed man, while dwelling for a few months in the middle parts of Ireland, founding, by Divine guidance, the monastery which, in the Irish tongue, is called Dairmaig [Durrow], was pleased to visit the brethren who dwelt in the monastery of S. Ceran, at Clonmacnoise. When his approach was known, all flocked together from the little farms in the neighbourhood of the monastery, and following the Abbot Alither and those who were found within it, with all alacrity, they issued beyond the enclosure of the monastery, and advanced with one accord to meet S. Columba, as if he were an angel of the Lord; they humbly bowed down with their faces to the earth in his presence, with all reverence, kissed him, and, singing hymns and praises, conducted him with honour to the Church. Over the saint, as he walked, was a canopy framed of wood, made to be supported by four men walking by his side, lest the holy Abbot Columba should be troubled by the multitude of brethren crowding around him. In that same hour a serving-boy, very mean in dress and appearance, and not yet acceptable to the elders, concealing himself as much as he could, came behind that he might stealthily touch even so much as the hem of the garment in which the blessed man was clothed, and if it were possible, without his knowing or feeling it. But this was not hid from Saint; for what he was unable to see done behind him with his bodily eyes, he saw with the eyes of his spirit. Suddenly therefore he stopped, and stretching his hand behind him, seized the boy by the neck, and pulling him round, set him before him. All who were standing by cried out: "Let him go, let him go: why hold that unhappy and naughty lad?" But the Saint, out of his pure heart, uttered these prophetic words: "Suffer it brethren; suffer it to be so now." But to the lad, who was quaking with fear, he said: "My son, open thy mouth and put out thy tongue." Then, as commanded, the boy opened his mouth in great terror, and put out his tongue; and the Saint, extending to it his holy hand, carefully blessed it, and spake prophetically, saying: "This lad, though he now appears to you very vile and worthless, let no one on that account despise him. For, from this hour, he will not only not displease you, he will greatly delight you. From day to day he shall gradually advance in good conduct and in the virtues of the soul; from this day also shall wisdom and prudence be more and more increased in him, and great shall be his progress in this your community; moreover, to his tongue shall be given sound and learned eloquence of God." This was Ernene, son of Crasen, who was afterwards famous, and most highly honoured among all the Churches of Ireland. All these words prophesied concerning himself, which are written above, he told to the Abbot Seghine, when my predecessor, Failbhe, was intently listening, who also was himself present with Seghine, and from whose revelation I myself have learned the things I have now narrated. Many other things, also, during those days in which he was entertained at the monastery of Clonmacnoise, did he prophesy by the revelation of the Holy Ghost; as, for instance, concerning the discord which, after many days, arose in the churches of Ireland on account of the difference in regard to the Feast of Easter; and concerning some angelic visitations manifested to himself; certain places within the enclosure of that monastery being at that time resorted to by angels.

CHAPTER IV.

Of the arrival of S. Cainnech, the Abbot, who had previously been announced in prophecy by S. Columba.

ON another occasion, when in the island of Iona, on a day of destructive tempest and exceedingly high seas, when sitting in his house and giving instructions to the brethren, the Saint said: "Prepare quickly the guest-chamber, and draw water to wash the feet of guests." Upon this one of the brethren said: "Narrow though it be, who can cross the sound safely on so stormy and perilous a day?" Whom hearing, the Saint thus answered: "To a certain holy and elect man, who will arrive amongst us before evening, the Almighty has granted a calm even in this tempest." And lo! the same day the ship, waited for by the brethren for some time, and in which was Cainnech, arrived according to the prophecy of the Saint, who went forth with the brethren to meet him, and received him with hospitality and honour. But the sailors who were with Cainnech, on being asked by the brethren what kind of a voyage they had had, told them, even as S. Columba had predicted, of the tempest and calm which God had given in the same sea and at the same time yet marvellously sundered. The tempest, which was seen in the distance, they said they did not feel.

CHAPTER V.

Of the peril of the holy bishop Colmann Mocusailni in the sea near the island called Rechru.

ON another day S. Columba, when sitting in his mother-Church, suddenly cried out, saying with a smile: "Columbannus, the son of Beogna has begun to sail over to us, and is now in great danger in the rolling tides of the whirlpool of Brecan. Seated at the brow he is raising both hands to heaven; he is also blessing that troubled and dreadful sea;

nevertheless the Lord thus alarms him, not that the vessel in which he is seated, may be overwhelmed by the waves in shipwreck, but rather to incite to more fervent prayer, that, by God's favour, he may reach us after escaping the peril."

CHAPTER VI.

Of Cormac.

ON another occasion, also, S. Columba thus prophesied concerning Cormac, grandson of Lethan, a man truly pious, who not less than three times patiently sought a desert in the ocean, yet did not find it, saying: " To-day again Cormac desiring to find the desert, is embarking from the district which is situated beyond the river Moy, and called Erris ; yet even this time he will not find what he seeks, and that for no other fault than this, that he has irregularly allowed to accompany him on his voyage the monk of a certain religious Abbot, who is going away without his consent."

CHAPTER VII.

A Prophecy of the Blessed Man concerning the tumults of Battles which were fought at a distance.

TWO years after the battle of Cooldrevny, as we have been told, at the time when the blessed man first set sail and took his departure from Ireland, one day, namely, in the same hour in which the battle, which in Irish is called Ondemone was fought in Ireland, the same man of God, who was then living with King Connall, the son of Comgill, in Britain, told him every thing, both concerning the battle which was being fought, and concerning the Kings to whom the Lord had granted victory over their enemies. In their own tongue the names of the Kings were Ainmire, son of Setna, and the two sons of Mac Erca, Domnall and Forcus. Also concerning the King of the Picts who was called Echoid Laib, how, when vanquished, he escaped riding in a chariot, the Saint prophesied in like manner.

CHAPTER VIII.

Of the Battle of the Miathi.

ON another occasion, many years after the above mentioned battle, when the holy man was in the island of Iona, he suddenly said to his servant Diormit: "Ring the bell." Startled by the sound, the brethren quickly ran to the Church, the holy president himself leading the way. There as they knelt he said to them: "Let us now earnestly pray to the Lord for this people and for King Aidan; for at this moment they are engaging in battle." And a little after he left the place of prayer and looking up to heaven, said: "Now are the barbarians being put to flight; and to Aidan, the victory, sad though it be, is given." The blessed man also prophetically declared that the number of the slain in Aidan's army would be three hundred and three men.

CHAPTER IX.

A Prophecy of S. Columba concerning the sons of King Aidan.

AT another time before the battle mentioned above, the Saint inquired of King Aidan concerning his successor to the kingdom. He said in answer that he knew not which of his three sons would reign after him, whether Artur, or Echoid Find, or Domingart. Thereupon the Saint prophesied as follows: "None of these three shall be the Ruler; for they shall all fall in battle, slain by their enemies; but if thou hast any younger sons, let them now come to me, and he whom the Lord shall choose from among them to be King, will straightway rush into my lap." And according to the word of the Saint, when they were called in, Echoid Buide drawing near lay in his bosom. Immediately the Saint kissed him, and blessed him, and said to his father: " This is the survivor ; he shall rule after thee as King, and his sons shall reign after him." And so afterwards were all these things fully accomplished in their own time. For Artur and Echoid Find were slain not long after the above-mentioned battle of the Miathi ; Domingart was defeated and slain in Saxonia ; and Echoid Buide succeeded his father in the kingdom.

CHAPTER X.

Of Domnall son of Aid.

DOMNALL son of Aid, while yet a boy, was brought by his fosterers to S. Columba at Druim Ceatt, who, looking at him, inquired saying : "Whose son is this whom ye have brought?" They answered : "This is Domnall, son of Aid, who is brought to thee that he may return enriched with thy blessing." When he had blessed him, the Saint immediately said : "This one shall survive his brothers and become a very famous king ; nor shall he ever be delivered into the hands of his enemies, but in his old age and in his own home, surrounded by a crowd of his familiar friends, he shall die in peace in his own bed. All these things were truly fulfilled concerning him, according to the prophecy of the blessed man.

CHAPTER XI.

Of Scandlan son of Colman.

AT the same time and in the same place, the Saint desiring to visit Scandlan, son of Colman, then a captive in bonds with King Aid, went to him ; and when he had blessed him, he comforted him, saying: "Son, be not sorrowful, but rather be of good courage and rejoice. For King Aid, with whom thou art now in bonds, will pass away from this world before thee; and after a while of exile, thou shalt rule among thine own people as King for thirty years. And again thou shalt be a fugitive from thy kingdom, and shalt dwell in exile for some days; after which, invited back by thy people, thou shalt reign for three short terms. All these things were fully accomplished according to the prophecy of the Saint; for after thirty years Scandlan was driven from his kingdom and lived some time in exile; but afterwards, when invited back by his people, he reigned not three years as he expected, but three months, and then died.

CHAPTER XII.

Of two other Rulers who were called the grandsons of Muiredach; Baitan, son of Mac Erc, and Echoid, son of Domnall—a prophecy of the Blessed Man.

AT another time, when travelling through a wild and rocky country which is called Ardnamurchan, and listening to his companions, Laisran, the son of Feradach, and Diormit his servant, discussing on the way respecting the two Kings mentioned above, he addressed to them these words: "O my children, why do you so foolishly talk together of these men? For both these Kings of whom you now speak, have just perished, their heads having been cut off by their enemies. To-day, moreover, some sailors coming here from Ireland, shall relate these same things to you concerning these Kings." And that same day sailors from Ireland arrived at a place called Muirbolc Paradisi, and told the two above-mentioned companions who were sailing in the same ship with the Saint, how the prophecy of the venerable man concerning the slaughter of these Kings had been fulfilled.

CHAPTER XIII.

A Prophecy of the Holy Man concerning Oingus, son of Aid Comman.

THIS man, when he was driven from his country with his two brothers, came as an exile to the Saint, who was then travelling in Britain, and who, when blessing him, uttered from his holy heart these words in prophecy concerning him: "This youth, surviving when his brothers are dead, shall rule in his native land for a long time; his enemies shall fall before him; neither shall he ever be delivered into his enemies' hands; but he shall die an old man among his friends a peaceful death. All which things were fully accomplished according to the word of the Saint. This was Oingus surnamed Bronbachal.

CHAPTER XIV.

A prophecy of the Blessed Man concerning the son of King Dermit who in the Irish tongue is called Aid Slane.

AT another time, when the blessed man was tarrying in Ireland for some days, he spake in prophecy the following words to the above mentioned Aid, who was then visiting him: "Beware, my son, lest through committing parricidal crime thou lose the prerogative of the monarchy of the Kingdom of all Ireland which has been foreordained for thee by God; for if at any time thou shouldst commit that crime, thou shalt not hold the whole of thy father's Kingdom, but only a part of it in thine own tribe for a little time." These words of the Saint were on this wise fulfilled according to his prophecy; for after Aid had treacherously slain Suibne, son of Columban, he did not reign, it is said, more than four years and three months, and then only as joint-ruler of the Kingdom.

CHAPTER XV.

A prophecy of the Blessed Man concerning King Roderc son of Tothal who reigned at Alcluith.

ON another occasion this same King, as a friend of the holy man, sent a secret message to him by Lugbe Mocumin, desiring to know whether he would be slain by his enemies or not. But when Lugbe was interrogated by the Saint respecting the said King, his kingdom and his people, he, responding as if he pitied him, said: "Why dost thou inquire concerning that wretched man who is in no wise able to tell at what hour he may be slain by his enemies?" The Saint then answered: "Never shall he be delivered into the hands of his enemies, but in his own house, and on his own pillow shall he die." Which prophecy of the Saint concerning King Roderc was fully accomplished; for according to his words, he died a peaceful death in his own house.

CHAPTER XVI.

A prophecy of the Saint concerning two boys, one of whom according to the word of the Saint died at the end of a week.

AT another time two peasants came to the Saint when he was residing in the island of Iona. One of them, named Meldan, whose son was with him, inquired of the Saint what would befall him in the future. To whom the Saint thus replied: "Is not this Saturday? Thy son on the sixth day at the end of the week will die, and on the eighth, that is, on Saturday, he will be buried here." Nevertheless, the other man, by name Glasderc, inquiring respecting his son, whom he likewise had with him, received from the Saint the following answer: "Thy son, Ernan, will see his grand-children, and will be buried in his old age in this island." All which things were in their own time according to the word of the Saint fully accomplished respecting both the boys.

CHAPTER XVII.

Prophecy of the Saint concerning Colga son of Aid Draigniche, descended from the grandson of Fechureg, and concerning a secret sin of his mother.

ON another occasion, the above mentioned Colga while staying with the Saint in the island of Iona, was interrogated by him concerning his mother, as to whether she was pious or not. In reply he said: "I have always known my mother to be well mannered and of good report." Then the Saint uttered this prophecy: "With the help of God, set out at once for Ireland and inquire diligently of thy mother concerning her very great hidden sin which she will not confess to any human being." Hearing this and obeying, he set out for Ireland. When closely questioned by him, his mother, though at first denying her sin, at last confessed it; and doing penance according to the judgment of the Saint, she was absolved, marvelling greatly at what was made known to the Saint concerning her. Colga, however, returned to the Saint and remained with him for some days; and inquiring concerning the end of his own days, received this reply from the Saint: "In thine own country, which thou lovest, thou shalt be the head of a church for many years; and if perchance thou shalt at any time see thy butler amusing himself at supper with his friends and twirling the ladle round by the neck, know then that thou shalt shortly die." What more need I say? This same prophecy of the blessed man was fulfilled in all things as was prophesied concerning this same Colga.

CHAPTER XVIII.

Of Laisran, the Gardener, a holy man.

ON a certain day the blessed man ordered one of his monks named Trena, of the tribe of Mocuruntir, to go to Ireland on a piece of business for him. In obedience to the command of the man of God he quickly prepared for the voyage, and complained in the presence of the Saint that he was in need of one sailor. Replying to him, the Saint immediately uttered these words from his holy breast : " The sailor who thou sayest is not yet present, I cannot now find ; go in peace ; thou shalt have favourable and prosperous breezes until thou reach Ireland. Thou shalt see a man about to run to meet thee from a distance, who before others shall be the first to take hold of the prow of thy ship ; he shall be the companion of thy journey for some days in Ireland, and when thou returnest thence, he shall accompany thee to us, a man chosen of God, who in this my monastery shall spend the rest of his days well." What more need I say ? Receiving the benediction of the Saint, Trena crossed over all the seas with full sails ; and lo, as his little ship reached the port, Laisran Mocumoie ran more quickly than the rest, and seized the prow. The sailors knew that he was the man concerning whom the Saint prophesied.

CHAPTER XIX.

Of a great whale which the Saint knew of beforehand, and spake about.

ONE day, when the venerable man was staying in the island of Iona, a certain brother, Berach by name, proposed to sail over to the island of Tiree, and coming to the Saint early in the morning, asked to be blessed by him. Looking at him the Saint said : " O my son, be very careful to-day not to attempt to cross by a direct course through the open sea to Tiree, but rather go about and sail round by the smaller islands, lest thou be terrified by some monstrous prodigy, and be hardly able to escape it." Having received the Saint's benediction, he left him, and embarking, transgressed the word of the Saint as if he lightly esteemed it. Then while crossing the larger arms of the sea near Tiree, he and the sailors who were with him, looked out, and lo, a whale of vast and astounding size raised itself like a mountain and swimming on the surface opened its wide mouth bristling with teeth. The rowers hauled down the sail, and rowed back greatly terrified, and could with difficulty escape from the agitation of the waves which the movement of the monster caused ; and recalling the prophetic utterance of the Saint, they marvelled. Moreover, on the same day, in the morning the Saint told Baithene, who was about to sail to the above mentioned island, of this same whale, saying : " Last night, at midnight, a great whale rose from the depths of the sea, and will to-day rise to the surface between the islands of Iona and Tiree." Baithene responding said : " The beast and I are under the power of God." " Go in peace," said the Saint, " thy faith in Christ shall protect thee from this danger." Baithene accordingly, having received a blessing from the Saint, sailed from the port, and before they had crossed but a little space of the sea, he and his companions beheld the whale ; and when all the rest were terrified, he alone was unmoved, and raising both his hands he blessed the sea and the whale ; and at the same moment the enormous monster sank beneath the waves and appeared to them no more.

CHAPTER XX.

Prophecy of the holy man concerning a certain Baitan who with others had sailed in search of a desert in the ocean.

AT another time a certain man named Baitan, by race a descendant of Niath Taloirc, when about to set out with others in quest of a desert in the sea, desired to be blessed by the Saint. Bidding him farewell the Saint uttered this prophetic word concerning him : " This man, who is going to seek a desert in the ocean, shall not lie buried in a desert, but shall be interred where a woman shall drive sheep over his grave. The same Baitan after long wanderings through stormy seas, not having found the desert, returned to his native land, and there remained many years the head of a small monastic house which in the Irish tongue is called Lathreginden. It came to pass in those days after he had died and was buried in the

Oakgrove of Calgach, that on account of a hostile inroad the people of the neighbourhood fled with their wives and little ones to the Church of that place. And hence it happened that on a certain day a woman was caught who was driving her lambs over the grave of this same man, who had lately been buried there. And a holy priest, who was among those who had seen this, said: "Now is the prophecy of S. Columba fulfilled, though first made known many years ago." And the aforesaid presbyter, Mailodran by name, a soldier of Christ, of the tribe of Mocurin, told these things to me, narrating them of Baitan.

CHAPTER XXI.

A Prophecy of the Holy Man concerning a certain Neman, who feigned penitence.

AT another time the Saint went to the Hinbina island (Eilean-na-naoimh), and on the same day gave instructions that even to the penitents indulgence shonld be permitted in respect of food. Now there was then among the penitents a certain Neman, son of Cathir, who, though ordered by the Saint, refused to accept the offer of this little indulgence. Him the Saint addressed in these words: "O Neman, dost thou not accept the indulgence in food permitted by Baithene and me? The time will come when thou wilt secretly eat mare's flesh in the wood with thieves." And accordingly this same man, after he had returned to the world, was found in a forest with robbers taking such flesh from a wooden griddle, and eating it according to the word of the Saint.

CHAPTER XXII.

Of a certain unhappy man who slept with his mother.

AT another time the Saint aroused the brethren at the dead of night, and when they were assembled in the Church, said to them: "Let us now pray earnestly to the Lord; for in this hour a sin unheard of in the world has been perpetrated, for which the vengeance of justice is greatly to be feared." Of this sin he spake on the morrow when a few inquired of him, saying: "After a few months, that unhappy creature will come to the island of Iona along with Lugaid, who is ignorant of the sin." Accordingly when the few months were passed, the Saint one day gave instructions to Diormit, saying: "Rise quickly, behold Lugaid approaches; tell him to send off the wretch he has with him in the ship to the island of Mull, that he may not tread the turf of this island." In obedience to the Saint's instructions, he put out to sea and told Lugaid on his drawing near all the words of the Saint concerning the unhappy man. On hearing these words the unhappy man swore that he would never eat food with others, until he had first seen S. Columba and spoken to him. Diormit on his return repeated this to the Saint, who on hearing it went to the port; and to Baithene who cited the evidences of Holy Scripture, and suggested that the penitence of the unhappy man should be received, S. Columba said: "O Baithene, this man has committed fratricide after the manner of Cain, and is an adulterer with his mother." Then the wretched man throwing himself on his knees on the shore promised that he would obey the requirements of penitence according to the judgment of the Saint. The Saint said to him: "If thou do penance with tears and weeping for twelve years among the Britons and never to the day of thy death return to Ireland, perchance God may pardon thy sin." Having said these things, the Saint turned to his companions and said: ("This man is a son of perdition, and will not perform the penance he has promised, but will soon return to Ireland and in a short time perish there, slain by his enemies.") All these things happened exactly according to the prophecy of the Saint; for the wretched man returned to Ireland in the same days, and falling into the hands of his enemies, in the district which is called Lea, was slain. He was of the descendants of Turtre.

CHAPTER XXIII.

Of the Vowel I.

ONE day Baithene coming to the Saint said: "I require some one of the brethren to look over and correct with me the Psalter I have written." Hearing this the Saint thus spake: "Why incur this trouble to us without cause? For in that Psalter of thine of which thou speakest not one superfluous letter will be found, nor is there one wanting except only a single vowel I." And so, when the whole Psalter had been read through, it was found to be as the Saint had said.

CHAPTER XXIV.

Of the book which fell into the water-vessel as the Saint had foretold.

IN like manner one day, when sitting at the hearth in the monastery, he saw Lugbe of the tribe of Mocumin at a distance reading a book, and suddenly said to him: "Take care, my son, take care; for I think the book thou art reading is about to fall into a vessel full of water." And so it immediately happened; for the said young man rising after a little to attend to some duty in the monastery, forgetful of the word of the blessed man, the book which he carelessly held under his arm suddenly fell into a waterpot full of water.

CHAPTER XXV.

Of the inkhorn, awkwardly spilled.

AMONG these, it is recorded, that on another day a shout was raised on the other side of the sound of Iona. The Saint who was sitting in a hut made of planks, hearing the shout, said: "The man who is shouting on the other side of the Sound is not quick witted ; for to-day he will upset my inkhorn and spill the ink. Hearing this, his servant Diormit, waited the arrival of this clumsy guest, and stood a little before the door in order to protect the inkhorn. But something soon arising he went away, and after his departure the troublesome guest arrived, and in his eagerness to kiss the Saint he upset the inkhorn with the hem of his garment and spilled the ink.

CHAPTER XXVI.

Of the arrival of another Guest foretold by the Saint.

AT another time, likewise, the Saint spake thus on the third day of the week : " On the morrow, which is the fourth day of the week, we intend to fast ; and yet by the arrival of a certain troublesome guest the customary fast will be broken. And so it came to pass as had been foreshown by the Saint ; for on the morning of the fourth day another stranger by name Aidan son of Fergno, who, as is said, ministered for twelve years to Brenden Mocualti shouted from the other side of the Sound. He was a very religious man, and by his arrival the fast of that day, was, according to the word of the Saint, broken.

CHAPTER XXVII

Of another man in distress who was calling out from the other side of the aforesaid Sound.

ALSO one day, hearing a certain man calling from the other side of the Sound, the Saint spake thus : " Much to be pitied is the man who is shouting ; he comes to us to ask something pertaining to the healing of his flesh. More suitable were it for him this day to do true penance for his sins ; for at the end of the week he shall die." Those who were present told this to the unhappy man when he arrived. But he, lightly esteeming it, when he had received the things he had asked, quickly returned, and according to the prophetic word of the Saint died before the end of the same week.

CHAPTER XXVIII.

Prophecy of the Holy Man concerning the Roman city burnt by a sulphurous fire which fell from heaven.

LIKEWISE at another time Lugbe of the tribe Mocumin, of whom we made mention above, came to the Saint one day, after the grinding of the corn, and could in no wise look upon his face, which was suffused with a marvellous ruddy brightness; and fearing greatly quickly fled. The Saint with a slight clapping of the hands called him back. When he returned, he was immediately asked by the Saint, why he had fled so quickly. He replied: "I fled, because I was greatly afraid." After a little, becoming more confident, he ventured to ask the Saint: "Has any awful vision been shown to thee just now?" The Saint replied: "A very terrible retribution has just now been exacted in a remote part of the world." "What retribution," asked the young man, "and in what part has it been executed?" Then the Saint thus spake: "A sulphurous fire has just been poured out from heaven upon a city under the Roman rule, situated within the confines of Italy; and about three thousand men, besides a number of women and children, have perished. And before the present year ends, Gallican sailors arriving from the provinces of Gaul, will relate these same things unto thee." His words, after a few months, were proved to have been true. For the same Lugbe, when going with the Saint to Kintyre, inquired of the captain and sailors of a bark just arriving, and heard all the things narrated by them concerning the city and its inhabitants, exactly as they were predicted by the illustrious man.

CHAPTER XXIX.

A vision of the Blessed Man concerning Laisran, son of Feradach.

ONE very cold day in winter, the Saint was troubled with great sadness, and wept. His servant, Diormit, asked him the cause of his sadness, and received this response: "Not without reason, O my child, am I now sad, seeing that my monks who are already wearied with heavy labour, are burdened by Laisran with the construction of a large house. This displeases me greatly." Strange to say, at that moment Laisran, who was then living in the monastery of the Oakwood Plain, was in some way compelled, and, as if incited by a fire within him, ordered the monks to cease from work, and some refreshments to be prepared for them, and besides, ordered them to rest not only for that day, but also on other days of severe weather. The Saint hearing in spirit these consolatory words addressed to the brethren by Laisran, ceased to weep, and greatly rejoiced, though dwelling in the island of Iona, and related all the circumstances to the brethren around him and blessed Laisran as the comforter of the monks.

CHAPTER XXX.

Of Fechna, a wise man, how he came as a penitent to S. Columba as he had foretold.

AT another time the Saint, when sitting on the top of the hill which in the distance rises up above our monastery, turned to his servant Diormit and addressed him, saying: "I wonder why a certain ship from Ireland is so long in drawing near. It carries a certain wise man, who having fallen into a certain sin, will soon arrive and promise amendment with tears. Not long after the servant, when looking towards the south, saw the sail of a ship approaching the harbour. The Saint, when its arrival was pointed out to him, rose up quickly, saying:

"Let us go to meet the stranger, whose sincere repentance Christ has received." But Fechna leaving the ship hastened to meet the Saint, who was coming down to the harbour, and falling on his bended knees, with tears and lamentations groaned most bitterly, and in the presence of all who were there confessed his sins. Then the Saint shedding tears equally with him, said to him: "Rise up, my son, and be comforted; the sins which thou hast committed are forgiven thee, because, as it is written, "God despiseth not a humble and contrite heart." He then rose up and was joyfully supported by the Saint; and some days after was sent to Baithene, who at the time was living, as Superior, at the monastery in the plain of Lunge, and made his journey thither in peace.

CHAPTER XXXI.

Prophecy of the Holy Man concerning his monk Cailtan.

AT another time, when sending two monks to another of the name of Cailtan, who at the time was superior in the cell which is now called by the name of his brother Diuni and is situated near the lake of the river Aba, the Saint gave them these instructions: "Go quickly to Cailtan, and tell him to come to me without delay." In obedience to the Saint's command they went, and arriving at the cell of Diuni, informed Cailtan of their errand. At once, without tarrying, he followed the Saint's messengers, and quickly came along with them to the Saint, who was then dwelling in the island of Iona. On making his appearance, the Saint spoke to him, addressing him in these words: "O Cailtan, thou hast done well by obediently hastening to me; rest a little. Loving thee as a friend, I sent to invite thee, in order that thou mayest in true obedience finish the course of thy life here with me; for before the end of this week thou wilt pass away in peace to the Lord." When Cailtan heard these words, he gave thanks to God and embraced the Saint with tears. After receiving the Saint's benediction, he went to the guest-chamber. That same night he fell sick, and according to the word of the Saint he departed during that same week to Christ the Lord.

CHAPTER XXXII.
Foresight and prophecy of the Holy Man concerning two brothers.

ONE Lord's day a shout was raised on the other side of the Sound we have so often mentioned. On hearing the shout the Saint said to the brethren who were present: " Go quickly and bring the strangers, who are come from a great distance, to us speedily." They obeyed at once; and, ferrying the guests across, they brought them in. The Saint embraced them, and immediately began to make inquiries of them as to the reason of their journey. In reply they said: " We are come that we may tarry this year with thee." To this the Saint responded: " With me you cannot tarry a year, as you say, without first taking the monastic vow." When those who were present heard these words addressed to newly arrived guests, they wondered greatly. But the elder brother answered in reply to the words of the Saint: " Although up to this moment we never had this thought in mind, yet we will follow thy advice, as we believe it to be divinely inspired." What more need I say? That self-same moment they entered the chapel with the Saint, and on bended knees devoutly took the monastic vow. The Saint then, turning to the brethren, said: " These two strangers who are presenting themselves a living sacrifice to God, and in a brief space are fulfilling a long period of Christian warfare, shall shortly, even during this present month, pass in peace to Christ the Lord." When they heard these words, both the brothers gave thanks to God, and were led away to the guest-chamber. After seven days the elder brother began to be sick, and, during the same week, passed away to the Lord. Likewise also the other, after seven days more, he also grew sick, and in the end of the same week passed with joy to the Lord. And thus, according to the true prophecy of the Saint, before the end of that same month both the brothers ended this present life.

CHAPTER XXXIII.

Prophecy of the Holy Man concerning Artbranan.

WHEN the blessed man was sojourning for some days in the isle of Skye he struck a piece of ground near the sea with his staff, and spoke thus to his companions: "Strange to say, O children, to-day in this spot a certain aged heathen, who has preserved his natural goodness through all his life, will here be baptized, and die, and be buried." And lo! about an hour after, there came into the harbour a vessel, on the prow of which sat a decrepit old man, the chief of the Geona cohort, whom two young men lifted out of the ship and laid in the presence of the blessed man. Having received the word of God from the Saint by means of an interpreter, he forthwith believed, was baptized by the Saint, and after the completion of the mystery of baptism, as the Saint prophesied, immediately died in the same place, and there his companions buried him, and raised a cairn over his body. To this day this cairn is seen on the sea shore; and the river of the place in which he received baptism was called by the inhabitants Dobur Artbranan, and is so named to this present day.

CHAPTER XXXIV.

Of the Boat that was removed by the Saint's order.

AT another time, when travelling beyond Drumalban, the Saint came to a village amid deserted fields, on the bank of a river where it enters a lake. Here he made a stay; and that same night, as they were falling asleep, he aroused his companions, saying: "Now, now, run out quickly, bring hither our boat, which you left in a house beyond the river, and place it in an adjoining hut." Obeying him forthwith, they did as he commanded them. When they were again settled down, the Saint, after a while, quietly nudging Diormit, said: "Stand now without the door and see what is happening in the village, where you first left your boat." In obedience to the Saint, Diormit went out, and looking back, saw the whole village burning with a devastating fire; and, returning to the Saint, told him what was taking place. The Saint then told the brethren of a certain envious foe who had that night set fire to the houses.

CHAPTER XXXV.

Of Gallan, son of Fachtna, who was in the jurisdiction of Colga, son of Cellach.

MOREOVER, on another day, when the Saint was sitting in his hut, he prophesied to the same Colga, who was reading beside him, saying: "Just now the demons are dragging down to hell a miserly chief from the district under thy jurisdiction." When he heard this, Colga marked down the day and hour on his tablet. After some months, having returned to his country and made inquiries among the inhabitants of the place, he found that Gallan, son of Fachtna, had died at the very moment the blessed man told him that he was being carried off by demons.

CHAPTER XXXVI.

Of Findchan, a priest, Founder of the Monastery which, in the Irish tongue, is called Artchain, in the island of Tiree.

AT another time the above-mentioned priest and soldier of Christ, Findchan, brought with him from Ireland to Britain, clad in the clerical garb and for the purpose of staying with him in his monastery for a number of years, Aid, surnamed the Black, a descendant of a royal family and an Irish Pict by race. This Aid the Black had been a very blood-thirsty man, and was the murderer of many. Among others he had slain Diormit, son of Cerbul, who by Divine authority had been ordained Ruler of all Ireland. Moreover, this same Aid, after spending some time in retirement, was, in the presence of the above-named Findchan, ordained a priest, though unlawfully, by a bishop who had been invited for the purpose. The bishop, however, would not venture to lay his hand upon his head unless the said Findchan, who loved Aid after the flesh, would first place his right hand upon his head as a mark of approval. When such an ordination was afterwards made known to the Saint, he was deeply grieved, and forthwith pronounced this terrible sentence against Findchan and Aid who had been ordained, saying : "That right hand which Findchan, contrary to the laws of God and the Church, laid on the head of that son of perdition, shall soon rot away and after great agonies of pain shall go before him to the grave; while he himself shall survive its burial for many years. But this unlawfully ordained Aid shall return as a dog to his vomit and live again as a bloody murderer, and at last, pierced in the neck by a lance, he shall fall from a beam into the water and die by drowning." Such was the end merited long before by him who slew the King of all Ireland. The prophecy of the blessed man was fulfilled concerning both; for the right hand of the priest Findchan putrified from the effects of a blow and preceded him to the earth, being buried in the island which is called Ommon; while he himself survived for many years according to the word of S. Columba. But Aid the Black, a priest only in name, turning again to his former evil ways, was treacherously pierced by a lance, and falling from the prow of a boat into a lake, perished.

CHAPTER XXXVII.

Of the consolation of the spirit of the Saint sent to the monks when wearied on a journey.

AMONG these remarkable manifestations of the spirit of prophecy it does not seem foreign to our little books to say something also of the spiritual comfort which the monks of S.

Columba once felt from his spirit meeting them in the way. For on one occasion, when the brethren were returning in the evening from harvesting, and were come to the place which in the Irish tongue is called Cuuleilne, which is said to be midway between the western plain of the Island of Iona and our monastery, each of them seemed to feel something strange and unwonted, which, however, none of them ventured to mention in any way to each other. And so for some days in the same place and at the same hour in the evening they had the same feeling. In those days, however, S. Baithene was among them, as the director of their labours, and one day he addressed them, saying: "Now brethren, if any of you feel any unwonted or unexpected sign in this middle place between the harvest and the monastery, you ought each to confess it." Then an elder brother said: "In obedience to thy command I will tell what has been shown to me in this place; for both in the past few days and even now I perceive a fragrance of such wonderful sweetness as if all the flowers of the earth were gathered into one place, also a glow of fire not painful but in a certain manner pleasing, and a certain unusual and incomparable gladness poured into my heart, which of a sudden comforts me in a wonderful way, and so refreshes me that I am able to remember neither grief nor weariness of any kind; but even the burden which I carry on my back, though heavy, from this place until the monastery is reached, is in some way I know not of, so lightened that I do not feel that I am bearing a burden." What more need I say? All the harvesters one by one declared that they had had the same experience in every thing, exactly as this one had openly declared, and all knelt down together and requested of S. Baithene that he would learn and inform them of the cause and origin of this wonderful relief which he himself as well as the rest was feeling. Thereupon he replied: "Ye all know that our father Columba is always anxiously thinking about us, and that mindful of our labour he is grieved when we are late in returning to him, and, therefore, though he has not come to meet us in person, his spirit is meeting us and comforting us as we walk along, and is in this way filling us with joy." On hearing these words, they knelt down, and spreading out their hands to heaven with great joy, venerated Christ in the holy and blessed man.

Moreover, we ought not to be silent respecting what has been unhesitatingly handed down to us by certain well informed men concerning the voice of the blessed man when engaged in singing the Psalms. The voice of the venerable man when he was in the church singing psalms with the brethren, was raised in so wonderful a manner that it was sometimes heard four stadia, *i.e.*, five hundred paces off, and sometimes even eight stadia, *i.e.*, a thousand paces away. And strange to say, in the ears of those who were standing beside him in the church, his voice did not exceed in the greatness of its sound the due measure of the human voice; and yet, at the same time, persons who were standing more than a thousand paces away heard the same voice so distinctly that they could distinguish the verses he was singing, even syllable by syllable. Whether they were near or afar off, his voice sounded the same in the ears of those who were listening. But it is admitted that this miracle in connection with the voice of the blessed man happened not often but seldom. Nevertheless, it could not have happened at all without the aid of the Holy Spirit.

And that also ought not to be passed over in silence which is said to have happened when he raised his voice in so great and wonderful a manner near the fortress of King Brude. For when the Saint was according to custom chanting the evensong with a few of the brethren outside the fortifications of the King, certain Druids coming near to them did all they could to prevent the sound of the divine praise from being heard out of their mouth among the heathen. On hearing this the Saint began to sing the forty-fourth Psalm, and at the same moment his voice was so wonderfully raised in the air that it became like pealing thunder, and both the King and the people were struck with intolerable amazement and fear.

CHAPTER XXXVIII.

Of a certain rich man who was called Lugud Clodus.

AT another time, when the Saint was staying in Ireland for some days, he saw a cleric seated in a chariot, and pleasantly driving along the plain of Breg, and inquired who he was. From the man's friends he received the following response concerning him: "This is Lugud Clodus, a man rich and honoured among the people." Thereupon the Saint replied: "Not such do I see; but a poor wretched creature who, on the day of his death, will have among his cattle, in one of his enclosures, three strayed cattle of his neighbour's. One of the three he will select and order to be slain for his own use, and when the flesh of it is cooked, he will request a part of it to be given to him as he lies on the same couch with a prostitute, and receiving but a morsel of it to eat, he will be there immediately choked and die." All these things, as we have heard from persons well informed, were fulfilled according to the prophecy of the Saint.

CHAPTER XXXIX.

Prophecy of the Saint concerning Neman, son of Gruthrich.

FOR this man, when the Saint reproved him for his faults, lightly esteemed and mocked the Saint. Replying to him the blessed man said: "In the name of the Lord, Neman, I will declare words of truth concerning thee. Thy enemies shall find thee lying in bed with a prostitute, and shall slay thee there. Moreover, demons shall snatch away thy soul to the place of torments." And this same Neman was, after some years, found in bed with a prostitute in the district of Cainle, and being beheaded by his enemies, died according to the word of the Saint.

CHAPTER XL.

Prophecy of the Holy Man concerning a certain priest who was in Trioit.

AT another time the Saint, when staying in that part of Ireland mentioned a little ago, came by chance on the Lord's Day to a little monastery in the neighbourhood, which is called in the Irish language Trioit. On the same day, when he heard a certain priest celebrating the holy mysteries of the Eucharist, whom the brethren residing there had chosen to perform the solemn offices of the Mass, because they deemed him very devout, he suddenly uttered this terrible declaration: "The clean and the unclean are seen now to be equally mingled together; that is, the clean mysteries of the Holy Sacrifice are offered by an unclean man who in his own conscience is concealing a great crime." When they heard these words those who were present were appalled. But he concerning whom they were said, was compelled to confess his sin in the presence of all. And the fellow soldiers of Christ, who stood round the Saint in the Church and had heard him making manifest the secrets of the heart, with great wonder glorified the divine knowledge which dwelt in him.

CHAPTER XLI.

Prophecy of the Holy Man concerning the thief Erco Mocudruidi, who dwelt in the island of Colonsay.

AT another time, when the Saint was staying in Iona, two of the brethren, by name Lugbe and Silnan, being summoned to him, he charged them saying: "Cross now to the island of Mull and on the open ground near the sea shore search for the thief Erc, who secretly came alone last night from the island of Colonsay, and during the day is trying to hide himself among the sandhills under his boat covered with hay, in order that at night he may cross over to the little island, where our young seals are brought forth and reared, and there filling his boat from those he has ruthlessly slain, the destructive thief may return to his own dwelling. As soon as they heard these words, they obeyed and sailed over and found the thief concealed in the place indicated by the Saint and brought him to the Saint as he had directed them. When he saw him the Saint said : " Why dost thou transgress the divine command so often and steal the things of others. Whenever thou art in want come to us, and thou shalt receive whatever needful things thou askest." And as he said this he commanded some wethers to be killed and given to the wretched thief in place of seals, that he might not go back home empty. And some time after the Saint, foreseeing in spirit the approaching death of the thief, sent to Baithene, who was at the time in charge in the plain of Lunge, to have conveyed to that same thief a fat sheep and six measures of corn as his last gift. Baithene having sent them as the Saint had desired, found that the wretched thief had suddenly died on the same day before their arrival, and the presents sent over were used at his funeral.

CHAPTER XLII.

Prophecy of the Holy Man concerning the poet Cronan.

AT another time, when the Saint was one day sitting with the brethren beside Lough Key, near the mouth of the river, which in Latin is called Bos, there came to them a certain Irish poet ; and when he had retired after a short interview, the brethren said to the Saint : " Why didst thou not ask the poet Cronan before he went away to sing us a song with accompaniment, according to the rules of his art." To which the Saint replied : " Wherefore do you also now utter useless words ? How could I ask a song of joy from that miserable creature, who even now has been slain by his enemies and has thus quickly come to the end of his life." When these words had been said by the Saint, lo, some man cried out from the other side of the river, saying, "The poet who just now left you in safety, has this moment been slain in the way by his enemies." Then all who were present, looked at each other in amazement, and wondered greatly.

CHAPTER XLIII.

Prophecy of the Holy Man concerning two Noblemen who died of wounds they had inflicted on each other.

AT another time, again, when the Saint was living in the island of Iona, very suddenly, while engaged in reading, and to the great surprise of all, he sighed very sorrowfully. On seeing this Lugbe Mocublai, who was present, began to ask the cause of his sudden grief. The Saint very sorrowfully replied : "Two men of royal descent in Ireland have just died from wounds they have inflicted on each other not far from the monastery called Cellrois in the province of the Maugdorna, and on the eighth day, when a week has passed, one coming from Ireland will call from the other side of the Sound, and tell you these things as they occurred. But O my child, as long as I live, tell this to no one." On the eighth day, accordingly, a shout was heard from the other side of the Sound. Then the Saint calling the above mentioned Lugbe to him quietly said : "He who is now calling from across the Sound is the aged traveller of whom I spoke to thee before ; go and bring him here to me." And he being speedily brought, among other things, told also this, saying : "Two noblemen in the district of the Maugdorna, near the confines of the territory where the monastery called Cellrois is situated, have died from wounds they inflicted on each other ; namely, Colman the Hound, son of Ailen, and Ronan, son of Aid, son of Colga, both descended from the Kings of the Airtheara. After these things had been narrated, Lugbe, the soldier of Christ, began to question the Saint in private, saying : "Tell me, I beseech thee, of these and such like prophetic revelations, how they are made to thee ; whether by vision or by hearing, or by other means unknown to men." To this the Saint replied: "Of the very difficult matter concerning which thou now inquirest, I can tell thee nothing whatever unless thou first strictly promise on thy bended knees by the name of the Most High God never to tell this most secret mystery to any one during all the days of my life." On hearing this, Lugbe immediately fell on his knees, and with his face bent down to the ground, promised every thing exactly according to the demand of the Saint. As soon as the promise was given, the Saint said to him as he arose: "Some there are, though very few, to whom the Divine grace has given when the bosom of their own mind is wonderfully enlarged, to behold clearly and most distinctly even the whole orb of the entire earth, with the surrounding sea and sky, in one and the same moment, as if beneath a single ray of the sun." The Saint, when speaking of this miracle, though he seems to be speaking of other of the elect, as shunning vain glory, did nevertheless in reality speak of himself, though indirectly, and no one can doubt this who reads the Apostle Paul, that vessel of election, where he narrates such visions as were revealed to him. For he did not write "I know that I," but "I know a man caught up even to the third heaven." Now although he seems to be here speaking of another, yet no one doubts that while preserving his humility, he is speaking of none other than himself. And our Columba, in narrating the spiritual visions mentioned above, imitated him, as in this also which the aforesaid man, whom the Saint greatly loved, could with difficulty extort from him after earnest entreaties, as Lugbe after the death of S. Columba did himself testify in the presence of other holy men, from whom we have learned those well authenticated incidents concerning the Saint, which we have narrated above.

CHAPTER XLIV.

Of Cronan the Bishop.

AT another time a traveller came to the Saint from the province of the Munstermen, and in his humility did all he could to disguise himself, so that no one might know that he was a bishop; but it was impossible to hide it from the Saint. For on the next Lord's Day, when requested by the Saint to consecrate according to custom the Body of Christ, he called the Saint to his side, that together, as two priests, they might break the bread of the Lord. Thereupon the Saint went up to the Altar, and suddenly looking him in the face thus addressed him: "Christ bless thee, brother; break this bread alone according to the episcopal rite. We know now that thou art a Bishop. Why hast thou until now tried to hide thyself, so that the veneration due to thee might not be rendered by us." On hearing the Saint's word the humble traveller was greatly astonished and venerated Christ in the Saint; and the bystanders in amazement glorified God.

CHAPTER XLV.

Prophecy of the Holy Man concerning Ernan the Priest.

AT another time, again, the venerable man sent Ernan, his uncle, an aged priest, to preside over the monastery which he had founded many years before in the island of Hinba (Eileanna-Naoimh). At his departure, the Saint embraced and blessed him, and uttered this prophecy concerning him: "This my friend who is now going from us, I do not expect to see alive again in this world." Accordingly Ernan after a few days fell ill and desired to be carried back to the Saint, who greatly rejoiced at his return and set out for the harbour to meet him. Ernan himself very boldly attempted, though with feeble steps, to walk without assistance from the harbour to meet the Saint. But when there was between them a space of about four and twenty paces, he was suddenly overtaken by death, and before the Saint could see his face in life, he fell to the ground and breathed his last, that the word of the Saint might not in any way be frustrated. Hence in that place before the door of the Kiln a cross was raised, and another cross was in like manner put up where the Saint stood when Ernan expired, which cross remains to this day.

CHAPTER XLVI.

Prophecy of the Holy Man concerning the family of a certain peasant.

AT another time also there came among others to the Saint while he was staying in the district which in the Irish tongue is called Coire Salchain, a certain peasant, of whom, when he saw him coming to him, one evening, he inquired: "Where dost thou live?" He replied: "I live in the district which borders on the shore of Lake Crogreth." "The district of which thou speakest," returned the Saint, "barbarous marauders are now devastating." When he heard this, the wretched peasant began to lament his wife and children; but the Saint, seeing him so deeply afflicted, comforted him, saying: "Go, my poor fellow, go; all thy family has escaped by flight to the mountain; but all thy cattle the marauders have taken away, and all the furniture of thy house the ruthless pillagers have in like manner carried off with their booty. When the peasant heard this, he returned home and found that all had happened as the Saint foretold.

CHAPTER XLVII.

Prophecy of the Holy Man concerning a peasant named Gore, son of Aidan.

AT another time, again, a certain peasant who at that time was by far the bravest of all the men among the Korkureti, asked the Saint by what death he would die. "Not on the battle field shalt thou die," replied the Saint, "nor at sea; a companion of thy journey of whom thou hast no suspicion, shall be the cause of thy death." "Perhaps," said Gore, "one of the friends who accompany me on my journey intends to murder me, or my wife because of her love for some younger man meditates my destruction by treachery." The Saint answered: "Not thus will it happen." "Why," said Gore, "wilt thou not now tell me of my murderer?" "Because," said the Saint, "I do not wish to tell thee anything more clearly just now concerning thy companion who is to injure thee, lest the frequent recollection of the fact should sadden thee too much before the day come when thou shalt prove the truth of this matter." But why delay longer with words? After the lapse of a few years this same Gore was by chance one day sitting under his boat scraping off the bark from his spear handle with his knife, when hearing others near him fighting among themselves, he rose quickly to separate them as they fought, and carelessly throwing his knife down to the ground in his haste, he was seriously wounded by it in the knee. And from such a companion did the cause of his death originate; and he himself trembling in spirit at once recognised it according to the prophecy of the holy man. After a few months he died in agony from the wound.

CHAPTER XLVIII.

The Saint's foreknowledge and prophecy concerning another matter, which though of less importance is so beautiful that I think it ought not to be passed over in silence.

FOR at another time when the Saint was dwelling in the island of Iona, he called one of the brethren to him and addressed him thus: "At the dawn of the third day from this when sitting on the shore of the sea on the western side of this island, thou oughtest then to look out. For a crane, a stranger from the northern part of Ireland, driven about by the winds through long flights, will come after the ninth hour of the day, fatigued and very weary, and with its strength almost spent will light on the shore and lie down before thee. Treat it tenderly and carry it to a neighbouring house, and there when it shall be kindly received, do thou nurse and feed it three days and nights; and when refreshed after the three days rest, it is unwilling to tarry longer with us, it will return with renewed strength to the pleasant part of Ireland from which it originally came. I earnestly commend it to thee, because it comes from our own native place." The brother obeyed, and on the third day after the ninth hour, he watched, as he was told, for the arrival of the presaged guest, and when it came and alighted, he lifted it from the shore, bore it in its weakness to a dwelling, and in its hunger fed it. On his return to the monastery in the evening the Saint not by way of inquiring but stating as a fact, said : "God bless thee, my son, because thou hast ministered to this foreign guest that will not tarry long on its journey, but after three days will return to its own country." As the Saint predicted the event also proved. For after being tended three days, the bird in the presence of its hospitable entertainer, first rose up on its wings to a great height, and then, having searched out its way for a little in the air, crossed the ocean, and flying by a straight course, returned to Ireland on a calm day.

CHAPTER XLIX.

The foreknowledge of the Holy Man concerning the Battle which was fought a long time afterwards in the fortress of the Cethirn and concerning the Well near the same place.

ANOTHER time, after the convention of the Kings at the Ridge Ceath ; namely, of Aid son of Ainmurech and Aidan son of Gabhran, the blessed man returned to the sea-coast, and on a calm day in summer, he and Abbot Congal sat down not far from the above-named fort. Then water from a well close by was brought in a bronze vessel to the Saint, that they might wash their hands. When S. Columba had received it, he thus addressed Abbot Congal who was sitting by his side : 'The well, O Congal, whence this water which has now been poured upon us, was drawn, will one day be no longer fit for human use.' 'From what cause,' said Congal, 'shall the water of this spring be polluted?' 'Because,' said S. Columba, 'it shall be filled with human blood, for thy relatives and mine according to the flesh, the people of the Cruithni and the race of Nial shall fight in battle against each other in this neighbouring fortress of the Cethirn, and at the aforesaid well an unhappy relative of mine shall be slain, whose blood with that of many others shall fill up its place.' After many years this veritable prophecy was in its own time fulfilled; for in the battle, as many are aware, Domnal, son of Aid, came off victorious, and at the said well according to the prophecy of the holy man a kinsman of his was slain.

Another soldier of Christ, Finan by name, who for many years lived blamelessly the life of an anchorite near the monastery of the Oakwood Plain, and was present when the battle was fought, in narrating some things to me, Adamnan, solemnly averred that he saw a dead body in the aforesaid well, and that on his return after the battle on the same day to the monastery of S. Comgel which is called in the Irish tongue Cambas, because he had thence first come, he found two aged monks of S. Comgel there, who, when he told them of the battle he had seen and of the well defiled with human blood, immediately said: 'A true prophet was Columba, who all these things which thou tellest us have to-day been accomplished concerning the battle and the well, many years before they have come to pass, he foretold in our hearing in the presence of S. Comgel when sitting with him near the fortress of the Cethirn.

CHAPTER L.

Of the difference between divers presents revealed to the Holy Man by Divine Grace.

ABOUT the same time Conall, Bishop of Coleraine, collected almost innumerable presents from the people of the Plain of Elne, in order to give to the blessed man a hospitable reception on his return, after the convention of the Kings mentioned above, and to the vast multitude accompanying him. Many of these presents from the people were laid out in the paved court of the monastery, that they might be blessed by the holy man on his arrival. While blessing them he examined them, specially pointing out me the gift of a wealthy man. 'The man whose gift that is,' he said, 'is, for his mercy to the poor and his liberality, attended by the mercy of God.' In like manner he distinguished another among the many presents, saying : 'Of this present of a wise and avaricious man I can in no wise taste, until he has first shown true penitence for the sin of avarice.' Hearing this saying, which was quickly circulated among the crowd, Columb son of Aid, conscious of his fault, ran up, and on his bended knees repented and promised that henceforward he would renounce his avarice and practice liberality with amendment of life. The Saint commanded him to rise, and from that hour he was cured of the vice of greed ; for he was a wise man, as was revealed to the Saint through that present. But the munificent rich man called Brenden, of whose present mention was made a little above, hearing the words spoken by the Saint concerning himself, knelt at the feet of the Saint, and besought him to offer up prayer for him to the Lord. When at the outset he was reproved by the Saint for certain of his sins, he repented of them, and promised to amend his life. And thus both these men were amended of their peculiar faults and cured of their vices.

With like knowledge the Saint also at another time distinguished among many presents, which had been collected at the Great Cell of Deathrib, on the occasion of his visit to that place, the present of a greedy man named Diormit.

To have written these things in the course of this book as a few instances out of many of the prophetic gifts of the blessed man, may suffice. I have said a few, for it cannot be doubted concerning this venerable man, that the things which, through being inwardly hidden sacraments, could not in any way come to the knowledge of men were much more numerous than those which as a few little drops oozed out, as it were, like newly fermented wine through the chinks of a full vessel. For holy and apostolic men, avoiding vain glory, strive to hide as far as they are able the inner secrets inwardly manifested to them by God. Yet God sometimes, whether they will or not, makes some of these secrets known and in many ways brings them forth to the world, desiring thus to glorify those Saints who glorify him; the Lord Himself, to Whom be glory for ever and ever. Amen.

Here endeth the First Book.

BOOK II.

OF HIS MIRACULOUS POWERS.

CHAPTER I.

Of the Wine which he made from Water.

AT another time, while the venerable man was yet a youth in Ireland, learning with S. Findbarr, the bishop, the wisdom of Holy Scripture, it came to pass one holy day that not the least drop of wine was found wherewith to celebrate the sacrificial mystery. When he heard the ministers of the altar complaining of their want among themselves, he took a vessel and went with it to the fountain, in order that as a deacon he might draw spring water for the celebration of the Holy Eucharist. At that time he was serving in the order of a deacon. Accordingly the blessed man blessed in faith the element of water which he drew from the spring, invoking the name of the Lord Jesus Christ, who turned water into wine at Cana of Galilee, by whose operation in this miracle also, an inferior element, namely water, was changed into one of a more acceptable kind, namely wine, by means of the hand of this remarkable man. The holy man then returned from the spring, and entering the church placed the vessel containing this liquid near the altar, and said to the ministers: 'You have wine which the Lord Jesus has sent for the celebration of His mysteries.' When this was known the holy bishop with the ministers gave great thanks to God. But the holy youth was wont to ascribe this not to himself but to S. Vinnian, the bishop. This first proof of his power Christ the Lord made manifest through his disciple in the same way as he wrought himself, when he made the beginning of miracles in Cana of Galilee.

Let this divine miracle manifested by means of our Columba shine in the beginning of this book as a light, that we may pass on to other miracles of power which were shown forth in him.

CHAPTER II.

Of the bitter fruit of a tree changed into sweet by the benediction of the Saint.

THERE was a certain very fruitful apple tree near the monastery of the Oakwood Plain, on its southern side. On a certain day in autumn, when the inhabitants of the place were complaining of the exceeding bitterness of its fruit, the Saint came to it, and seeing the boughs uselessly bearing abundant fruit which injured rather than pleased those who tasted of it, he raised his holy hand and blessed it, saying : ' In the name of Almighty God, let all thy bitterness, O bitter tree, depart from thee, and let thy apples hitherto so very bitter, be now changed into the sweetest.' Strange to say ; quicker than the word, and at the same instant, every apple of the tree lost its bitterness and became wonderfully sweet according to the Saint's word.

CHAPTER III.

Of corn sown after Midsummer and reaped in the beginning of the month of August at the Saint's prayer while he was residing in the island of Iona.

AT another time the Saint sent his monks to fetch from the little farm of a peasant some bundles of withes to build a guest house with. When they returned to the Saint with a freight ship filled with the foresaid bundles of withes, and told him that the peasant was very sorry on account of the loss, the Saint immediately gave directions, saying : ' Lest we do the man any injury, let there be taken from us to him twice three measures of barley and let him sow it now in his arable land.' According to the command of the Saint the three measures of barley were sent to the peasant, whose name was Findchan, and delivered over to him with the above instructions. He received them thankfully, but said : 'What good can corn do which is sown after midsummer contrary to the nature of this soil ? ' His wife on the other hand urged : ' Act according to the command of the Saint, to whom the Lord will give whatsoever he shall ask of Him.' And those also who were sent likewise added thus, saying : 'Saint Columba who sent us to thee with this gift, entrusted us also with this instruction concerning thy corn, saying : ' Let the man trust in the Omnipotence of God; his corn, though sown now when twelve days of the month of June are passed, shall be reaped in the first days of the month of August.' The peasant therefore obeyed, ploughing and sowing ; and to the amazement of all his neighbours, the harvest which he sowed against hope at the aforesaid time, he gathered in ripe in the beginning of the month of August according to the word of the Saint, in the place which is called Delcros.

CHAPTER IV.

Of a Pestilential Cloud, and the curing of many people.

AT another time, again, when the Saint was staying in the island of Iona, and was sitting on the hill, which in Latin is called Munitio Magna, he saw in the North a heavy rain cloud rise up from the sea on a bright day. As the Saint saw it ascending, he said to one of his monks, named Silnan, son of Neman-don Mocusogin, who was sitting beside him : " That cloud will be very baneful to men and beasts, and after swiftly passing to-day over a considerable part of Ireland, that is, from the river which is called Ailbine (Delvin, in Meath) as far as the Ford Clied (Dublin), it will discharge in the evening a pestilential rain, which will cause large and putrid ulcers to grow on the bodies of men and on the udders of cows, from which men and cattle will sicken and labour till worn to death. But we, commiserating with them, ought, with the merciful aid of God, to relieve them in their sufferings. Do thou, therefore, Silnan, descend now with me from this hill, and make ready for a voyage on the morrow, when, life being spared and God willing, thou shalt receive from me bread blessed by the invocation of the name of God. This thou shalt dip in water, and with the water thou shalt then sprinkle man and beast, and they shall quickly recover their health." But why delay? On the morrow, having quickly prepared the things which were requisite, Silnan, after he had received from the hand of the Saint the bread which had been blessed, sailed away in peace. As he was setting out, the Saint gave him this word of consolation, saying, " Be of good courage, my son, thou shalt have favouring and prosperous breezes, day and night, till thou come to the place which is called Ard Ceannachte, so that thou mayest succour the sick there the more speedily with the healing bread." What more? Silnan, obeying the command of the Saint, had a quick and prosperous voyage, through the help of God, and coming to the above-mentioned part of that country he found the people, of whom the Saint had spoken, destroyed by the pestilential rain falling down from the aforesaid cloud, which had passed rapidly on before him. In the first place, twice three men were found in one house by the sea, reduced to the last agonies of approaching death, but when sprinkled by Silnan with the water of benediction, they were the same day happily healed. The fame of this sudden healing was quickly noised abroad through all the region devastated by this very pestilential disease, and drew all who were sick to S. Columba's messenger, who, following the Saint's instructions, sprinkled man and beast with the water in which the consecrated bread had been dipped, when they were immediately restored to perfect health. Then the men, finding that they and their cattle were saved, praised Christ in S. Columba with the utmost expressions of thankfulness. In the narrative above written, these two things, I think, are clearly associated, namely, the gift of prophecy concerning the cloud, and miraculous power in healing the sick. That these things are in every particular true, the above-named Silnan, a soldier of Christ, the messenger of S. Columba, testified in the presence of Abbot Seghine and other elder brethren.

CHAPTER V.

Of Maugina, a holy virgin, daughter of Daimen, who had dwelt in a place which in Irish is called Clochur of the sons of Daimen.

AT another time the Saint, while dwelling in the island of Iona, one day at prime called to him a certain brother, named Lugaid, surnamed, in the Irish tongue, Lathir, and addressed him thus, saying: "Get ready quickly for a rapid voyage to Ireland, for it is of the utmost importance that I should send thee on an errand as far as Clochur of the sons of Daimen. For last night, by some accident, Maugina, a holy virgin, daughter of Daimen, stumbled when returning home from the chapel after Mass, and her thigh-bone is broken in two. She is now crying out, and often mentions my name, hoping that through me she will obtain some comfort from the Lord." Why need I say more? Lugaid obeyed at once, and as he was setting out, the Saint gave to him, with his benediction, a little pinewood box, saying: "Let the blessed gift which is contained in this little box, be dipped in a vessel of water when thou comest to meet Maugina, and let the water thus blessed be poured over her thigh-bone, and immediately on the name of the God being invoked, her thigh-bone shall be joined and made strong, and the holy virgin shall be restored to perfect health." This also the Saint added: "Lo here, in thy presence, I write on the lid of this box the number of twenty-three years, which the holy virgin shall live in this present life after receiving her health." All these things were fulfilled exactly as the Saint predicted, for as soon as Lugaid came to the holy virgin, and her thigh was washed, as the Saint had enjoined, with the blessed water, without the slightest delay the bone closed together, and her thigh was perfectly healed. On the arrival of the messenger of S. Columba, she rejoiced with much giving of thanks, and after her restoration lived, according to the prophecy of the Saint, twenty-three years in the constant practice of good works.

CHAPTER VI.

Of the cure of divers diseases which were wrought in the Ridge of Ceatt.

THIS man of remarkable life, as we have been told by those who were well-informed, healed the disorders of divers sick persons by invoking the name of Christ, during the days he dwelt for a short time at the Ridge of Ceatt attending the Convention of the Kings. For either by the stretching out of his holy hand, or by sprinkling many sick with water he had blessed, or even through touching the hem of his garment, or some other thing, as salt, or bread which had received his blessing and been dipped in water, those who believed recovered perfect health.

CHAPTER VII.

Of a lump of salt blessed by the Saint which fire could not consume.

AT another time, again, Colga son of Cellach asked and received from the Saint a lump of salt, which he had blessed for the cure of his sister, who had been his nurse and was now suffering greatly from a severe attack of ophthalmia. This same sister and nurse, when she received so great and blessed a gift from the hand of her brother, hung it up on the wall over her bed. Some days after it happened by accident that the same village, together with the dwelling of the aforesaid woman, was wholly consumed by a destructive fire. But strange to say, in order that the gift of the blessed man might not be destroyed, the portion of the wall on which it hung remained standing uninjured after all the rest of the house had been consumed; nor did the fire venture to touch the two uprights on which the lump of salt was suspended.

CHAPTER VIII.

Of the volume of a book written by the Saint which could not be destroyed by water.

ANOTHER miracle which was wrought by means of the contrary element, ought not, I think, to be passed over in silence. For many years after the blessed man's departure to the Lord a certain youth falling from his horse into the river which is called in the Irish tongue Boend, sank and was drowned, and remained under the water twenty days. When he fell, he had under his arm a number of books packed up in a leathern satchel, and so, when he was found after the above mentioned number of days, he was still holding the satchel with the books between his arm and his side. When the dead body was brought to the dry ground and the satchel opened, the volume which had been written by the sacred fingers of S. Columba, was found among the other books, which were not only destroyed but had also rotted away, dry and wholly uninjured, as if it had been laid away in a box.

CHAPTER IX.

Of another miracle under similar circumstances.

AT another time a book of hymns for the office of every day in the week and in the Saint's own handwriting dropped with the leathern satchel that contained it, from the shoulder of a boy who fell from a bridge, into a certain river in the province of Leinster, and sank. This same book remained in the water from the Feast of the Nativity of our Lord until the end of the Paschal season, and was afterwards found in the bank of the river by certain women who were walking there, and was by them carried in the same satchel, which was not only soaked but also rotted away, to a certain priest named Iogenan, a Pict by race, to whom it formerly belonged. On opening the satchel this same Iogenan found his book uninjured and as clean and dry, as if it had remained as long a time in his desk and had never fallen into the water. Other similar incidents which have occurred in different places, we have also indubitably learned from persons well informed, respecting books written by the hand of S. Columba, which books, indeed, by immersion in water could not in any degree be injured. But in regard to the above mentioned book of Iogenan, we have received the narrative without the slightest ambiguity from certain veracious and upright men of good reputation, who saw the book itself, perfectly white and beautiful after it had been immersed for as many days as stated above. These two miracles, though wrought in matters of small moment, and shown by opposite elements, namely, fire and water, attest the honour of the blessed man, and of what and how great merit he was esteemed before God.

CHAPTER X.

Of water which at the prayer of the Saint was drawn from the hard rock.

AND because a little ago mention was made of the element of water, we must not be silent respecting other miracles which the Lord wrought by the Saint, though in divers times and places in connection with the same element. For at another time, when the Saint was on one of his journeys, an infant was presented to him by its parents for baptism as he was travelling ;

and because there was no water to be found in the neighbourhood, the Saint turning aside to a rock that was near, knelt down and prayed a little; and rising up after prayer, he blessed the face of the rock, from which the bubbling water immediately flowed abundantly, in which he at once baptized the infant. Prophesying, concerning the child which was baptized, he uttered these words, saying: "This child shall live to an extreme old age; in the years of his youth he will serve freely his carnal desires, and then devoting himself to the Christian warfare until the end of his life, he will depart to the Lord in a good old age." All these things happened to the man according to the prophecy of the Saint. He was Lugucencalad, whose parents had been in Artdaib Muirchol, where to this day is seen a fountain called by the name of S. Columba.

CHAPTER XI.

Of another poisonous fountain of water to which the Blessed Man gave his blessing in the country of the Picts.

AT another time, the blessed man, when tarrying some days in the province of the Picts, heard that there was spread among the heathen people the fame of another fountain which foolish men, whose senses were blinded by the devil, worshipped as a god; for those who drank of this fountain or purposely washed their hands or feet in it, were, with the permission of God, smitten with demoniacal art, and returned leprous, or blind of an eye, or even crippled, or they were seized with some other ailments. And because of these things, the Pagans were seduced, and were paying divine honour to the well. When he learned these things, the Saint went boldly one day to the well; and the Druids, whom he had often sent away vanquished and confounded, were greatly rejoiced, thinking, forsooth, that he would suffer similar things from the touch of the hurtful water. But having first raised his holy hand with an invocation of the name of Christ, he washed his hands and feet; and then with his companions drank of the water he had blessed. And from that day the demons departed from the fountain, and not only was it not permitted to do harm to any one, but even many diseases were healed among the people by this same fountain, after it had been blessed and washed in by the Saint.

CHAPTER XII.

Of the Blessed Man's peril at sea and the sudden stilling of the tempest at his prayer.

AT another time the holy man began to be in great peril at sea; for the whole vessel in which he was, was violently shaken and heavily struck by huge waves, while a great storm of winds raged on every side. The sailors then chanced to say to the Saint as he was trying with them to bail the vessel: "What thou art now doing is of little use to us in our present straits; thou ought rather to be praying for us as we are perishing." On hearing this he ceased to throw out the bitter water of the green sea wave, and began to pour forth sweet and earnest prayer to the Lord. And wonderful to relate, the very moment the Saint stood up in the prow, with his hands outstretched to heaven, and prayed to the Almighty, the whole storm and fury of the sea, subsiding more quickly than can be told, ceased, and a most serene calm ensued. But those who were in the ship were amazed, and giving thanks with great admiration, they glorified God in the holy and illustrious man.

CHAPTER XIII.

Of another similar peril to him, at sea, in the Brecain whirlpool.

AT another time, also, when a furious and dangerous storm was raging, and his companions were crying out that he ought to pray to the Lord for them, the Saint made them this answer:

"On this day it is not for me to pray for you in your present peril, but the holy man, Abbot Cainnech." And wonderful are the things I am about to relate. At that same hour S. Cainnech was residing in his monastery, which in Latin is called Campulus Bovis, but in Irish, Ached-bou, and had heard with the inward ear of the heart, through the revelation of the Holy Spirit, the above saying of S. Columba. And when by chance he had begun to break the blessed bread, after the ninth hour, in the refectory, he hastily left the table, and with one shoe on his foot and the other left behind in his very great haste, he went hurriedly to the church, saying: "This is not the time for us to eat, when the vessel of S. Columba is in great peril at sea. For at this moment he is lamenting and calling on the name of Cainnech to pray to Christ for him and his companions in peril." After saying these words, he went into the chapel, and prayed for a little on his bended knees, and the Lord hearing his prayer, the storm immediately ceased and the sea became quite calm. Thereupon S. Columba, seeing in spirit, though away at a great distance, Cainnech's great haste in going to the church, to the amazement of all uttered these words from his pure heart, saying: "Now I know, O Cainnech, that God has heard thy prayer; now has thy swift running to the church with a single shoe greatly profited us." In such a miracle as this, as we believe, the prayer of both Saints co-operated.

CHAPTER XIV.

Of the staff of S. Cainnech, which was forgotten in the Harbour.

AT another time, the Cainnech mentioned above, when embarking at the port of the island of Iona for Ireland, forgot to take with him his staff. After his departure it was found on the shore and placed in the hands of S. Columba, who returned home and carried it into the chapel, where he continued alone a long time in prayer. Cainnech, meanwhile, was drawing near to the island of Oidech, when he was suddenly pricked at heart on account of his forgetfulness, and was greatly disturbed in mind. But after a little while, when he disembarked from his vessel, and was bending his knees in prayer on the ground, he found the staff, which in his forgetfulness he had left behind him in the port of the island of Iona, lying before him on the turf in the little land of Aitech. And greatly surprised at its conveyance to him by the divine power, he gave thanks to God.

CHAPTER XV.

Of Baithene and Columban, the son of Beogna, holy priests; how on the same day prosperous winds were given to each, when they asked them to be given through the prayer of the Blessed man, though they were sailing different ways.

AT another time, also, the above-mentioned holy men came to the Saint, and together with one accord asked that he would seek and obtain from the Lord a favourable wind for them, though they were about to set out in different directions. In answer the Saint gave them this reply: "To-morrow morning, Baithene, when setting sail from the harbour of the island of Iona, shall have a favourable wind until he reaches the harbour of the Plain of Lunge." And so the Lord granted it according to the word of the Saint. For Baithene, on the same day, crossed the whole of the great sea, until he came to Tiree, with full sails. But in the third hour of the same day the venerable man called the priest, Columban, to him, saying: "Baithene has now prosperously reached his desired haven; make ready to sail to-day; the Lord will soon change the wind to the north." The same hour the wind from the south, in obedience to the word thus spoken by the blessed man, changed into a wind from the north; and thus on the same day the two holy men departed from each other in peace, and both made their voyages with full sails and a favouring breeze, Baithene setting out in the morning for Tiree, and Columban in the afternoon for Ireland. This miracle, the Lord granting it, was wrought in virtue of the prayers of this illustrious man; because, as it is written, "All things are possible to him that believeth." After the departure of S. Columban, on the same day S. Columba uttered this prophetic word concerning him: "The holy man, Columban, whom we blessed as he departed, will never in this world see my face again." This also was afterwards fulfilled, for in the same year S. Columba passed away to the Lord.

CHAPTER XVI.

Of the driving away of a Demon which was lurking in a Milk-pail.

AT another time, a certain youth, called Columban, grandson of Briun, came up himself and stopped at the door of the hut in which the blessed man was writing. This same man when on his return home after milking the cows, was carrying on his back a vessel full of new milk, which he asked the Saint to bless according to his wont. The Saint who was then sitting at some distance opposite to him raised his hand, made the sign of the cross in the air, and invoking the name of God, blessed the vessel, which was at once greatly disturbed, and the bar of the lid being pushed back through the two holes that received it, was shot away to a great distance, the lid fell to the earth, and the greater part of the milk was spilled on the ground. The young lad set the vessel with what little milk remained in it down on its bottom on the ground, and humbly bowed his knees in prayer. The Saint said to him: "Rise, Columban, to-day thou hast done thy work carelessly; for thou didst not drive away the demon that was lurking in the bottom of thy empty vessel by making upon it the sign of the cross of our Lord before pouring the milk into it, and now not enduring the power of that sign, but stricken with terror and having troubled every corner of the vessel, he has quickly fled away after spilling the milk. Bring hither, therefore, to me thy vessel that I may bless it. When this had been done, the half empty vessel which the Saint had blessed, was found the same moment divinely filled; and the little which at first had remained in the bottom of the pail, under the blessing of his holy hand quickly rose up to the brim.

CHAPTER XVII.

Of a vessel which a certain Sorcerer called Silnan filled with milk taken from a bull.

IT is said that the following occurred in the house of a rich peasant, named Foirtgirn, who dwelt in Mount Cainle. When the Saint was staying there as a guest, he discerned justly in a dispute between two rustics of whose coming he knew beforehand. One of them, who was a sorcerer, at the command of the Saint, took milk by means of his diabolical art from a bull which was near. This the Saint ordered to be done, not that he might confirm these sorceries, which God forbid, but to destroy them in the presence of the multitude. The blessed man, therefore, quickly asked the vessel, full as it seemed to be of such milk, to be given to him, and with this sentence he blessed it, saying: " In this way shall it be proved that this is not that true milk which it is thought to be, but blood deprived of its colour by the artifice of demons for the deception of men." And immediately the milky coloured fluid was changed into its own nature, *i.e.*, into blood. The bull also, which for the space of an hour had pined and wasted away with a hideous leanness and was near to death, when sprinkled with water, blessed by the Saint, was healed with marvellous celerity.

CHAPTER XVIII.

Of Lugne Mocumin.

ONE day a certain youth of good parts, named Lugne, who afterwards in his old age was president of the Monastery in the Elena island (Eilean Naomh), came to the Saint, complaining of a flow of blood, which frequently during many months had issued profusely from his nostrils. Having asked him to come nearer, the Saint blessed both his nostrils, pressing them together with the fingers of his hand. From the hour in which he received the blessing unto the last day of his life, blood never again flowed from his nose.

CHAPTER XIX.

Of a great salmon found in the river Sale according to the word of the Saint.

AT another time, when some hardy fishermen, companions of this renowned man, had taken five fish in a net in the river Sale, which abounds in fish, the Saint said to them: "Go again, cast your net into the river, and immediately you shall find a large fish, which the Lord has prepared for me." They obeyed the word of the Saint, and caught in the net a salmon of amazing size, which had been prepared for him by God.

Of two fish found, by his prophecy, in the river which is called Boo.

AT another time, also, when the Saint was staying some days beside Lough Key, his companions desiring to go afishing, he delayed them, saying: "To-day and to-morrow no fish will be found in the river. On the third day I will send you, and you shall find two large river-salmon caught in the net." Accordingly, after two days, when they cast the net, they landed two of the most extraordinary size. The river in which they were found is called Bo. In the capture of fish on these two occasions the power of the miracle appears accompanied at the same time by prophetic foreknowledge, for which graces the Saint and his companions gave fervent thanks to God.

CHAPTER XX.

Of Nesan the Crooked, who dwelt in the country bordering on the Lake of Apors.

THIS Nesan, although very poor, on one occasion joyfully received the holy man as his guest. When he had hospitably entertained him according to his ability for the space of one night, the Saint asked him the number of his heifers. He replied: "Five." Thereupon the Saint said: "Bring them to me that I may bless them." When they were brought to him, the Saint raised his holy hand and blessed them, saying: "From this day thy five little heifers shall increase to the number of a hundred and five cows." And because the same Nesan was a man of humble condition with a wife and children, the blessed man added even this further blessing, saying: "Thy seed shall be blessed in thy children and grandchildren." All these things without any failure were completely fulfilled according to the word of the Saint.

But concerning a certain rich and very greedy man named Uigene, who had despised him, and did not receive him with hospitality, S. Columba, on the other hand, uttered this prophetic sentence, saying: "The riches of that avaricious man, who has despised Christ in the strangers who came to be his guests, shall from this day gradually diminish, until they are reduced to nothing, and he himself shall be a beggar; and his son shall go about from house to house with a half empty wallet, and he shall die, slain by a rival beggar with an axe in the pit of a threshing floor." All these things concerning both were fully accomplished according to the phophecy of the holy man.

CHAPTER XXI.

Of Columban, a man of equally humble condition, whose very few cattle the Holy Man blessed, how and after his blessing they increased to a hundred.

AT another time, also, when the blessed man had one night been hospitably entertained by the aforesaid Columban, who was then poor, early next morning the Saint asked his humble host, as he had done before in the above account of Nesan, as to the amount and value of his goods. When asked, he said: "I have only five small cows, but if thou wilt bless them, they will grow to more." Being immediately ordered by the Saint to bring them to him, in like manner as was related above concerning the five cows of Nesan, the Saint gave as rich a blessing to the five cows of Columban, saying: "By the gift of God, thou shalt have a hundred and five cows, and an abundant blessing shall be on thy children and on thy grandchildren." All which things were abundantly fulfilled in his lands and cattle and offspring according to the prophecy of the blessed man, and in a wonderful way the number of cattle of each of the above-mentioned men when it reached one hundred and five, as fixed by the Saint, could not in any way be increased. For those which exceeded this fixed number were carried off by various accidents, and could never be found except in so far as any of them might be used for the family, or spent in almsgiving. In this narrative, as in others, then, a miracle of power together with prophecy is clearly shown. For in the large increase of cattle the virtue of his blessing and of his prayer is equally manifest, and in the fixing of the number his prophetic foreknowledge.

CHAPTER XXII.

Of the death of some wicked men who had despised the Saint.

THE venerable man had a great affection for the above mentioned Columban, whom the virtue of his blessing had raised from povery to wealth, because he had done for him many acts of kindness. Now there was at the same time a certain wicked man, an oppressor of the good, named John, son of Conall, son of Domnall, sprung from the royal race of Gabhran. This man was oppressing the aforesaid Columban, the friend of S. Columba; and, making a hostile incursion, not once but twice, had destroyed his dwelling and taken away everything he could find in it. Hence it not undeservedly happened to this wicked man that, after he had plundered the house of the same person for the third time, and was returning to the ship with his associates laden with plunder, he met the blessed man, whom he had despised as being far away, coming towards him. When the Saint rebuked him for his evil deeds, and advised, and besought him to lay down the plunder, he remained hardened and obstinate, and scorned the Saint, and went on board his vessel with the plunder, and mocked and derided the blessed man. The Saint followed him to the edge of the water and wading up to the knees in the clear sea-water, raised both his hands to heaven and earnestly besought Christ, who glorifies His own elect who are glorifying Him. Now the haven, in which for some time after the departure of the oppressor he continued standing and praying to the Lord, is at a place which in Irish is called Ait-Chambas Art-Muirchol. As soon as he had finished his prayer, the Saint returned to the dry land and sat down in the higher ground with his companions, to whom he then uttered these very terrible words, saying: "That miserable wretch, who has despised Christ in his servants, will never return to the port from which he has just set out in your presence; neither shall he nor his wicked associates reach any other place they seek, for sudden death shall prevent it. This day, as you will soon see, a furious storm proceeding from a cloud rising in the North shall overwhelm him and his companions; not even one of them shall be left to tell the tale." After a little, while the day was exceeding bright, behold, a cloud rose up from the sea, as the Saint had said, and caused a great hurricane, which overtook the robber with his booty between the islands of Mull and Colonsay, and overwhelmed them in the midst of the sea which was suddenly lashed to fury; and as the Saint had said, not even one of those who were in the ship escaped; and in this wonderful way, by such a singular storm, were the robbers, miserably indeed, but justly, overwhelmed and sunk in the deep, while the whole sea round about remained tranquil.

CHAPTER XXIII.

Of the death of a certain Feradach, a dishonest man, foretold by the Saint.

AT another time, also, the holy man specially commended to the care of one Feradach, a rich man, who lived in the isle of Islay, a certain exile, of noble race among the Picts, by name Tarain, that he might pass some months in his retinue as one of his friends. When he had received the person thus highly recommended at the hand of the holy man, he after a few days acted treacherously towards him, and by a cruel order put him to death. This enormous crime having been made known to the Saint by travellers, he in reply thus prophesied: "Not to me, but to God has this unhappy wretch lied, whose name will be blotted out from the Book of Life. I am speaking these words now in the midst of summer, but in autumn, before he shall taste the flesh of the swine fattened on the fruit of the trees, he shall be seized with sudden death and be carried off to the infernal regions!" When this prophecy of the holy man was made known to the miserable wretch, he scorned and laughed at the Saint: and when a few days of the autumn months were passed, he ordered a sow which had been fattened on the kernels of nuts to be killed; none of the other swine of the man having as yet been slaughtered; he ordered also that the entrails should be at once taken out, and a piece quickly roasted for him on the spit, so that by tasting of it the impatient man might falsify the prediction of the blessed man. As soon as the piece was roasted, he asked that a very small morsel might be given him to taste, but before the hand which he had stretched out to take it could be turned to his mouth, he expired, and fell on his back a corpse. And all who saw and heard this were greatly terrified and amazed and glorified Christ, honouring him in his holy prophet.

CHAPTER XXIV.

Of another persecutor whose name in Latin was Manus Dextera.

AT another time when the blessed man was staying in Eileanna-Naiomh, and had begun to excommunicate some destroyers of the churches, namely, the sons of Conall, son of Domnall, one of whom was the John of whom we spoke above, one of their wicked associates at the instigation of the devil rushed on the Saint with a spear to kill him. To prevent this, one of the brethren named Findlugan who was prepared to die for the holy man, put on the Saint's cowl and threw himself between them. But in a wonderful way the Saint's garment, as if it had been a most secure and impenetrable protection, could not be pierced by the strong thrust of a very sharp spear, though made by a powerful man, but remained uninjured; and he who was clad in it was preserved safe and untouched under such a defence. But the ruffian, who was called Manus Dextera, went back thinking that he had transfixed the holy man with the spear. A year after from that day, when the Saint was dwelling in the island of Iona, he said: "To-day exactly a year has passed since the day on which Lam-dess did what he could to kill Findlugan in my place, but he himself is, I believe, being slain this very hour." And so it happened at that same moment according to the revelation of the Saint, in the island which in Latin may be called Longa, where, in a battle fought between a number of men on both sides, this Lam-dess alone was slain by Cronan son of Baithene, being transfixed by a dart shot in the name, as it is said, of S. Columba; and after his death the men ceased to fight.

CHAPTER XXV.

Of another oppressor of the innocent, who, in the Province of Leinster, being terribly reproved by the Saint, fell dead at the same moment, like Ananias in the presence of Peter.

WHEN the blessed man, while yet a youth in deacon's orders, was living in the country of the Leinstermen, learning divine wisdom, it came to pass one day that a certain ruthless and cruel oppressor of the harmless was pursuing a young girl, who fled before him, on a level plain. By chance she saw the aged Gemman, the teacher of the above-mentioned young deacon, reading on the plain, and ran straight to him as fast as she could. Alarmed at such an unexpected occurrence, Gemman called to Columba, who was reading at a distance, that together, as far as they were able, they might protect the girl from her pursuer. He immediately coming up, paid no respect to them, but stabbed the girl with his lance under their cloaks, and leaving her lying dead at their feet, turned away and began to depart. Then the old man in great affliction turned to Columba and said: "How long, holy youth Columba, shall God, the Just Judge, suffer this crime and our dishonour to go unavenged?" The Saint at once uttered this sentence against the perpetrator of the crime, saying: "The same moment that the soul of this girl murdered by him ascends into heaven, the soul of her murderer shall go down to hell." And quicker than it can be said, at the word, as Ananias before Peter, so also that murderer of the innocent fell down on the same spot, before the eyes of the holy youth, dead. The report of this sudden and terrible avenging was immediately spread throughout many districts of Ireland, and with it the wonderful fame of the holy deacon.

Let what we have hitherto said be sufficient concerning the terrible avenging of the adversaries. We will now relate a few things concerning wild beasts.

CHAPTER XXVI.

Of the death of a wild boar which the Saint slew from a distance, striking it down with the sign of our Lord's Cross.

AT another time the blessed man, when staying a few days in the isle of Skye, separated himself from the brethren and went alone a little further to pray; and having entered a thick wood, he met a huge wild boar, which the hounds chanced to be pursuing. As soon as he saw it, at a distance, the Saint stood looking intently at it. Then, having invoked the name of God and raised his holy hand in fervent prayer, he said to it: "No further shalt thou come; perish on the spot on which thou now standest." When these words of the Saint sounded in the woods, the terrible brute was not only unable to advance further, but through the efficacy of his word quickly sank down dead before his face.

CHAPTER XXVII.

Of an aquatic monster, which at his prayer and on raising his hand against it, was driven back, that it might not hurt Lugne, who was swimming in the vicinity.

AT another time, again, when the blessed man was staying for a few days in the province of the Picts, he had occasion to cross the river Ness. When he came to its bank, he saw some of the inhabitants burying an unfortunate man, whom, as those who were burying him said, an aquatic monster had seized a little before while he was swimming and bitten very savagely. His wretched body, though too late, certain who had come to his assistance in a boat, had taken out with long hooks. The blessed man, on the other hand, hearing this, directed one of his companions to swim across and rowing over in the coble that was standing on the other shore bring it to him. When he heard the order of the excellent man, Lugne Mocumin made no delay, but obeying, took off his clothes with the exception of his tunic and threw himself into the water. But the monster, which before had been not so much satiated as excited for prey, was lurking in the bottom of the river, and feeling the water disturbed above by the man swimming, suddenly rose up and with a tremendous roar darted with open mouth at the man as he swam in the middle of the stream. Then the blessed man observing this, while all present, the brethren even as well as strangers, were stricken with terror, raised his holy hand and having made the saving sign of the cross in the empty air and invoked the name of God, commanded the ferocious brute, saying: "Thou shalt advance no further, nor touch the man; go back quickly." Then the monster, on hearing the voice of the Saint, was terrified and fled backward very swiftly just as if it had been drawn back with ropes, though before it had approached so near to where Lugne was swimming, that there was not more than the length of a spear-shaft between the monster and the man. The brethren when they saw that the monster had gone back and that their fellow soldier Lugne had returned to them in the boat safe and sound, with great wonder glorified God in the blessed man. And even the barbarous heathens who were present, were compelled by the greatness of the miracle, which they themselves had seen, to magnify the God of the Christians.

CHAPTER XXVIII.

Of the poisonous serpents of the Island of Iona, which from the day the Saint blessed the island, could harm neither man nor beast.

ON a certain day of the same summer in which he passed to the Lord, the Saint went, being conveyed in a cart, to visit the brethren who were engaged on some heavy work in the western plain of the island of Iona. After addressing to them some words of comfort, the Saint stood on the higher ground and thus prophesied: "My children, I know that from this day you will never again be able to see my face anywhere in this field."

Seeing the brethren in great sorrow at hearing this, he tried as much as he could to console them; and raising both his holy hands, he blessed the whole of this our island, saying: "From this moment the poisons of all reptiles shall in no wise be able to hurt either man or cattle in this island so long as the inhabitants continue to observe the commandments of Christ."

CHAPTER XXIX.

Of the knife blessed by the Saint with the sign of our Lord's Cross.

AT another time a certain brother, called Molua, grandson of Briun, coming to the Saint while he was writing, said to him: "I beseech thee to bless this knife which I hold in my hand." The Saint, without turning his face from the book out of which he was copying, extended his holy hand a little, and, making the sign of the cross with his pen, blessed it. When the aforesaid brother was going away with the knife thus blessed, the Saint began to inquire, saying: "What sort of a knife have I blessed for that brother?" Diormit, his faithful attendant, answered: "Thou hast blessed a knife used for killing bulls or oxen." The Saint, on the contrary, replied: "The knife which I have blessed will, I trust in my Lord, hurt neither man nor beast." This word of the Saint was most strongly confirmed in that same hour. For the same brother went beyond the enclosure of the monastery intending to slay an ox, and tried three times with a strong and powerful thrust; nevertheless he could not pierce even the hide. When the monks, who were skillful, knew this, they melted the iron of this same knife with the heat of fire, and spread a thin coating of the liquid metal over all the iron tools in the monastery; and such was the abiding virtue of the Saint's blessing that after that they could inflict a wound on no flesh.

CHAPTER XXX.

Of the cure of Diormit when sick.

AT another time, Diormit, the Saint's faithful servant, was sick nigh into death, and the Saint went to see him in his extremity. Having invoked the name of Christ, he stood by the bed of the sick man, and praying for him, said: "Be propitious unto me, O my Lord, I beseech Thee, and take not away the soul of my faithful servant from the tabernacle of this flesh whilst I live." And having said this, he was silent for a little. Then he uttered these words from his sacred mouth: "My child shall not only not die now, but he shall even live many years after my death." His prayer was heard, for immediately after the Saint's audible prayer, Diormit was restored to complete health, and lived also for many years after the departure of the Saint to the Lord.

CHAPTER XXXI.

Of the cure of Finten, son of Aid, when he was on the point of death.

AT another time, also, when the Saint was making a journey across Drumalban, a certain youth, named Finten, one of his companions, was seized with a sudden illness and reduced to the last extremity. His fellow soldiers besought the Saint, with sorrow, to pray for him. Sympathising with them, he immediately spread out his holy hands to heaven in earnest prayer, and blessing the sick youth, said: "This youth, for whom you plead, shall live a long life; he shall remain alive after all of us who are now here have passed away, and shall die in a good old age." This prophecy of the blessed man was in all things fully accomplished; for this same youth, afterwards the founder of the monastery which is called Kailli-au-inde, ended this present life in a good old age.

CHAPTER XXXII.

Of a boy whom the venerable Man raised to life in the name of the Lord Christ.

AT the time when S. Columba was sojourning for some days in the province of the Picts, a certain peasant with all his family hearing the word of life when the holy man was preaching through an interpreter believed, and believing was baptized—the husband with his wife and children and domestics. And after the short interval of a few days one of the sons of this householder was seized with a dangerous illness, and brought down to the confines of life and death. When the Druids saw him in a dying state, they began to upbraid his parents with great bitterness, to magnify their gods as more powerful than the God of the Christians, and to despise God as weaker than their own gods. When all these things were made known to the blessed man, he burned with zeal for God, and went with his companions to the house of the friendly peasant, where the parents were celebrating the sad obsequies of their child, who had just died. The Saint on seeing them deeply affected strove to comfort them with words of consolation, and exhorted them not in any way to doubt the Divine Omnipotence. He then inquired, saying: "In which room is the body of the dead child?" The bereaved father then led the Saint under the sad roof, who immediately, leaving all the crowd without the door, entered the chamber of mourning alone, where instantly, on bended knees and with his face bathed in abundant tears, he prayed to the Lord Christ. Then rising from his knees, he turned his eyes to the dead child, saying: "In the name of the Lord Jesus Christ rise up and stand on thy feet." At this glorious word of the Saint the soul returned to the body, and the dead child opened his eyes and lived again. The apostolic man then taking him by the hand raised him up, and placing him in a standing position, led him forth out of the chamber, and restored him to his parents. A shout then arose from the people; wailing was turned to joy, and the God of the Christians was glorified.

We must believe that this our Columba had the gift of miracles like the prophets Elijah and Elisha, that like the Apostles Peter and Paul and John he had the honour bestowed upon him of raising the dead to life ; and that among both, that is, among the company of the prophets and of the apostles, this prophetic and apostolic man now enjoys a glorious and eternal throne in the heavenly land with Christ, Who reigneth with the Father in the Unity of the Holy Ghost for ever and ever. Amen.

CHAPTER XXXIII.

Of the illness with which the Druid Broichan was visited because of his retention of a female slave, and of his cure on her release.

ABOUT the same time the venerable man requested Broichan the Druid, out of compassion for humanity, to set at liberty a certain Irish female slave ; and when he very cruelly and obstinately refused, the Saint spoke to him and addressed him as follows : " Know, O Broichan, and be assured, that if thou refuse to set this captive stranger free, as I desire, before I depart again from this province, thou shalt suddenly die." This he said in the presence of King Brude, and going out from the King's dwelling, he came to the river Ness ; and taking from it a white stone, said to his companions : " Observe this white stone ; by means of this the Lord will effect the cure of many diseases among this heathen people." And having uttered this saying, he immediately added: " Broichan is now greviously chastised ; for an angel sent from heaven is striking him severely, and has broken into many fragments the glass cup in his hand from which he was drinking, and has left him gasping heavily for breath and nearly dead. Let us wait here a little for the two messengers of the King, who have been sent after us with all haste to request us to return quickly to the help of the dying Broichan, who now that he has been terribly punished is ready to set the girl free." While the Saint was yet speaking these words, behold, there came, as he had said, two horsemen sent by the King, who related all that had occurred to Broichan in the King's fortress according to the prediction of the Saint, both the breaking of the drinking cup, and of the chastisement of the Druid, and his readiness to set his captive free. They then added: "The King and his friends have sent us to thee to request thee to come to the assistance of his fosterer Broichan who is fast dying." On hearing these words of the messengers S. Columba sent two of his companions to the King with the stone he had blessed, saying : " If Broichan shall first promise to liberate the maid, then let this stone be dipped in water, from which let him drink, and he shall be immediately restored to health. But if he break his promise, and refuse to set the maid free, he shall die at once."

Obeying the Saint's instructions, the two who were sent came to the royal palace and related to the King the venerable man's words. When made acquainted with them, the King and his fosterer Broichan were utterly dismayed. They immediately liberated the maid, and delivered her to the Saint's messengers. The stone was then immersed in water, and in a wonderful manner, contrary to its nature, it floated on water like an apple or a nut ; nor could it, on account of the holy man's blessing, be made to sink. Broichan drank of the water as the stone floated on it, and instantly returned from the brink of the grave, recovering the perfect health of his body. This remarkable stone was afterwards preserved in the King's treasury, and, through the mercy of God, floated in the same manner when immersed in water, and effected many cures of sicknesses among the people. Wonderful to relate, however, when this same stone was in request for any who were sick whose term of life had arrived, it could never be found. Thus on the day King Brude died it was sought for, but could not be found in the place in which it had been previously preserved.

CHAPTER XXXIV.

Of the Holy Man's opposition to the Druid Broichan and of the contrary wind.

ONE day after the above mentioned events, Broichan addressed the holy man, saying: "Tell me, Columba, when dost thou propose to set sail?" The Saint replied: "On the third day, God willing and preserving my life, I propose beginning my voyage." Broichan on the other hand said: "Thou shalt not be able; for I can make the wind unfavourable to thee and bring down upon thee the shadow of a thick darkness." The Saint replied: "The Almighty Power of God rules all things, and in His name and under His control are all our movements directed." What more need I say? The same day, the Saint as he purposed in his heart, came with a great concourse attending him, to the long lake of the river Ness. Then the Druids began to exult, seeing that a thick darkness was resting upon all things, and that the wind was contrary and tempestuous. Nor should we wonder that God permitting them, they are sometimes able, with the aid of demons, to raise tempests and to agitate the sea. For thus legions of demons once met the holy Bishop Germanus in the middle of the sea, when sailing from the Gallican Gulf to Britain, for the salvation of men, and opposed him with perils, raising violent storms and obscuring the heavens and the light of day with clouds of thick darkness. But all these things were dispersed at the prayer of S. Germanus, more quickly than his words were uttered, and the darkness ceased. Accordingly, our Columba, seeing that the elements were violently agitated against him, invoked Christ the Lord, and embarking in his small boat, while the sailors hesitated, he, made more confident, ordered the sail to be hoisted against the wind. On this being done, and while the whole crowd was looking on, the vessel ran against the adverse winds and was carried along with marvellous rapidity. And after no great interval the winds which had been against them, veered round to help them on their voyage to the astonishment of all. And thus during all that day the skiff of the blessed man was driven along by gentle and favouring breezes, and borne to the desired haven. Let the reader therefore consider what and how great this venerable man was, in whom God Almighty manifested His own illustrious name in the presence of the heathen people, by bestowing upon him the power of working such great miracles as those we have now recorded.

CHAPTER XXXV.

Of the Gate of the Royal Fortress which suddenly opened of its own accord.

AT another time, that is, when the Saint was weary at the end of his first journey to King Brude, it happened that this same King, elated with pride of royalty and acting haughtily, would not open the gates of his fortress on the first arrival of the blessed man. When the man of God observed this, he went up with his companions to the folding gates, and having first marked them with the sign of the Lord's Cross, he next knocked at, and then laid his hand upon them, when they immediately flew open of their own accord with great celerity, the bolts having been violently driven back. Immediately they were opened, the Saint and his companions entered. On this becoming known, the King and his Senate were greatly alarmed, and issuing out of the palace, went to meet the blessed man with reverence, and addressed him with the most respectful and conciliating words; and from that day, ever afterwards, that same ruler as long as he lived, honoured the holy and venerable man with the greatest honour as was meet.

CHAPTER XXXVI.

Of a similar unclosing of the Church of the Field of the Streams.

AT another time, again, when the blessed man was staying a few days in Ireland, he went to visit the brethren who were dwelling in the monastery of the Field of the Two Streams, having been invited by them. But from some accident it happened that on his arrival at the church, the keys of the chapel could not be found. But when the Saint heard some of them complaining among themselves about the keys not having been found yet and of the doors being bolted, he went up to the door, and said : "The Lord is able to open His house to His servants without a key." When this was said, the bolts were driven back with great force and the door opened of its own accord. The Saint with the admiration of all entered the church before them. He was hospitably entertained by the brethren and regarded by all with the utmost respect and veneration.

CHAPTER XXXVII.

Of a certain Peasant, who was a beggar, for whom the Saint made and blessed a stake for killing wild beasts with.

AT another time a certain very poor peasant who was dwelling in the country which borders on the shores of the Aporic Lake, came to the Saint. To this miserable man who had nothing wherewith to feed his wife and little ones, when he was begging, the blessed man showed pity, and having given him what he could, said : " Poor creature, take a branch from the neighbouring wood and bring it to me at once." The miserable man obeying, brought the branch as according to the Saint's command ; and the Saint taking it from him, sharpened it into a stake ; and when he had sharpened it with his own hand and blessed it, he gave it back to the destitute man, saying : " Take great care of this stake, which, as I believe will hurt neither man nor cattle, but wild beasts and fish alone ; and as long as thou hast this stake there shall never be lacking in thy house abundance of venison." On hearing this, the wretched beggar rejoiced greatly and returned home, and fixed the stake in a remote place frequented by the wild beasts of the forests; and when the night was passed, early next morning he went to see the stake, and found that a stag of great size had fallen upon it and had been transfixed by it. What more need be said? Not a day could pass, so tradition says, on which he did not find that either a stag or a hind or some other wild animal had fallen upon the spit and been transfixed. His whole house being thus filled with the flesh of the wild animals, that which was over, which the chamber of his own house could not hold, he sold to his neighbours.

Nevertheless, as with Adam, the envy of the devil found out even this wretched man by means of his wife, who, not as wise but as foolish, thus addressed her husband: "Take the stake," she said, "out of the earth, for if men, or even cattle, should perish upon it, thou and I, with our children, will either be put to death or led captive." To this her husband replied: "It will not so happen, for the holy man said to me, when he blessed the stake, that it would never injure men nor even cattle." After saying this, however, he yielded to his wife, and went and took the stake out of the earth, and, as if demented, placed it within his house, leaning it against the wall, when immediately his house-dog, falling upon it, was killed. On its death his wife said: "One of thy children will fall upon the stake and perish." On hearing her words the husband removed the stake from the wall, and carried it back into the forest and placed it in a very dense thicket, where, as he thought, it could not be lighted upon by any living creature. But, returning on the following day, he found that a roe had fallen upon it and perished. Removing it thence, he placed it in the river, which may be called in Latin Nigra Dea, hiding it near the bank, under the water, but when he visited it the next day he found transfixed, and still held upon it, a salmon of great size, which he was scarcely able by himself to lift from the river and carry home. The stake he took out of the water, and, carrying it back with him at the same time, placed it outside on the top of his house, when a crow, having alighted upon it, was killed by the force of its fall. After this the miserable man, perverted by the counsel of his foolish wife, took the stake down from the house-top, and, having procured an axe, cut it into many pieces and threw them into the fire. And after this, the rich solace against his poverty being lost, he began, as he deserved, to be in want again. This solace against poverty depended entirely on the stake so often mentioned above, which the blessed man had blessed and given him, and which, so long as it was preserved, would have sufficed for snares and nets, and for every kind of hunting and fishing, but now that it was lost, the wretched peasant, though enriched by it for a season, with his whole family, bewailed it, though too late, all the remaining days of his life.

CHAPTER XXXVIII.

Of the leathern milk-vessel which was carried away by the ebb, and brought back to the same place by the return of the tide.

AT another time the blessed man's messenger, who was called Lugaid, and surnamed Laitir, when preparing, in obedience to the Saint, to set sail for Ireland, found among the utensils of the Saint's ship a leathern milk-vessel, which he had sought for, and put it in the sea, under a heap of large stones, for the purpose of moistening it, and then going to the Saint told him what he had done with it. The Saint smiled and said: "The skin which, as thou sayest, thou hast put under the waves, will not, I think, accompany thee this time to Ireland." "Why," inquired Lugaid, "can I not have it with me in the ship?" The Saint replied: "Thou shalt know the reason to-morrow, as the event will prove." Accordingly, on the following morning, Lugaid went to take the skin out of the sea, but during the night the ebb of the tide had carried it away. Not finding it, he returned in grief to the Saint, and on his bended knees on the ground confessed his carelessness. The Saint consoled him, saying: "Be not grieved, brother, for perishable things; the skin which the retiring tide carried away, the returning tide will bring back to its place after thy departure." The same day, after Lugaid had set out from the island of Iona, when the ninth hour was passed, the Saint said to those who stood near him : "Let one of you now go to the sea; the skin for which Lugaid was grieving, and which the ebbing tide carried away, the returning tide has now brought back and restored to the place from which it was taken away." On hearing these words of the Saint, a certain active youth ran to the sea-shore, and found the skin as the Saint had predicted, and, hastening at full speed, bore it back, rejoicing greatly, and delivered it openly to the Saint, amid the great admiration of all who were present. In the two narratives which we have just related, though touching on small matters, namely, a stake and a skin, as often said, the gifts of prophecy and of miracles are seen accompanying each other. Let us now turn to other matters.

CHAPTER XXXIX.

Of Libran of the Rush-ground, a prophecy of the Holy Man.

AT another time, while the holy man was residing in the island of Iona, a certain man of humble birth, who had lately assumed the clerical habit, sailed over from Ireland and came to the island monastery of the blessed man. The Saint having one day found him sitting alone in the guest house, he inquired of him first concerning his country and race and the object of his journey. He replied that he was born in the country of the Connaught men, and that he had undertaken his long and weary journey in order to atone for his sins by a pilgrimage. The Saint, then, in order to test the character of his penitence, set before his eyes the hardness and severity of the monastic discipline, whereupon he immediately replied : "I am ready for whatever thou mayest desire to command me, however hard or humiliating." Why need I add more? That same hour he confessed all his sins, and on his bended knees on the ground promised to fulfil the rules of penance. The Saint said to him :

"Rise and sit down." Then he thus addressed him as he sat: "Seven years thou must do penance in the island of Tiree; thou and I, God willing, shall survive that period of seven years." Comforted by these words of the Saint, the man gave thanks to God, and, turning to the Saint, asked, "What ought I to do on account of an oath I have violated? For while living in my own country I murdered a certain man, and after his murder, as guilty of the crime, I was held in bonds. But a certain very wealthy blood relation came to my aid, and promptly loosing me from the chains with which I was bound, rescued me from the death to which I was condemned. After my release I bound myself by a great oath to serve him, who had rescued me, all the days of my life. But I had passed but a few days in his service when, disdaining to serve man, and preferring rather to obey God, I deserted my master according to the flesh, and, violating my oath, fled, and, God granting me a prosperous journey, came to thee." To this the Saint, seeing him very much grieved for these things, first prophesying, said: "At the end of the seven years, as I said to thee, thou shalt come to me here during the Forty Days, that in the Paschal Festival thou mayest approach the altar and receive the Eucharist."

But why delay with words? The penitent stranger obeyed the Saint's commands in every thing. He was sent at the time to the monastery on the Plain of Lunge, and when he had completed the seven years of penance there, he returned during the Forty Days to the Saint, according to his previous command and prophecy. When the celebration of Easter was over, during which he drew near, as directed, to the altar, he came again to the Saint inquiring of him with regard to the above-mentioned oath. Then the Saint gave this prophetic response to his inquiry: "Thy earthly master, of whom thou spakest some time ago, is still living, and thy father and mother and brethren are still alive. Now, therefore, thou must prepare thyself for a voyage." And, while saying these words, he drew forth a sword, ornamented with carved ivory, and said: "Take this gift to carry with thee, and offer it to thy master as the price of thy ransom; nevertheless, he will in no wise accept it, for he has a kindly disposed wife, and, guided by her wholesome counsel, he will on that same day, without recompense or ransom, set thee free, unloosing, according to custom, the captive's girdle from around thy loins. But when relieved from this anxiety, thou shalt not escape another arising from a different source. For thy brethren on all sides will press thee to make good the support due to thy father for so long a time as thou hast neglected it. Nevertheless do thou, obeying their will, without any hesitation, dutifully take in hand to cherish thine aged father. But this burden, though it may seem to thee heavy, must not grieve thee, because thou shalt soon lay it down. For in the end of the week in which thou beginnest to minister to thy father, thou shalt lay his dead body in the grave. But after the burial of thy father, thy brethren, again, will sharply require of thee to pay the expenses also due for thy mother. But from the necessity of doing this thy younger brother will free thee, by engaging to perform in thy stead every duty and obligation which thou owest, serving thy mother on thy behalf."

After these words the above-mentioned brother, Libran by name, having received the gift, set out enriched with the Saint's blessing; and, arriving at his native country, found everything turn out exactly in accordance with the Saint's prophecy. For, immediately on his showing and offering the price of his freedom to his master, his wife opposed his wish to accept anything, saying: "What need have we to accept this ransom which S. Columba has sent? We are not worthy of it. Set this dutiful servant free without payment. The blessing of the holy man will profit us more than this payment which is offered." Accordingly the husband, hearkening to this wholesome counsel of his wife, immediately set the slave free without a ransom. Libran was next, in accordance with the Saint's prophecy, compelled by his brothers to undertake the care of his father, and buried him at his death on the seventh day. After his burial he was compelled to discharge the duties owing to his mother, but his younger brother coming to his assistance, as the Saint had foretold, relieved him from the obligation by fulfilling the duties in his stead, and said to his brothers: "On no account ought we to detain our brother at home, who for seven years has laboured with S. Columba in Britain for the salvation of his soul."

After being released from all the things by which he was troubled, and bidding farewell to his mother and brethren, he returned a free man, and came to the place which, in Irish, is called Daire Calgaich. There he found a ship under sail just leaving the port, and, shouting from the shore, he asked the sailors to receive him among them that he might sail into Britain. But they refused, because they were not of the monks of S. Columba. Then, addressing the venerable man, who, though far distant, was nevertheless present in spirit, as the event speedily proved, he said: "Is it thy will, O holy Columba, that these sailors, who do not receive me, thy companion, should sail away with full sails and favourable winds?" At this saying the wind, which before was favourable to them, was changed, quicker than it can be said, into the contrary direction. Meanwhile the sailors, seeing the same man running in the same direction with them along the river, hastily took counsel with each other, and cried out to him from the ship, saying: "Perhaps on this account, because we refused to receive thee, the wind has quickly veered round against us. But if even now we were to invite thee on board amongst us, couldst thou make the winds, which are now against us, favourable?" On hearing this the wayfarer said to them: "S. Columba, to whom I am going, and whom I have obeyed during the past seven years, is able, by virtue of his prayers, to obtain from his Lord, if ye receive me, a favourable wind." When they heard this they brought the ship to land and invited him on board with them. As soon as he was on board, he said: "In the name of the Almighty, whom S. Columba blamelessly serves, spread your sail on the extended yards." When this was done, the contrary gales of wind were immediately changed into favourable, and a prosperous voyage was made under full sail to Britain. And Libran, after the shores of Britain were reached, blessed the sailors and left the ship, and came to S. Columba in the island of Iona, where he was then dwelling.

The blessed man received him with joy, and, without obtaining the information from another, told him all that had happened to him during his journey, also concerning his master, and the wholesome counsel of his master's wife; how by her persuasion he was set free; likewise concerning his brothers; of the death of his father, and his burial at the end of a week; of his mother, and of the timely assistance of his younger brother; of the things which occurred as he returned; of the wind adverse and favourable; of the words of the sailors, who at first refused to take him on board; of the promise of a fair wind, and of the favourable change in the wind on his being taken on board the ship. But why need I add more? Everything the Saint foretold, he now described after it had been exactly fulfilled.

After these words the traveller gave back the price of his ransom which he had received from the Saint. At the same time, the Saint addressed to him this word, saying: "Inasmuch as thou art free, thou shalt be called Libran." In those days Libran took the monastic vow with much fervour. And when he was being sent back by the holy man to the monastery, where he had previously served the Lord during the seven years of penance, he received in farewell from the Saint this prophetic announcement concerning himself: "Thou shalt live a long life, and shalt finish this present life in a good old age. Nevertheless, thou shalt not rise from the dead in Britain but in Ireland." When he heard these words, he wept bitterly on his bended knees, and the Saint, seeing that he was very sad, began to comfort him, saying: "Arise, and be not grieved. Thou shalt die in one of my monasteries, and thy lot shall be among my chosen monks in the Kingdom, and with them shalt thou awake from the sleep of death unto the resurrection of life." When he received this great consolation from the Saint he rejoiced exceedingly, and departed in peace, enriched with the blessing of the Saint. This truthful prophecy of the Saint concerning this man was afterwards accomplished. For when, through many revolving years, he had obediently served the Lord in the monastery of the Plain of Lunge, after the departure of S. Columba from the world, he was sent, in extreme old age, on a mission to Ireland in connection with certain affairs belonging to the monastery, and proceeded as soon as he landed through the Plain of Breg until he came to the monastery of the Oakwood Plain; and there, being received as a guest in the guest chamber, and suffering from a certain disease, he passed to the Lord in peace on the seventh day of his sickness, and was buried among the chosen monks of S. Columba, according to his prophecy, to await resurrection to life eternal.

Let it suffice that we have written these true prophecies of S. Columba concerning Libran, who was called Libran of the Rush-ground, because for many years he had worked on the rush-ground gathering rushes.

CHAPTER XL.

Of a certain little woman who suffered great and very dangerous pains in childbirth.

ON a certain day, while the Saint was dwelling in the island of Iona, he rose from reading and smiling said: "I must now hasten to the chapel to pray to the Lord for a certain poor woman in Ireland, who is at this moment crying out and mentioning the name of Columba and suffering in the great pains of a most difficult child-birth, and is hoping that deliverance will be given to her from the Lord from her suffering through me, because she is a blood relation to me, and is lineally descended from the house of my mother's parentage." Saying this, the Saint moved with pity for the little woman, ran to the church and on bended knees prayed for her to Christ who was Himself born of human kind. After prayer he went out from the chapel, and addressed the brethren who came running to him, saying: "Now hath the Lord Jesus, born of woman, mercifully given timely help to the miserable woman, delivered her from her distresses; and she hath safely brought forth her child; nor shall she die on this occasion." The same hour, as the Saint prophesied, the poor woman, on invoking his name, was safely delivered and restored to health. So it was afterwards made known to us by some travellers who came from Ireland and from the same district in which the woman lived.

CHAPTER XLI.

Of one Lugne, surnamed Tutida, a Pilot, who lived on the island of Rechrea, and whom, because he was deformed, his wife hated.

AT another time, when the holy man was sojourning on the island of Rechrea, a certain man of humble birth came to him and complained of his wife, who, as he said, so hated him that she would on no account allow him to come near her for marriage rights. On hearing this, the Saint summoned the wife and, so far as he could, began to reprove her on account of it, saying: 'Why, O woman, dost thou attempt to withdraw thy flesh from thyself, when the Lord says 'They two shall be one flesh?' The flesh of thy husband therefore is thy flesh." She answering said: "Whatever thou shalt require of me I am ready to do, however hard it may be, this one thing excepted, that thou dost not in any way urge me to sleep in the same bed with Lugne. I refuse not to perform every household duty, or if thou commandest me, I will even cross the seas and dwell in a monastery for women." The Saint then said: "What thou sayest cannot lawfully be done; for thou art bound by the law to thy husband so long as he liveth. What God hath lawfully joined it is impious to separate." And when he had said these words, he immediately added: "This day let us three, that is, the husband with his wife and I, pray to the Lord with fasting." But the woman replied: "I know, because nothing is impossible with thee, that the things which seem difficult or even impossible will, when asked by thee from God, be granted. But why say more?" The woman agreed to fast with the Saint that night, and likewise the husband; and the following night the Saint passed without sleep, praying for them. Next day he thus addressed the woman in the presence of her husband: "O woman, art thou still ready, as thou saidst yesterday, to go away to a convent of women?" She replied: "Now I know that thy prayer for me has been heard by God: for him whom I hated yesterday, I to-day love; for my heart was last night, in some way I know not of, changed from hate to love." Why linger? From that day to the day of death the soul of the wife was indissolubly joined to that of her husband in love, so that she in no wise refused those mutual marital rights, which she was before unwilling to allow.

CHAPTER XLII.

Of the voyage of Cormac, the grandson of Lethan, a prophecy of the Blessed Man.

AT another time, Cormac, a soldier of Christ, of whom, in the first part of this little book, we briefly mentioned a few particulars, attempted again, a second time, to discover a desert in the ocean. After he set out under full sail from the land along the boundless ocean, S. Columba, who was then staying beyond Drumalban, commended him to King Brude in the presence of the ruler of the Orkneys, saying: "Some of our brethren have lately set sail, desiring to find a desert in the pathless sea; should they chance, after many wanderings, to come to the Orkney islands, do thou carefully commend them to this prince, whose hostages are in thy hand, that no evil may befall them within his territories." The Saint spake thus because he foresaw in spirit that after a few months Cormac would arrive at the Orkneys. And so it came to pass; and to the aforesaid commendation of the holy man Cormac owed his escape from impending death.

After the lapse of a few months, when the Saint was staying in the island of Iona, Cormac's name was one day unexpectedly mentioned in his presence by some persons in conversation. They were observing that it was not yet known whether Cormac's voyage had been successful or not. Hearing this the Saint joined in the conversation, and said: "Cormac, of whom you are now speaking, you will presently see arriving here to-day." And after the space of about an hour, wonderful to relate, behold Cormac unexpectedly arrived, and, amid the admiration and thanksgiving of all, proceeded to the chapel. And because we have briefly mentioned the blessed man's prophecy respecting the second voyage of this Cormac, it is requisite that another and equally remarkable instance of his prophetic knowledge should be related respecting his third voyage.

When Cormac was wearily pursuing his third voyage in the ocean, he began to be in imminent danger of death. For, when for fourteen summer days and as many nights his vessel sailed with full sails before the south wind in a straight course from the land into the regions of the north, his voyage seemed to be extended beyond the limits of human wanderings and return impossible. Then it came to pass that, after the tenth hour of the fourteenth day, certain terrors, most formidable, and almost insupportable, arose on every side. Loathsome and annoying creatures, such as had never been seen before, covered the sea in swarms, and struck the keel and sides, the prow and the stern, of the vessel with such fearful violence that it seemed as if they would wholly penetrate the leathern covering of the vessel. As those who were there afterwards narrated, they were nearly as large as frogs; they gave great trouble with their stings, and, though not able to fly, they could swim; they also crowded upon the blades of the oars. When Cormac and his fellow-sailors saw these and other monsters, which it is not now our province to describe, they were filled with fear and alarm, and, with tears, prayed to God, who is a faithful and a very present help in time of trouble.

At that same hour our holy Columba, though far distant in body, was nevertheless present in spirit with Cormac in the vessel. Therefore, at that moment, he gave the signal, assembled the brethren in the chapel, and entering the church, addressed those who were present, and uttered the following prophecy in his usual manner, saying: "Brethren, pray with all earnestness for Cormac, who, by sailing too far, has passed beyond the limits hitherto reached by men, and is now suffering horrible fear and alarm in the presence of monsters never before seen and well nigh indescribable. We ought, therefore, to sympathise with our brethren and associates in their anxiety and danger, and to pray the Lord with them. For, behold, at this moment Cormac and his sailors are shedding copious tears, and praying to Christ with intense fervour; let us assist them with our prayers that Christ, having compassion upon us, may cause the wind, which for fourteen days past has blown from the South, to blow from the North, and this North wind will draw back Cormac's vessel from the perils." When he had said this, with a tearful voice, on bended knees before the altar, he prayed to the almighty power of God, the Ruler of the winds and all things. And after prayer he rose quickly, and wiping away his tears, joyfully gave thanks to God, saying: "Now, brethren, let us congratulate our dear friends for whom we are praying; for God will now change the South wind into one from the North, and delivering our associates from their perils, bring them here to us again." And as he spoke the South wind immediately ceased and a North wind blew for many days; and Cormac's vessel was brought back to land. And Cormac came to S. Columba, and, God granting it, they saw each other face to face to the great joy and wonder of all. Let the reader then consider how great and of what character the blessed man must have been, who possessed such prophetic knowledge, and by invoking the name of Christ, could control the winds and waves.

CHAPTER XLIII.

Of the Venerable Man's journey in a Chariot which was not secured with proper linch-pins.

AT another time, when the Saint, compelled by some matters of ecclesiastical business, was spending some days in Ireland, he mounted a yoked cart which he had previously blessed, but in which, from some unaccountable negligence, the requisite linch-pins had not been fixed in the holes at the ends of the axles. On that day it was Columban, the son of Echud, a holy man, and founder of the monastery which in the Irish tongue is called Snam-luthir, who performed the office of driver in the carriage with S. Columba. The jolting of that day through the long reaches of the journey was great, yet the wheels did not come off the axles, nor slip from their proper places, though, as said above, there were no linch-pins to secure them, nor fastenings to prevent them. Divine grace alone so favoured the venerable man that the vehicle in which he was advantageously seated, should proceed without being upset or meeting with any obstacle to prevent its progress.

Let that which we have thus far written suffice in respect to the miracles which the Divine Omnipotence wrought through this remarkable man, while he lived in this present life. We must now mention a few of those well authenticated miracles which the Lord granted unto him to perform after his departure from the flesh.

CHAPTER XLIV.

Of the Rain which after some months of Drought the Lord bountifully poured out upon the earth in honour of the Blessed Man—a miracle which we are now by God's favour going to relate as we saw it happen in our own day with our own eyes.

FOR about fourteen years ago there occurred in these marshy regions during the spring a great drought, long-continued and severe, insomuch so that there seemed to impend over the people the threat of the Lord against sinners in the book of Leviticus, which says: "I will give to you the heaven above as iron, and the earth as brass. Your labour shall be spent for naught; the earth shall not bring forth her increase, nor the trees their fruit," etc. We, therefore, reading these words, and fearing the impending plague, took counsel together and resolved that some of our elder brethren should go round the newly-ploughed and sown field, carrying with them the white tunic of S. Columba and the books which he had written with his own pen, and that they should raise them in the air and three times shake the tunic which the Saint wore at the time of his death, and that they should open his books and read them on the little Hill of the Angels, where the citizens of the heavenly country were sometimes seen to descend to hold communion with the blessed man. When all these things had been done in the manner prescribed, then, wonderful to relate, on the same day, the heavens, which during the past months of March and April had been bare of clouds, were suddenly covered with dense vapours, rising up from the sea with marvellous rapidity; a copious rain fell day and night; and the land, previously parched, being sufficiently moistened, brought forth its fruits and a most abundant harvest in the same year. And thus the very commemoration of the name of the blessed man, by the exhibition of his tunic and books, obtained seasonable relief at the same time for many places and much people.

CHAPTER XLV.

Of adverse winds changed into favourable breezes through the virtue of the Venerable Man's prayers.

OUR belief in such miracles as were performed in past times, and which we ourselves did not see, is confirmed beyond doubt by those which have been wrought in the present, and which we ourselves have seen. For on three occasions we have seen unfavourable gales of wind changed into propitious breezes.

On the first occasion, when our long boats of hewn pine and oak had to be drawn over land, and a great quantity of materials for building ships to be brought home in the same way, taking counsel together, we placed the garments and books of the blessed man upon the altar, and at the same time fasted and prayed and invoked his name, in order that he might obtain for us from the Lord a favourable wind. And this was done for us by the holy man, through God's favour. For on the day that our sailors had made all things ready and were prepared to convey the wood, for the purposes above mentioned, in skiffs and curachs, the wind, which for several days before had been contrary, suddenly became favourable. Then by long and dangerous ways, the favouring breezes blowing the entire day, and under full sails, the whole fleet of boats arrived, without the slightest hindrance, safely at the island of Iona.

On the second occasion when, a few years later, some oak trees were being conveyed, in twelve vessels which we took with us for the purpose, from near the mouth of the river Shiel for the repair of our monastery, our sailors one day rowed out to sea with their oars, the sea being calm, when suddenly a westerly wind, which is also called Zephyr, sprang up against us, and we turned aside to the nearest island, which is called in Irish Airthrago, seeking shelter in a harbour in it. But meanwhile we began to complain of this inopportune contrariness of the wind, and in a certain manner as it were to blame our Columba, saying: "Is this our unfortunate detention pleasing to thee, O Saint? Hitherto we had hoped that, through the Divine favour, we might have received some aid and comfort in our labours from thee, thinking that thou wert great and honoured before God." A little after, as it were a single moment, wonderful to relate, behold the adverse westerly wind fell, and more quickly than it can be said, a most favourable south-easterly wind blew. The sailors then as directed raised the yards in the form of a cross and spread the sails upon them, and with steady and favouring breezes we, that same day, reached our own island, being borne thither without the slightest fatigue, and rejoicing in our cargo of wood, in company with all those who were engaged in assisting us in the ships. This querulous blaming of the holy man, though slight, profited us not a little; and in what and how great esteem the Saint is held before God is evident in His hearing him so quickly and changing the wind.

The third occasion was when in the summer, after the convention of the Irish Synod, we were detained some days by adverse winds among the people of the tribe of Lorn, and had reached the island of Shuna, where the vigil and feast of S. Columba found us delayed and very sad, because we wished to celebrate that joyous day in the island of Iona. Then, as on a former occasion, we were complaining and saying, "Is it pleasing to thee, O Saint, that we should spend the morrow, the day of thy festival, among strangers, and not in thine own church? Easy is it for thee on the morning of such a day to obtain from the Lord that contrary winds be changed into favourable, and that we celebrate the solemn Mass of thy birth in thine own church." When that night was passed, we arose at daybreak, and, observing that the adverse winds had ceased, we went on board and put to sea when there was no wind blowing, and lo, immediately there sprang up behind us a wind from the South. Then the sailors, rejoicing, raised the sails, and thus on this day also, without any exertion on our part, so quick and so favourable was our passage, God granting it to the blessed man, that we reached the haven of the island of Iona after the third hour of the day, as we had before anxiously desired. After washing our hands and feet, we entered the church at the sixth hour with our brethren, and celebrated at once the sacred service of the Mass on the festival day, which is the birth-day of SS. Columba and Baithene, at the daybreak of which day, as we said above, we set sail from the island of Shuna, which is situated afar off. The witnesses of the incidents just related are not merely two or three, as the law requires, but hundreds and more, who are still living.

CHAPTER XLVI.

Of the Plague.

AND this also, in connection with the Plague which in our own time twice devastated the greater part of the world, ought to be accounted, I think, among not the least of his miracles. For not to mention the other and greater countries of Europe, that is, Italy, the Roman States and the Cisalpine provinces of Gaul, with the provinces of Spain also, which lie beyond the Pyrenees, these islands of the sea, namely Ireland and Britain, have throughout their whole extent, except among two tribes, the Picts and Scots of Britain, who are separated from each other by the Dorsal mountains of Britain, been twice ravaged by a dreadful pestilence. And although neither of these tribes was free from those great sins by which the wrath of the Eternal Judge is very frequently provoked, yet hitherto both of them have been patiently borne with and spared. And to whom else can this favour, granted to them by God, be attributed but to S. Columba, whose monasteries have been founded within the territories of both these peoples, and are regarded by both with the greatest respect up to the present time. But that which we are now about to say cannot, we think, be heard without a sigh, because there are many very stupid people in both tribes, who, in their ignorance that they have owed their immunity from the plagues to the prayers of the Saints, ungratefully and wickedly abuse the patience of God. But we give frequent thanks to God for having, through the intercession of our holy patron, preserved us in these our islands from the ravages of the plagues, and that in Saxonia also, when visiting our friend, King Aldfrid, where the pestilence was still raging and laying waste many villages, our Lord, both in the first visitation, after the war of Egfrid, and in the second, two years later, so delivered us from such danger, though walking in the midst of death, that not even one of our companions died of the plague, nor was any one of them attacked by any other disease.

Here the Second Book of the miracles must end; but it is right to inform the reader that in it, even of well authenticated miracles, many have been omitted in order to avoid fatiguing those who read it.

Here endeth the Second Book.

BOOK III.

Here beginneth the Third Book.

OF ANGELIC VISIONS.

CHAPTER I.

IN the First of these three little Books have been described, with the assistance of God, briefly and concisely, as was observed above, some of the prophetic revelations. In the Second have been recorded the miracles of power which were wrought by the blessed man, and with which, as was frequently remarked, the gift of prophecy was often associated. But in this Third Book, which treats of Angelic Apparitions, we shall narrate those which were made to others regarding the blessed man, and those which were made to him regarding others, and those also which were made to both parties, though in a different manner; that is, to the Saint directly and more fully, but to others indirectly and in part, that is, externally and tentatively, yet in the same visions, whether of angels or of heavenly light. But whatever discrepancies may at first sight appear in such visions, will be cleared away when they are narrated below in their proper places. We shall begin as from the beginnings of the birth of the blessed man by describing those angelic apparitions which occurred then.

The Angel of the Lord appeared to the mother of the venerable man one night, between his conception and his birth, in dreams, and, standing by her, delivered to her a certain robe of marvellous beauty, on which the most beautiful colours, as it were of the whole world of flowers, seemed to be depicted. After a little he asked it back, and took it out of her hands, and, lifting it up and opening it out, sent it forth into the empty air. But she, deeply grieved at the robe being taken from her, spake thus to the man of venerable mien: "Why takest thou the beautiful cloak away from me so soon?" He immediately replied: "Because this mantle is of such great honour that thou mayst not longer retain it with thee." When this was said, the woman saw the aforesaid mantle gradually receding from her in its flight, and expanding till it exceeded in width the breadth of the plains, and surpassed in all its dimensions the mountains and forests. Then she heard a voice addressing her thus: "Be not grieved, O woman, for to the man to whom thou hast been joined in bonds of wedlock thou shalt bear a beautiful son, who shall be numbered among his people as one of the prophets of God, and is predestinated by God to be the leader of innumerable souls to the heavenly country." On hearing these words the woman awaked out of sleep.

CHAPTER II.

Of the bright ray of Light seen resting upon the face of the sleeping boy.

ON another night the fosterer of the same blessed boy, Cruithnechan, a priest, a man of blameless life, upon returning home from the church after Mass, found his whole house illumined with a bright light, and saw a globe as of fire standing over the face of the little boy as he lay asleep. On seeing this he shook with fear, and fell down with his face to the ground, marvelling greatly, and perceiving that the grace of the Holy Spirit had been poured out from heaven upon his young charge.

CHAPTER III.

Of the Apparition of the holy Angels whom S. Brenden saw accompanying the Blessed Man along the Plain.

FOR after an interval of many years, when S. Columba was excommunicated by a certain Synod for some pardonable and very trifling reasons, though unjustly, as was afterwards made clear in the end, he came to the Assembly which had been convened against him. When S. Brenden, the founder of the monastery which, in Irish, is called Birra, saw him approaching in the distance, he suddenly rose up, and, with his head bowed down, reverently kissed him. When some of the elders in the Assembly, who took him aside from the rest, found fault with him, saying: " Why didst thou not refuse to rise in the presence of the excommunicated and to kiss him?" he replied to them on this wise: " If you had seen what the Lord has this day thought fit to show to me concerning his chosen one, whom you dishonour, you would never have excommunicated him whom God not only doth in no wise excommunicate according to your unjust sentence, but even more and more magnifies." They, in reply, said: " In what way, we should like to know, does God honour him whom we have excommunicated, and not without cause?" "I have seen," said Brenden, "a most brilliant pillar, wreathed with tresses of fire, going before that same man of God whom you despise. Holy angels also were his companions as he journeyed across the plain. Him, therefore, whom I see to be ordained by God to be a leader of the people to life, I dare not spurn." On hearing these words from him, not only did they cease, not daring to persist in excommunicating him any longer, but they also honoured him with the greatest reverence. This was done at Tiltown.

CHAPTER IV.

Of the angel of the Lord whom S. Finnio saw accompanying the Blessed Man on his journey.

ON another occasion the holy man went to the venerable Bishop Finio, who had formerly been his teacher, the young going to visit the aged. When S. Finnio saw him drawing nigh to him, he beheld an angel of the Lord accompanying him; and as it has been handed down to us by well informed persons, he made known the same to certain brethren who were standing by, saying, "Behold, look now at S. Columba as he draweth near; he has been deemed worthy to have an angelic inhabitant of heaven for his companion on the way." About the same time the Saint sailed over into Britain with his twelve fellow-soldiers and disciples.

CHAPTER V.

Of the Angel of the Lord who appeared in a vision to S. Columba while he was staying in the island of Eilean-na-naoimh, and was sent that he might ordain Aidan king.

AT another time, when this illustrious man was staying in the island of Eilean-na-naoimh, on a certain night, he saw in an ecstacy of mind an angel of the Lord sent to him from heaven, and bearing in his hand the glass book of the ordination of Kings. Having received the book from the hand of the angel, the venerable man, as commanded by him, began to read therein; and when he refused to ordain Aidan King, as the book directed, because he preferred Iogenan, his brother, the angel suddenly stretching forth his hand smote him with a scourge, the livid marks of which remained in his side all the days of his life. And he added these words: "Know for certain that I am sent to thee from God with the glass book that, in accordance with the words thou hast read therein, thou shouldst ordain Aidan unto the kingdom. And if thou refuse to obey this command, I will smite thee again." When, therefore, this angel of the Lord had appeared for three successive nights, holding in his hand the same glass book, and had given him the same commands respecting the ordination of the same king, the Saint, in obedience to the word of the Lord, sailed over to the island of Iona. Aidan arriving in the same days, he then ordained him to be King, as he had been commanded. And among the words of ordination he made known the future concerning the children, grand-children, and great-grand-children of Aidan, and laying his hands upon his head ordained and blessed him.

Cummene the Fair, in the book which he wrote on the virtues of S. Columba, thus records what S. Columba began to prophesy concerning Aidan, his posterity and his kingdom, saying: "Believe implicitly, O Aidan, none of thy adversaries shall be able to withstand thee unless thou first act unjustly towards me and my posterity. Instruct, therefore, thy children, that they instruct their children, their grand-children, and their posterity, that they let not the sceptre of their kingdom perish from their hands through evil counsels. For at whatever time they turn against me or against my relatives who are in Ireland, the scourge which I endured of the angel because of thee, shall be turned in great disgrace upon them by the hand of God upon them, and the hearts of men shall be turned away from them, and their foes shall be greatly strengthened against them."

Now this prophecy was fulfilled in our own times, at the battle of Roth, when Domnall Brece, the grandson of Aidan, devastated the territory of Domnall, the grandson of Ainmureg, without cause. And from that day until this they have been trodden down by strangers, which pierces the heart with sighs and grief.

CHAPTER VI.

Of the apparition of Angels carrying the soul of the blessed Brito to heaven.

AT another time, when the holy man was staying in the island of Iona, Brito, one of his own monks, who was always bent on good works, being seized with bodily illness and brought down nigh unto death, he stood for a little at his bedside and blessed him, and then suddenly went out of the house, not wishing to see him die. And the same moment after the holy man had left the house, the monk ended this present life. Then the illustrious man, walking about in the little court of the monastery with his eyes directed to heaven, was for a long time lost in wonder and admiration. But a certain brother, Aidan by name, the son of Liber, a man truly virtuous and religious, who alone of the brethren was then present, began to ask the Saint, on his bended knees, to tell him the reason of his great astonishment. The Saint replied: "Just now I saw holy angels warring in the air against the adverse powers, and I give thanks to Christ the Judge, because the victorious angels have borne away the soul of this pilgrim, who was the first to die among us in this island, to the joys of the heavenly country. But I beseech of thee to reveal this secret to no one while I live."

CHAPTER VII.

Of the vision of Angels vouchsaved to the same Holy Man when they were leading the soul of one Diormit to heaven.

AT another time a certain stranger from Ireland came to the Saint and remained some months with him in the island of Iona, to whom the blessed man one day said: "One of the clerics of thy province, whose name I do not yet know, is at this moment being borne by angels into heaven." Then the brother, on hearing this, began to search within himself concerning the life of the Anterii, who are called, in Irish, Indairthir, and concerning the name of that blessed man, and immediately replied, saying: "I know a soldier of Christ, named Diormit, who has built himself a little monastery in the same district as that in which I dwell." The Saint said to him: "It is he of whom thou speakest who has now been carried by the angels of God into Paradise." But this ought to be noted most carefully, that there were many secret things entrusted to him by God, but concealed from others, which this venerable man would in no wise suffer to go forth to the knowledge of men; and this for two reasons, as he one day hinted to a few of the brethren—one was that he might avoid vainglory, and the other that he might not, through the fame of his revelations being spread abroad, invite the intolerable crowds who were anxious to ask some questions about themselves, to come and inquire of him.

CHAPTER VIII.

Of the brave fight of the Angels against the Demons, and how they opportunely came to his assistance in the same conflict.

ON another day, when the holy man was living in the island of Iona, he sought a place in the woods more remote from men and suitable for prayer; and there, when he had begun to pray, he suddenly, as he afterwards told a few of the brethren, beheld a very black host of demons fighting against himself with iron darts. As it had been revealed by the Spirit to the holy man, these wicked spirits desired to assail his monastery and to slay many of the brethren with the same spears. But he, though but one man against an innumerable multitude of such foes, having received the armour of the Apostle Paul, fought bravely in the conflict. And so the battle was contested on both sides during the greater part of the day; nor could they, who were innumerable, overcome him who was but one; neither could he, who was but one, of his own strength expel them from the island, until the angels of God, as the Saint afterwards related to a certain few, came to his aid, when the demons, overcome with fear, left the place. The same day the Saint, when returning to the monastery after the flight of the demons from his island, uttered these words concerning the same hostile legions, saying: "These deadly foes who this day, through the mercy of God and the assistance of the angels, have been put to flight from this small tract of land, have fled to the island of Tiree, and there these ruthless invaders will attack the monasteries of the brethren, and carry with them pestilential diseases, and being attacked by them many will die." And so in those days it came to pass, as the blessed man had foreseen. And, two days after, he thus spake by the revelation of the Spirit: "Well has Baithene managed, through the help of God, that the congregation of the Church, over which he was appointed by God to preside in the Plain of Lunge, should be defended by fastings and prayers from the attack of the demons, where no one, except him who is now dead, shall at this time die." And so it came to pass according to his prophecy. For when many died from that disease in other monasteries of the same island, no one, except the one of whom the Saint spoke, died with Baithene in his own congregation.

CHAPTER IX.

Of the Apparition of Angels whom the man of God saw carrying the soul of a blacksmith named Columb, and surnamed Coilrigin, to heaven.

A CERTAIN blacksmith, greatly devoted to works of charity, and full of other good works, dwelt in the midland district of Ireland. When the above-mentioned Columb, surnamed Coilrigin, was dying in a good old age, at the very moment when he departed from the body, S. Columba, who was residing in the island of Iona, thus addressed a few of the elder brethren who were standing around him: "Columb Coilrigin, the blacksmith, has not laboured in vain; he who was desirous of profit is now happy, having obtained eternal wages by the labour of his own hands. For lo! his soul is now being carried by holy angels to the joys of the heavenly country. For whatever he could obtain by the exercise of his trade, he spent in alms for the needy."

CHAPTER X.

Of a like vision of Angels whom the Blessed Man saw carrying the soul of a certain virtuous woman to heaven.

AT another time, again, when the holy man was staying in the island of Iona, on a certain day he suddenly lifted his eyes to heaven and spake these words: "O happy woman, happy, because pious, whose soul the angels of God are now carrying to paradise." Now there was a certain religious brother, a

Saxon, Genere by name, a baker, working at his trade, who heard these words spoken by the mouth of the Saint. And on the same day of the month, at the end of the same year, the Saint said to this same Genere, the Saxon: "I see a wonderful thing; behold, the woman of whom I spake last year, when thou wert present, is now meeting in the air the soul of her husband, a poor and holy man, and with the holy angels is fighting for it against the adverse powers; by their united aid, and by the aid of the uprightness of the man himself, his soul is rescued from the assaults of the demons, and brought to the place of eternal refreshment.

CHAPTER XI.

Of the apparition of the holy Angels whom S. Columba saw meeting in its passage the soul of the blessed Brenden, founder of the monastery which is called in Irish, Birra.

ON another day, again, while the venerable man was residing in the island of Iona, very early in the morning he called his servant Diormit, who has been so often mentioned, and commanded him, saying: "Make ready in haste for the celebration of the Holy Eucharist: for to-day is the birth-day of the blessed Brenden." "Wherefore," his servant asked, "dost thou order such solemnities of the Mass to be prepared to-day; for no messenger has come to us from Ireland announcing that holy man's death?" "Go," said the Saint; "it is thy duty to obey my commands. For during the past night I saw the heavens suddenly open, and choirs of innumerable angels descend to meet the soul of S. Brenden, and by their bright and incomparable splendour the whole orb of the world was in that same hour illumined.

CHAPTER XII.

Of the vision of holy angels who bore the soul of the Bishop Columban Mocu Loigse to heaven.

ON another day, also, when the brethren were putting on their shoes in the morning, and preparing to go to the various labours of the monastery, the Saint, on the contrary, ordered them to rest that day and preparations to be made for celebrating the holy sacrifice, and some additions to be made to their dinner as on the Lord's Day. "I, though unworthy," he said, " must to-day celebrate the holy mysteries of the Eucharist out of reverence for the soul, borne amid holy choirs of angels, which ascended during the night beyond the starry realms of the heavens to Paradise." When they heard these words, the brethren obeyed, and spent the day in rest, according to the Saint's command ; and the preparations for the sacred services having been duly made, clothed in their white robes, as on a festival, they went with the Saint to the Church. But it came to pass that when, in the course of chanting the offices, the prayer was as usual being sung, in which the name of S. Martin is commemorated, the Saint, when the chanters came to the place of that name, suddenly said to them : "To-day you must pray for the Bishop S. Columban." Then all the brethren who were present understood that Columban, a bishop in Leinster, and a dear friend of Columba, had departed to the Lord. And after a time, some who came from the province of Leinster announced that the Bishop had died the same night in which it was so revealed to the Saint.

CHAPTER XIII.

Of the apparition of Angels who descended to meet the souls of the monks of S. Comgell.

AT another time the venerable man, when residing in the island of Iona, became suddenly excited, and, sounding the bell, collected the brethren. "Now," he said, "let us help with our prayer the monks of the Abbot Comgell, who this moment have been plunged into the Lake of the Calf [now Belfast Lough]; for lo! they are now fighting against the adverse powers in the air, and are striving to rescue the soul of a stranger who, with them, is in danger of drowning." Then, after many tears and fervent prayers, he stood up quickly before the altar with a joyful countenance, while the brethren were still prostrate in prayer, and said: "Give thanks to Christ, for now the holy angels, coming to the aid of the holy souls, have rescued this stranger from the assaults of the demons, and delivered them as victorious warriors.

CHAPTER XIV.

Of the manifestation of Angels who came to meet the soul of one Emchath.

AT another time, when the holy man was travelling beyond Drumalban, near the lake of the river Ness, he was suddenly inspired by the Holy Spirit, and said to the brethren who accompanied him: "Let us hasten to meet the holy angels, who have been sent out from the highest realms of heaven to bear away the soul of a heathen, and are now awaiting our arrival at the place that we may in time baptize this man before his death, who, through his whole life up to an extreme old age, has preserved his natural goodness." And having said this, the holy old man hastened on before his companions as much as he could, until he came to a district which is called Aircardan, where was found a certain old man named Emchath, who, hearing the word of God preached by the Saint, believed and was baptized, and immediately thereafter, full of joy and secure against evil, and accompanied by the angels who came to meet him, passed to the Lord. His son, Virolec, also believing, was baptized with all his house.

CHAPTER XV.

Of the Angel of the Lord who so quickly and opportunely came to the assistance of a brother who fell from the top of the round monastery in the Oakwood Plain.

AT another time, when the holy man was sitting in his hut writing, his countenance suddenly changed, and he poured forth from his pure heart this cry, saying: "Help! help!" Two brothers who were standing at the door, namely, Colgu, son of Cellach, and Lugne Mocublai, asked him the cause of so sudden a cry. The venerable man gave the following reply, saying: "The angel of the Lord, who was just now standing among you, I commanded to go quickly to the assistance of one of the brethren who had fallen from the highest point of the great house which is now being built in the Oakwood Plain." The Saint immediately thereafter added these words: "Very wonderful and almost unspeakable is the swiftness of the angelic flight, similar, as I think, to the speed of lightning. For the heavenly being who just now flew away from us when the man was beginning to fall, arrived there to his assistance, as it were in the twinkling of an eye, before his body could touch the ground; nor was he who fell able to feel any fracture or bruise. How astonishing, I say, is that most swift and timely help which, swifter than a word, can be given so very quickly, even though so many seas and lands intervene."

CHAPTER XVI.

Of the multitude of Holy Angels which were seen to descend from heaven to hold converse with the Blessed Man.

AT another time, again, while the blessed man was dwelling in the island of Iona, he one day, when the brethren were assembled together, enjoined them with great earnestness, saying: "To-day I desire to go alone to the western plain of our island. Let none of you, therefore, follow me." They obeyed, and he went alone as he wished. But a certain brother, a crafty spy, going by another path, secretly placed himself on the top of a little hill which overlooks the plain, anxious to find out the reason why the blessed man went alone. When this spy was looking at him from the top of the hill as he stood on a mound on the plain, with his hands stretched upwards in prayer and raising his eyes to heaven, then, strange to relate, behold a wonderful sight suddenly appeared, which the above-mentioned man, not, as I think, without Divine permission, saw even with his bodily eyes from his place on the neighbouring hill, that the Saint's name and the honour due to him might afterwards, though much against his will, be more widely made known among the people because of the vision thus vouchsaved. For holy angels, citizens of the heavenly country, clad in white robes and flying with wonderful swiftness, began to stand around the holy man as he prayed; and after a little intercourse with him that heavenly host, as if conscious of being watched, quickly flew back to the highest heavens. The blessed man himself, after the angelic meeting, returned to the monastery, and again assembling the brethren, demanded, with no slight menace, who among them had been guilty of violating his command. While all were protesting that they were entirely ignorant of the matter, the brother who knew that he himself was the inexcusable transgressor, no longer able to hide his guilt, fell on his knees before the Saint in the midst of the brethren, and humbly prayed for forgiveness. The Saint then, taking him aside, commanded him with a heavy threat, as he knelt, never during the life-time of the blessed man to disclose to any person even the least hint of the secret regarding that angelic vision. But after the departure of the holy man from the body he, with great protestations, made known to the brethren the apparition of that heavenly assembly. Whence, even to this day also, the place where that angelic assembly was held, bears witness to the event which occurred on it, by its name; this in Latin may be said to be "Colliculus Angelorum," but in Irish it is called Cnoc Angel.

Hence, therefore, we must notice and carefully inquire how

great and of what kind those sweet visits of the angels to the blessed man were. They occurred most frequently during winter nights, when he was watching, and in lonely places, where he was praying whilst others slept; and could in no wise come to the knowledge of men. That they were very numerous is beyond all doubt; and even though several which happened by night or by day might in some way be discovered by men, yet in comparison with the angelic visions which could be known by no one, they are doubtless very few. The same remark must be made in respect to certain bright manifestations, which have been examined by a few, and shall be described below.

CHAPTER XVII.

Of the bright Pillar which was seen to glow upon the Holy Man's head.

AT another time, four holy founders of monasteries came from Ireland to visit S. Columba, and found him in the island of Eilean-na-naoimh. The names of these distinguished men were Comgell, Mocu Aridi, Cainnech Mocu Dalon, Brenden Mocu Alti, and Cormac, grandson of Lethan. They all with one accord agreed that S. Columba should consecrate in their presence in the Church the holy mysteries of the Eucharist. In compliance with their request, the Saint went with them into the Church on the Lord's Day according to custom after the reading of the Gospel; and there, while the solemn offices of the Mass were being celebrated, S. Brenden Mocu Alti, as he afterwards told Comgell and Cainnech, beheld a ball of fire like a comet, and very bright, glowing on the head of S. Columba, and rising upward from it like a pillar, as long as he stood before the altar consecrating the holy oblation, and until the holy mysteries were completed.

CHAPTER XVIII.

Of the descent or visitation of the Holy Spirit which in the same island continued with the Venerable Man during three days and as many nights.

AT another time, when the holy man was staying on the island of Eilean-na-naoimh, the grace of the Holy Ghost was abundantly and incomparably poured out upon him, and continued with him in a wonderful manner, so that he remained for three days and as many nights without eating and drinking, and allowing no one to approach him, in a house shut close, and filled with heavenly brightness. From this house beams of intense brightness escaped through the chinks in the doors and through the key-holes, and were seen at night. Certain spiritual songs also, which had never been heard before, were sung by him. Moreover, as he afterwards admitted in the presence of a very few, he beheld many mysteries kept secret from the beginning of the world fully revealed. Obscure passages of the Holy Scriptures also, and passages very difficult to understand, were made plain, clearer even than the light to the eyes of his very pure heart. He grieved that his disciple Baithene was not present, because if he had chanced to have been with him during those three days, he would have been able to explain, from the lips of the blessed man, many mysteries regarding past or future ages unknown to others, and to have interpreted numerous passages also in the Sacred Volume. Baithene, however, was detained in the island of Eigg by contrary winds, and was not able to be present until the three days and nights of that incomparable and glorious visitation were ended.

CHAPTER XIX.

Of the splendour of the angelic light which Virgno—a youth of good disposition, and afterwards appointed by God Superior of this church, in which I, though unworthy, now serve—saw descending upon S. Columba in the church, one winter's night, while the brethren were at rest in their cells.

ONE winter night the above mentioned Virgnous, burning with the love of God, entered the church alone to pray while the others were asleep; and there, in a certain chapel attached to the wall of the church, was engaged in fervent prayer. After a while, as it were the space of an hour, the venerable man Columba entered the same sacred house, and along with him a golden light, which came down from the highest heaven and filled the whole of that part of the church. Even the separate recess of the little chapel, where Vignous was trying as much as he could to hide himself, was, to his great alarm, completely filled by the splendour of that heavenly light which broke in through the inner door of the chamber which was standing ajar. And as no one can look at the midday sun in summer with open and steady eye, so Vignous could not in any wise endure that celestial splendour which he saw, because of the brilliant and incomparable radiance which beat upon his eyes. The brother spoken of was so much terrified by the fierce and surpassing brightness which he saw, that no strength remained in him. But, after a short prayer, S. Columba left the church. On the following day he called Virgnous, who was greatly alarmed, and addressed him in these few encouraging words: "Thou art sighing to good purpose, my child, for last night thou didst make thyself well pleasing in the sight of God by keeping thine eyes fixed on the ground when overwhelmed with fear at the brightness; for hadst thou not done so, thine eyes would have been blinded by that inestimable light which was then seen. But this thou must carefully observe, that as long as I live, thou shalt never make this manifestation of light known to any one." This remarkable and wonderful circumstance, therefore, became known to many after the blessed man's death, from the narrative of this same Virgnous Comman. It was related to me, Adamnan, by the son of Virgnous' sister, a respected priest, who assured me of the truth of that which I have now here written of the vision. He had even heard the story of the vision, as far as it was seen by him, from the lips of the Abbot Virgnous himself, who was his uncle.

CHAPTER XX.

Of another almost similar vision of heavenly light.

ANOTHER night, again, one of the brethren, whose name was Colge, the son of Aido Draigniche, of the grandsons of Fechrech, of whom we made mention in the First Book, came by chance to the door of the church while the other brethren were asleep, and there stood for a time in prayer. Then suddenly he saw the whole church filled with celestial light, which, more quickly than he could tell, flashed like lightning from his gaze. He did not know that S. Columba was then within the church praying. After so sudden a manifestation of light he returned home greatly alarmed. The next day the Saint called him and rebuked him sternly, saying: "Beware above all things, child, that thou attempt not, as a curious spy, to investigate that heavenly light, which is not granted to thee, for it will flee from thee; see also that thou tell no one during my lifetime what thou hast seen.

CHAPTER XXI.

Of another similar apparition of Divine Light.

AT another time, again, the blessed man one day gave strict orders to a disciple who was receiving instruction with him, and whose name was Berchan, and surname Mesloen, saying: "Take care, my son, that to-night thou come not, as is thy custom, to my hut." But though he heard this, contrary to the command, Berchan went in the dead of night, when the rest were quiet, to the blessed man's dwelling, and cunningly prying about, placed his eyes in a line with the keyholes, thinking, as indeed the event proved, that some heavenly vision would be vouchsaved to the Saint within. For in that same hour, that little hut of the blessed man was filled with the splendour of the heavenly glory, and the young transgressor, not being able to endure it, at once fled from the spot. On the following day the Saint took him aside and reprimanded him with great severity, and addressed to him these words: "Last night, my son, thou didst sin before God, for thou didst vainly imagine that the prying of thy secret inquisitiveness could be covered or hid from the Holy Ghost. Did I not see thee at that hour approaching the door of my hut and then going away? Unless I had then prayed for thee, thou wouldest there, before the door, either have fallen down dead or had thine eyes plucked from their sockets. But the Lord spared thee this time for my sake. And be thou assured of this also that, whilst thou art living in luxury in thine own country of Ireland, thy face will bear the marks of thy reproach all the days of thy life. Nevertheless, by my prayers, I have obtained from the Lord that, as thou art my disciple, thou shalt repent in tears before the end and obtain mercy from the Lord." All these things, according to the saying of the blessed man, afterwards happened to Berchan as they were foretold concerning him.

CHAPTER XXII.

Of another vision of angels whom the Holy Man saw coming to meet his holy soul, as if it were about to leave the body.

AT another time, while the blessed man was living in the island of Iona, his holy countenance was one day lighted up with a marvellous and joyful cheerfulness, and raising his eyes to heaven he was filled with gladness and rejoiced exceedingly. Then, after an interval of a few seconds, that sweet and pleasant joyfulness was changed into mournful sadness. And two men, who were then standing at the door of his hut, which was built on the higher ground, and were themselves also much afflicted with him—of whom one was Lugne Mocublai, and the other a Saxon called Pilu—inquired of him the cause of his sudden joy and of the sorrow which followed. The Saint thus addressed them: "Go in peace; ask me not now to explain the cause either of the joy or of the sorrow." On hearing this they fell on their knees, and with their faces bowed to the earth, entreated him with tears, desiring to learn something concerning the matter which had in that hour been revealed to the Saint. Seeing them deeply afflicted, he said: "Because I love you, I desire you not to be afflicted, but you must first promise me that you will never during my lifetime tell to any one the secret you seek to know." They at once, according to his request, promised; and then, after the promise had been given, the venerable man spake to them thus: "On this present day thirty years of my sojourn in Britain have been completed. Meanwhile, for many days past, I have earnestly asked of the Lord that in the end of this thirtieth year He would deliver me from my dwelling here and call me thither to the heavenly country. And this was the cause of my joy concerning which you are now sorrowfully inquiring. For I saw holy angels sent from the Lofty Throne to meet me, to lead my soul from the flesh. But behold now, they have suddenly stopped, and are standing on a rock on the other side of the sound of our island, though anxious to come near and call me away from the body. But they are not permitted to come nearer, and are shortly about to fly back to the highest heavens, because that which the Lord granted me, after praying with my whole strength, that I might pass from the world to Him on this day, He, hearkening to the prayers of many Churches for me, has suddenly withheld. That is to say, the Lord, in answer to the prayers of these Churches, though against my will, has granted that four years from this day be added to me for continuing in the flesh. Such a sad delay as this was not unfitly the cause of my grief to-day. These four years in this life being by God's favour ended, I shall suddenly, and with no preceding sickness of body, depart with joy to the Lord, accompanied by His holy angels, who will come to meet me." According to these words which the venerable man uttered, not, it is said, without great sighs and grief and with much weeping, he afterwards abode in the flesh four years.

CHAPTER XXIII.

Of the departure to the Lord of our Patron, S. Columba.

WHEN the end of the above-mentioned four years was approaching, after the completion of which he knew, as a true prophet, that his death would follow, the old man, worn out with age, one day in the month of May went in a cart, as we have already narrated in the Second Book, to visit some of the brethren who were at work. And while they were working that day in the western part of the island of Iona, he began to speak to them, saying : " During the Paschal services, which were recently held in the month of April, with desire, have I desired to depart to Christ the Lord, as he had conceeded to me if I preferred it. But in order that the festivity of joy might not be turned for you into sorrow, I preferred to delay the day of my departure a little longer." While listening to these sad words from him his beloved monks were greatly afflicted, and he endeavoured as much as he could to cheer them with consolatory words. Then having done this, as he was sitting in the vehicle, he turned his face to the East and blessed the island and its inhabitants ; and from that day to the present, as we have already stated in the Book mentioned above, the venom of vipers with three forked tongues is unable to do any manner of harm either to man or beast. After pronouncing these words of blessing, the Saint was carried back to his monastery.

Then, again, when a few days had passed, while the solemn offices of the Mass were according to custom being celebrated on the Lord's day, the face of the venerable man, as his eyes were raised to heaven, suddenly appeared as if suffused with a ruddy glow; for, as it is written, " A glad heart maketh a cheerful countenance." For in that same hour, he alone saw the angel of the Lord flying above within the walls of his chapel ; because the lovely and tranquil aspect of the holy angels pours joy and exultation into the hearts of the elect, this was the cause of the sudden joy which was infused into the blessed man. When those who were present in the same place made inquiries as to the cause of the joy with which the Saint was inspired, he, looking up to heaven, made this reply: "Wonderful and incomparable is the subtilty of the angelic nature. For behold an angel of the Lord, sent to demand a deposit dear to God, after looking down upon us within the church and blessing us, returned again through the roof of the church without leaving any trace of his passage through." Thus spoke the Saint; but none of those around him could understand anything of the nature of the deposit which the angel was sent to demand back. Our Patron, however, gave the name of a deposit to his own soul, which had been entrusted to him by God; and after an interval of six days from that time, he departed to the Lord during the night of the Lord's Day, as shall be related further on.

In the end of that same week, that is on the Saturday, the venerable man and his faithful servant Diormit, went to bless the barn which was close at hand. When the Saint had entered the barn and blessed it, and also the two heaps of winnowed corn that were in it, he added these words and gave thanks, saying: "Heartily do I congratulate my beloved monks that in this year also, although in it I am called to depart from you, you will have bread sufficient for the year." On hearing this, Diormit, his servant, began to be sorrowful and thus spake: "This year, O Father, thou often makest us sad, because thou frequently makest mention of thy departure from us." The Saint made this reply: "I have a little secret communication to make to thee; if thou wilt faithfully promise me not to reveal it to any one before my death, I shall be able to speak with thee more explicitly concerning my departure." When his attendent had, on bended knees, given the promise in accordance with the Saint's desire, the venerable man continued thus: "In the Holy Scriptures this day is called the Sabbath, which being interpreted is called rest. And a true Sabbath is this day to me, because it is the last day of my present laborious life; in it I rest after the fatigues of my labours; and to-night, at midnight, when the holy day of the Lord begins, according to the words of the Scriptures, I shall go the way of our fathers. For already my Lord Jesus Christ condescends to invite me; and to Him, I say, in the middle of this ensuing night, I shall depart at His invitation. For thus has it been revealed to me by the Lord Himself." As he listened to these sorrowful words, Diormit began to weep bitterly; and the Saint tried to console him as well as he could.

After this the Saint left the barn and when returning to the monastery, rested half way at a place where a cross was afterwards erected, which may be seen to this day standing by the wayside and fixed in a millstone. And there, while the Saint, as I have said, wearied with old age, sat and rested for a little, behold there ran towards him a white pack-horse, a faithful servant, that used to carry the milk vessels between the cowhouse and the monastery. It came to the Saint, and, wonderful to relate, placed its head in his bosom, inspired, as I believe, by God, as every animal is endowed with the knowledge of things according to the will of the Creator, and knowing that its master was soon about to leave it, and that it would see him no more, it began to utter plaintive cries and, like a human being, to shed abundant tears on the Saint's bosom, foaming and weeping greatly. The servant seeing this began to drive the weeping mourner away, but the Saint forbade him, saying: "Let it alone, let our friend alone, let him pour out his bitter grief into my bosom. Behold thou, as thou art a man, and hast a rational soul, canst know nothing of my departure beyond what I myself have just told thee; but to this brute beast, devoid of reason, the Creator Himself has in some way manifestly made it known that its master is about to leave it." And saying this the Saint blessed the horse as it turned away from him in sadness.

And leaving this place the Saint ascended a little hill which overlooks the monastery, and stood for a while on the top, and as he stood there he raised both his hands and blessed the monastery, saying: "On this place, though small and mean, shall not only the Scotic kings and their peoples, but also the Rulers of foreign and barbarous nations and their subjects, confer great and unusual honour; by the saints also, even of other churches, shall it be held in no common reverence."

After these words he descended from the hill, and having returned to the monastery, sat in his hut transcribing the Psalter; and coming to that verse of the Thirty-third Psalm, where it is written—" They that seek the Lord shall not want any good thing" [A.V., Ps. xxxiv. 10], he said: "Here at the end of the page I must stop, but let Baithene write what follows." The last verse he had written was very applicable to a Saint who was about to depart, and to whom eternal goods shall never be wanting; but the one which follows it, is equally applicable to the father who became his successor and the instructor of his spiritual children—" Come, ye children, hearken unto me; I will teach you the fear of the Lord;" and, as he appointed him his successor, he did succeed him not only in teaching but also in writing.

After he had written the above-mentioned verse at the end of the page, the Saint entered the church at vespers on the night before the Lord's Day. When the service was over he returned to his chamber and reclined the rest of the night upon his bed, where he had a bare flag for his couch, and for his pillow the stone which, to this day, stands as the title of his monument beside his grave. While reclining there he gave his last instructions to the brethren, in the hearing of his attendant alone, saying: "These, O my children, are the last words I address to you—that ye have mutual and unfeigned charity among yourselves with peace; and if ye thus observe these things after the manner of the holy fathers, God, the Comforter of the Good, will be your Helper, and I, abiding with Him, will intercede for you; and not only will the things needful for this present life be sufficiently administered unto you by Him, but there will also be rendered unto you those good and eternal rewards which are prepared for them that keep His commandments." Thus far have the last words of our venerable Patron, as he was passing from this weary pilgrimage to the heavenly country, been preserved for recital in our brief narrative.

After these words, as the happy hour of his departure was gradually drawing nigh, the Saint became silent. Then, as soon as the bell rang at midnight, he rose hastily and went to the church, and running more quickly than the rest, he entered alone, and knelt down in prayer beside the altar. At the same moment, Diormit, his servant, who followed him more slowly, saw from a distance the whole of the interior of the church about the Saint filled with angelic light. As he drew near to the door the light he had seen, and which was also seen by a few more of the brethren who were standing at a distance, suddenly disappeared. Diormit, therefore, entering the church, cried out in a mournful voice: "Father, where art thou?" And feeling his way through the darkness, as the lamps of the brethren had not yet been brought in, he found the Saint lying before the altar, and raising him a little, sat down beside him and took his holy head into his bosom. Meanwhile the rest of the monks ran in with lights, and seeing their father dying burst into lamentations. And the Saint, as we have learned from some who were present, before his soul departed, opened wide his eyes and looked round him from side to side, with a countenance full of wonderful joy and gladness, seeing, doubtless, the holy angels coming to meet him. Diormit then raised the holy right hand of the Saint that he might bless the assembled monks. And the venerable father himself moved his hand at the same time as well as he was able, that, as he could not in words, he might at least by the motion of his hand be seen to bless the brethren as his soul was departing. And having in this way given them his holy blessing, he immediately breathed his last. When he had departed from the tabernacle of the body, his face still continued ruddy and lit up in a wonderful way by the angelic vision, insomuch so that it seemed to be the face not of the dead but of one sleeping. Meantime the whole church resounded with mournful lamentations.

I ought not to omit to mention the revelation made to a certain saint in Ireland at the very time the blessed soul passed away. For in the monastery, which in the Irish tongue is called Clonifinchoil, there was a holy man, an aged soldier of Christ, named Lugud, the son of Tailchan, and known for his integrity and wisdom. This man had a vision which, at the first dawn of day, he told in great sorrow to one named Fergnous, who was, like himself, a Christian soldier, saying:

"In the middle of this last night, S. Columba, the pillar of many churches, departed to the Lord, and in the hour of his blessed departure I saw in spirit the whole island of Iona, where in the body I never was, resplendent with the brightness of angels, and the whole space above, up to the pure air of heaven, lit up with the brilliance of the same heavenly messengers, who descended in countless numbers, and were sent from heaven to bear away his holy soul. Also, I heard the loud hymns and entrancing songs of the angelic hosts at the moment of the departure of his holy soul among the ascending choirs of angels." This angelic vision which, as has been said, he undoubtedly learnt from the lips of the aged Saint to whom it was revealed, Fergnous, who about that time came over from Ireland, and abode the rest of his days in the island of Eilean-na-naoimh, used often to narrate to the monks of S. Columba. This same Fergnous, after living for many years in blameless obedience among the brethren, led the life of a hermit in the hermitage of Muirbulcmar, finishing his course as a victorious soldier of Christ. This vision mentioned above we have not only found in writing, but we have also heard it related without the slightest hesitation by several well informed old men, to whom Virgnous himself had told it.

Another vision, also given at the same hour, under a different form, was related to me, Adamnan, who was then a young man, by one of those who saw it, and solemnly assured me of its truth. He was a very old man, a soldier of Christ, whose name in Latin may be called Ferreolus, but, in Irish, Ernene, of the race of the Mocufirroide, who, as being himself a monk, is buried amid the remains of other monks of S. Columba in the Ridge of Tomma, and awaits the resurrection with the saints. He said: "On the night in which S. Columba, by a happy and blessed death, passed from the earth to the heavens, I, and others with me, were engaged in fishing in the valley of the river Fend, which abounds in fish, when we saw the whole vault of heaven suddenly illuminated. Struck by the suddenness of the miracle we turned our uplifted eyes to the East, and lo! there appeared, as it were, an immense pillar of fire, which seemed, as it rose up in the darkness, to illumine the whole world like the summer sun at noon, and after the pillar penetrated the heavens, darkness followed as after the setting of the sun. And not only did we, who were together in the same place, see with great surprise the brightness of this remarkable and luminous pillar, but many other fishermen also, who were here and there engaged in fishing in different deep pools along the same river, were greatly terrified, as they afterwards related to us, by an apparition of the same kind. These three miraculous visions, then, which were seen at the very hour of our venerable Patron's departure, show clearly that eternal honours have been conferred upon him by the Lord. Let us now return to our narrative.

Meanwhile, after the departure of his holy soul, when the morning hymns were sung, his sacred body was borne, amid the chanting of psalms by the brethren, from the church back to the chamber from which a little before he had come alive, and his obsequies were celebrated with all due honour and reverence for three days and as many nights. And when these sweet praises of God were ended, the venerable body of our holy and blessed Patron was wrapped in clean clothes of fine linen and placed in a coffin which had been prepared for it, and was buried with all due reverence, to rise again in lustrous and eternal glory.

And now, near the close of this book, will be related what has been told us by well-informed persons regarding the above-mentioned three days in which his obsequies were celebrated according to ecclesiastical custom. One of the brethren, speaking one day in the presence of the venerable man, with great simplicity said to him: "After thy death all the people of these provinces will row over to this island of Iona to celebrate thy obsequies, and will entirely fill it." On hearing this the Saint immediately replied: "No, my child, the event will not turn out as thou sayest, for a mixed multitude of people will not in any way be able to come to my obsequies. My beloved monks alone will perform my funeral rites and grace the last offices bestowed upon me." And this prophetic word, immediately after his departure, the Omnipotence of God caused to be fulfilled. For during the three days and nights of his obsequies a great and stormy tempest, without rain, arose, and by reason of its violence no one could in any direction cross the Sound in his little boat. And immediately after the interment of the blessed man, the tempest fell, and the wind ceased, and the whole ocean became calm.

Let the reader therefore consider in what and how great honour our illustrious Patron was held with God, seeing that while he was yet dwelling in mortal flesh God was pleased at his prayer to still the storms and calm the seas; and again, when he found it necessary, as on the occasion mentioned above, gales arose when he wished, and the sea was lashed into fury, and this storm, as was said above, when his funeral services were completed, subsided into a great calm.

Such, then, was the end of our illustrious Patron's life, and such is an earnest of his merits, who, according to the statements of the Scriptures, is now a sharer in eternal triumphs, added to the Patriarchs, associated with the Prophets and Apostles, numbered amongst the thousands of white-robed saints who have washed their robes in the blood of the Lamb, and is now following the Lamb, his Leader; a virgin immaculate, freed from every blemish through the grace of our Lord Jesus Christ; to Whom be honour, power, praise, and glory, and everlasting dominion in the Unity of the Holy Ghost, for ever and ever.

After reading these three little Books let the diligent reader observe of what and how great merit, of what and how high honour in the sight of God our holy and venerable President, often mentioned above, must have been deemed worthy, how great and many were the bright and angelic visitations to him, how full he was of the spirit of prophecy, how efficacious was the working of his divine powers, how often and to what great extent the brightness of the divine light shone around him while he was still dwelling in mortal flesh, and how, even since the departure of his most holy soul from the tabernacle of the body, even up to the present day, as has been clearly shown to certain chosen persons, the place where his bones repose does not cease to be illumined by that same heavenly brightness or to be haunted by the visits of the holy angels. And this unusual favour has also been conferred by God upon this same man of blessed memory, that though he lived in this small and remote island of the British sea, his name has been found worthy to be clearly proclaimed not only throughout the whole of our own Ireland and Britain, the largest island of the whole world, but has reached even to triangular Spain, and into Gaul and to Italy, situated beyond the Pennine Alps, and also to the city of Rome itself, which is the head of all the cities. Such and so great honourable celebrity, among other gifts of divine favour, is known to have been conferred upon this same Saint by God, who loveth the diligent, and raiseth to immense honour, by glorifying them more and more, those who with praises magnify Him who is blessed for ever. Amen.

I beseech those who wish to transcribe these little Books— yea, rather, I adjure them by Christ, the Judge of the world— after they have diligently copied, carefully to compare and correct their copies with that from which they have written them, and also to subjoin here this adjuration—Whosoever readeth these little Books on the virtues of Columba, let him pray to the Lord for me, Dorbbene, that after death I may possess eternal life.

These are the names of the twelve men who sailed over from Ireland with S. Columba on his first voyage to Britain : the two sons of Brenden ; Baithene, who is also called Conin, the successor of S. Columba, and Cobthach, his brother ; Ernaan, the uncle of S. Columba ; Diormit, his servant ; Rus and Fechno, two sons of Rodain ; Scandal, the son of Bresail, the son of Endei, the son of Neil ; Luguid Mocuthemne ; Echoid ; Tochannu Mocufir-cetea ; Cairnaan, the son of Branduib, the son of Meilgi ; Grilaan.

The parents of S. Columba were—Aedelmith, his father, the son of Ferguss ; Eithne, his mother, the daughter of Mac Nav.

Iogen was the younger brother of Columba. His three sisters were : Cuimne, the mother of the sons of Meic Decuil, who are called Mernooc, Cascene, Meldal, and Bran, who was buried in Dairu Calchaich, the cousins of S. Columba ; Mincholeth, mother of the sons of Enain, one of whom was called Calmaan ; Sinech, mother of the men of Mocuni, in Cuile-aque, whose names are—Aidan, a monk, who was buried in Cuil-uisci ; Chronrii Moccucein, who was buried in Dairmagh ; and Tocummi Mocucein, a holy priest, who in extreme old age ended this present life in the island of Iona.

THE LIFE OF S. KENTIGERN.

BY

JOCELIN, A MONK OF FURNESS.

LIFE OF S. KENTIGERN.

HERE BEGINS THE PROLOGUE, IN THE FORM OF AN EPISTLE, TO THE LIFE OF S. KENTIGERN, BISHOP AND CONFESSOR.

TO his most reverend lord and dearest father, Jocelin, the anointed of the Lord Jesus Christ, Jocelin, the least of the poor of Christ, animated and sustained by filial love and obedience, wishes the salvation of body and soul in our Saviour.

Since your great name, high office, and equal judgment, your life untarnished by any breath of evil fame, and your long tried religion, persuade me, after most careful consideration, that you love the beauty of the House of the Lord over which you preside, I have deemed it fitting to present to you the first fruits of my gleanings, which are redolent of the beauty and glory both of yourself and your Church. For, according to your command, I have wandered through the streets and lanes of the city seeking a record of the life of S. Kentigern, in whom your soul delights, and in whose chair the grace of Divine condescension, by the adoption of sons, by ecclesiastical election, and by succession of ministry, has caused your sanctity to preside. Wherefore I sought diligently for a life of him, if perchance one might be found, which seemed to be supported with greater authority and more evident truth, and to be written in a more graceful style than the one which your Church has hitherto used, because that, as it seems to many, is stained throughout, being discoloured by an uncouth diction, and obscured by an uncultivated style; and, what above all these things a wise man would still more abhor, in the very beginning of the narrative there are matters which are manifestly contrary to sound doctrine and the Catholic Faith. But another little volume I have found, written in the Celtic dialect, which, though abounding from beginning to end with solecisms, contains the life and acts of the holy pontiff at greater length. Seeing the life of so precious a pontiff, glorious with signs and wonders, and most illustrious in virtues and doctrine, perversely narrated and marred by unsound doctrine, or greatly obscured by barbaric language, I confess I was grieved and took it ill. I resolved, therefore, to put together the materials I had collected from either volume for its restoration, and as far as I could, and in obedience to your command, season what had been rudely composed with Roman salt. It is absurd, I think, that so precious a treasure should be swathed in such vile wrappages, and I have endeavoured, therefore, to cover it, if not with tissues of gold or silk, at least with pure linen. I have attempted, moreover, to so pour the life-giving liquid from the old vessel into the new, that, drawing it out according to the scanty capacity of the vessel, it may be acceptable to the more simple, and neither useless to those of moderate ability, nor contemptible to those who are more richly endowed. Assisted, therefore, by the prayers and merits of our holy President, if the favour of the Inspirer from on High, encourage me, I shall so temper my style that the work I have undertaken shall not be obscured by creeping in the darkness through poverty of language, nor swell with rhetorical phrases beyond what is fitting, through aiming too high, lest I should seem to have planted a grove in the temple of the Lord contrary to His command. Hence the whole aim of this work, all the fruit of my labour, ought, it has seemed to me, to be consecrated to your name and to be submitted for your consideration. If, however, any thing inelegant or insipid be put forth, let it be seasoned with the salt of your discretion; if by chance there be anything in it which sounds scarcely consonant with the truth, though I do not think there is, let it be shaped and adjusted to the rule of your judgment. But if nothing be found in it failing in either of these respects, let it be supported by your testimony and confirmed by your authority. And in all these things, if any thing come to light proceeding from my pen otherwise than becoming the subject, let it be imputed to the slenderness of my skill. And if any thing appear in it worthy of being read, let it be ascribed to your Eminency. Of the translation of this Saint, or of the miracles he performed after his death, I have been unable anywhere to find an account; they either have not been recorded, because they have escaped the memory of those who were present, or they have been multiplied beyond enumeration and have been omitted, that the multitude of facts collected might not weary feeble readers. May your sanctity always live and flourish in the Lord.

Here ends the Prologue.

CHAPTER I.

Here beginneth the Life of S. Kentigern, Bishop and Confessor.

THE beginning of the record of the glorious life of the most illustrious Kentigern, very dear to God and men, a Nazarite of our Nazarene Jesus Christ, is consecrated by the divine oracle in which the Lord, anticipating in His gracious benedictions the blessed prophet Jeremiah, foretells that he should be a vessel of election sanctified to the work of his ministry, by such praise as this: "Before I formed thee in the belly I knew thee, and before thou camest forth out of the womb I sanctified thee and gave thee a prophet unto the nations." Truly the blessed Kentigern, who was known to God before he was born into the world, and bedewed with the grace of election before he came forth from his mother's womb, was made great by miracles before he became great either in his members or his merits. For him who was sanctified, and was to be yet more sanctified, the Holy of Holies Himself, while he was still shut up within the gates of the maternal womb, began to cause to shine forth in his very beginning the splendour of His virtues, that he might prove that the special gift of the Holy Ghost is not constrained by the chain of original sin. This man, I say, famous for his race and beauty, and distinguished in many ways by signs, and prodigies, and presages, was, by a decree of the Redeemer, destined to be a prophet, yea, also a teacher and chief ruler, to many nations.

Wherefore this most holy man, though he drew his original germ from a royal stem, came forth as a rose from the thorn, as a sweet smelling tree from filthy ground, since his mother was the daughter of a certain King, very pagan in his creed, a ruling prince in the northern parts of Britain. But when the sound of the preaching of the Christian Faith went forth in the land of that region, and the words of holy preachers advanced into those northern confines, whence every evil used to be spread, she heard with her ears those things which were to be heard, how the Brightness of the Eternal Light, the Sun of Righteousness, having risen by the Star of Virginity, illumined the world with the rays of His knowledge and love, and proclaimed salvation to them that were near and to them that were afar off, leading His own into all the fulness of the truth more efficaciously by the arguments of manifest signs; then her heart burned within her, and in her meditation that fire burned which the Lord sent upon the earth, and she earnestly desired that it should be kindled. Her soul thirsting to come to the knowledge of the truth, she received the engrafted word which was able to save her soul from everlasting death. Though not yet washed in the water of the saving laver, she was nevertheless running in the way of the commandments of God with an enlarged and diligent heart. She persevered continually in frequent almsgiving, in devout prayers, in learning the faith of the Church and in practising its discipline, as far as she might, for fear of her pagan father. With special devotion, however, did she, among these things, admire the fruitful purity of the Virgin Mother; through admiring, she venerated, and, through venerating and loving, she desired to imitate it, and with a certain presumptuous boldness of feminine rashness, she desired to be like her in conceiving and in giving birth, and on this account she earnestly laboured to entreat the Lord.

After the lapse of some time she was found to be with child, and her soul magnified the Lord, believing in her simplicity that her desire had been accomplished. That, however, which was born in her she received from the embrace of man, but, as she often asserted, binding herself by an oath, by whom, or when, or in what way she conceived, she was unconscious. But though the fact of this secret was hid from her, or had escaped her memory, the truth of the matter ought by no means to perish from the mind of any discreet person, nor should any scruple arise from it. For though at present we bury in silence things which we find recorded in poetic songs or in histories which are not canonical, when we turn to the Sacred Volumes we read in the Book of Genesis that the daughters of Lot not only secretly stole for themselves their father's embraces, but also that each of them conceived by him when he was drunk, and entirely unwitting of the fact. It is certain, moreover, that many, through taking the draught of oblivion, which physicists call Letargion, have slept; and when they suffered incisions in their members, and sometimes burning and abrasion in vital parts, have not in the least felt it, but have been ignorant, when awakened, of the things which were done to them. We frequently have heard that maidenly chastity has been stormed by tricks of jugglers, and that the deflowered has never known her deflowerer. It may be that something of the sort happened to this girl by the secret judgment of God, that she might not feel the mixture of the sexes, and so, when impregnated, might think herself undefiled.

We do not think that this has been mentioned here in vain, because the foolish and stupid people who live in the diocese of S. Kentigern do not shrink from asserting even that he was conceived and born of a virgin. But why should we delay with these things? Indeed, we deem it both absurd and irrelevant to inquire further who the sower was, or how he ploughed or sowed the land, when the Lord, bestowing His favour, the land brought forth good and rich fruit—the fruit, I say, of this land which received a blessing from the Lord, whereby many generations are blessed by the Lord and receive from Him the fruit of eternal salvation. Meanwhile the woman went about,

and the signs of her seduction were apparent to all. . . . .
. . . .
When her condition was made known to the King, her father,
. . . .
he began more earnestly to try to learn from her—now urging her with terrors, now coaxing her with blandishments—who had caused her to be with child. But she, interposing with an oath in the name of Christ, protested that she was innocent of all intercourse with man. But the King hearing this, and moved with a more vehement rage, both because of the name of Christ, which had been uttered by her mouth, and because he could not find out the violator of his daughter, swore, and resolved to keep his righteous judgment, that he would not in any respect swerve from the law ordained by his ancestors in such matters for the love or life of his own daughter.

CHAPTER II.

Of the law established in those days among the Cambrian people concerning Girls who committed fornication.

THERE was among that barbarous people a law, promulgated of old, that a girl who committed fornication in her father's house, and was found with child, should be cast down from the top of the highest mountain, and that her paramour should be beheaded. Similarly among the ancient Saxons, almost down to these modern times, the law continued that every virgin deflowered of her own will in her father's house should, without any remission, be buried alive, and her violator be hanged over her tomb. What shall we say to these things, or what can we conjecture concerning them? If such zeal for chastity burn in the heathen, who are ignorant of the divine law, solely for the sake of integrity, and out of respect for the traditions of their fathers, what shall the Christian do who is constrained to the preservation of chastity by the divine law, which promises as the reward of it the joy of heaven, and likewise, on the other hand, metes out for the transgression of it eternal punishment?

Behold, both sexes and every condition are now plunged in every slough of carnal pollution almost as boldly as willingly, because with impunity; and not only is the vilest herd polluted with the contagion, but those who are maintained by ecclesiastical benefices and attached to divine offices deem themselves happier, the more filthy they are. But now the Hammerer of the whole earth, even the Spirit of Fornication, passes through them. They who exhibit outwardly a certain fancied form of godliness, but deny the power thereof by their works, paying allegiance to this present world, are known by their impure life to lie before God by their sacred habit and tonsure. Verily they ought to fear that which the Lord threatens by His prophet, saying: "He who hath done iniquity in the land of the saints shall not look upon the glory of God." Even now what is to be bewailed with every river of tears? That sin of sins, which is now committed with impunity, than which nothing more detestable can be conceived, on account of which the sulphurous flame, a heavenly judgment, destroyed the guilty in the Five Cities of the Plain. Nor can he easily be found who will willingly reprove the perpetrator. For if any one, however rarely, be found whom the zeal of the Lord's house consumeth, and who burneth with the love of justice and integrity, so that he should seem to censure such monstrous sins, he is straightway resisted to his face as a sycophant, and denounced by all as a traducer; his mouth is closed, as of one speaking wickedly, his tongue is decreed to be tied up.

Why is this? Plainly because the body of Leviathan, as it is written, is shut close up with scales, pressing upon one another, and the shadows cover his shadow; because the criminous and guilty, who are members of the devil, are mutually protected by others who labour in the same vice, that the arrow of correction cannot pierce them. Verily, as I think, this is done as a proof of their inexcusable damnation, that such men, being given over to a reprobate mind, neither receive nor accept the rod of correction. And the multitude, labouring in the same vice, mitigates not in the least their punishment because the many, not less than they themselves, individually burn, as if cast into a furnace. But what shall we say of those on whom the duty is conjoined of binding and loosing, of shutting and opening, who are placed upon a candlestick, that in the House of the Lord they may shine by word and example? Do not the greater number in the present represent smoke rather than flame, and stench rather than brightness? Are they not dumb dogs, not able, yea, not willing, to bark? When they see manners more than bestial, they do not dare to rebuke them, especially since they themselves are conformed to their habits, yea, are worse deformed. For, as the people, so the priest; as the subject, so the prelate; yea, as the first in dignity, so the worse in iniquity, and they who excel in office excel also in vice. What the Scripture mystically says of such is to be feared for them : " If so much as a beast touch the mountain, it shall be stoned." The beast touches the mountain when any one of bestial life mounts to the chair of prelacy, and lays an impure hand on purifying sacrifices. Yet such is he who is commanded to be stoned, since it is clearly taught in the opinions of the holy Fathers that he ought to be subjected to a hard and heavy condemnation. That I have said these things by way of digression will, I trust, be burdensome to none. The zeal of this pagan man who spared not his own daughter, but for the fault of simple fornication delivered her to such a doom, ought to cause great shame to the worshippers of Christ to the planting and propagating of modesty.

CHAPTER III.

How the divine favour delivered the mother of S. Kentigern from the precipice and from shipwreck.

ACCORDINGLY the aforesaid girl was led by the command of the King to the summit of a very high mountain, called Dumpelder, in order that she might be cast down from thence and be broken limb from limb or dashed to pieces. But she, groaning heavily, and looking up to heaven, said in complaining words: "Justly do I suffer this, because I have acted as one of the foolish women, desiring to be equalled to the most holy, most serene Bearer of Salvation, the parent who brought forth her Father. But I beseech thee, O Lady! blessed among women, take away the iniquity of thine handmaid, for I have done very foolishly. O Mother of mercy! show the light of thy compassion towards me, and deliver me from the oppression which surrounds me. I beseech thee, O Lady, that as He, the Flower of the Angelic Mountains, without injury to thy snow white purity, vouchsaved to become in thee, the lowly valley, fertile in every virtue, the lily of our valleys, and as out of thee, the most firm mountain of the faith, the stone was hewn without hands, which grew into a great mountain and filled the whole earth; so me, thine handmaid, though not yet washed in the sacred laver, yet firmly believing in thy Son, and hoping in the shadow of thy wings, do thou deliver from the imminent precipice, that the blessed name of thy Son may for ever be magnified in the sight of these people. Moreover, the offspring which I bear in my womb I promise to thy Son and to thee as a peculiar possession, to be thy servant all the days of his life."

When she had prayed in this manner with devout heart and mouth, the servants of the King cast her, continually invoking Christ and His mother, down from the top of the mountain. Then a thing, wonderful and unheard of from the past, occurred. When she fell she was not bruised, because the Lord supported her hand, therefore she felt no hurt. As it seemed to her, she descended to the earth like a winged bird, with a gentle gliding, lest, perchance, she should dash her foot against a stone. Thanksgiving and the voice of praise sound in the mouth of many who beheld these wonderful works of God. The holy and terrible name of Christ is magnified. The innocent is judged both to be deemed free from all further punishment, and in every way to be held in reverence. But, on the other hand, the idolaters and adversaries of the Christian Faith ascribed this miracle not to divine virtue but to magical arts; and with unanimous voice proclaimed her a witch and a sorceress. Therefore there was a division among the people concerning her. Some said: "She is a good woman and innocent." Others said: "Nay, but by her artifices she deceiveth the people, changeth her countenance, and deludeth their senses." The crowd, therefore, in the whirl of its own words confused itself; but the sacrilegious multitude prevailing, they moved the King, who was wholly given up to idolatry, to pronounce a new judgment concerning his daughter. At length, by the general connivance of the assembly of the wicked and of those who oppose the name of Christ, it was decreed that the little pregnant woman should be placed alone in a boat and exposed on the sea. In order, therefore, that the sentence thus resolved upon might be carried out, the servants of the King embarked and took her far out to sea, and there, placed alone in a very little boat of hides, put together after the manner of the Irish, they committed her to fortune without a single oar, and then rowed back to the shore, and related what they had done to the King and the people, who were awaiting the issue of the event. But these, mocking, said: "She calls herself the handmaid of Christ. She professes that she has His power as her protector. Let us see if her words are true. She trusteth in Christ, let Him deliver her, if He is able, from the hand of death and from the peril of the sea."

But the girl, destitute of all human help, commits herself to Him alone who made the sea and the dry land, devoutly beseeching that He who had already saved her from the precipice would save her from the imminent peril. Wonderful to relate —but with God nothing is impossible—that little boat in which the pregnant girl was detained, ploughed the watery vortices and the eddies of the waves towards the opposite shore in a much swifter course than if it had been borne onward by a wind filling the sails or propelled by the effort of many rowers. For He who preserved Jonah the prophet unhurt amid the whirlpools of the ocean when swallowed up in the huge belly of the whale, who likewise by His right hand upheld the blessed Peter when walking upon the waves that he might not sink, and delivered his co-Apostle, who thrice suffered shipwreck, from the depths of the sea, brought the woman safe to a haven of safety, for the sake of the child whom she bore in her womb, whom He predestinated to be a chief steersman of His own ship, that is, an excellent teacher and ruler of His Church.

CHAPTER IV.

Of the birth of S. Kentigern, and of his education with S. Serf.

THE aforesaid woman landed on the sand near to a place called Culross. In this place S. Serf was then dwelling, and teaching many boys, who were to be trained to the Divine service, and in sacred literature. When she had landed on the shore, the pangs of labour at once took hold upon her. Raising her eyes, she saw afar off, though in the darkness, the sign of the ashes of a fire near the shore, which, perhaps, some shepherds or fishermen had left. She therefore crawled to the place, and as best she could kindled for herself a fire. But when the dawn, the harbinger of the divine light, began to whiten, the time was fulfilled that she should be delivered. And she brought forth a son, about to be a herald and messenger of the true Light.

Now, at the same hour, S. Serf, while intent upon prayer after Mass in the morning matins, and drawing in his breath with the sweetness of holy contemplation, heard the angelic companies chanting their sweet praises on high, and rejoicing together with them in their praises, he with his disciples exulted and eagerly offered in spirit to the Lord the sacrifices of jubilation by singing: "We Praise Thee, O Lord." The clerics were astonished at the novelty of the event, and when they inquired what had happened, he told them all in order the whole matter, and the hymning of the angels, and sedulously exhorted them that they themselves should offer the calves of their lips to the Lord. But there were in the neighbourhood shepherds keeping watch over their flocks by night, and they going forth at the break of day, when they saw a fire burning close at hand, made haste and came to it, and found the young woman newly delivered of a child, and the infant wrapped in rags and lying in the open air. They were moved with pity, took care of them by increasing the fire and supplying them with food, and by obtaining other necessaries; and bringing them in as suitable a way as they could, they presented them to S. Serf, and rehearsed the matter to him in order.

When he heard these things, and saw the little boy, the mouth of the blessed old man was filled with spiritual laughter, and his heart with joy. Wherefore also in the language of his country he exclaimed: "Mochohe! Mochohe!" which in Latin means "Care mi, Care mi," adding: "Blessed art thou who hast come in the name of the Lord." He therefore took them to his dwelling, nourished and educated them as if they had been his own kindred. Accordingly, after certain days had elapsed, he bathed them in the laver of regeneration and renovation, and anointed them with the sacred chrism; calling the mother Taneu, and the boy Kyentyern, which, being interpreted, is The Capital Lord. That this new name with which the mouth of S. Serf named him was not received in vain shall be clearly set forth in its place in the following pages. Therefore the man of the Lord educated the child of the Lord, like another Samuel, commended and assigned to him by God. The child grew and waxed strong, and the grace of God was with him. But when the age of understanding and the time fit and acceptable for learning came, he delivered him to be instructed in letters, and, that he might profit in these things, spent much labour and care upon him. Nor was he in this respect defrauded of his desire; for the boy, in acquiring and retaining, responded well and richly to his training, like a tree which is planted near the running waters, which bringeth forth its fruit in due season. The boy advanced, the unction of a good hope and a holy disposition teaching him, in the discipline of letters, and not less in the exercises of the sacred virtues. For there were bestowed upon him by the Father of Lights, from Whom cometh down every good and every perfect gift, a docile heart, a mind quick to understand, a memory tenacious in retaining what he had learnt, a tongue persuasive in setting forth what he willed; a voice, high, sweet, harmonious, and almost unwearied, in singing the divine praises. A praiseworthy life gilded all these gifts of grace, and therefore beyond all his companions he was precious and beloved in the eyes of the holy old man. Wherefore, also, he was accustomed to call him, in the language of his country, Mungher, which in Latin means Karissimus Amicus ; and by this name, down to the present day, the common people are frequently used to call him, and to invoke him in their necessities.

CHAPTER V.

Of the little bird which was killed and then restored to life by Kentigern.

THE fellow pupils of S. Kentigern, seeing that he was loved by their teacher and spiritual father more than all the rest, hated him, nor could they say anything peaceably to him either publicly or in private. Wherefore in many ways they lay in wait for him, abused, envied, and slandered him. But the child of the Lord always had the eyes of his heart towards the Lord, and grieved more for them than for himself, caring little for all the unjust machinations of men. Now, a little bird, which on account of the redness of its body is called the redbreast, by the will of the Heavenly Father, without whom not one sparrow falleth to the ground, was wont to receive its daily food from the hand of Serf, the servant of God, and in consequence of this had become familiar and at home with him. Sometimes it was even wont to rest upon his head, or face, or shoulder, or in his bosom, or to sit by his side as he prayed or read ; and by the flapping of its wings, or by the sound of its inarticulate voice, or by some other little gesture, it showed the affection which it had for him. So that sometimes the face of the man of God assumed the joy which was shadowed forth in the motion of the bird, as he wondered at the great power of the Creator in this little creature, to Whom the dumb speak, and irrational things are known to have understanding.

And because this bird frequently, at the command or beck of the man of God, came to him or departed from him, it brought to light the unbelief and hardness of heart of his disciples, and showed clearly their disobedience. Let not this seem strange to any one, seeing that the Lord, by the voice of an animal dumb and a beast of burden, reproved the foolishness of the prophet ; and Solomon, the wisest of men, sends the sluggard to the ant, that, by considering its labour and industry, he may shake off his torpor and sloth. Moreover, a holy and wise man called his religious to consider the work of the bees, that in their little bodies they might learn the beautiful discipline of service. But perhaps it will seem marvellous to some that a man so holy and perfect should take delight in the play or ways of a little bird. But let such know that perfect men ought at times to have the severity of their discipline mitigated by something of this kind, in order that they who mentally rise up to God may at times lower themselves to us ; because even the bow requires occasionally to be unbent from its daily strain, lest at the needful time it be found nerveless and useless for the discharge of the arrow. For birds in passing through the air rise with outstretched wings, and again closing them, descend to the lower parts of the earth.

Therefore on a certain day, when the aged man entered his oratory to offer up to God the incense of prayers, the boys took advantage of his absence, and began to indulge in play with the aforesaid little bird ; and, while they handled it among themselves, and tried to snatch it from each other, it died in their hands, and its head was torn from its body. When this was done, their play was changed into sorrow, and they already, in imagination, saw the strokes of the rods which are wont to be the greatest torment of boys, hanging over them. At length, having taken counsel among themselves, they laid the blame on the boy Kentigern, who had kept himself entirely aloof from the affair, and they showed him the dead bird, and threw it from them before the old man arrived. The old man took the destruction of the bird very ill, and threatened to avenge its death upon its destroyer very severely. The boys, therefore, rejoiced, thinking that they had escaped, and that they had turned on Kentigern the punishment due to themselves, and that they had lessened the grace of friendship which Serf had hitherto entertained towards him.

When Kentigern, the most pure child, learned this, he took the bird into his hands, put the head to the body, and impressed upon it the sign of the cross, and raising his pure hands in prayer to the Lord, said: "O Lord Jesus Christ, in whose hand is the breath of all Thy creatures, rational and irrational, give back to this little bird the breath of life, that Thy blessed name may be glorified for ever." These words spake the Saint in prayer, and immediately the bird was restored to life; and not only rose safely with untrammelled flight in the air, but flew forth in its usual way to meet the old man with joy as he returned from the church. On seeing this prodigy the heart of the holy old man exulted in the Lord, and his soul magnified the child of the Lord in the Lord, and the Lord who alone doeth marvellous works, and was working in the child. By this remarkable sign, therefore, the Lord signified, nay, in a way presignified, Kentigern to be His own, and began to announce him whom He afterwards, and in manifold ways, made more remarkable by wonders.

CHAPTER VI.

Of the fire put out through envy by the companions of S. Kentigern and by his breath brought down from heaven on a little branch of hazel.

IT was a rule with S. Serf that each of the boys whom he trained and instructed should, during the course of the week, carefully attend to arrange the lamps in the church while the divine office was being celebrated there by day and by night, and that for this purpose, when the rest had gone to sleep, one of them should diligently attend to the fire, lest any neglect should occur in the divine service on account of the want of light. It came to pass that S. Kentigern was appointed to this service in the order of his course, and while he was performing it diligently and in order, his rivals, inflamed with the torches of envy, yea, blinded, as it is the way with the perverse to envy the progress of their betters, and to persecute or prevent or depreciate the good in others which they do not, or will not, or can not have in themselves, secretly on a certain solemn night extinguished all the fire within the habitations of the monastery and the places in its neighbourhood; and then, as if ignorant and innocent sought their couches. And when about cockcrow, Kentigern rose according to custom at the sacred vigils, in order that, as custom required, he might attend to the lights, he sought for fire all around and found none.

At length, becoming aware of the wickedness of his rivals, he determined to give place to envy, and began to leave the monastery. And when he came to the hedge which surrounded that habitation, he came to himself and stood still, and armed his soul to endure perils among false brethren and to bear the persecution of the froward. Then returning to the house, he laid hold of and drew out a branch of a growing hazel which had come up beside the hedge, and, animated by faith, besought the Father of Lights to lighten his darkness by the pouring in of new light, and in a new way prepare a lamp for him by which he might clothe with wholesome confusion his enemies who were persecuting him. Therefore, raising his pure hand, he made upon the branch the sign of the cross, and blessing it in the name of the Holy and Undivided Trinity, he breathed upon it. A marvellous and wonderful thing happened. Straightway fire sent down from heaven fell upon the branch, as if the boy had breathed out flame instead of breath, and sent forth rays, vomiting fire far and wide, and dissipating the darkness all around, and so in His light he saw light and went into the House of the Lord. God, therefore, sent forth His light, and led him and brought him into the monastery, unto His holy hill and unto His tabernacles. So also he went unto the altar of God, who gladdened his youth with so clear a sign, and kindled the lamps of the Church that the Divine Office might be celebrated and performed in due season. The Lord, therefore, was his light and his salvation, that he might no longer fear any of his rivals, because He judged him and pled his cause against those unjust, envious, and deceitful boys, that their malice might no more prevail against him.

All were astonished beholding this great vision, when that torch burnt without injury to him, as once the bush which appeared to Moses was seen to burn and was not consumed. Nevertheless it was one and the same Lord who wrought the sign both in the bush and in the hazel bough; for He who appointed Moses to be a Lawgiver to the people of the Hebrews, that he might lead them out from the Egyptian bondage, deigned to appoint Kentigern a preacher of the Christian law to many peoples among the nations, that he might rescue them from the dominion of the devil. At last that torch was extinguished, after the lamps of the church were lighted, and every one wondered more and more as they saw these great works of God. For that hazel tree from which the little branch was taken, received a blessing from S. Kentigern, and afterwards began to grow into a grove. If from that grove of hazel, as the country folk say, even the greenest twig be taken, it kindles like the driest material at the touch of fire, which as it were laps it up, and when beaten upon by but a little breath, by the merit of the Saint, it sheds from itself a fiery spray. And truly, a miracle of this kind deserved to continue, yea, to perpetuate itself in his case in whom, in the verdure of the springtime of his youth, the delight of the flesh, though outwardly flourishing, was inwardly despised, and all the glory of the world like the flower of the grass altogether withered, because the Spirit of the Lord blew upon it, and the Word of the Lord which endureth for ever, by enlightening, consecrated to Himself that most dear soul and undefiled body, and the fire of the Holy Spirit consumed him as a whole burnt offering, accepted in an odour of sweet savour.

CHAPTER VII.

Of the cook raised from the dead by the prayers of S. Kentigern.

S. SERF had a certain man deputed to the office of the kitchen, who was very necessary for him and for those who were living with him, inasmuch as he was skilled in his art and active and carefully attended to this frequent ministry. It came to pass that he was seized with a very severe illness and lay in bed; and the disease increasing and prevailing, he yielded up the breath of life. Sorrow at his death filled the heart of the old man; and all the multitude of his disciples and all his household mourned for him, because any one equal to him in such a ministry was not easily found. Discharging the duty of nature, they consigned his native dust to the womb of all, and sustained no small loss on account of his decease. On the day after his burial, all the disciples and servants, the jealous as well as the friendly, came to the blessed Serf, earnestly beseeching him that he would by his prayer summon his Munhu, and compel him, in virtue of his obedience, so far as to endeavour to raise his cook from the dead. For those who were envious asserted that the magicians in Egypt had, by means of their enchantments, shown forth signs from heaven, and on the testimony of John in the Apocalypse, the disciples of Antichrist would send down fire from heaven, and that many wizards had in the eyes of all done what seemed wonderful things by their wicked arts, but that no one of the human race could bring back from death to the breath of life any one who was really dead, unless he were perfect in holiness.

In season and out of season they persisted, urging with persuasive words that he should prove his holiness with such a work, and that his merit would be proclaimed for ever if he recalled to life him who was dead and buried. At first the holy old man hesitated to presume to enjoin so extraordinary a work on the youth, but at length, overcome and constrained by the importunity of their wickedness, he talked to the young man of the Lord on such a matter with gentle words and prayers, but found him reluctant, asserting that he had not merit for it. Then S. Serf adjured him, by the holy and terrible name of the Lord, that he should at least attempt to do what he could in this matter, and this he commanded in virtue of holy obedience. The young man, then, fearing that adjuration, and deeming obedience better and more pleasing to God than all sacrifices, went to the grave where the cook had the day before been buried, and caused the earth wherewith he was covered to be dug up and cast out. Then falling down upon the ground alone, shedding many tears, and having his face covered with them, he said: "O Lord Jesus Christ! Who art the life and the resurrection of Thine own who faithfully believe in Thee, Who killest and makest alive, who bringest down to the grave and bringest up; to Whom life and death are servants, Who didst raise up Lazarus when he had been dead four days, raise again this dead man, that Thy holy name may be glorified above all things, blessed for ever."

Then a thing exceedingly astonishing occurred. While S. Kentigern poured forth many prayers, the dead man, prostrate in the dust, straightway rose again from the dead, and came forth, though bound in grave clothes, from the sepulchral house. He verily rose from death as the other rose from prayer, and along with him, and a great crowd following him, he proceeded safe and active, first, to the church to give thanks to God, and then, by the command of Kentigern, to his accustomed office of the kitchen, every one applauding the miracle and praising God. But he that was raised from the dead afterwards described the punishments of the wicked and the joys of the righteous which he saw, and turned many from evil to good, and strengthened in their holy purpose many who were endeavouring to advance from good to better. On being urged by many he likewise unfolded the manner of his resuscitation. He asserted that he was torn from things human with unspeakable pain, and led before the tribunal of the terrible Judge, and that there he saw many who, on receiving their sentence, were cast into hell, others destined to purgatorial places, and some raised to celestial joys beyond the heavens. And when he, tremblingly, expected his own sentence, he heard that he was the man for whom Kentigern, beloved of the Lord, was praying; he was ordered by a being, streaming with light, to be led back to the body and brought back to his former life and health, and he was sedulously warned by the same being who conducted him, that in future he should be watchful to live a stricter life. And the same cook, preferring sacred religion in habit and in act, and profiting, and going on from strength to strength, lived seven years longer, and then, yielding to fate, was buried in a noble sarcophagus. Likewise there was engraven on the lid of his tomb how he was raised from the dead by S. Kentigern, that by all who see or shall see it in time to come, the wonderful God may be glorified in his Saint.

CHAPTER VIII.

How S. Kentigern secretly departed from S. Serf, and what sort of miracle was wrought at his departure.

WHEN the holiness of S. Kentigern shone forth with such increasingly remarkable signs, and the fragrance of his virtues spread far and wide as the savour of life, his rivals drew unto themselves from these life-giving odours a savour of death; and the holy reputation which furnished to many an incentive to holy conversation, fostered in them the seeds of a greater hatred towards the saint of God. The boy, prudent in the Lord, knew that the measure of their malice towards him was filled up, and that the inveterate envy that had entered into their bowels and marrow could find no rest in their unquiet hearts. Nor did he deem it safe to slumber longer beside a venomous crowd of serpents, lest, perchance, he should suffer the loss of inward sweetness. Moveover, he weighed the breath of popular fame, serenely and sweetly breathing on him and calling from every side: "Well done! well done!" Accordingly he resolved forthwith to leave the place, that he might in humility forsake the company of those who were hating and envying him, and prudently avoid vain glory. Upon this he took counsel, with the earnestness of the most fervent prayer, with the Angel of Good Counsel, that his good spirit might lead him in the right way, lest by any means he should run, or had run, in vain. The Lord, therefore, inclined His ear to the prayers of His servant, revealing to him by the Holy Spirit that that which he had settled in his mind would be well pleasing in the eyes of the Lord.

Therefore he secretly withdrew from the place, having God as the guide of his journey and as his protector in every place. Journeying on he came to the Friscan shore, where the river, called Mallena, overflowing its channel from the influx of the tide, took away all hope of crossing. But the good and mighty Lord, who divided the Red Sea into parts, and led Israel through the midst dry shod, under the leadership of Moses, and again turned back to its sources the perpetual flowing of the Jordan, so that the children of Israel might cross dry shod into the Land of Promise under Joshua, and who the stream of the same Jordan, at the prayer of Elijah and his disciple Elisha, divided, in order that they pass through with dry feet, He Himself now, with the same mighty hand and outstretched arm, divided the river Mallena, that Kentigern, beloved of God and men, might pass through on dry land. Then the tide flowing back in a wonderful way, and being, as I may say, afraid, the waters as well of the sea as of the river, were as walls on his right hand and on his left. He next crossed a little arm of the sea by a bridge, which is called by the inhabitants the Pons Servani, and on looking back to the bank saw the waters, which before stood as in a heap, now flowed back, and filling the channel of the Mallena, and even overflowing the afore-mentioned bridge, and entirely denying a passage to any one.

And behold S. Serf, supporting his aged limbs with a staff, having followed the fugitive, stood above the bank, and beckoning with his hand, shouted and lamented saying: "Alas! my dearest son! light of mine eyes! staff of mine old age! why dost thou desert me? Wherefore art thou leaving me! Call to mind, I beseech thee, the days that are past, and remember the years that are gone by: how I took thee up when thou camest forth from thy mother's womb; how I have nourished thee, taught thee, trained thee even unto this hour. Despise me not; neither forsake my gray hairs; but return that shortly thou mayest close mine eyes." Kentigern, moved by these words of the old man and melted to tears responded: "Thou seest, O Father! that what is done is according to the Divine Will; neither ought we, nor can we change the counsel of the Most High; nor ought we to fail to obey His Will. Besides there is this sea which as a great gulf is fixed between us; so that if I would pass from hence to you I cannot, neither can you pass from thence to me. I pray thee, therefore, have me excused." Then the old man said: "I pray thee that by thy prayer thou wouldest make, as thou hast just done, the liquid again solid, divide the sea, make bare the ground, that at least I alone may cross and come to thee on dry ground. With willing mind will I become a son instead of a father to thee, and a disciple instead of a teacher, that until the evening of my days I may be thine inseparable companion." Then again Kentigern, bedewed with tears, said: "Return, I beseech thee, O my Father, to thine own, that in thy holy presence they may be trained in sacred doctrine, guided by thy example and corrected by thy discipline. The Rewarder of all reward thee for all the benefits thou hast shown toward me, and since thou hast fought a good fight, even now thou hast finished thy course, and hast maintained the faith living and fruitful; henceforth there is laid up for thee a crown of righteousness, which the Lord, the Righteous Judge, will shortly render thee. But I, destined to the work of the ministry, will go to that to which He Who separated me from my mother's womb and called me by His grace, has sent me.

When these words were said, and each had given the other his blessing, they separated, no more to look upon each other again in this world. Serf returned to his home and awaited in a good old age the day of his call. And thus grown old in good days, he was gathered to the holy fathers and rested in the Lord, and as a good labourer in the vineyard in the evening, he received from the Lord the penny of eternal reward. And what sort of a man and how great and in what miracles he shone, a little book written concerning his life will clearly show to those who read it. Now the place by which S. Kentigern crossed was afterwards entirely impassable. For the bridge was always after that covered with the waters of the sea, and afforded to no one any longer the means of crossing. Even the Mallena changed the force of its current from its proper place, and from that day until the present turned back into the channel of the river Ledon. So that henceforward the rivers which until then had been divided from each other, were mingled and united.

CHAPTER IX.

Of the sick man who desired and sought in prayer and obtained from the Lord that before his death he should see S. Kentigern, and tasted death in his presence, and obtained sepulture by his forethought.

THERE was a man of venerable life, Fregus by name, tormented by much and long continued sickness. The same lived in a town called Kernach (Carnoch), detained upon a bed of pain, strong in faith, wholesome in holy conversation, intent upon heaven. This man, just and full of fear, when the south wind was blowing over his garden so that the odour of its breezes reached him, felt in his heart the sweetness of the sanctity flowing from the great reputation of S. Kentigern. Whence also the desire kindling within him, both his heart and eye thirsted, so that it might have been thought that the desire which S. Simeon had to see the Lord, was renewed. For Simeon with panting spirit desired to see with the eyes of the flesh the salvation of God, the Lord's Christ clothed in flesh. Fregus, with a fixed faith, unwearied desire, and many prayers, desired of the Lord that he might see the servant of the Lord Christ, Kentigern. Christ heard the desire of both, and the ear of God hearing the preparation of their heart, fulfilled it.

Simeon's desire and joy was fulfilled to his salvation in the day in which Christ was presented in the Temple. To his consolation Fregus saw Kentigern the same day in which he departed from S. Serf, and was glad. For Fregus had received a promise from the Holy Ghost that he should not see death until he had first seen Kentigern the Nazarite of the Lord. And when Kentigern came to the dwelling place of the holy sick man and knocked at the door, the sick man instructed by a divine oracle called from within, saying: "Open the gates, for God is with us. Come is the herald of my salvation, promised me by God, and long waited for by me, and to-day shown me." And when he saw him he exulted in spirit, and giving thanks, blessed God and said: "Lord, now lettest Thou Thy servant depart in peace according to Thy word; for mine eyes have seen Thy salvation which Thou hast prepared before the face of all people, a Light for the revelation of the True Light which lighteth every man coming into the world and to declare the glory of eternal life to the peoples of these and many nations." And turning to him, he again said: "Dispose of my house and of my life to-day, and to-morrow attend to my burial, as it pleaseth thy providence, God inspiring thee." Then by the advice of S. Kentigern, whatever of earthly substance he possessed he dispersed and gave to the poor, and having made a pure confession, he was anointed with the oil of remission, and being purified with the sacraments of the life-giving Body and Blood of the Lord, he commended his spirit into the hands of the Lord, and with eyes and hands stretched out to heaven expired during the words of prayer. On the morrow Kentigern yoked two untamed oxen to a new cart on which he placed the dead body, and having offered up prayer in the name of the Lord, he enjoined the brute beasts to convey the burden placed upon them to the place which God had provided for it. And the bulls, which were not in the least restive, nor in anything disobedient to the voice of S. Kentigern, without any tripping or falling and without a guide, came by a straight course, with Kentigern and many others who were accompanying him following, to Cathures, which is now called Glasgow, and there with all gentleness halted with the burden of sacred earth laid upon them (a beautiful sight) near a certain cemetery which had long before been consecrated by S. Ninian. Indeed, with no less a miracle, in no dissimilar way, and with no unequal power was this chariot by ruling and threatening directed to the aforenamed place by Him who once, when Dagon was cast down and broken, brought from Ekron to Bethshemesh, the Ark of the Covenant, which had been taken by the Philistines, placed on a new cart and drawn by milch cows which had never borne the yoke. The Saint therefore in the same place took the holy body down from the cart and having celebrated the obsequies, buried it in that cemetery, wherein was never yet man laid. This was the first burial in that place in which afterwards many bodies were buried in peace. The greatest reverence was paid to the tomb of the man of God : nor did any rash fool ever venture to trample upon or to pass over it with impunity : for within the space of a year many who trod upon it or refused to honour it were overtaken by some grevious misfortune, and some were even punished with death. That tomb is even to the present surrounded by a delicious density of overshadowing trees in token of the sanctity of him who is buried there and of the reverence due to him.

CHAPTER X.

Of two brothers, one of whom was punished by the judgment of God, the other with all his family was deemed meet to be blessed by God for many generations.

WHEN the man of God, Fregus, had been buried, S. Kentigern, as enjoined upon him by a revelation from the Lord, dwelt with two brothers who were living in the same place before his arrival, and, ordering his life in much sanctity, went on with great virtues unto perfection. One of the brothers with whom he lived was called Telleyr, the other Anguen. Anguen received God's Saint as an angel of the Lord and loved him out of the most generous affection of his heart, and with all reverence and veneration obeyed his commands, submitting himself to all his injunctions. And not in vain. For the servant of the Lord blessed him in the name of the Lord. And succoured by that benediction of graciousness not only he himself but almost the whole of his posterity received a blessing from the Lord, and mercy from God our Saviour, and seemed to possess it as if by hereditary right. For He magnified them in the sight of kings and made them of great name like unto the name of the great ones who were in the earth, so that they grew and increased both in abundance of wealth, and in the culture of the Christian Religion, insomuch so that it was justly said, these are the seed which the Lord hath blessed by the prayers of his servant Kentigern.

But the other, Telleyr by name, was very troublesome to him, secretly detracting from his religion, depreciating all his actions, often openly resisting him to his face, doing him insults and injuries. Either by minishing from the good he did or by perverting it, he obscured every thing by evil interpretation. But the servant of God, who by daily custom had taught himself with blessed Job to be a brother to dragons and a companion to ostriches, and like Ezekiel to dwell with scorpions, possessed his soul in patience and was peaceful with him who hated peace. When he spoke to him of the things that belong to peace, Telleyr, perverse and ungrateful as he was, only fought against him. But God, the Lord of Vengeance, the patient Rewarder, did not finally suffer the injury done to his servant to go unavenged. For on a certain day, after many revilings by which he had embittered the soul of the just, he went forth to his work. And because he was of great strength he placed upon his shoulders a beam of great weight beyond the measure of his strength, rejoicing and thinking that he had acquired for himself the triumphal reputation of having surpassed asses in the bearing of burdens. And when he had gone a little way he tripped upon a stone and fell, and so, being crushed beneath his burden, he gave up the ghost. He learned what Solomon says: " Woe to him that is alone, for when he falleth, he hath none to lift him up." And again : " He hath fallen once for all who continually doeth evil."

Kentigern, when he heard that his adversary had fallen, afflicted himself with great lamentations and procured for him a place of burial; imitating in this matter holy David the good King of the Hebrews who mourned over the death of his persecutor Saul and lamented him with a great lamentation. But because, as Solomon testifies, where the fool perishes the wise man will be more prudent, we have in the case of this man sufficiently clear evidence that we ought to beware of offending against the servants and friends of God, and not to dare to inflict upon them trouble, or grievance, or injury. For the elect are the temple of God, and the Holy Ghost dwelleth in them. They are the more therefore to be deferred to, and we should abstain from injuring them, inasmuch as He who dwelleth in them is most powerful in vindicating their wrongs and impartial in rendering justice to those who suffer wrong.

CHAPTER XI.

Of the election of S. Kentigern, and of his consecration as a bishop.

AND when S. Kentigern, dwelling in the above mentioned place, became abundant in the affluence of many miraculous gifts, it pleased Him Who had separated him from his mother's womb, that he should no longer be hid under a bushel but rather that he should be set upon a candlestick, that by bringing forth his righteousness as the light and his judgment as the noonday, he might give light to all that are in the house of God. Therefore by Divine prompting the king and clergy of the Cambrian region with other Christians, though they were but very few, came together; and after taking into consideration what was to be done in order to restore the state of the Church which had been well-nigh destroyed, with one consent they came to S. Kentigern and chose him, notwithstanding his great resistance and many objections, as the shepherd and bishop of their souls. He objected to their election of him, that he was not fit on account of his youth; but they urged the gravity of his manners and the riches of his wisdom and knowledge. He pled that he could not with equanimity endure the diminution of his inward peace and holy contemplation. They alleged, on the contrary, that it was healthful to break in on the Sabbath of the contemplative life for the salvation of many souls. In the end, he judged himself insufficient for this honour, yea, rather for this burden ; but the voice of all proclaimed that his sufficiency had been declared by God with many indications of signs and wonders. Invoking therefore for him prosperity, and blessing him in the name of the Holy Trinity, and committing him to the Holy Ghost, the Glorifier and Distributor of all the orders and offices and dignities in the Church, they enthroned him ; and having called one bishop from Ireland, after the manner of the Britons and Scots of that period, they caused him to be consecrated bishop. The custom had grown up in Britain in the consecration of bishops to anoint only their heads by pouring on them the sacred chrism, with invocation of the Holy Ghost and benediction and the laying on of hands ; which rite these ignorant people alleged they had received by the institution of the Divine law and by the tradition of the Apostles. But the sacred canons ordain that no one shall be consecrated a bishop except by at least three bishops, to wit, one who acts as consecrator, who shall say over him who is to be consecrated the sacramental benedictions and the prayers for each of the episcopal ornaments ; and two others, who shall lay on hands along with him, shall be witnesses, and hold the text of the Gospels supported on his neck. Yet although the consecration to which the Britons were accustomed, seems to be little consonant with the sacred canons, it is nevertheless agreed that it does not destroy the power or efficacy of the Divine mystery or of the episcopal ministration. But because these islanders, as placed beyond the civilized world, were, by reason of the attacks made upon them by the pagans, ignorant of the canons, the judgment of the Church, condescending to them, admits in that respect their excuse. But in these times it permits no such rite as this to be used by any one without grave censure. But S. Kentigern, though he was consecrated in this manner, took pains to correct it in every possible way, as we shall state further on. He established his cathedral seat in a town called Glesgu, which is interpreted The Dear Family, and is now called Glasgow, where he united to himself many servants of God, a family famous and dear to God, who practised continence and lived after the manner of the primitive Church under the Apostles, with no possessions, in holy discipline, and in divine service.

The diocese of that episcopate was extended to the borders of the Cambrian kingdom, which reached from sea to sea like the rampart once built by the Emperor Severus. Afterwards by the advice and assistance of a Roman legion, in order to prevent the incursions of the Picts, a wall was built in the same place as this rampart, eight feet in breadth, and twelve in height. It stretched to the Forth, and by division separates Scotia from Anglia. This Cambrian region over which Kentigern now ruled with episcopal honour, had formerly, in the time of Pope Eleutherius, when King Lucius was reigning, received the Christian Faith, as had also the whole of Britain; but in consequence of the pagans infesting the island and asserting their rule in it, the islanders lapsed into apostasy and cast away the faith they had received. Many had not even been washed in the saving laver. Many were tainted with the contagion of manifold heresies. Many, in name only Christians, were plunged in the slough of numerous vices; very many had been taught by a ministry of men who were unskilled in and ignorant of the law of God. All the provincials therefore were in need of the counsel of a good pastor and the healing of a good ruler. God, therefore, the Disposer and Dispenser of all good things, provided, promoted and proposed S. Kentigern as the remedy of all their diseases, their support and their example in life.

CHAPTER XII.

How S. Kentigern conducted himself by his example and teaching in his Episcopacy; and how he bore himself both in public and in private.

THE blessed Kentigern, having taken possession of his government, as he excelled others in dignity, so he sought to exceed all in sanctity. And as he was higher in rank, so he endeavoured to appear more excellent than others in the increase of holy virtues and manners. For he thought it unworthy for him, who was bound by a Divine command to go up upon the mountain to bring good tidings to Zion, to creep on the ground and to lie at the foot. And truly it is not becoming for him who, from his office, is called to announce high things to live meanly ; wherefore the Saint of God, after accepting the Episcopal dignity, always sought to exercise a greater humility and strictness than previously in food and clothing, in vigils and couches, and in the mortification of his body. And that I may briefly describe his whole life from the time of his ordination, which occurred in the twenty-fifth year of his age, down to the extreme end of his life, which lasted the space of one hundred and sixty years—breaking his fast after three and often four days, he used to revive rather than recruit his body by tasting cheap and very light foods, such as bread and milk, or cheese, or butter and some slight relish, lest his bodily frame should entirely perish after the way of this mortality ; yea, that I may speak more fittingly, mortifying his members which were upon the earth by the crucifixion of a daily cross, he would by slaying offer himself for a sweet savour, a living sacrifice, acceptable unto God. From flesh and blood, from wine and from all that could inebriate he abstained altogether as one of, nay, as a chief among the Nazarites. But if at any time it happened that he was on a journey or dining with the King, he refrained from abstaining with his usual strictness. Afterwards, when he returned home, as if punishing himself for a serious crime, he increased his abstinence.

CHAPTER XIII.

Of S. Kentigern's mode of dress.

HE wore the roughest hair-cloth next to his naked body; then a garment of leather made from the skins of goats; next a cowl tied on like a fisherman's. Over this he was clad in a white alb, and always wore a stole placed upon his neck. He bore also a pastoral staff, not rounded, gilded and gemmed as may be seen now, but of simple wood, and merely bent. In his hand he had the Manual Book, always ready for the exercise of his ministry when necessity or reason required. And so by the whiteness of his dress he expressed the purity of his inner life and avoided vain glory.

CHAPTER XIV.

Of the couch of S. Kentigern and his vigils, and his bath in cold water.

WHAT shall I say of his bed? I hesitate whether to call it a bed or a tomb. He lay on the rock hollowed out like a monument; having for his head a stone in place of a pillow, like another Jacob. Verily, he was a strong wrestler against the world, the flesh, and the devil. Throwing in a few ashes, and taking off his hair-cloth, he shook off his drowsiness by destroying rather than by taking sleep. And to express myself more clearly, in a certain similitude of snatching sleep he used to bury himself with Christ. Then, when he had taken a moderate amount of sleep he rose in the night time, at the beginning of his vigils, and poured out his heart as water in the sight of the Lord his God. And thus in psalms and hymns and spiritual songs celebrating the night watches of the Lord, he exulted in the Lord and rejoiced in God our Saviour, until the second cock-crowing. Then entering into conflict with a sharper wrestling against that great and malignant dragon, which, according to the prophet, lieth in the midst of his rivers, he was wont to strip himself of his clothes, and naked following a naked Christ, making himself naked and bare, he plunged into the swift-flowing and cold water. Then, verily, as the hart thirsteth after the water brooks, so his soul thirsted after God, the living water; and there in cold and nakedness, with his eyes and hands lifted towards heaven, he with devout heart and lips chanted the whole Psalter from beginning to end. Thereby made like one of the flock of sheep that are even shorn which came up from the washing to Mount Gilead, emerging from the water like a dove bathed in milk, yea, as a Nazarite whiter than snow, brighter than milk, ruddier than ancient ivory, fairer than a sapphire, he sat down, drying his limbs, on a stone on the brow of a mountain called Gulath, by the river-side, near his own hut. And then, when his body was dried, he put on his clothes, as if preparing his going forth at the dawn, and showed himself as an example to his disciples. Of this practice of bathing neither the fire of the flashing lightning, nor hail, nor snow, nor the spirit of the storms ever deprived him, unless a journey unavoidably undertaken or a very serious sickness prevented him. But even then he was wont to redeem the work by some other divine and spiritual exercise. Wherefore, by the daily use of this salutary bath, as of a new Jordan, his flesh was restored as the flesh of a little child; because the law of sin which warreth in the less honourable members was so weakened in him, and the fire of concupiscence so mortified and extinguished, that no corruption of the rebellious flesh, either watching or even sleeping, ever polluted or stained the lily of his snow-white modesty. Nor did he feel even its simple motion either rage or stir within him. For through the grace of Christ working with him, his flesh with its passions stilled, continued in the innocence of childhood's purity. Yea, this holy one grew up before the Lord like an unfading lily. And hence on one occasion he plainly declared to his disciples that he was no more moved at the sight or touch of the most beautiful girl than at the sight or touch of the hardest flint.

CHAPTER XV.

Of the mode of speaking the man of God used.

IN speaking, however, he was able to control his spirit and had learned to set a watch before his mouth and to keep the door of his lips that he might direct his words with discretion. Nor did any one of his words fall lightly to the ground, nor was the word he uttered given to the winds that when found it might return unto him void. Wherefore he spoke in weight, in number, and in measure as the necessary occasion required. His speech was seasoned with salt and suited to every age and sex. Honey and milk were under his tongue and his storehouse was filled with spiritual wine ; yea, even from his lips the babe in Christ sucked milk, the more advanced honey and the perfect wine, each unto his health. In judging or condemning or reproving he had not by him divers weights, nor was there respect of persons with him, but he studied the cause ; and according to the name of the fault in due time and place he administered the measure of ecclesiastical discipline with the greatest discretion. Besides, this Saint preached more by his silence than many teachers and rulers do by loud speaking. For his look, countenance, mien, gait, and the bearing of his whole body proclaimed discipline and by certain signs bursting forth like water interpreted the purity of the inner man, which lay hid there. Of his munificence which gave itself wholly to almsgiving and works of mercy, it is superfluous to commit anything to writing ; since all the substance which the Divine Bounty had conferred upon him, was the common treasury of the poor.

CHAPTER XVI.

With what grace he was deemed meet to be adorned, while he celebrated the sacred mysteries of the Mass.

BUT although in the preceding, and in similar holy exercises, he showed himself as a man, or sometimes as above man, yet it was when celebrating the sacred mysteries of the Mass, that he in a manner putting off the man and withdrawing himself from earthly things, assumed something of a divine character wholly above the human. For while with his hands raised in the form of a cross he repeated the Sursum Corda, he lifted his own unto the Lord, as he exhorted others. So from the golden censer of his own purest heart filled with the live coals of virtue, kindled with divine love, like the clearest sweet smelling incense, his prayer, passing beyond the clouds penetrated the heavens, and rising into the light which no man can approach unto, was directed into the presence of God, so that the Most High Himself vouchsafed by signs manifest to the eyes of men to declare that He had accepted it as an odour of a sweet savour well-pleasing to Himself. For many times while handling the Divine Sacraments, a snow white dove having a beak as it were of gold was seen to settle upon his head and with the transparent fluttering of its wings to overshadow him and that which was laid upon the altar like a ray of sunlight. Frequently also as he stood as a sacrificer, sacrificing at the holy altars, a bright cloud overshadowed his head. At times too when the Son was being immolated to the Father, it was not he that seemed to stand there, but a fiery pillar, by the brightness of which the sight of the beholders was blinded. Not to all, however, was it given to know or see this ministry, but to those only to whom it was granted by the Father of Lights. For on one occasion when the priest of the Lord was celebrating the Holy mysteries, a sweet smelling cloud filled the whole house, when many were hearing the sacred mysteries of the Lord. The odour, exceeding all perfumes, bathed all who had assembled themselves together in an exceeding sweetness, and infused perfect health into many who were there labouring with divers diseases. Verily, while I record these things sorrow fills my heart as I see the priesthood in the present defiled in so many ways. For while in the meantime I am silent concerning those who simoniacally come to sacrifice, or with Judas sell the Lord's body, since forsooth they will not offer it except for a price, I speak of those who, entangled in crimes and dissolute in vices, polluted in body and soul, presume to touch and to contaminate with impure hands the Sacrifice of Purification. Alas! in how many in the present is the stench of foulness felt rather than the odour of spiritual sweetness! O how more are now seized upon and blinded by the dark whirlwind than overshadowed by the bright cloud! Woe! woe! I say to many in the present whom the sulphurous flame rather the surrounding pillar of fire awaits! But now I turn back my eyes to myself and to others like unto me, who in any way are discharging the office of the priesthood, and for whom instead of a snow white dove at the time of sacrifice, flies sufficiently tormenting come up from the river of Egypt; that is, thoughts unclean, vain, unprofitable rush into the memory from the imagination of this perishing world. Wherefore fear and trembling come upon me, for, as Solomon testifies, dead flies cause the ointment to stink, since minds occupied with thoughts of this kind know little of how great the delight is of that inward sweetness which proceeds from the visitation of the Holy Ghost.

CHAPTER XVII.

Of the way in which S. Kentigern withdrew himself during the whole of Lent into more secret places in the desert and returned to his own Church before Maundy Thursday and sometimes before Palm Sunday.

THE man of God persevered in the manner of life we have described up to an extreme old age almost all the year round, except during the days of Lent; for in those days he was wont beyond his ordinary way to walk in a certain newness of life. For emulating the fervour of certain holy fathers, or rather following in the footsteps of Elijah and John the Baptist and of the Saviour Himself, he withdrew during every Lent into desert places, and thus separating himself by flight from the sight of the sons of men and remaining in solitude of body and mind, he dwelt alone; and thus more freely devoting himself to God, away from the disturbance of men, the contradiction of tongues and the conversation of the world, he hid himself in the secret presence of God. Therefore sitting alone he raised himself above himself, and often dwelling in dens of the earth or standing at the entering in of his cave, and praying, after the rushing of the great and strong wind and of the fire, he heard the still small whisper of thin air breathing upon him and shedding over him and filling him with a certain unspeakable sweetness. Wherefore he walked about the streets of the heavenly Jerusalem seeking for himself Him in whom his soul delighted, and offering in his heart a sacrifice of joy, mortifying, nevertheless, his most holy members which were upon the earth. Presenting his most innocent body by a daily martyrdom as an odour of sweet savour, he offered himself a living sacrifice, holy and acceptable unto God. With what and what sort of food he sustained his life during those days he revealed to none or at least only to a few. These, however, he forbade with episcopal authority to disclose that mystery to mortal man.

Nevertheless he once spake, and two of his disciples heard the word once and simply uttered from his lips, and not to be recalled. "I knew," he said, "a certain man, who during Lent sustained his life on the roots of herbs only, and sometimes, the Lord granting him strength, passed the whole of that time without the support of earthly food." Neither of them doubted that he spake this of himself, but the man of God suppressed his own name, in order that he might avoid vain glory which he everywhere sought to shun. At first he used for a long time to return home and to his disciples on Maundy Thursday, and afterwards on the Saturday before Palm Sunday, in order to fulfil his episcopal duties, when he was received by all as an angel of light and peace. Accordingly he was wont to pass that week with his disciples, and on Maundy Thursday, after the preparation of the holy chrism and oil, washing with his own hands and tears the feet, first of the poor and then of the leprous, and wiping them with his hair and soothing them with many kisses,* he afterwards diligently

---

* Osculis demulcens, B. M.

waited upon them at table. Then for their consolation he sat at a banquet with the reconciled penitents and refreshed himself and them with bodily and with spiritual food ; and from that hour until after the celebration of the Mass on Easter Sunday he remained continually fasting. Truly on Good Friday he crucified himself with the Crucified with an incredible crucifixion, and with scourgings and in nakedness and with frequent kneeling, scarcely ever sitting down, he passed the day and the night bearing about in his own body the marks of the Lord Jesus with an exceedingly heavy cross of the soul and body.

But on holy Saturday, as if dead to the world, he buried with himself in a double tomb the true Abraham the ancient of days, and entering the sepulchre in the abundance of inward contemplation, he rested from the strifes of this stormy world, except that he appeared to celebrate the office of the day. At length, renewed in the spirit of his mind he awaited, with the sweet spices of holy virtues so diligently prepared, the most holy day of the Lord's resurrection. Then in a certain manner rising together with Christ, he feasted on the flesh of the unspotted lamb with the unleavened bread of sincerity and truth. And in the day which the Lord had made a day of joy on earth and in heaven, he rejoiced with all spiritual joy, and feasted with the brethren and a great multitude of the poor. This he was said to do at the other great festivals also. But if from any urgent cause it chanced, and it happened rarely, that he had to dine with seculars, while he slightly tasted the food set before him, he filled the guests with spiritual dainties, and, restraining the vain conversation which is wont to prevail at feasts, he concealed his own abstinence under the veil of sacred preaching.

CHAPTER XVIII.

What a bright countenance he had, and what he thought about hypocrites.

S. KENTIGERN is said to have been of middle stature, though inclining to be tall. It is asserted also that he was of robust strength, and almost unwearied in the endurance of any labour whether of body or mind. He was fair to look upon and graceful in form. Having a countenance full of grace and reverence, dovelike eyes, and cheeks like the turtle-dove, he drew towards him in love the affections of all who beheld him. And presenting the cheerfulness of his outward man as the most faithful interpreter and sign of his inward gentleness, he shed over all a certain feeling of spiritual joy and exultation with which the Lord had enriched man. For shunning hypocrisy as well in manner as in act himself, he taught all who followed him to shun it with the greatest care. And showing by examples that hypocrites are the most loathsome class of men, he instructed them with such words as these: "Beware, beloved," he said to his disciples, "of the vice of hypocrisy, which in a way is the renunciation of the Faith, the abandonment of hope, the death of charity, the cancer of chastity, the blinding of truth, the prison-house of sobriety, the fetter of righteousness, the little fox of obedience, the scant mantle of patience. And, that I may speak briefly, it is the moth of religion, the extinction of the virtues, the covert of vices, the asylum of all iniquity, the habitation of crimes. That hypocrisy is the nourisher of all evils our Lord teaches when he says that hypocrisy is the leaven of the Pharisees. For as leaven mixed with food makes it light, puffed up, and sour, so hypocrisy makes the heart of which it takes possession, void of religion, puffed up, and elated with the false praises of men, and sharp, hard and bitter against the truth of conscience, against good, against the righteous, and against those who seek after purity and holiness. And truly, beloved, while all iniquity by itself and in itself is single, hypocrisy alone in itself is double, yea, manifold. For the hypocrite, as far as in him lies, tries to blind Him who sees all things, while turning his eyes away from himself, he conceals his vices before human onlookers, under the appearance of an ostensible sanctity. And although other impious, wicked and criminal men are members of Antichrist, yet hypocrites alone are singularly and specially his followers and forerunners, as the simple followers and lovers of truth and purity are members and disciples of Jesus Christ. For Antichrist himself, as it is written, shall sit in the temple of God and by false signs show himself as if he were God. Yea, the very angel of Satan transforms himself into an angel of light ; and therefore it is not to be wondered at if his special servant and member transform himself into a servant of righteousness, since he is himself a synagogue of Satan. Believe me, for I speak to you in the truth, that the wrath of God never rages more fiercely in the Church of God than when he causeth a hypocrite to rule over it, because of the sins of the people. For also in the Apocalypse a more hurtful persecution is described as raging on the pale horse than on the rest which precede it ; because in truth the Holy Church is injured much more severely by hypocrisy, which is signified by the pale horse, than in the time of open persecutions wherein the faithful and unfaithful, the just and the unjust were made manifest and a multitude of martyrs were crowned. But clearly hypocrites by their gestures and by the bearing of their outward man make known to those who watch carefully and judge all spiritual things what kind of things lie hid within them. For while they feign the gait and bearing of the turtle-dove, contracting the shoulders, and hanging down the head, fixing the eyes upon the earth, disfiguring their faces, breathing with compressed lips, and speaking in I know not what feminine way, they by such signs make manifest their inner state. For with their gait they simulate peacocks, nay thieves ; by the contraction of their shoulders they show that they bear not in the least the easy yoke of Christ and His light burden ; by the hanging down of the head and the direction of their eyes they show that with the heart they cleave more to the dust than to the heavens, that they mind earthly things, love earthly things, and yearn with earthly desires ; but with their disfigured faces they show that they turn their backs rather than their faces to God ; and by their feminine mode of speaking, they prove that they live dissolutely and not in a manly way. To whom shall I say such are like save to jugglers, who exhibit fire, water, men, beasts, etc., in an imaginary way, where there is no reality ? But though pretenders, and cunning hypocrites, who provoke against themselves the wrath of God, may escape the opinion of those who judge according to appearance, they will in no wise deceive Him Who trieth the heart and the reins, or escape His just judgment." "These things," said the man of God, " I have said to you, beloved, not that I may make known a snare to you, or that you should not exhibit maturity of countenance, gesture, bearing, and discipline, but this I admonish you, in every way to seek God in simplicity of heart, to associate external with internal purity, and everywhere fleeing hypocrisy, to do all things with spiritual cheerfulness. Thus in all your works man shall be edified, God glorified, for God loveth a cheerful teacher and doer of good.

CHAPTER XIX.

How Kentigern converted the people over whom he was placed, and who for the most part had apostatised, to the Faith of Christ, and brought back those who had profaned the faith with unrighteous works to a more correct life.

THEREFORE the blessed Kentigern, when he had assumed the episcopacy, zealously endeavoured to discharge the duties laid upon him. And seeing that the northern enemy, that is, the prince of this world, had placed his seat in those parts and was ruling there, he took up spiritual arms to fight against him. Accordingly clad with the shield of faith, the helmet of hope, the breastplate of righteousness, and girt with the sword of the Spirit which is the word of God, he attacked the house of that strong man armed and spoiled his goods, supported by the help of the Lord of might, who is manifestly strong in battle. And to be brief, neither his foot, nor his hand, nor his tongue ceased from the completion of the journey he had undertaken, from the working of miracles, nor from the preaching of salvation, until all the ends of that land remembered and were converted unto the Lord. Those who had not yet been regenerated in the water of life, like thirsty harts, ran to the living fountain of baptism with burning desire. By this herald of salvation teaching the way of God in truth, those who had fallen away or wandered from the true faith in some erroneous doctrine of an heretical sect, when they came to themselves, and returned from the snares of the devil in which they were held captive, into the bosom of the Church, were incorporated into Christ.

Wherefore this renowned warrior began to overthrow the shrines of demons, to cast down their images, to build churches, to dedicate those which were built, to mark out parishes by fixed boundaries with the line of distribution, to ordain clergy, to dissolve incestuous and unlawful marriages, to change concubinage into lawful matrimony, to introduce as far as he could ecclesiastical rites, and to endeavour to establish whatever was consonant with the Faith, with Christian law and with righteousness. Wherever he journeyed, he was not borne on horseback, but even to an extreme old age he travelled after the manner of the Apostles on foot. When he had set all these things in order, he returned home, and betook himself to his own, and there, after his accustomed way, led a life glorious with virtues and miracles, in the perfection of the highest religion. Concerning his miracles we shall now say something which deserves to be recorded, because we do not doubt that it will be profitable to very many.

CHAPTER XX.

How S. Kentigern placed under one yoke in the plough a stag and a wolf, and how, sowing sand, he reaped wheat.

THUS, as we have said, the man of God joined to him a great number of disciples, whom he instructed in the sacred literature of the Divine Law and trained by word and example to holiness of life, and from whom he hoped to secure fellow-labourers in the harvest of the Lord. They all emulated with the emulation of God his life and doctrine, accustomed themselves to fastings and sacred vigils, were intent on psalms and prayers, and on meditation in the Divine Law, were content with sparing diet and clothing, and at certain times and seasons engaged in manual labour. For after the manner of the Primitive Church under the Apostles and their successors, they possessed nothing of their own; they lived soberly, righteously, godly, and very continently, and dwelt, as did also S. Kentigern himself, in separate huts from the time when they had become mature in age and wisdom; and hence these "singulares clerici" were commonly called Calledei (Culdees). Thus the servant of Jesus Christ went forth to his work in the morning and sometimes to his labour till the evening, labouring chiefly in husbandry that he might not eat the bread of idleness, but rather in the sweat of his brow, both that he might set an example of industry to his disciples and have to give to him that was in need.

It happened on a certain occasion that he was altogether without oxen and that from the want of these there was no ploughing, and the land lay fallow. When the man of God saw this, he lifted up his eyes, and saw on the edge of a wood, situated close by, a herd of stags bounding along here and there through the forest. Straightway offering up a prayer, by the mighty power of his words, he summoned them to him, and in the name of the Lord, whom all dumb and unreasoning beings, animals and all the beasts of the field obey, ordered them to be yoked instead of oxen to the plough, and to plow the land. They immediately obeyed the command of the man of God, and as oxen trained and accustomed to agriculture, to the astonishment of many they ploughed the land. When unyoked from their toil, they went to their usual pastures, and at the fitting hour, like tame and domesticated, yea, like trained animals, they returned to their accustomed work. When therefore the stags had been going and returning for some time, after the manner of domestic animals, a ferocious wolf rushed upon one of them, which was wearied with labour and was cropping some food as it lay on the grassy turf, strangled it, and filled its voracious stomach with its carcass. When this came to the knowledge of the Saint, he extended his hand towards the wood, and said : " In the name of the Holy and Undivided Trinity I command that the wolf which has wrought this injury, which I have not deserved, upon me, come hither to me to make reparation." Wonderful in word, but more wonderful in deed! At the voice of the man of God the wolf forthwith came leaping from the wood, and with a howl fell before his feet, and with such signs as it was able to make, declared that it begged forgiveness and was willing to make reparation. But the man of God upbraiding the wolf with threatening voice and look, said : " Rise ; and I command thee, by the authority of Almighty God, that thou set thyself to the plough in the place of our labourer the stag which thou hast devoured, and plough over all that remains unbroken of the little field." The wolf obeyed the word from the lips of the Saint ; and with the remaining stag yoked to the plough, ploughed up nine acres. The Saint then freely gave it permission to depart.

In this act, as it seems to me, the prophecy of Isaiah, " The wolf also shall dwell with the lamb, and the leopard shall lie down with the kid ; and the calf and the young lion and the fatling together, and a little child shall lead them," which he spiritually uttered concerning the time of our Lord's advent, was by a certain similitude fulfilled to the letter. For let the reader consider whether it is more wonderful to see a wolf lying down with a lamb or ploughing with a stag. Nevertheless, Kentigern, a most pure child, very mild in his own eyes and lowly in heart, brought this about ; yet he wrought this sign not by himself, but by the power of that Child who is born unto us, and of that Son who is given unto us. It was right that he should do this bodily who often subdued many spiritually, recalling them from wolfish cruelty and bloody slaughter, animal ferocity and a coarse life, to the yoke of faith and the plough of holy conversation.

Very many gathered together at such a sight as this, and were astonished at so unwonted a miracle. But the Saint opened his mouth and taught them, saying: "Men, brethren, why wonder ye at beholding this word? Believe me, before man became disobedient to his Maker, not only all the animals, but also all the elements, were obedient to him. But now, because of his transgression, all things are wont to be against him, for the lion to tear, the wolf to devour, the serpent to wound, water to drown, fire to burn, the air to taint, and the earth often made like iron to overwhelm with famine. And in rivalry of this wonted evil, man not only of his own accord rages against man, but man himself, by sinning against himself, also rageth against himself. But since many saints were found perfect in true innocence, in pure obedience, faith, and love, in holiness and in righteousness before the Lord, they obtained again from the Lord this power, as an ancient and natural and primordial right, and with authority commanded the beasts and elements the diseases and deaths of many."

While the holy man said many other things of this kind, those who were present were not less edified by his discourse than they were before astonished by the miracle they had seen. When the field which had been ploughed required to be sown, the Saint sought seed and found none, since all his grain had been used as food for the poor. Whereupon he betook himself to his accustomed weapons of prayer, and in faith, nothing doubting, took up sand instead of seed, and scattered it on the ground. This being done, in due season the herb grew, the seed sprouted, the blade produced the stock, and in the time of harvest brought forth the best and richest wheat, at which all who saw and heard were struck with the utmost astonishment, and his fame already great became much greater. Truly this Saint, in the power of that Grain of Wheat, which falling into the earth and dying and by rising again, brought forth much fruit, gathered corn from the sand which was sown. Moreover, he hid in the bowels of Holy Mother Church, as in the best ground, broken up by the ploughshare of the gospel, many, yea, an innumerable multitude, who were before unstable in mind and carried about by every wind of false doctrine, whose folly was heavier than the sand of the sea, and caused them, with the co-operation of God, to bring forth the corn of salvation in faith and in charity and in the performance of good works, and the Chief Householder himself deemed them worthy to be translated to the heavenly barns and fit for His own table.

CHAPTER XXI.

How St. Kentigern, assisted by Divine aid, and causing the force of the river Clyde to serve him, without any detriment transferred the barns of the King, which were full of wheat, to his own dwelling-place.

AFTER the lapse of many days, a certain tyrant, by name Morken, had ascended the throne of the Cambrian Kingdom, whom power, honour, and riches had persuaded to walk in matters which were great and strange and above him. But his heart, as, on the one hand, it was lifted up with pride, so, on the other, it was contracted and blinded by greed. The life and doctrine of the man of God he scorned and despised, slandering him in secret and sometimes withstanding him to his face, ascribing his signs to magical illusions, and esteeming all he did as nothing. But the man of God, when on a certain occasion he was in need of corn for the food of the brethren of the monastery, went to the King, and gently hinting at the poverty of himself and his disciples, desired him to come to their aid, and, according to the injunction of the Apostle, out of his abundance to supply their need. But he, elated and inflated, returned insults for prayers and threatened injuries to him who begged assistance. Then with a blasphemous mouth he ironically said to him : "Cast thy care upon the Lord and He will sustain thee, as thou hast often advised others, for there is no want to them that fear Him, but they that seek the Lord shall not want any good thing. Thou, therefore, though thou fearest God and keepest His commandments, art in need of everything, even of thy necessary food. But I, who seek not the kingdom of God nor His righteousness—to me are added all good things, and plenty of every kind smiles upon me." Finally he said: "Thy faith therefore is vain, and thy preaching false."

But the holy man, arguing on the other side, proved from the testimonies of the Holy Scriptures and from the instructive declarations of reason, and by examples, that many just and holy men were in many ways in this life afflicted with thirst and want, and that reprobates were exalted by opulence, affluence of delights, and the highest honours. And when with power and clearness he taught that the poor would be the patrons of the rich by whose benefits they are sustained, and that the rich need the support and protection of the poor as the vine that of the elm, the barbarian was unable to resist his wisdom and the Spirit who spoke through him, but angrily responded : "What more dost thou desire ? If, trusting in thy God, thou canst without human hand transfer to thy house all my corn which is contained in my barns which thou seest, I willingly yield and bestow it upon thee, and for the rest I will be devoutly obedient to your demands."

As he said this he retired joyfully, as one who by such an answer had mocked the holy man. But when the evening was come, the Saint, with his eyes and hands raised to heaven and weeping profusely, prayed very devoutly to the Lord. In the very hour when from the inmost depths of the Saint's soul tears rose up and flowed from his eyes, the river Clyde, which flowed beneath him, by the will of Him who has power in heaven and on earth, in the sea and in all deep places, suddenly came down and became swollen, and overpassing its banks flowed round the barns which stood there, and licking them up drew them into its channel, and swiftly transported them to dry land at a place called Mellingdenor, where the Saint was at that time in the habit of residing. Then the river at once ceased from its fury, and broke down within itself its swelling waves, because the Lord placed gates and bars that they should not advance further nor pass beyond their appointed bounds. These barns were found there whole and uninjured, and not only not a sheaf, but not even a blade appeared to have been wetted. Lo! in this, though in a different element, we see the sign repeated which we read of as having already been wrought in the Chaldaean furnace, into which the three children, free in their religion, but otherwise bound, were cast. For as there the fire had power to burn only their bonds, not their bodies or their clothes, so here, water was able to transpose the barns filled with corn, but not to wet them. When the multitude had seen that in the name of the Lord His servant had wrought so great a sign, they said: "Truly great is the Lord, and greatly to be praised, who has thus caused His Saint to be magnified."

CHAPTER XXII.

How the aforesaid King Morken, at the instigation of his military follower Cathen, struck S. Kentigern with his foot, and with what punishment both of them were visited.

AFTER the current of the river had, by thus carrying across the fruits of the earth, made glad the city of God, in which those who had been enrolled as fellow citizens of the Saints and of the household of God were assembled together to serve the living God, that faithful and wise servant, made steward in the house of the Great Householder, distributed the measure of wheat to each of his fellow servants, dividing to every one according to his need. What was over he dispersed abroad and gave to the poor; nor did he send any needy one who begged empty away. But the aforesaid King Morken, though very rich and great in the eyes of men, yet being a vile slave of Mammon, bore ill the loss, as it seemed to him, of his stock of corn, and from the sign which had happened to him by the will of heaven, whence he ought to have had joy and gladness to his own advantage, he took scandal to his soul. Just as the solar ray is pleasant and delightful to healthy eyes and lends its aid to their sight, yet ministers the material of darkness to the diseased and to those under the influence of hemlock ; therefore his eye being consumed because of his fury, he belched forth many reproaches against the holy bishop, calling him a magician and a sorcerer. And he commanded that if ever he appeared again in his presence, he should suffer the heaviest penalties as one who had ridiculed him. For a certain very wicked man who was the King's confidential friend, Cathen by name, had urged him on to hatred and injury of the bishop, because the life of the good is wont to be hateful and burdensome to the wicked, and the mind inclined to evil readily yields to one who persuades it to that which it embraces. For an impious leader, according to Scripture, has all his servants wicked, and very often chooses such for his counsellors, as pour venomous whispers into ears which willingly listen to unjust things, and diligently blow up the fire of malice with the breath of accusations, adding fuel to make the flame burn higher, so that it does not die away of itself, but rages the more fiercely. But the man of God, wishing to extinguish malice by wisdom, approached the presence of the Prince in the spirit of meekness rather than with the rod of severity ; and, instructing and warning him after the manner of a most gentle father, sought to correct the folly of a son. For he knew that by the melodies of the sweetly sounding harp of David the madness of Saul had been allayed, and that, according to the sentence of Solomon, the King's wrath is appeased by patience. But the man of Belial, like the deaf adder that stoppeth her ears lest she should hear the voice of the charmer, charm he never so wisely, yielded not to the warning word, the counsel of safety. Nay, excited by fiercer madness, he rushed upon him, struck him with his heel, and smote him to the ground upon his back. But the Saint, that his doctrine might be known by his patience among the bystanders, bore most patiently the hurt and the ignominy, committed his cause to the vindication of the Supreme Judge, and so departed from the presence of this sacrilegious King, rejoicing that he was deemed worthy to suffer reproach for the word of the Lord. Cathen, the instigator of this sacrilege, mounted his horse, laughing loudly, and departed full of joy, as one who seemed to himself to have triumphed over the Saint. But behold judgment went forth from the face of the Lord to do justice on behalf of his servant who had suffered injury. He had not gone far from the crowd assembled in the place when the prancing steed on which he sat, struck its foot on I know not what stumbling-block, fell down, and its rider, falling backwards before the gate of his lord, broke the neck which he had raised so proudly against the Lord's bishop, and expired. Also a swelling attacked the feet of the King, pain followed the swelling, and death the pain. He died in the royal town, which is called after his name, Thorp-Morken, and was buried. Nevertheless, the disease was not cut off or buried in the succession of his family. For, from the beginning of that time forward, the weakness ceased not, gout became hereditary in his family, and his descendants take after him, though not in look or habit of body, yet in this kind of disease. For the fact that this royal race has become extinct through this kind of disease, proclaims by the witness of death how the Lord, who is zealous for His own and the avenger of such, visits the sins of the fathers upon the children for many generations, and how great the retribution is which he inflicts upon the proud. After this the Saint dwelt for many days in great quietude in his city of Glasgow and in his own diocese, and had peace in the circuit thereof, because the divine vengeance which had been shown forth upon his persecutors, ministered to others motives of fear, reverence, love, and obedience towards the Saint of God, and afforded him the opportunity of doing whatever he wished according to the will of God.

CHAPTER XXIII.

How S. Kentigern, avoiding the snares of those who lay in wait for his death, departed from the borders of his own country, and went to S. David, who was dwelling in Wales.

AFTER some time had elapsed, certain sons of Belial, a generation of vipers, of the kindred of the above-named King Morken, incited by the sting of intense hatred, and infected with the poison of the devil, took counsel together to take Kentigern by craft, and to put him to death. But, fearing the people, they did not dare to go about that evil deed openly, because all held him as their teacher, and as the bishop and shepherd of their souls, and loved him as an angel of light and peace. Frequently they laid many snares for him in order that they might suddenly shoot their arrows against him, but the Lord became unto him a strong tower, that his enemies, the children of iniquity, might not prevail against him. At last they bound themselves by a strong oath not to cease until they had accomplished the wicked compact in which they had conspired against his life, nor through fear of any one to fail in one unjust or treacherous word they had resolved upon against him. When the man of God learned this, although he might have repelled force with force, he thought it better for a time to leave the place and give place to wrath, and to seek elsewhere a richer harvest of souls, rather than to bear about with him a conscience seared as with a hot iron, or even darkened on account of the death of any man, however wicked. For the blessed Paul, the chosen vessel, gave him an example of acting in the same way, when at Damascus he saw a death without fruit hanging over him, and sought the basket and rope to escape and avoid it, and yet afterwards at Rome joyfully submitted to it with great gain.

At length, taught by divine revelation, he departed from those regions, and journeyed towards Wales, where at that time the holy bishop David was shining forth in his episcopal work like the star of the morning, when, with its rosy face, it brings in the day. Wheresoever the Saint went, virtue went forth of him to the healing of very many. And when he had come to Carlisle he heard that many in the mountains were given to idolatry or were ignorant of the Divine Law. Thither he turned, and God helping him and confirming the word with signs following, he converted to the Christian religion many who were alien from the faith and others who had erred in the faith. O, how beautiful upon these mountains were the feet of him that brought good tidings, that published peace, that brought good tidings of good, that published salvation, that saith unto Zion, Thy God reigneth. He tarried some time in a certain thickly crowded place to confirm and strengthen in the faith the men who were dwelling there, where he also erected a cross as the sign of their salvation, from which the place received in English the name of Crosfeld, that is, Crucis Novale. In this same locality a basilica, which has recently been built, is dedicated to the name of the Blessed Kentigern ; and in order that he might show forth his sanctity, he is not doubted to have shone forth in many miracles.

Departing from this place, the Saint next directed his steps along the sea-shore, and scattering the seed of the Divine Word wherever he journeyed, he gathered a great and fruitful harvest in the Lord. At length he reached S. David, safe and sound, and found in him greater works than fame reported. But the holy bishop David rejoiced with exceeding joy at the arrival of such and so great a guest. With eyes overflowing with tears, and with many mutual embraces, he received Kentigern as an angel of the Lord, dear to God, and retaining him with him for some time, he always honoured him to a wonderful extent. These two sons of light, therefore, dwelt together, attending upon the Lord of the whole earth, as two lamps shining before the Lord, whose tongues became the keys of heaven, that by them a multitude of men might be deemed meet to enter therein. These Saints were joined opposite to each other as the two cherubims in the Holy of Holies in the temple of the Lord, having their faces bent down towards the mercy-seat. In frequent contemplation of heavenly things they stretched out their wings on high ; in the ordering and dispensing of earthly things they folded them down. They touched each other mutually with their wings, while, by the instruction of each other in the doctrine of salvation, and in the alternate exercise of virtues, they excited each other to the more earnest perfecting of holiness. Thus these Saints, whether beside themselves unto God, or whether sober for our cause, they have left to posterity an example of laying hold on and attaining to eternal life.

When S. Kentigern had abode there for some time, the fame of him spread through the mouths and ears of very many, and led him to the acquaintance, familiarity, and friendship of many, not only of the poor and middle class and nobility of that land, but also of King Cathwallain, who governed the country. And the King, knowing him to be a holy and righteous man, heard him willingly, and after hearing him did many things which pertained to the salvation of his soul. And when the King on several occasions asked him the reasons why he had left his own country, and he had made them known to him, and said that he wished to have the power of building a monastery in which he might unite a people acceptable to God, and zealous of good works, the King replied: " My land is before thee ; wherever it suits thee and it seems good in thine eyes, construct the habitation of thy dwelling-place and build a monastery. Yet, as it seems to me that the place which is called Nautcharvan is more suitable than all others, inasmuch as it abounds in everything necessary, I assign it to thee." The man of God gave frequent thanks to the King, and chose for his building and habitation that place which had even already been marked out for him by a divine intimation. Therefore, blessing the King, he departed, and bidding farewell to S. David, each bestowing upon the other his benediction, he betook himself to the aforesaid place with a great multitude of disciples, who had flocked around him, preferring to lead a life of poverty with him in a strange land rather than to live luxuriously without him in their own.

CHAPTER XXIV.

How S. Kentigern, following a wild boar, found a suitable place.

THUS the most holy Kentigern, separated from S. David in bodily presence but by no means absent from his love, and from the vision and observation of the inward man, gave no sound sleep to his eyes, nor quiet rest to his eyelids, until he found a place fit for building a tabernacle to the Lord God of Jacob. Therefore, with a great crowd of disciples with him, he went round the land, and walked through it, exploring the situations of the places, the quality of the air, the richness of the soil, and the sufficiency of the meadows, and pastures, and woods, and the other matters which pertain to suitability for the erection of a monastery. And while they proceeded together over steep mountains, hollow valleys, and caves of the earth, through thickets of briers, dark woods, and open glades in the forests, they talked together as they went of the things which pertained to the matter they had in hand, when lo! a solitary wild boar from the wood, entirely white, met them, and approaching the feet of the Saint, moving its head, sometimes advancing a little, and then standing still and looking back, motioned to the Saint and his companions with such gesture as it could that they should follow it. On seeing this they marvelled and glorified God, who works things marvellous and past finding out in His creatures, and followed step by step their leader, the boar, which went before them.

When they came to the place which the Lord had predestinated for them, the boar stood still, and frequently striking the ground with its foot, and making the gesture of tearing up with its long tusk the soil of the little hill that was there, by shaking its head again and again and grunting, it showed clearly to all that that was the place designed and prepared for them by God. The place is situated on the bank of the river which is called Elgu, from which to this day, as it is said, the district takes its name. Then the Saint, on bended knees, giving thanks adored the Almighty Lord, and rising from prayer, he blessed the place and its surroundings in the name of the Lord ; and then, in testimony, and as the sign of salvation and as an earnest of future religion, he there erected a cross and pitched his tents. The boar, however, seeing what was done, approached with frequent grunts as if about to request something from the bishop. But the Saint, scratching the head of the beast, and stroking his mouth and teeth, said : "God Almighty, in whose power are all beasts of the forests —the oxen, the fowls of the air, and the fish of the sea—grant thee such reward for thy conduct as He knoweth is best for thee." Then the boar, as if well remunerated, bowed its head to the priest of the Lord, departed, and sought again its well-known woods.

On the following night, when the man of God, yearning after divine things, lifted up his hands in the sanctuary and blessed the Lord, it was revealed to him from on high that he should dwell in that place, and that he should there construct a monastery in which the sons of God, who were scattered abroad, might be gathered into one, so that coming from the east and from the west, and from the north and from the south, they might be deemed meet to sit down with Abraham, Isaac, and Jacob in the kingdom of heaven, and that God Himself would provide for them, and be the protector of the place and of them that dwelt therein. With what truth this revelation was sustained, the issue of events by its manifest fulfilment showed. For at the dawn of day he made known to others the oracle which had been divinely shown to him, and cheered on the souls of those who heard him to set about the building. For, like bees making honey, they did not slumber in ease, but all in the sweat of their brow laboured strenuously at the work. Some cleared and levelled the ground; others, when the ground was levelled, laid the foundations. Some felling trees, others carrying them, others fitting them together, they began, as the father had marked out for them by measurement, to build a church and the other offices of planed wood, after the manner of the Britons, for of stone they were not yet able to build, nor was it then the custom.

While they were pressing on the work, and the building was growing under their hands, there came a certain heathen prince,

Melconde Galganu by name, with his soldiers, and a great multitude with them. A fierce man and ignorant of God, in the indignation of his wrath he demanded who and whence they were, and how they had dared to presume to do such things upon his land. To his questions the Saint humbly replied, that they were Christians from the northern parts of Britain, and were come thither to serve the living and true God. He asserted that he had begun to build the house there by the permission, yea, rather through the kindness, of King Cathwalain, his master, in whose possession he believed the place lay. But he, furious and raging, ordered them all to be driven away from the place, and whatever they had built to be pulled down and scattered, and then began to return to his own house. Thus the man departed, breathing out threatenings against the servants of Christ, and lo! the chastening hand of the Lord touched him, and smote him with a sudden blindness. Nevertheless, as was clear in the end, this happened to him not for foolishness to himself; for, while he sat in the utter darkness, the true morning star shone into his heart, and when the outward light was for a time taken away, drew him out of the darkness and shadow of death and led him with the light of truth. Wherefore inwardly enlightened and induced by penitence, he caused himself to be conveyed by his servants to the man of God, whom he began to entreat devoutly to dispel the blindness by his prayers, and wash him in the font of salvation.

Then the Saint who studied not to be overcome by evil, but to overcome evil with good, desired to render to the man good for evil. For having offered up prayer, he laid his healing hand upon the blinded man in the name of the Lord, and signing him with the cross of salvation, both turned his night into day, and again, after darkness, poured into him the light he hoped for and eagerly desired. Thus the Lord smote that He might heal, and making the new Paul out of the old Saul, He blinded that He might give light. Immediately, therefore, on receiving his sight, he was washed by the holy bishop in the saving water, and thenceforward he was an active and devoted fellow-worker in all that he desired of him. Taking an account of all things in his possession, he bestowed them with royal munificence on S. Kentigern for the construction of his monastery, and, aided by his assistance, he speedily brought the work he had begun to completion. In the church of the monastery he established the Cathedral Chair of his bishopric, the diocese of which was the greater part of the adjacent country, which by his preaching he won for the Lord. In truth, he led back to the way of salvation a countless number who were either ignorant of the Christian faith or averse from it, or had been depraved by profane teaching, or debased by wicked works; and, by his labours, made vessels of wrath vessels of mercy, and vessels of dishonour vessels of glory. For he went forth from his monastery to perform the episcopal office, travelling through his diocese as time permitted. But, as he never found where the foot of his desire might long rest, as the dove to the ark from the face of the deluge of the world, so he returned to the beloved quiet of his monastery. Yet he bore with him the olive branch with its green leaves, because he received the fruit of the peace and mercy he preached to others.

CHAPTER XXV.

With what number of brethren the monastery flourished, and how the holy boy Asaph carried fire without being burnt.

THERE flocked to the monastery of the man of God old and young, rich and poor, to take upon them the easy yoke and the light burden of the Lord. Nobles and men of the middle class brought their children to the Saint to be brought up in the nurture of the Lord. The multitude of those who renounced the world increased from day to day both in number and quality, so that the number of those who enlisted in the army of God amounted to nine hundred and sixty-five, who professed in act and manner the monastic rule according to the institution of the holy man. He divided this company, which had been gathered and devoted to the divine service, into a threefold division for the observances of religion. To three hundred, who were illiterate, he assigned the duty of tilling the ground, herding the cattle, and other necessary labours outside the monastery. Another three hundred he appointed to duties within the walls of the monastery, such as preparing food and building the offices. The remaining three hundred and sixty, who were lettered, he appointed to celebrate the divine services in the church day and night; nor did he readily allow any of them to cross the threshold from the holy places, but directed them to remain together within as if in the sanctuary of the Lord. Those whom he found to be more advanced in holiness and wisdom, and apt for the teaching of others, he was accustomed to take with him when, from necessity demanding or reason requiring, it behoved him to go forth for the discharge of his episcopal duties. But, dividing into bands and choirs those whom he had set free for the divine service, he ordained that when one choir finished the service of God in the church, another immediately entering should begin it, and when that had finished, another should thereupon enter to celebrate. Thus the sacred choirs being conveniently and discreetly arranged, and following each other in turns, while he performed the work of God continually, prayer was regularly made to God without ceasing by the Church there, and by praising the Lord at every time, the praise of God was continually resounding in their mouth. Truly, glorious things were said in and of that City of God, for in it was the habitation of all who were joyful, so might fittingly be said of it that prophecy of Balaam: "How goodly are thy tents, O Jacob! and thy tabernacles, O Israel. As the valleys are they spread forth as gardens by the river's side."

There flourished in that glorious monastery men holy and perfect, shining wrestlers, like Jacob, against the world, the flesh, and the devil. By faith, love, contemplation, yearning intently after the vision of God, like true Israelites, fruitful in good works, humble in their own eyes, and therefore as well-wooded valleys fragrant with holy thought and bathed in rivers of Scripture, and thus also, like the cedars beside the waters, glorious in all those many virtues and signs. Among them was one Asaph by name, distinguished by birth and presence, shining in virtues and miracles from the flower of his earliest youth. He sought to follow the life and teaching of his master, as may be learnt more fully by reading a little book of his Life, from which I have thought fit to insert in this work one miracle, because the perfection of the disciple is the glory of the master. For on one occasion, in the time of winter, when the frost had contracted and congealed everything, S. Kentigern, having according to his custom recited the Psalter naked in the coldest water, and having after putting on his clothes gone out in public, he began to be greatly oppressed by the intensity of the cold, and in a manner to become entirely rigid, so that it was clearly given to be understood what was of himself and what was of the power of the divine condescension. For, since when naked in the water, he endured for so long a space the icy cold without being frozen, it is clear that in the frail vessel of his human body divine virtue operated, and in the fact that he became rigid, though clad in skins and other garments, human fraility is recognised. The holy father therefore ordered the boy Asaph to bring fire to him, at which he might warm himself. The Lord's child ran to the oven and begged that coals might be given to him. And when he had nothing in which to carry the burning coals, the servant said to him either in joke or seriously: "If thou wish to take the coals, spread out thy dress, for I have nothing at hand in which thou mayest carry them." The holy boy, fervent in faith, and trusting in the sanctity of the master, without hesitating, having gathered up his dress, held it out, and received into his lap the live coals, and carrying them to the old man cast them forth in his sight from his bosom, without any sign of burning or corruption being apparent on his dress. The greatest astonishment, therefore, took hold upon all who were present because the fire carried in the dress had not in the least burnt combustible material. A friendly dispute arose between the father and his holy disciple concerning this sign, for the one seemed to maintain his ground by assertions to which the other as justly objected. The bishop ascribed the working of the sign to the innocence and obedience of the holy boy; the boy asserted that it was done on account of the merits and sanctity of the bishop, obeying whose command and trusting in whose holiness he had ventured to attempt it. And indeed, without prejudice, I think that this miracle is more correctly to be attributed to the merits of each wise one, inasmuch as each of them had always from his earliest years preserved the members of his body, which are the garment of the soul, white in virgin chastity, and because the oil of divine charity was never wanting from the head of either. The dress of the disciple suffered neither hurt nor injury from the fire in order that the integrity of both might be rightly made manifest. For if the fire of unchaste love had been hid in their bosoms, their clothes, according to the words of Solomon, would have been burnt. And if their garments had been rolled in blood, that is, if the members of their bodies had been stained with the pollution of prurient lust from the will of the flesh or of blood, doubtless, according to Isaiah, it would have been the presage of burning and the fuel of fire. S. Kentigern, therefore, who up to this time had held the venerable boy Asaph dear and beloved, from that day henceforward regarded him as the dearest and best loved of all, and as soon as he conveniently could, raised him to holy orders. In due season, moreover, he delegated to him the care of the monastery, and made him his successor in the episcopate, as we shall hereafter relate.

CHAPTER XXVI.

How he saw S. David crowned in heaven by the Lord, and what he predicted concerning Britain.

ON a certain occasion, while the man of God continued longer and more intently in prayer than was usual with him, his face seemed as if glowing with fire, so that the bystanders were filled with amazement and ecstasy. They beheld his countenance as the countenance of an angel standing among them, and as they saw his face shining as the face of another Moses, wonder and amazement took hold upon them all. When his prayer was finished, he withdrew apart and sat down and gave himself up to the most vehement grief. His disciples, knowing that his grief would not be without great cause, drew near to him with fear and trembling, and humbly besought him, if it were permissible and not displeasing to his paternity, to reveal to them the cause of such great grief. The Saint was silent for a little, but as they perseveringly knocked at the ears of that most pious father, he at length gave way, and responded in these words: "Be it known to you, my dearest sons, that the most holy David, the honour of Britain, the father of his country, the most precious carbuncle of prelates, has just left the prison of the flesh, and rich in merits has been introduced among the splendours of the saints, and penetrated into the Holy of Holies. I say unto you, believe me, that not only has a multitude of holy angels, flooded with light, conducted him as he entered with heavenly music into the joy of the Lord, but the Lord Jesus Christ Himself, meek and lowly in heart, went forth, as I saw, to meet him at the gates of Paradise, and crowned him with glory and honour. Behold, like a matchless light to his generation, and a most brilliant star which shone by word and example, he has become present to him who under his charge calls upon him that he may shine with delight for Him who made him, and assist all who ask his protection, seek his help, and celebrate his sacred memory. And truly, dearest ones, it behoves me to rejoice in the glory of such a father, who loved us beyond others, but the ardent affection of devoted love permits me not to abstain from tears. Know that the world of Britain, deprived of such a light, of a patron so devoted, and of one so powerful before God and with all the people, will feel the absence of him, who ever placed himself between that region and the sword of the Lord, half-drawn on account of the wickedness of those who dwell therein, lest when entirely drawn it should smite even to destruction. The Lord will surely deliver Britain up to strange nations who know not God, pagans in religion, and the island will be emptied of its original inhabitants, and the religion of the Christian law there is in it will be scattered until the appointed time ; but again, by the mercy of God, the Ruler of all things, Christianity shall be restored to its former state, yea to a better." These things the Saint said and was silent ; fear seized upon all who heard him, and the shower of their tears poured forth. But desiring to be further informed on this matter, they quickly sent a messenger to the church over which S. David presided as bishop, and they found that the Saint of God had passed away from this world in that same hour in which the man of the Lord, instructed by a divine oracle, had announced it to them. In this matter it must be considered how great was the merit of that man in the sight of God, who beholding not with the eye of flesh but by the vision of the heart, was deemed meet to see such glory, and delivered so true a prophecy concerning the Britons and the Angles, which all England was able, by a faith which sees, to verify.

CHAPTER XXVII.

How S. Kentigern went seven times to Rome and consulted the blessed Gregory concerning his orders.

THE blessed Kentigern, knowing that Britain was smitten in in many provinces by the Gentiles, and that the Church of God established therein was in many ways perverted from the faith of Christ by idolaters, and divided ; discovering, moreover, that it was frequently assailed by heretics, and that there were many things contrary to sound doctrine and alien from the integrity of the faith of our Holy Mother, the Catholic Church, deliberated within himself for a long time what remedy he could apply for all these evils. He resolved at last to visit the seat of S. Peter, which was founded on a rock, and that the tares might not grow up among the wheat, he endeavoured by means of the sound teaching of the Holy Roman Church, and through the knowledge of the articles of the faith, to cast away from his mind every scruple of doubt, so that he might arrive by careful investigation at the light of the truth. For Britain, during the reign of the most holy King Lucius, had received, under the papacy of Eleutherius, the faith of Christ through the preaching of the most excellent teachers, Faganus and Divianus, and others, whom Gildas the Wise, the historian of the Britains, commemorates ; and the Christianity thus received, it preserved whole and undefiled down to the time of the Emperor Diocletian. Then the moon was turned into blood, and the flame of persecution against the Christians burnt brightly through the whole world. Then that scourge inundated Britain and vehemently oppressed it, and a pagan hand mowing the firstfruits of that island, namely Alban, took him out of the midst thereof to be recorded in the Book of the Eternal King ; and shortly after innumerable others, voluntarily and in ignorance, it also offered up to heaven.

From that time the worship of the idols began to spread in the island, and brought in rejection and forgetfulness of the Divine Law. Nevertheless, after this Christianity in some way revived and flourished. But in process of time, first the Pelagian heresy springing up, and then the Arian creeping in, defiled the face of the Catholic Faith. Yet it renewed itself, and again grew when these heresies were cut down and cast out by S. Germanus, Bishop of Auxerre, a man truly Apostolic, and made illustrious by many signs ; but the invasion of the neighbouring Picts and Scots, hostile to the recognition of the name of Christ, entirely drove away the faith and the faithful from the northern parts of Britain.

Afterwards, Britain was conquered by the Angles, who were at that time pagans, after whom it was called Anglia. By them the natives were driven out, and the land was made subject to idols and idolatry. The natives of the island, however, fled beyond the sea into Little Britain or into Wales, and though driven from their own country they did not all altogether abandon their faith. But the Picts, first chiefly through S. Ninian, and afterwards through S. Kentigern and S. Columba, received the faith. Then relapsing into apostasy, through the preaching of S. Kentigern not only the Picts but also the Scots and innumerable people settled in divers parts of Britain, were again, as we have already said, and as we shall say more at length, either converted or confirmed in the faith.

S. Augustine, however, noted for his monastic life and habit, and other religious servants of God, who were sent by the Supreme Pontiff, the blessed Gregory, came to Anglia, and being rich in showers of preaching and glittering with the lightning of miracles, either by themselves or by means of their disciples, converted the whole island to Christ, instructed them fully in the rules of the faith and in the institutes of the Holy Fathers, and filled the whole land of Anglia with the sweet savour of Christ.

Because therefore Britain had been crushed by so many misfortunes, and because Christianity had so often been obscured or even destroyed in it, there had arisen in it at divers times divers rules contrary to the form of the Holy Roman Church and the decrees of the Holy Fathers. In order, therefore, that he might learn and be able to meet and remedy all these, the blessed Kentigern left the abovementioned monastery, visited Rome seven times, and brought home what he there learned was needed for the correction of Britain. But as he returned the seventh time to his fatherland, a most grievous malady seized him, and he reached home with the greatest difficulty.

On one occasion he visited Rome when the blessed Gregory was presiding in the Apostolic seat, a man apostolic by office, authority, doctrine, life, and the special Apostle of Anglia, for the Angles are the signs of his Apostleship. As a vessel of solid gold adorned with all manner of precious stones, he was rightly called the Golden Mouth, for when expounding he elucidated many parts of Scripture by his clear and highly polished style. His memory is as the work of the apothecary in making up an unguent, and as music at a banquet of wine. For by his mellifluous writings and the hymns which he composed according to the laws of music, he gladdened, and by his canonical institutions he strengthened and adorned the House of God, the Holy Church scattered throughout the world. To this most holy Chief Pontiff he laid bare his whole life, and set before him in order his election to the episcopacy and consecration, and all things that had happened to him. But the holy Pope, strong in the spirit of counsel and discretion, as filled with the Holy Ghost, and knowing him to be a man of God and full of the grace of the Holy Ghost confirmed his election and consecration, because he knew that both had come from God. And on the bishop on many occasions seeking it, and with difficulty obtaining it, he supplied the things which were wanting to his consecration, and set him apart to the work of the ministry which had been laid upon him by the Holy Ghost. The holy bishop Kentigern having received the Apostolic absolution and benediction, returned home, bringing with him precepts, codes of the canons, and many other books of Holy Scripture, as well as privileges and many relics of the saints, ornaments of the Church, and other things which belong to the adornment of the House of God. And he gladdened his own by his return, both by religious gifts and blessings. He dwelt there for some time in great peace and [holy] conversation, and ruled holily and firmly both his see and his monastery with great care.

CHAPTER XXVIII.

What he knew, by revelation of the Spirit, of two clerics, and what happened to them according to his prediction.

IT came to pass that the holy president had to confer sacred orders by ordaining clergy and promoting some to the priestly office. Among others, there was brought to him for promotion to the priesthood, a certain cleric of elegant appearance, great eloquence, and much learning, a Briton by birth, but educated among the Gauls. When the Saint saw him, he summoned the archdeacon, and ordered him to be immediately removed and separated from the clergy. For to the eyes of the Saint, as it were, a sulphurous flame seemed to proceed from the bosom of this cleric, and to assail his nostrils with an unbearable stench. By this vision, revealed to him by the Holy Spirit, he was made aware of the vice which reigned in his body. For he was, as was then made known to the man of God alone, but afterwards to all others, addicted to that most foul crime for which the Divine vengeance overthrew and destroyed with fire and brimstone the sons of unbelief in the Five Cities. And the Saint said to those around him: "If the sacred canons forbid women on account of the infirmity of their sex, which is no wise in blame, to be promoted to the rank of the priesthood, much more are we bound to banish from a rank and office so sacred men who are perverters of their own sex, abusers of nature, who, in contempt of the Creator, in degradation of themselves, in injury of all creatures, cast off that in which they are created and born, and become as women. Nowhere do we read of a heavier penalty being decreed than against that monstrous race of men among whom that execrable crime was first conceived. Not only did it overthrow those cities with their inhabitants with fire, on acccunt of the burning of libidinous passion, and with brimstone because of the stench of that abominable sin, but it also turned them into a lake horrid to the sight, full of brimstone and bitumen, and intolerable stench, receiving nothing living into itself, having indeed on its shores trees that produce fruits outwardly sound, but inwardly full of smoke and ashes, and presenting an image of the punishments of hell. And this indeed shows distinctly enough how horrible so dreadful a pleasure is, and how it ought to be avoided by all in this life, and with what torments it will be visited in the future; while the fire expresses the heat of the passion, the brimstone the stench of the crime, the bitumen the bondage of the vice, the smoke the blindness of heart in this world, and in the world to come the unquenchable fire, the intolerable stench, the indissoluble chains, the horror of darkness, everlasting death." After this the aforesaid cleric went his own way, and, as fame has noised abroad, died, cut off by a sudden death.

But when the holy man had finished the office, and was returning, there met him, among others, a cleric, a most eloquent foreigner. Beholding him the man of God gazed at him with burning eye and asked who he was, whence he came, and for what purpose he had come into those parts. He replied that he was a preacher of the truth, teaching the way of God in truth, and asserted that he had come into those parts for the salvation of souls. But when the Saint had conversed with him, he convicted him of being intoxicated with the poison of the Pelagian pestilence. Willing, therefore, that he should return rather than perish, he earnestly warned and reasoned with him to renounce the pernicious sect, but found his heart stony as to conversion. Then the Saint ordered him to be expelled from his diocese, and denounced him as a son of death, and that the death of body and soul was in his gates. He remembered also the saying of the Apostle: "A man that is a heretic after the second admonition, reject; knowing that he that is such is subverted." The same son of hell departed, expelled from those borders, and attempting to cross a certain river, was choked in the water and descended into hell; and thus, by an evident proof, showed the exceeding trustworthiness of the veracious prophecy of the most holy man.

CHAPTER XXIX.

How the Divine vengeance smote the adversaries of S. Kentigern, and bore down upon his countrymen who had apostatised.

HITHERTO we have related, as carefully as we could, what S. Kentigern did when he withdrew from his own country and dwelt in a foreign land. Let us now turn back and show point by point what his adversaries suffered, how he returned to the Cambrian region, and what he did there. When the man of God, yielding to malice, departed, his enemies were not long suffered to rejoice over his departure. For the Lord visited them with a heavy hand and a strong arm, and with fury poured out, holding over them a rod that was vigilant for evil and not for good, smiting them with the blow of an enemy and with cruel chastisement, even to destruction. For some, darkness obscured, the gloom of blindness following ; others paralysis enervated, enfeebling all their strength, and rendering them effete as to their bodily powers. Some an incurable madness seized, and retained its hold upon them even to the grave ; others a contagious leprosy devoured or struck down, making them, as they breathed in their half-dead bodies, like unto the putrescent dead. Many of them became epileptic, and exhibited a dreadful spectacle to those who saw them. Some in one way and some in another were consumed by various kinds of incurable diseases, and died. So great was the indignation of the wrath of God, and so suddenly did He destroy them, that all who knew their power and numbers before, hissed over at them, saying : " Wherefore hath the Lord done thus to this people? since lo! they have suddenly come to an end and perished on account of the iniquity which they wrought against the holy one of the Lord, striving to take away from the earth his life and memory."

Even his countrymen quickly abandoned the way of the Lord, which the good shepherd and true teacher had shown them ; and, as dogs returned to their vomit, had relapsed into the rites of idolatry. But not with impunity. For the heavens and the earth, the sea and all that is therein, withdrew from them their obedience, use, and wonted aid, so that, according to the Scripture, the whole world seemed to fight against these foolish ones, and the elements were thought unable to bear with equanimity the absence of so great a man when banished from that land. For, according to that prophecy, "All men departed, all the cattle died, the heaven above was as brass, the earth as iron, devouring the inhabitants thereof, and a consuming famine prevailed for a long time over all the earth."

But when the time came for having mercy, that the Lord might remove from them the rod of his indignation, and that they might be converted to the Lord, and that He should heal them, He raised up over the Cambrian kingdom a King Rederech by name, a most Christian King, who had been baptized into the faith in Ireland by the disciples of S. Patrick, and who sought the Lord with his whole heart, and endeavoured to restore Christianity. And truly it is a great sign of the Divine pity when the Lord ordains for the government of the holy Church and for the dominion of the earth, rulers and kings who judge righteously and live holily, who seek the good of their people, who execute judgment and justice in the earth. So, moreover, on the other hand, it is an evident proof of the wrath of God when He causes a hypocrite to reign because of the sins of a people, when He calls the King apostate and the rulers unjust, as it is written in the book of Job, and when, according to the prophet, He gives kings in his wrath and princes in his anger.

CHAPTER XXX.

How holy Rederech invited S. Kentigern by messengers and letters to return to his own see in Glasgow, and how the holy prelate, taught by a divine oracle, acquiesced in the petition of the King.

KING REDERECH, therefore, seeing that the Christian religion was almost entirely destroyed in his kingdom, anxiously considered how he might restore it. And after deliberating about it for a long time in his own mind, and with other Christians who were in his confidence, he found no plan by which it would more surely be brought about than to send messengers to S. Kentigern to recall him to his first see. The fame of the Saint going forth smote on the ears and mind of the King, for his light could not be hid, although it was shining in regions more remote. The King, therefore, despatched his messengers to the holy prelate with letters deprecating his refusal, warning, praying, exhorting, and adjuring him by the name of God as a shepherd no longer to withdraw his care from the sheep of his pasture, long desolate and destitute, by longer absence, lest he should expose them to be carried off and torn to pieces by the open mouth of the infernal wolf; but rather to hasten to them before they were altogether swallowed by the throat of the roaring lion seeking whom he might devour, since none but he can deliver them, and there is none more justly bound to do so. He declared that it was wrong for the spouse to desert his bride, the shepherd his flock, the prelate his church, for the love of whom he ought to lay down his life, so that he might not be a hireling. He intimated also that those who had sought his life had died by the vengeance of God, and he swore that in all things, as a son his father, he would obey his will, his teaching, his commands.

When the holy father received this he was silent, nor did he on that day return any definite answer. For he had proposed to nourish his grey hairs to the evening of his life, and to end his days in that glorious monastery which he had built with long and great labour; to lay himself down to sleep in peace, and to take his rest in the sight of them, his sons, whom he had begotten in the Gospel and brought forth in Christ. But because he sought not his own, but the things which are of Jesus Christ, and came not to do his own will but the will of Him that sent him, and desiring it to be done concerning himself in himself and towards himself, as it would be in heaven, he submitted himself entirely to the Divine disposition. And when, on the following night, he prostrated himself in prayer and consulted the Lord on the matter, the angel of the Lord stood beside him, and a light shone in the part of the oratory in which he was, and the angel smote him on the side and commanded him to arise. And when he stood up the heavenly messenger said to him: "Return to Glasgow to thy church, and there thou shalt be for a great nation, and the Lord will make thee to increase among his people. Thou shalt acquire for the Lord thy God a holy nation, an innumerable people to be won unto the Lord thy God, and from Him thou shalt receive an everlasting crown. For there thou shalt end thy days in a good old age, and shalt pass from this world to thy Father who is in heaven. Thy flesh shall rest there in hope, buried with glory and honour, much honoured by the frequent visits of the peoples, and by the exhibition of miracles, until, in the last day, by receiving a double robe at the hand of the Lord, thou possessest a double reward in the general resurrection." These words being said, the angelic vision and address ceased. But he, weeping copiously, gave thanks to the Lord, frequently groaning : " My heart is ready, O God ; my heart is ready for whatsoever may be pleasing to Thee."

CHAPTER XXXI.

How the Saint, addressing his disciples concerning his return, appointed S. Asaph as his successor in the government.

WHEN the day dawned, he assembled his disciples together, and said unto them : " I speak as a man to you, dearly beloved, I wished, after long yearning and deliberation, according to the infirmity of my flesh, these, mine aged eyes, to be closed by you, and my bones to be hidden in the womb of the mother of all in the sight of all of you. But since it is not in man to direct his steps, it has been enjoined upon me by the Lord to return to mine own church of Glasgow ; nor ought we, nor dare we, nor will we contradict the words of the Holy One, as Job saith, or in any wise go against it, but rather in all things obey His will and command, even to the end of life. You, therefore, dearly beloved, stand fast in the faith ; quit you like men, be strong, and seek always to do all your things in charity.' These and many similar things he said in their presence, and lifting up his hand he blessed them all. Then, with the unanimous consent of all, he appointed the aforesaid S. Asaph to the government of the monastery, and by petition of the people, and by canonical election of the clergy, successor of his bishopric, and again delivered a profound and lengthy sermon concerning faith and hope and charity, on mercy and justice, humility and obedience, on holy peace and mutual patience, on avoiding vice and acquiring virtue, on observing the institutes of the Holy Roman Church, on the regular discipline and exercises which he had established to be observed with all diligence, and on constancy and perseverance unto the end in all good things.

When the sermon was ended he enthroned S. Asaph in the cathedral seat, and again blessing and bidding them all farewell, he went forth by the North door of the Church, because he was going forth to combat the Northern enemy. When he had gone out that door was closed, and all who saw or heard of his going out or departure bewailed his absence with great lamentations. Hence the custom grew up in that church that that door should not be opened except once a year, on the festival of S. Asaph, that is, on the kalends of May, for two reasons. First, in deference to the sanctity of him who had gone forth; secondly, because thereby was indicated the great grief of those who had bewailed his departure. Therefore, on the day of S. Asaph that door is opened, because when he succeeded the blessed Kentigern in the government their mourning was turned into joy. From that monastery a great part of the brethren, to the number of 665, being in no wise able or willing, so long as he lived, to live without him, went with him. Only three hundred remained with S. Asaph. With such troops, as if compassed about by the host of the heavenly court, he returned to fight the old enemy, and from the ends of the North, in which the apostate angel had placed his seat, to drive him out. And truly those who accompanied him were counted by such a number, who multiplying the senary exercise of good works by fulfilling the decalogue of the Law, arrived at the centenary perfection of virtues, and maintained the quinary guard over the discipline of the senses so far as they were able.

When King Rederech and his people heard that Kentigern had come from Wallia into Cambria, from exile into his own country, the King with great joy, and a great multitude of people rejoicing and praising God, went out to meet him. On account of his arrival there sounds in the mouth of all thanksgiving and the voice of praise and gladness, while in the mouth of the holy prelate there resounded glory to God in the highest, peace on earth, and good will towards men.

CHAPTER XXXII.

Of the devils miraculously driven away, and of the place where he stood to preach, and of the fertility of the land which ensued.

BLESSED Kentigern, when he saw the concourse and approach of a great multitude hastening towards him, rejoiced in spirit, gave thanks to God, and knelt down in prayer. When he had finished praying he rose up, and, in the name of the Holy Trinity, blessed the assembled multitude. Then, as if fortifying those who stood around him with the sign of the Holy Cross, he addressed them as follows: "Whoever envy the salvation of men and oppose the word of God, I command them, by virtue of that same word of God, that they forthwith depart and present no obstacle to them that would believe." Whereupon, with exceeding speed, a vast multitude of phantoms, horrible in stature and appearance, issued out of that crowd and fled away in the sight of all, and great fear fell upon all who saw them. The holy champion, comforting and strengthening them, laid bare the natures of those in whom they had believed, and encouraged the hearts of all who stood around him to believe in the living God. For by clear reason he showed that idols are dumb, vain inventions of men, fitter for the fire than for worship. He showed, likewise, that the elements in which they believed as gods are creatures and formations adapted by the disposition of their Maker to the use, service, and help of men. But Woden, whom they, and especially the Angles, had believed to be their principal God, from whom they derived their origin, to whom they had consecrated the fourth day, he affirmed, with probability, had been a mortal man and King of the Saxons, by faith a pagan, from whom they and many nations had derived their descent. His body, he said, many years having passed, was turned into dust, and his soul, buried in hell, endures the eternal fire.

By these and similar arguments he cast out the worship of idols from their hearts, and proved to them the Almighty God, Three and One, to be the Creator of all things, from the very beauty of the visible creation; and afterwards preaching to them the faith that is in Christ Jesus and the Sacraments of the Faith, he showed by the most true and lucid demonstrations that there is none other name under heaven whereby believing men may be saved, save the name of our Lord Jesus Christ. And when, by the instruction and dictation of the Spirit, he had taught many things in this way which pertain to the Christian Faith, in the flat field which is called Hoddam, the ground on which he sat grew, in the sight of all, into a high hill, and remains there even to this day. Therefore those who had come together, beholding so sudden and so great a miracle, obeyed the word of faith in their inmost hearts, and believed firmly and faithfully that Jesus Christ is God, who had revealed Himself to them by His servant Kentigern. All eagerly therefore, both men and women, old men and young, rich and poor, as one man, flocked to the man of God and were instructed in the rules of the faith. After being catechised, they renounced Satan and all his pomps and works, and were washed in the saving laver in the name of the Holy Trinity; and so, anointed with the sacred chrism and oil, were incorporated into the body of the Church and made members of Christ.

The Bishop, therefore, rejoiced with great joy in that a great salvation had been wrought, and great happiness increased among the people ; nor was there less joy in the presence of the angels of God in heaven, because so great a multitude had been converted unto God. Appropriately by such a sign as the elevation of the mountain at the beginning of his preaching did the Lord will to magnify His saint, who, by that same preaching, did effectually bring all to believe as unto that same mountain, compacted and fruitful, in which God was well pleased to dwell. That Stone first cut from the mountain without hands grew into a great mountain, and filled the face of the whole earth, for the Omnipotent God, born of the Virgin, without human passion, clearly shone forth throughout the breadth of this world. Christ, I say, is that Mountain exalted on the top of the mountains, even the Lord Himself, who surpasses all the power and greatness of all the saints, in whose ways, paths, and light, by the instruction of Kentigern, these natives walked much more devoutly and consistently than that carnal house of Jacob, who, loving darkness rather than light, and going back from the ways of the truth, have scorned to be enlightened by the Supreme Light.

But after the inhabitants of Cambria had turned to God and were washed in the laver of salvation, all the elements which seemed to have conspired together for their ruin, to avenge the wrong done to God, now put on a new face towards them for the salvation both of their bodies and their souls. For as the Lord turned away from the apostates and opposed them by forbidding even the dew to fall, and commanded the clouds not to rain upon the earth, and summoned a devastating famine upon them, so when He turned to those who had returned to Him, He commanded the heaven to yield rain, and the earth to bring forth green herb, and to produce its fruits for those who dwelt thereon. Thus, by the Lord causing His face to shine upon them, the sun was seen to be brighter than usual, the vault of heaven clearer, the air more wholesome, the earth more fruitful, the sea calmer, the abundance of all things greater, peace surer, the aspect of all things more joyful, and therefore the devotion of all in the observance of Divine worship was more profuse.

CHAPTER XXXIII.

How King Rederech conceded to him power over himself and his posterity.

KING REDERECH, therefore, seeing that the good hand of God was with him, and was working according to his desires, was filled with great joy, and made no delay in openly showing with what great devotion he was animated. For, stripping himself of his royal robes, he, on bended knees and joined hands, with the consent and advice of his lords, did homage to S. Kentigern, and handed over to him the dominion and princedom over all his kingdom, and desired him to be the King, and himself to be appointed the ruler of the country under him, in like manner as he knew the great Emperor Constantine had formerly done to S. Silvester. Hence the custom arose that, during the course of many years, so long as the Cambrian kingdom lasted in its own right, the Prince was always subject to the Bishop. Frequently was this saying inculcated by the King that not in vain, but rather of set purpose, had he been called Kentigern by S. Servanus, because, by the will of God, he ought to become the head lord of all, for "Ken" is "caput" in Latin, and the Albanic "tyern" is interpreted "dominus" in Latin.

S. Kentigern made, as it were, a new Melchizedeck, did not hesitate to receive what the King so devoutly offered to the honour of God, because he foresaw that in the future even this would be to the advantage of the Church of God. Moreover, he had the privilege sent to him by the Supreme Pontiff that he should be subject to no bishop, but should rather be styled and should actually be the Vicar and Chaplain of the Pope. But the King, who exalted the holy bishop with glory and honour, received grace for grace, and greater honours and riches from the Lord. Likewise his Queen, Languneth by name, bowed down by the opprobium of long continued barrenness, by the blessing and intercession of the holy bishop, conceived and bare a son, to the consolation and joy of their whole kindred. The Saint baptized him and named him Constantine in commemoration of the act which his father had done to him in resemblance of that which the Roman Emperor had done, as we have already said, to S. Silvester. He grew up a boy of good disposition, in stature and grace, beloved of God and men, and by hereditary right, when his father yielded to fate, he succeeded him in the kingdom, but was always subject to the Bishop, even as his father before him. And because the Lord was with him he overcame all the neighbouring barbaric nations without bloodshed. All the Kings who ruled in the kingdom of Cambria before him he surpassed in riches, glory, and dignity, and, what is better, in holiness. Whence also famed for his merits, and finishing his course in peace, he was deemed worthy to triumph over his age, and to be crowned with glory and honour in heaven, and even to the present day he is wont to be called by many S. Constantine. We have said this as it were by anticipation, because we have made mention of Constantine as begotten by the prayers of S. Kentigern, and baptized and educated by him. The holy prelate Kentigern built churches and ordained priests and clerics in Hodelm, and fixed his see there, for a certain reason, for some time. Afterwards, warned by a Divine revelation, justice demanding it, he transferred his seat to his own city of Glasgow.

CHAPTER XXXIV.

How many nations the Saint, now by himself, now by means of his disciples, cleansed from the foulness of idolatry, and how he was distinguished by many miracles.

BLESSED Kentigern, like a burning torch, in his days endeavoured, by the radiant flames of his virtues and the burning and shining word of God, to enlighten the hearts blinded by the error of ignorance, to kindle in the cold the love of God, to burn up the thorns of sins and the tares of vices which, because of the ancient curse, had grown up upon the face of the earth and covered it. Nor was there any one who could easily hide himself from his heat. For he carefully visited his diocese, removed all strange gods from the midst of them, and cast forth all ceremonies of foreign worship. And so preparing the way for the Lord, and making the paths of our God straight, he restored the whole of Christianity there to a better state than it had been in before.

Then the soldier of God, consumed with the fire of the Holy Spirit, like a fire which burns the wood, and as a flame setting on fire the mountains, after he had corrected that which was nearest to himself, namely, his diocese, went forth to more distant places, and cleansed from the foulness of idolatry and the contagion of heretical doctrine the land of the Picts, which is now called Galwiethia, with the adjacent parts; and with shining miracles, brought back to the rule of truth whatever he found contrary to the Christian Faith and sound doctrine, and amended it as far as lay in his power. In all these things the fervour of his devotion was not turned aside, but his hand was stretched out still to greater works and to the increase of the glory and honour of the name of the Most High, his feet having been shod with the preparation of the Gospel of Peace.

For he went to Albania, and there with great and well-nigh intolerable labour, often exposed to death by the snares of the barbarians, but standing in the faith undeterred, the Lord working with him and giving power to the voice of his preaching, he converted that country from the worship of idols and profane rites, which are almost equal to idolatry, to the ways of faith, to the customs of the Church and to canonical institutions. For there he built many churches, dedicated them when built, ordained priests and clerics, and consecrated many of his disciples bishops. Moreover, in those parts he founded many monasteries, and placed fathers over them from the disciples whom he had instructed.

In all these things his spirit, yearning for the salvation of the many, did not rest unless as a glorious standard-bearer of the Lord of Hosts, and a wrestler of unconquered mind, he were fighting the battle of the Lord. Therefore he sent forth those of his own whom he knew to be strong in faith, fervent in charity, eminent for doctrine, and lofty in religion, to the isles which are afar off, towards the Orkneys, Norway, and Iceland, to proclaim among them the name of the Lord and the faith of Jesus Christ, because in those places the harvest was indeed great, but there were no labourers. And since he was now old and unable to go to them himself, he desired that this work should be accomplished by his disciples.

These things being duly performed, he returned to his own Church in Glasgow, where, as also elsewhere, yea everywhere, he is known to have shone with many and great miracles. For wheresoever his lips disseminated the knowledge of salvation, the virtue of God working in His servant manifested its efficacy by manifold signs. For to the blind he gave sight, to the deaf hearing, to the lame the power of walking, to the dumb speech, to the insane reason. He drove away fevers, cast out devils from the bodies possessed, gave strength to the paralytic, healed lunatics, cleansed the lepers, cured all manner of diseases. But in works of this kind was his daily employment, his accustomed play, his assiduous custom, which in a manner became common from so frequent occurrence, and which, lest their number should beget weariness, have not here at least been written down. Frequently, also, many sick were taken to the bishop to be healed by the touch of the hem of his garments, often by mouthfuls of food or drink given or received ; also men, borne on a bed, were healed by the shadow of his body as he passed by, so that he might have been thought another Peter.

CHAPTER XXXV.

How the Lord preserved the clothes of the Saint untouched by any particle of rain, snow, and hail.

ALTHOUGH the hand of the Lord wrought by blessed Kentigern many miracles not commonly vouchsaved to other saints, He wrought one particular work in him at which all men wondered. For as all bare witness who knew the man, as well as those who conversed with him, never during his lifetime were his clothes wetted with showers of rain, or with snow, or with hail pouring down and falling upon the earth. For often standing in the open air, while the inclemency of the weather increased, the rain pouring down like bilge-water and flowing in different directions, and the spirit of the storm raging around him, he from time to time stood immovable, or went where he would, and yet always remained uninjured and untouched by any drop of rain from any quarter. And not on him alone did the Lord vouchsafe to work this prodigy, which was the Lord's doing, and wonderful in the eyes of all, but also the whole crowd of his disciples who were going along with him, by his merits oftentimes, though not as in his own case always, experienced the same grace on themselves and for themselves. For the sanctity of the holy teacher Kentigern, who was bedewed with Divine grace, was for his followers a shadow in the daytime from the heat and a refuge from the wind and rain.

Let no one, therefore, disbelieve that the Lord bestowed the blessing of the miracle we have described upon his most devoted servant, to the praise of his name and in commendation of his holiness, since in a manner similar to this, yea in a manner greater than this, He vouchsaved in the desert to confer a boon upon the whole of the Hebrew people to show the favour which they had found in His sight. The garments of that people, as we read, were not worn away, nor grew old; the garments of this man alone were never wetted with drops of rain from heaven. Therefore, to none let this seem incredible, for, as the Lord says, all things are possible to him that believeth, and with God nothing is impossible. Likewise, also, the sign which in the smiting of Egypt, as in a certain place we find written concerning the children of Israel, we know was frequently repeated in the case of blessed Kentigern. For when darkness covered the whole land of Egypt, and thick darkness the people, as it is written, where the children of Israel dwelt there was light; so, often, when a cloud covered the whole land, bringing a darkness that might be felt, where the Saint was preaching, around himself and the place, and all the inhabitants thereof, light shone. Rightly, therefore, as we believe, never wet with rain were the garments of this Saint, who endeavoured with all care to preserve the members of his body clean and untouched by any defilement of flesh and blood. With justice also did a light shine forth upon the darkness around him in the place of his preaching while he taught the people; in his heart the Sun of Righteousness, the True Light that knows no setting, ever shone, and he himself, like a lamp in a dark place, gave light in the midst of a wicked and perverse generation, according to the word of the Apostle Peter.

CHAPTER XXXVI.

How the Saint miraculously restored to the Queen a ring which she had improperly given away, and which had been thrown by the King himself into the river Clyde.

S. KENTIGERN, therefore, having returned home, as we have said, intending to live alone in mental solitude, apart from the throngs of men, willed not to be readily seen in public or to go abroad except in case of great urgency, yet he ceased not, though against his will, to shine forth in wondrous signs. Queen Langueth, whom we mentioned above, rich in wealth and pleasures, was not faithful, as she ought to have been or as it became her, to the royal chamber or marital bed, for the abundance of her treasures, the superfluity of her luxuries, and the pride of power, were wont to minister incentives and fuel to the will of the flesh. She cast her eyes upon a certain youth, a soldier, who, after the perishable beauty of this perishing flesh, seemed to her fair to look upon and of great beauty beyond many who were with him at Court. And, as one who of himself is ready for such service without incitement from another, he was easily induced to sin with her.

And when the days passed, and the unlawful pleasure, frequently repeated, had become more and more pleasing to both, for bread eaten in secret and stolen waters, according to Solomon, seemed to be sweeter to them, so from a rash act they were overmastered by a blind love. And a royal ring, set with a precious gem, which her lawful husband had intrusted to her as a special mark of his conjugal love, she imprudently and impudently gave to her paramour. But he more impudently accepted the ring and placed it on his finger, and by such a sign opened the door of suspicion to all who were acquainted with the matter. A faithful servant of the King discovering the secret of the Queen and soldier, took care to instil it into the King's ears. But the King did not easily lend his ear or mind to him who told him of his disgrace and the unworthiness of his wife. An old and true proverb is: " It is difficult for a cuckold to put faith in one who reveals the failings of a beloved wife; and he is more apt to turn his hatred back upon the accuser than against the accused." But the informer of the adultery, in proof of the matter, showed the ring on the finger of the soldier, and by this persuaded the King to believe him, and kindled in him the spirit of jealousy more fiercely.

The King, therefore, being assured of this secret, veiled under a calm demeanour the wrath of his soul against the Queen and the soldier, and bore himself towards them with more than his wonted cheerfulness and familiarity. But when a day more serene than usual occurred, he went to hunt, and summoning the soldier to accompany him, he sought the woods and the forests with a multitude of hunters and dogs. The dogs being uncoupled, and the hunters being scattered in divers places, the King came down alone with the soldier to the banks of the river Clyde, where, in a shady place and on the green turf, they each thought it would be pleasant to sleep a little. The soldier, worn out with fatigue, and suspecting no danger, reclining his head, stretching out his arms, and opening his hand, straightway slept; but the spirit of jealousy exciting the King, who feigned to be sleeping, did not suffer him either to sleep or rest. Accordingly, seeing the ring on the finger of the sleeper, his eye was blinded with madness, and he could scarcely keep his hand from his sword and refrain from shedding his blood. Nevertheless he controlled his rage, and drawing the ring from the sleeper's finger, threw it into the neighbouring river, and then rousing him up, ordered him to join his companions and return home. The soldier awoke from sleep thinking nothing of the ring, and obeyed the King's command, and never noticed what he had lost until he entered his house.

But when, on the return of the King, the Queen went forth from her chamber to salute him as usual, she received from the mouth of him she saluted, invectives, threats, and continual reproaches, and with flashing eyes and menacing countenance he demanded where the ring was which he had entrusted to her keeping. She replied that she had it deposited in a casket. The King, in the presence of all his courtiers, commanded her to bring it to him with all haste. She, still full of hope, entered into the inner chamber as if to seek the ring, but straightway sent off a messenger to the soldier telling him of the enraged King's demand, and bidding him send the ring with all haste. The soldier sent back word to the Queen that he had lost the ring, and could not tell where he had lost it; and, fearing the face of the King, he took refuge in concealment, and absented himself from the Court. Meanwhile, as she sought further delay, and was slow in producing what she was of course unable to find, vainly seeking an empty nothing, the King, incensed with rage, and frequently calling her an adulteress, broke into curses, saying: "God do so to me and more also if I do not judge thee according to the law of adulteresses, and if I do not condemn thee to a most disgraceful death. Thou, clinging to a young adulterer, hast neglected the King, thy husband, yet I had made thee the sharer of my bed and the mistress of my kingdom. Thou hast acted in secret; I will act openly, and in the sight of the sun I will make manifest thy ignominy, and reveal thy most shameful deeds before thy face."

And when he had said many things of this kind, all his courtiers prayed for some delay, and he with difficulty conceded three days, but ordered her to be imprisoned. Cast into a dungeon, she was already anticipating the death which, as it were, was hanging over her, but none the less did her guilty conscience torment her. O heavy and intolerable punishment, the damning testimony of a guilty conscience! Although one condemned to punishment may have outward peace, yet is he acknowledged to be wretched and disturbed whom a gnawing conscience ceaselessly persecutes. The spirit, therefore, of the guilty woman was vexed within her, and with a lowly and contrite heart, and with tearful prayers, she implored God that He would not enter into judgment with His handmaiden, but that according to His great mercy, as He formerly had pity on the woman taken in adultery and placed in the midst before Him, He would design to pity her in the same case. By the inspiration of the Lord, therefore, the woman in her great strait found out a wise devise. Sending a trusty messenger to S. Kentigern, she told him all her misfortune, and from him, as her only deliverer, earnestly desired help. She also begged that he would at least use his influence with the King and beseech pardon for her, because there was nothing so great that he would or could or ought to deny him.

The holy bishop, instructed by the Holy Spirit and with virtue from on high, and acquainted with the whole story in order before the messenger arrived, ordered him to go with a hook to the banks of the aforesaid river Clyde, and to cast the hook into the stream, and to bring back to him immediately the first fish that was caught with it and taken out of the water. The messenger did what the Saint told him, and exhibited in the presence of the man of God a large fish which he had caught, and which is commonly called a salmon. He ordered the fish to be cut open and gutted, when there was found in it the aforesaid ring, which he immediately sent by the messenger to the Queen. When she saw and received it, her heart was filled with joy, her mouth with exultation and thanksgiving ; her mourning was turned into joy, the expectation of death into the dance of exultation and safety. The Queen therefore rushed into the midst, and before the eyes of all, restored to the King the ring he had demanded back.

The King, therefore, and all his Court with him, were sorry for the injuries intended against the Queen, and humbly on his knees he sought her forgiveness, and swore that he would inflict a very heavy punishment, even death or exile, if she willed it, upon those who had informed against her. But she, wisely understanding that pity rather than the award of judgment was what she had to do with, was desirous that he should shew mercy, as it becomes a servant always to do to a fellow-servant. "Far be it, my lord, O King," she said, "that any one should suffer anything of the kind on account of me ; but if thou desirest that from my heart I should forgive, what thou hast done towards me, I desire that thou wouldst put away all angry feeling from thy heart, as I do, against my accuser." And all, when they heard this, wondered and were glad. And so the King and Queen and the accuser were recalled into the grace of peace and mutual love with each other. The Queen, as soon as she could, went to the man of God and confessed her guilt to him, and making satisfaction by his advice, carefully corrected her life for the future, and kept her feet from a similar fall. Nevertheless the sign by which the Lord magnified His mercy towards her she never made known to any one during her husband's lifetime, but after his death she told it to all who wished to know it.

Behold the Lord, sitting in heaven, repeated by His saint, Kentigern, what He deigned to do while He was clothed in the flesh and dwelt upon the earth. Peter, casting a hook into the sea, at His command drew out the first fish which came, in the mouth of which he found the piece of money, which he gave in tribute for the Lord and for himself. So by the command of S. Kentigern, in the name of the Lord Jesus Christ, the Queen's messenger casting a hook into the river, took a fish, and bringing it to the Saint, found in it when brought and opened a ring with which he saved the Queen from a double death. In both cases, as it seems to me, there was rendered unto Caesar the things which are Caesar's, and to God the things which are God's. For in the piece of money there was returned to Caesar his image, and in the ring restored to the flesh, the flesh was redeemed from destruction, and the soul made in the image of God was washed from sin and restored to God.

CHAPTER XXXVII.

How a Jester, despising the King's gifts, demanded a dishful of fresh mulberries after Christmas, and how he received them through the instrumentality of S. Kentigern.

KING REDERECH was magnified by the Lord because he clung to Him, by serving Him in faith and good works, and by obeying the will of S. Kentigern. For glory and riches were in his house, generosity was in his heart, urbanity in his mouth, and munificence in his hand, because the Lord had blessed the work of his hands. Hence not only within the confines of his own country was the fame of his liberality spread, but also beyond the sea in Ireland. Wherefore a jester from one of the Kings of Ireland, who was skilled and clever in his art, was sent to Cambria to the court of the aforesaid King, that he might see whether the truth responded to his fame so far and widely spread. Admitted to the court, the jester played with his hand on the tympanum and cithera, and rejoiced the King and his paladins all the days of the festivity of Christmas. When the feast of the Lord's holy Epiphany was ended, the King commanded gifts to be brought forth and bestowed upon the jester as became his royal munificence. The jester refused them all, asserting that he could have enough of such things in his own country. Being asked by the King what he would be willing to accept, he replied that he had no need at all of gold or silver, vestments or horses, in which Ireland abounded. "But if thou desirest," he said, "that I should leave thee well remunerated, let there be given to me a dish full of fresh mulberries." Those who heard this speech proceed from the mouth of the man burst into laughter, because they thought he was joking and speaking playfully. For a servant of this kind is wont to be more highly esteemed in proportion as excites to laughter and to words that move to mirth. But he, with an oath, declared that he had demanded the mulberries in all seriousness and not as a joke; nor could he in any way be moved from his purpose either by prayers, promises, or the offer of the most ample gifts, and rising, he intimated that he wished to retire from the midst and to carry off, as the saying is, the King's honour. But the King took this very ill, and inquired of his companions what could be done in the matter that he might not be dishonoured. For it was then winter, and not a mulberry could be found anywhere. Therefore, acting on the advice of his courtiers, he went to S. Kentigern, and humbly begged that by prayer he would obtain from God what was demanded. The man of God, although he thought that his prayer would not be fitly offered for such trifles, yet because he knew that the King had a great devotion to God and to Holy Church, and recognised his imperfection in this matter, the holy prelate resolved to condescend to his petition, since he hoped that by such means he might be able to advance him in virtue. Therefore, deliberating with himself for a little, and praying briefly, he said to the King: "Rememberest thou in what place during the summer thou didst cast away the garment in which thou wast girded because of the great heat, when thou wast hunting, that thou mightest follow the hounds more quickly, and then forgetting or slighting it, thou didst not return to take up what thou hadst cast off?" The King replied: "I know, O Lord, my King and bishop, the time and the place." "Go," said the Saint, "quickly to the place, and thou shalt find the garment still whole spread out over a bush of thorns, and beneath it mulberries sufficiently ripened, still fresh and fit for gathering. Take them and satisfy the demand of the jester, and in all things concern thyself that thou more and more honour God, who will not allow thy honour to be harmed or diminished in so slight a thing." The King did as the bishop directed him, and found all as he predicted. Taking a dish, therefore, and filling it with the mulberries, he gave it to the actor, saying: "See, take that which thou askest for; for by the hand of the Lord working with us, thou canst not in any thing injure the fame of my liberality. And that I may not appear more niggardly to thee than to others, remain with us as long as it pleaseth thee." The actor, seeing the charger full of mulberries, contrary to the season of the year, grew pale with wonder, and when he knew how it had happened, he cried out and said: "Truly there is none like thee among the kings of the earth munificent in thy liberality, and none like Kentigern, glorious in holiness, fearful in praises, doing wonders, who doeth such things in my sight beyond my expectation. Henceforth I will not leave thy house or thy service; but I will be unto thee a servant for ever as long as I live." The actor therefore remained at the King's court, and served him for many days as jester. Afterwards by the instigation of the fear of God, he set himself against his own face, gave up the profession of an actor, and, entering the ways of the better life, gave himself up to the divine service.

CHAPTER XXXVIII.

Of the two vessels filled with milk which were sent by S. Kentigern to a certain workman; how the milk, when poured out into the river, was formed into cheese.

THERE was a certain man, skilled in the smith's craft, who served by hammering and forging in the works of the man of God, and in employments of the monastery, and received from the Saint the necessary wages. Now, the Saint was wont to use milk as food and drink, because, as we said above, he was in the habit of abstaining from all liquor by which a man can be intoxicated. He therefore ordered vessels full of new milk to be carried to the smith, because he knew that workmen and hired servants are gratified by partaking of the food prepared for the lord and householder. But when the porter was crossing the river Clyde, the covers of the vessels accidentally became open and all the milk was poured out into the water. But strangely and wonderfully, the milk poured out did not mix with the water, and was not changed either as to taste or colour, but all at once became curdled and turned into cheese. Not less properly was this cheese consolidated by the beating of the waves than any other is wont to be by the pressure of the hands. The porter snatched the little shape of cheese from the water and went to the smith, to whom the Saint had sent him, and related the whole matter to him. Many saw this remarkable sign, and were amazed when they saw how the fluid element was not turned into fluid or liquified. But the smith and many others tasted of that cheese, and also distributed little particles of the same, piece by piece, to many to be kept as relics. Relics of this sort have been received and preserved in many places and at many times, and have declared the dear and famous merits of S. Kentigern, making them dearer and more famous still. But although this sign bears much that is wonderful on the face of it, yet to those who view it subtilly, and gather spiritual things from corporeal, and invisible from visible, it affords much instruction. In the milk, which fell into the water but was not mixed with it or changed into water, or sunk in it, it, we have an example of the preservation of innocence and justice, which are relics to a peaceful man among those who swell with pride, who sow to themselves many kinds of evil, who seek to drown us with bad examples and persuasions, who dissipate themselves in pleasure. That the milk in the stream was hardened into cheese gives us an example of maintaining constancy under the pressure of tribulation and difficulties. For the just and the innocent hardens among the waves as the milk did into cheese, when, in obedience to the words proceeding out of the mouth of God, he perseveres in the hard paths, and through many tribulations seeks to enter into the kingdom of God. And if he endures threats, insults, losses, injuries from wicked and froward men, as if he did not feel them, but in patience possesses his soul, and endeavours to persevere in good, knowing of a surety that he who perseveres unto the end here, he shall be saved.

CHAPTER XXXIX.

How S. Columba visited blessed Kentigern and saw a crown that came down from heaven upon his head and a celestial light shining around him.

AT the time when Blessed Kentigern, placed in the Lord's candlestick, like a lamp burning with heavenly desires, and shining with life-giving words, in the examples of virtues and with miracles of power, gave light to all who were in the House of God, S. Columba, the Abbot, whom the Angles call Columkillus, wonderful in doctrine and virtues, celebrated for his presages of future events, yea rather, full of the spirit of prophecy, and living in that glorious monastery which he had built in the Island of Iona, desired earnestly not once but continually to rejoice in the light of S. Kentigern. For, hearing for a long time of the esteem in which he was held, he desired to approach, visit, and behold him, and to come into his closer intimacy, and to consult the sanctuary of his holy breast concerning the things which lay near to his own heart. And when the opportune moment came the holy Father Columba went forth, and a great crowd of disciples and others accompanied him, desiring to behold and look upon the face of so great a man. And when he approached the place which is called Mellindenor, where the Saint was then staying, he divided all his people into three bands, and sent a messenger before him to announce to the holy prelate his arrival and that of those who were with him.

The holy bishop rejoiced at the things which were told him concerning them, and calling to him his clergy and people, he, in like manner, divided them into three bands, and went forward with spiritual songs to meet them. In the forefront of the procession were placed the juniors in order of time, next the more advanced in years, then with himself there walked those who had grown old in good days, white and hoary, venerable in countenance, gesture, and bearing, yea, even in grey hairs. And all sang: "In the ways of the Lord, how great is the glory of the Lord." And again they answered: "The way of the just is made straight, and the path of the saints is prepared." On S. Columba's side they sang with tuneful voice: "The saints shall go from strength to strength: unto the God of gods every one of them shall appear in Sion," with Alleluia. Meanwhile some who had come with S. Columba asked him, saying, "Has S. Kentigern come in the first chorus of singers?" The Saint replied: "Not in the first, nor in the second, but in the third comes the genial bishop." And when they inquired how he knew this, he said: "I see a fiery pillar in fashion as of a crown of gold, set with sparkling gems, descending upon his head from heaven and a light of heavenly brightness encircling and shining around him as a veil, and covering him, and again returning to the skies. Wherefore it is given to me to know by this manifest sign that as Aaron he is the elect of God and sanctified; who clothed with the light as with a garment and with a gold crown represented on his head appears to me with the sign of sanctity. When these two godlike men met, they embraced and kissed each other, and having first satiated themselves with the spiritual banquet of Divine words, they refreshed themselves with bodily food. But how great was the sweetness of Divine contemplation within their holy breasts is not for me to say, nor is it given to me or to such as me to reveal the manna which is hidden and which, methinks, is entirely unknown except to those who taste it.

CHAPTER XL.

Of the head of S. Kentigern's ram that was cut off and how it was turned into stone.

WHEN the two men we have just mentioned were mutually joined together as two pillars in the court of the temple of the Lord, firmly founded in faith and love and confirmed therein, by the imitation and instructions of whom many peoples, tribes and tongues have entered, and are still entering, into the heavenly temple, which is the joy of the Lord, some sons of the stranger who had come with S. Columba were hardened in their evil habits and halted away from the paths of the man of God. For as the Ethiopian cannot change his skin, so he who is accustomed to theft or rapine with difficulty changes his malice. There came, therefore, with Blessed Columba some with no dovelike innocence, but merely by the advances of their feet, with no affection of devotion and no progress in morals. While they journeyed they saw one of the flocks of the holy bishop feeding in the distance, and leaving the path and going by dark ways, as it is said in the Book of Proverbs of such, they turned aside thither, and notwithstanding the resistance and remonstrances of the shepherd, seized the fattest wether. But the shepherd in the name of the Holy Trinity and by the authority of S. Kentigern forbade them to commit such robbery, nay sacrilege, in the flock of the holy prelate, admonishing them that if they would but ask a ram from the Saint, they would without doubt receive one. But one of them drove away the shepherd, whom he insulted and even threatened with death, and took away a ram; while the other taking out a knife cut off its head. They had debated how they should carry off the carcass with them, and, at a time and place suitable for their crime, skin and prepare it more carefully, as they well knew how, for their uses.

But a thing wonderful to relate, and yet more wonderful to behold, occurred. The ram with its head cut off ran back with marvellous speed to its own flock, and there fell down; while its head, changed into stone, stuck firmly, as if fastened by some indissoluble glue, to the hands of him who held it and had struck it. Those who were able to pursue, catch, hold, and cut off the head of the ram when living and whole, now when it was beheaded were unable by following or pursuing to overtake it; nor could they cast away the head, already become a stone, from their hands, though they tried with all their might. The men became rigid and their heart died within them and became as stone, as they were carrying a stone, and at length, taking wholesome counsel, they went to the Saints, and lying prostrate at the feet of S. Kentigern, penitent and suffused with tears, they besought him to forgive them. But the holy prelate, chiding them with gentle reproof, and warning them never again to presume to perpetrate fraud, theft, robbery, and, what is more detestable, sacrilege, unloosed them from the double bond, of sin and the hold of the stone. He ordered the carcase of the slain ram to be given to them and permitted them to depart. But the head which was turned into stone, remains there to this day as a witness to the miracle and, though mute, declares the merit of S. Kentigern.

Assuredly this miracle, as it seems to me, is, in the main, not inferior to that which the book of Genesis relates to have been wrought in the case of Lot's wife. After the avenger of the injury done to God, the fire from heaven was ordered to destroy the wicked subverters of the natural use of human generation and was already hanging over them, being instructed by an angelic oracle and assisted by its help, Lot escaped the fire of the overthrow and overwhelming of Sodom. But his wife, on looking back, contrary to the command given from heaven, was changed into a rock, into an image of salt, to be a relish to the food of brute animals. Here the head of a ram is transmuted into stone to condemn the hardness and cruelty of them who carry off the property of others. In the figure of Lot's wife, by the Lord's own teaching, every faithful man is taught and warned not foolishly to draw back from any holy purpose once taken in hand. In the head turned into stone every Christian is taught not to commit theft or fraud, or robbery or any violence on the property of the Church or on the substance of the servants of God. In the place where this miracle wrought by S. Kentigern, in the sight of S. Columba and many others, became known, they exchanged staves in pledge and testimony of mutual love in Christ. The staff which S. Columba gave to the holy bishop Kentigern was for a long time preserved in the church of S. Wilfrid, bishop and confessor, at Ripon, and on account of the sanctity of both the giver and receiver was held in great reverence. Wherefore for some days these Saints passed the time together conversing on the things which are of God and on those which belong to the salvation of souls: after bidding each other farewell in mutual love, they departed to their own homes never to meet again.

CHAPTER XLI.

How the man of God erected crosses in many places, by which even to the present day miracles are wrought.

THE venerable father and bishop Kentigern was in the habit of erecting the triumphant standard of the Holy Cross in the places where he had won the people to the dominion of Christ by preaching and imbued them with the faith of the Cross of Christ, or where he had dwelt for any length of time, that all might learn that he was not in the least ashamed of the Cross of our Lord Jesus Christ, which he carried on his forehead. But, as it seems to me, this very holy custom of the holy man is in many ways supported by sound reason. Because the Saint was wont to erect this life-giving and holy and terrible sign, in order that, as wax melts before the fire, so the enemies of the human race, the powers of the darkness of this world, melting away before this sign, might flow down, and terrified and routed, might flee afar off. It is fitting, moreover, that the soldiers of the Eternal King should recognise at a glance the invincible standard of their Commander, and flee to it, as to a tower of strength, from the face of the enemy and from the face of the wicked who afflict them, and that they may have that which they adore, and in which they boast before their eyes. And because, according to the Apostle, the wrestling against spiritual wickedness in high places and against the fiery darts of the evil one is continual, it is fit and healthful that they should fortify and protect themselves by signing themselves with this sign, and by imitating the passion of Christ, and with the Apostle bearing about in their bodies the prints of the wounds of Christ, crucify for the love of the Crucified One their own flesh with its vices and lusts and the world to them and themselves unto the world.

Among many crosses, therefore, which the man of God erected in divers places, there are two which to the present time work miracles. One in his own city of Glasgow he caused to be cut by quarriers from a block of stone of extraordinary size, which by the united exertions of many men and by the use of machines, he ordered to be set up in the cemetery of the Church of the Holy Trinity in which his episcopal chair is placed. But all their labour was spent in vain, every machine was powerless, human industry and strength were of no avail to erect it, though they toiled much and long. But when human ingenuity and help failed, the Saint had recourse to Divine aid. For on the following eve, which chanced to be Sunday, while the servant of Jesus Christ was pouring out prayers on behalf of this matter to the Lord, the Angel of the Lord descended from heaven and coming near, rolled back the stone cross and erected it in the place where it is to this day, and blessing it, signed it with the sign of the cross, hallowed it, and departed. The people, when they came to the church in the morning and discovered what had been done, were astonished and glorified God in his Saint. The cross was very large and from that time has never been wanting in great virtue. For many maniacs and those vexed with unclean spirits are wont to be tied to that cross on the night preceding the Lord's day and on the morrow they are found of a sound mind, delivered and cleansed, or sometimes dead or on the point of death.

Another cross, which it would be incredible to describe had it not been tested by sight and touch, he constructed merely of sea sand at Lothwerverd, while meditating justly and religiously on the Resurrection. In this place he remained for the space of eight years. Who ought to doubt that the Lord will not raise our mortal bodies, though they be resolved into dust, since He has so promised with His own blessed mouth, when in His name this Saint, of like passions with ourselves, raised up a cross from the sand of the sea while praying to the Lord? Truly, it ought to be believed by all that, at the Lord's will, the bones of the dead will be joined bone to his bone, according to the prophecy of Ezekiel, and that the Lord will give them sinews and make flesh to come upon them and skin to cover them and put breath into them and they shall live for ever, seeing that at the prayer of a man still mortal a mass of sand was condensed into a solid and perfect substance from the smallest particles, or as I may say atoms, and formed into a cross, which neither the burning sun by day nor the frost by night nor any inclemency of weather can dissolve. That cross therefore stands as a proof of our faith, showing that this corruptible must put on incorruption, and that the multitude of the children of Israel, though they be as the sand of the sea, a remnant shall be saved by the faith of the cross of Christ, and that the friends of God shall be multiplied beyond the number of the sand by Him who numbereth the stars of heaven, and the sand of the sea, and the drops of rain, and the days of the age. To this cross also many afflicted with divers diseases, and especially madmen and those vexed by the devil are bound in the evening and in the morning are often found safe and sound, and being set free return to their friends.

There are many other places in which he lived and especially during Lent, unknown to us, which the Saint sanctified by the presence of his holy indwelling Spirit. Yet many persons relate numerous instances regarding these which by some tokens diffuse his sanctity to this day, and by his merits afford to the infirm many blessings and have the efficacy of working miracles.

CHAPTER XLII.

How he tied up his chin with a certain bandage, and prepared for the departure of his soul.

BLESSED Kentigern, overcome by extreme old age, perceived from many rents in it that the ruin of his earthly house was at hand; but the foundation of his faith, which was founded on a Rock, comforted his soul. For he trusted that when his earthly house of this tabernacle was dissolved, he had an house not made with hands prepared for him in heaven. And because both by reason of his extreme old age, and because he was touched with infirmity, the fastenings of his nerves throughout his whole body were almost entirely withered and loosened, he bound up his cheeks and chin with a certain linen bandage which went over the middle of his head and under his chin, neither too tight nor too loose. This the most refined man did, that by the falling of his chin nothing indecent might appear from the opening of his mouth, and that such a support might render him more ready in bringing forth what he could or would.

At length, this man, beloved by God and men, knowing that the hour approached when he should pass from this world to the Father of Lights, fortified himself with the sacred unction which is efficacious for the remission of sin and with the life-giving sacraments of the Lord's Body and Blood, in order that that ancient serpent seeking to bruise his heel should be unable to fix therein his poisonous tooth and inflict a deadly wound, but that with bruised head he might retreat in confusion. In

this way the Lord treading Satan under his feet, in order that
his holy soul might not be speedily confounded, when at his
going out from Egypt he spake with his enemies in the gate,
he waited patiently as hitherto, like an excellent under-pilot,
for the Lord who had saved him from the tempest of this age.
And now close to the shore, driven into the port of a certain
inward quiet by gentle navigation, after so many dangers of
the sea, he cast out the anchor of hope bound with the ropes of
his desires into the solid and sure ground, reaching of a truth even
within the veil, whither the Precursor, the Lord Jesus, entered
before him. Henceforth he awaited alone the departure from the
tents of Kedar and the entrance into the land of the living, so
that as a successful wrestler, he might in that City of The Virtues, that is, in the Heavenly Jerusalem, receive from the hand of
the Heavenly King the crown of glory and the diadem of the
Kingdom which fadeth not away. His own disciples gathered
around him he warned, as far as his strength permitted, concerning the observance of holy religion, the maintenance of
mutual charity and peace, the grace of hospitality, and of continuing instant in prayer and holy reading. But above all
things, he gave to them and left behind him short but peremptory commands to avoid every evil appearance of simoniacal wickedness, to shun entirely the communion and society
of heretics and schismatics, and to observe strictly the decrees
of the holy Fathers, and especially the laws and customs of
Holy Church, the Mother of all. Then, as was meet, he gave
to each of them, as they humbly knelt before him, the kiss of
peace, and raising his hand, as best he could, he blessed them,
and bidding them a last farewell, he committed them all to the
care of the Holy Trinity and to the protection of the Holy
Mother of God, and gathered himself together, on that glorious
stony couch of his. Then one voice of mourners sounded everywhere; then fell as a horror of confusion deep sadness on the
face of all.

CHAPTER XLIII.

Of his disciples who sought a speedy journey to heaven, and of his warm bath.

BUT some of them, who loved the Saint of God more closely, prostrated themselves in tears before him and said: "We know, O Lord Bishop, that thou desirest to be dissolved and to be with Christ. For thine old age, venerable, very protracted and measured by the number of many years as well as thy spotless life demand it; but, we pray thee, have pity upon us whom thou hast begotten in Christ. For in whatsoever we have erred through human frailty we have always confessed it in thy presence, and have made amends, giving satisfaction to the judgment of thy discretion. Since then we have no power to retain thee any longer with us, seek from the Lord that it may be given to us to depart from this vale of tears to the joy of thy Lord with thee. For as to this we believe, even as we assert, that whatever thou askest the Divine Mercy will vouchsafe to thee, for the will of God has been to us directed in thy hand from thy youth. It seems to us improper that the bishop without his clergy, the pastor without any of his flock, the father without his sons, should enter into those festal and sublime places; yea rather the more festal and sublime they are, the greater the company of his own that should attend him." And when they had urged many things in this way with tears, the man of God, overflowing with bowels of mercy, collecting his breath as well as he was able, said: "The will of God concerning us all be done; let Him do with us as He knows best and as is well-pleasing to Him."

After these things the Saint was silent, and sighing in his soul for heaven awaited the passage of his spirit from the body; and his disciples watching by him took care of him as of one nigh unto death. And behold, while the morning star, the herald of the dawn, the messenger of the light of day, tearing through the pall of the darkness of night, shone forth with flaming rays, the Angel of the Lord appeared in unspeakable splendour and the glory of God shone around him. For fear of him the guardians of the holy bishop were afraid and greatly amazed, and being but earthly vessels and unable to bear the weight of so great a glory they became as dead men. But the holy old man, comforted by the vision and the angelic visit, and forgetting as it were his age and infirmity and being made strong, experienced some foretastes of the blessedness now near at hand, and held close intercourse with the angel as with a most dear and familiar friend.

Now the heavenly messenger said to him these words : " O Kentigern, elect and beloved of God ! rejoice and be glad, and let thy soul magnify the Lord, since He has magnified His mercy toward thee. Thy prayer is heard, and the Divine ear has heard the preparation of thy heart. For it shall be to thee concerning the disciples who desire to accompany thee, as thou willest. Therefore be steadfast, and you shall see the help of the Lord toward you. On the morrow ye shall go forth from the body of this death to the unfailing life, and the Lord shall be with you and ye shall be with Him for ever. And because thy whole life in this world has been a perpetual martyrdom, it has pleased the Lord that thou shalt have an easier passage from life than other men. Cause to be prepared for thee therefore on the morrow a warm bath and going into it, thou shalt fall asleep in the Lord without pain, and therein rest in peace in Him. But after thou hast paid the debt of nature in it, immediately before the water cools, while it is yet warm about thee, let thy brethren enter after thee into this bath, and straightway loosed from the bonds of death they shall migrate with thee as the companions of thy journey, and being introduced into the splendours of the Saints, they shall enter with thee into the joy of thy Lord."

With these words the angelic vision and voice ceased, but a fragrance of marvellous and indescribable odour in some strange way spread through all the place and over all who were there. But the Saint calling his disciples to him, revealed to them in order the angelic mystery, and ordered his bath to be prepared as the Lord commanded by the angel. The brethren above mentioned gave unmeasured thanks to God Almighty and to their holy Father Kentigern, and assured of the oracle, in every way they could, and fortified with the Divine Sacraments, they prepared for what awaited them.

CHAPTER XLIV.

How he passed out of this world and how he shone forth after his death in many miracles.

WHEN the octave of the Lord's Epiphany, on which the gentle bishop himself had been wont every year to wash in sacred baptism a multitude of people, was dawning—a day very acceptable to S. Kentigern and to the spirits of the sons of his adoption, the Saint borne by their hands entered a vessel filled with hot water which he had first hallowed with the sign of salvation, and a circle of brethren standing round him waited the issue of the event. And when the Saint had been some little time in it, after raising his hands and eyes to heaven and bowing his head, as if falling into a calm sleep, he yielded up his spirit. For he seemed as free from the pain of death as he stood forth spotless and pure from the corruptions of the flesh and the snares of this world.

The disciples seeing what was taking place, lifted the holy body out of the bath and eagerly strove with each other to immerse themselves in it. And so, one by one before the water cooled, they slept in great peace in the Lord, and having tasted death with their father, the holy Bishop, they passed with him to the heavenly mansions. And when the water had become cold not only the fear of death but also every spark of discomfort wholly disappeared.

This bath is in my opinion to be compared with the sheep-pool in which, after the descent of the angel and the troubling of the water, one sick man was healed of whatsoever infirmity he had ; but he was still liable to death. But in this ablution a very great company of Saints were cured of every sickness, to live for ever with Christ. The water of that laver was distributed to divers persons in divers places ; and from its being drunk or sprinkled health was conferred on many sick persons in many ways.

The brethren stripped the Saint of his ordinary clothes, which they partly preserved and partly distributed as precious relics, and clothed him in the sacred vestments which became so great a bishop. Then he was carried by the brethren into the choir with hymns and psalms, and the Life-giving Victim was offered to God for him by many. Diligently and most devoutly, as the custom of the Church at that time required, they celebrated his obsequies, and on the right side of the altar they laid beneath a stone with as much becoming reverence as they could, that home of virtues, that precious stone, by whose merit, as it was a time for collecting stones for the edifice of the heavenly temple, many elect and lively stones, along with that pearl, were taken up and laid in the treasuries of the Great King. The sacred remains of all the brethren were decently and separately consigned to the cemetery for sepulture in the order in which they followed the holy prelate from this world.

Blessed Kentigern therefore full of years, for he was a hundred and eighty-five years old, matured in merits, famous for signs, wonders and prophecies, on such wise passed from this world to the Father—from faith to sight, from labour to rest, from exile to the Fatherland, from the course to the crown of victory, from the present misery to the eternal glory. Blessed, I say, is the man to whom the heavens are open, who penetrated the sanctuary, who entered into the powers of the Lord, received by the angelic hosts, admitted into the ranks of the patriarchs and prophets, joined to the choirs of the Apostles, mingled in the ranks of the martyrs who are crowned with the purple of their rosy blood, associated with the sacred confessors of the Lord ; crowned with the snow-white choirs of virgins. And no wonder. For he was in office and merit an angel of the Lord who announced to those who were afar off and to them that were near peace and salvation in the blood of Jesus Christ ; his lips kept true wisdom, from his mouth many sought and found the law of God. He was also a prophet of the Highest, who knew many things which were not, and foresaid and foretold many things to come. Rightly moreover is he called and is the Apostle of the region of Cambria, for its inhabitants and many other peoples are the signs of his Apostleship. Deservedly also is he called a martyr who in a constant and unceasing martyrdom mortifies himself for Christ, and is proved to have had his heart prepared for every kind of death if the occasion had offered. For, for the name of Christ and for the defence of truth and righteousness he frequently offered himself to persecution, proscription, the snares and swords of the enemies of the cross of Christ, and bravely, and happily triumphed over the world, the flesh, and the devil and his satellites. He by change of name is called the Confessor of Christ, who confessing the name of Christ before peoples and Kings, confidently preached, and invited all men to the profession of the name of Christ, and to the confession of the Christian Faith, of the praise of God and of their own sin.

Moreover by a certain special prerogative he obtained a virginal honour and glory, who from the tamarisk extracted balsam, from the nettle the lily, and while in the vessel of this fragil and frail body never disturbed, as they say, even by a look his angelic celibacy, and preserved in a vessel of clay the heavenly treasure of chastity. Wherefore from a virgin body he soared in white to the white-robed company, that without spot he might stand before the throne of God and the Lamb, and following Him whithersoever He goeth, sing the new song, unknown to all save to those who have not defiled their garments. Justly, therefore, that holy man lives as a companion, fellow-citizen and partaker with all the Saints, who in this life had communion with all Saints, and always sought to please, obey and follow and to be united in spirit with the Saint of all Saints, the Sanctifier of all, and being united to them, lives and rejoices with Him now and for ever.

The spirit of S. Kentigern being translated to the starry realms, that which the earth, the mother of all, had bestowed, she gathered into her womb. Nevertheless the power of miracles, which grew in him when living, could not be buried beneath the turf or hid by the stony mound, but burst forth.

For from the day of his burial down to the present, his sacred bones are known to have there germinated into very many miracles, and they do not cease to announce, by benefits bestowed in respect to many kinds of infirmities, that both in heaven and on earth the just is had in everlasting remembrance. At his tomb sight is restored to the blind, hearing to the deaf, the power of walking to the lame, speech to the dumb, cleanness of skin to the leprous, strength of limb to the paralytic, sense to the insane. The impious, the sacrilegious, the perjured, violators of the peace of his Church and profaners of the holy place are justly punished.

Moreover on one occasion a certain man by night stole away from Glasgow a cow which in the morning was found living and bound to the foot of the thief who was dead, which struck him who sought it with both astonishment and joy. Likewise many, who, though guilty of sins of the flesh, did not hesitate to pollute the holy place with their impure steps, were sometimes punished with sudden death, often mutilated, and at times visited with some incurable and protracted disease in their limbs. Thus also the breakers of his peace often suffered. Many, likewise, have often experienced in themselves the punishment of their sin, who have presumed by any servile work to dishonour the festival of the Saint, during which at the Church in Glasgow, where his most sacred body rests, a great multitude is wont to assemble from divers parts, to seek his interccssion and to behold the miracles which are here wont to be wrought.

CHAPTER XLV.

Of the prophecy of a certain man, and of the burial of the Saints in Glasgow.

IN the same year that S. Kentigern was freed from earthly things and migrated to the heavens, King Rederech, who has been so often named, remained much longer than usual in the royal town which is called Pertnech (Partick). In his court there lived a certain fool called Laloecen, who received the necessaries of food and clothing from the munificence of the King. For the chiefs of the earth, the sons of the kingdom, are given to vanity and are wont to retain men of this kind about them, who by their foolish words and gestures may excite to jokes and laughter the lords themselves and their household. This man after the death of S. Kentigern gave himself up to the heaviest grief and would not receive consolation from any one.

When they asked him why he mourned so inconsolably, he answered that his lord King Rederech and another of the chiefs of the land, Morthec by name, would not continue long in this life after the death of the holy Bishop, but would die during the present year. That the saying of the fool was uttered not foolishly but rather prophetically, the death of those whom he mentioned within the same year clearly proved. Nor is it much to be marvelled at, that the Creator of all things allowed to be announced by the mouth of a fool what had been determined of the Lord, since even Balaam, the soothsayer, by His inspiration foresaw many and great things in his seer's mind and foretold them, and Caiaphas prophesied that the redemption of the people would come from the death of Christ, and by the mouth of a she-ass the madness of a prophet was rebuked, and the destruction of Jerusalem was foretold by the mouth of a madman, as Josephus writes. So in the same year that the holy Bishop Kentigern passed away, the King and Prince aforesaid died, and were buried in Glasgow.

In the cemetery of the Church of this city as the inhabitants and countrymen assert, 665 saints rest, and all the great men of that region have long been wont to be buried there. O how much is that place to be feared and to be had in reverence, which so many pledges of the Saints adorn as their resting-place! which so precious a Confessor decorates with his sacred spoils, and illustrates with so many miracles that if all were committed to writing they would be seen to fill great volumes. Not only in the place where he rests in the body, though there more frequently, and especially on his anniversary, is he used to shine forth in signs, but in almost all places in which he is had in remembrance, in churches and chapels, and at altars, he is present as a most powerful helper in necessities to those placed in tribulations, to those who love him, trust in him, cry to him. And where faith or some reason demands it, he does not cease to shine in miracles to the praise and glory of our Lord Jesus Christ; whose is the glory, praise, honour and power, for ever and ever. Amen.

Thus endeth the Life of the Most Holy Kentigern, Bishop and Confessor, who is also called Mungu.

THE LIFE OF S. SERVANUS.

THE LIFE OF SERVANUS.

CHAPTER I.

THERE was a certain noble king in the land of Canaan by by name Obeth, the son of Eliud; and the name of his wife was Alfia, the daughter of the King of Arabia. They lived together twenty years but had no offspring. Therefore they very frequently besought God and offered unto Him oblations and sacrifices that He would grant unto them a worthy child, in order that their reproach might be taken away. For this cause the King ordained through all His kingdom that all men from the least unto the greatest should fast three days and three nights and earnestly entreat the pity of God for the King and Queen, that the shame of sterility might be turned away from them. On the third night, at the last crowing of the cock, the angel of the Lord suddenly appeared to the King in a dream as he slept, saying: "Go to the city which is called Heliopolis and in it thou shalt find a very beautiful fountain and in it bathe three times. Afterwards you shall have what you desire." And departing, they came to the aforesaid fountain and did according to the saying of the angel. And the Queen desiring an herb growing by the fountain, which is called mandragon, she ate of it. After she had eaten thereof her husband went in unto her and she conceived. On the following night the angel appeared unto the Queen comforting her, and saying: "Be not sad nor sorrowful, O Queen! for lo, thou bearest in thy womb two sons who shall excel in faith and works. The name of the one shall be Generatius; that is, Shining Gem, and he shall be a great king over all the land of the Canaanites. The name of the other shall be Malachias or Servanus. And after he has finished the course of this secular life, these names will prove to have suited him well. For Malachias being interpreted is Angel of the Lord. This is a fit name for him, in that he lived as the ambassador of the Apostolic see, proclaiming the Word of God to the four quarters of the world. But he is called Servanus from serving God, in that he served our Lord Jesus Christ, labouring in every good work night and day." After saying these words the angel departed, and the Queen awoke and told her husband the words of the angel. Both therefore rejoiced and gave great thanks to God.

CHAPTER II.

AFTER the boy was born he was taken to the Bishop of the city of Alexandria, Mayonius by name, to be baptized by him. The Bishop baptized him and gave him the name Servanus. Blessed Servanus was accordingly nurtured seven years; and his father died. Now when his father was dead, they conferred upon him the government of the whole of their kingdom. But he, cleaving to God from his youth, opposed all their wishes; and his brother Generatius reigned in his stead. Now S. Servanus went to the city of Alexandria to devote himself there to divine study and to learn the arts. And there he remained thirteen years and received the habit of a monk from the bishop of that city. After thirty years, he was earnestly advised by the aforenamed Bishop that he ought to be promoted to sacred orders, inasmuch as he was deserving. Accordingly he was advanced to the order of the priesthood, though unwilling and gainsaying. Now after he was ordained he came into his own land, and all the Canaanites elected him with great joy to the bishopric. That bishopric he ruled in peace for twenty years, building monasteries and churches in it, and serving God day and night. Then the angel of the Lord came to him, saying: "Thou art commanded by the Lord God to go out and depart from thy country and from thy kindred." Blessed Servanus answered: "Freely will I go, but I know not whither my Lord desires me to go." The angel on this said to blessed Servanus: "I will be with thee whithersoever thou goest, delivering thee from every temptation of the devil; and I will be thy companion, prospering the way of thy journey on sea and on land, from this day until the day of the dissolution of thy body." Then S. Servanus took leave of all the clerics and laity of his see and of his kindred and his friends, and blessed them. But they, lamenting his departure, earnestly besought him that he would not send them away desolate. But he, heeding not their tears and prayers, took his journey with a great multitude of companions, the angel guiding him.

CHAPTER III.

S. SERVANUS, afterwards, with fifty and ten thousand, came to the bank of the river Nile, and with all his company he safely crossed the river. Next, he arrived with them at the shore of the Red Sea, and they all crossed that sea with dry feet. Then after two months he came to the city of Jerusalem, and was there the honourable patriarch for seven years, in the place of James the Bishop, patriarch of the people of Jerusalem. Now, on a certain day the Angel said to S. Servanus; "Ascend Mount Sion, and go round about it." S. Servanus ascended Mount Sion and went round about it. There was shown to him the tree from which the health-bringing Cross of Christ was hewn. Then the Angel said unto him:—"Cut from this tree four staves and carry them away with thee, and they shall be held in great virtue and reverence after you." At the voice of the Angel S. Servanus cut three staves. But the wood for a larger staff the Angel himself cut off and handed it to S. Servanus, and entrusted it to him. Thereafter the Saint held and preserved this staff in the greater honour and reverence. After these things he returned to Jerusalem with joy. And there the Angel said to him:—"It is time to leave this city and to go to the city of Constantinople, for this place is near to thy country and kindred." Blessed Servanus therefore arose and blessed all the inhabitants of Jerusalem, taking leave of them. After this he came to Constantinople with all the multitude of his companions, and was there honourably entertained for three years. Then being warned by the same Angel, he came to the land and to the island of Salvatoris. Now the island is called Salvatoris because in it our Saviour graciously came to us. Afterwards he came to Rome with a very great company. And the Romans learning his fame, which was noised abroad through all the countries and regions round about, received him with great honour. Now in these days the Romans were without a Pope and without a teacher. But the assembly of the clergy and people of Rome chose him to the Apostolate. And he was thus in the chair of Peter, ruling and teaching the Roman people, and doing signs and wonders seven years.

CHAPTER IV.

THE Angel of the Lord speaks with S. Servanus, saying, "Thy God commandeth thee to go out from this place, for it is too pleasant for thee to be here." Then Blessed Servanus addressed the Roman clergy and people, saying ;—" Men, brethren, I take leave of you all and leave you all my benediction. For it behoves me, being warned of the Lord, to go into distant parts and to obey the Lord Jesus Christ in all things." On hearing this all the Romans were greatly displeased, for all the Roman people were of one mind to go with him, because they greatly loved a man so glorious in doctrine, manner and nobility. For they would rather endure hardness and privation in wandering through the world with him than be deprived of his presence and mellifluous doctrine. Nevertheless, he departed from the city of Rome with a great multitude of clergy and of the people, both men and women, sorrowing greatly over his departure, and came to the Hill of Tears. Blessed Servanus stood in this place, and turning to the people, said: "Men, brethren, and people beloved of God, grieve not over my departure nor be sorrowful, but divide yourselves into two companies; let one remain here at Rome; let the other lay aside all worldly care and follow me in this pilgrimage; for those who remain and for those who come with us I will pray God that He Himself may be with you, pardoning all your sins, and that He may have mercy upon us." All responded, "Amen." And the companies were separated and he blessed them with tears, and kissing them, said,—" Farewell, and abide in Christ."

CHAPTER V.

Now after Blessed Servanus with all his company ascends the Alps, he comes to the valley which is called Nigra, or the Valley of Beasts. And because Servanus knew that during that night he would be tempted of the devil, he passed the night in that valley. Then the angel said to the blessed man: "I make known to thee the pains which thou and all thine are about to suffer this night." And he said to him: "Comfort the crowds, and say to them that when the pains and torments of this night are passed, they will no more suffer the pains of hell." After this the angel departed, and S. Servanus came to the crowd, and comforting them, said: "Strengthen yourselves, and be ready to endure the pains which will this night come upon you." He set a verse before them as an example of prophecy, viz.: "Thou shalt tread on the asp, and the basilisk and the lion and the dragon shalt thou trample under foot." That is, You shall all, if you persevere in the faith of the Holy Trinity, tread on the asp and the basilisk, that is, on the devil and his pomps, and nothing shall harm you. Then the Saint said: "Eat and prepare yourselves for the coming wars." Now when they had finished eating and had repeated the verse, immediately there came a most black thick darkness over the valley in which they were. Then there came great earthquakes, thunders and lightnings, hail and sulphurous fires; and divers kinds of beasts, two-footed and four-footed, filled the valley round about them. Then came gnats having horny beaks, dragons, winged serpents, and every torment which the Prince of Darkness can show to man. When they saw all these things, great part of the crowd died. But S. Servanus, seeing that his companions were unable to endure these things, arose and blessed the valley, when all vanished and returned to nothing, and did no more hurt to any one. Then S. Servanus came with seven thousand thousands to the Ictean Sea which separates England from France, and they crossed it dry-shod. Thus God granted them a way and support on the sea. And afterwards he went from place to place until he came to the stream which is called the Forth. Now S. Edhennanus (Adamnan) was abbot in Scotland at that time, and he went to meet Servanus as far as the island of Keth (Inchkeith), and received him with great veneration because he had heard much good concerning him. When the space of one night was passed there, and after a time which it pleased them to enjoy in sweet conversation, S. Servanus said: "How shall I dispose of my household and companions?" S. Adamnan replied: "Let them dwell in the land of Fife and from the sea of the Britains as far as the mountain which is called Okhel." And so it was done.

CHAPTER VI.

AFTERWARDS S. Servanus, with only a hundred companions in his train, came to Kinel, and threw the branch which he held across the sea, and from it there grew an apple tree, which among the moderns is called Monglas. Then the Angel said to the blessed man: "There where that very beautiful tree has grown shall be the resting place of thy body." S. Servanus then came to the place which is called Culenros (Culross), desiring to dwell there, and cleared away all the thorns and thickets which abounded in the place. But the King of Scotia, namely, Brude, son of Dagart, who then held the kingdom of the Picts, was greatly enraged because without his permission he was dwelling there. Now the King sent his spearmen to slay S. Servanus with his whole household. Meanwhile a violent disease had attacked the King so that he had well nigh given up the ghost. He therefore hastily sent to the Saint of the Lord. The sick King spoke to the Saint as he came, saying: "O Saint of God, for the sake of Christ in whom thou believest, restore me to health and thou shalt have the place in which you dwell as a perpetual gift." The Saint, moved with the prayers and piety of the King, restored him to health. S. Servanus after this founded and dedicated a cemetery and his own Church in Culenros. The time there being fulfilled, he went to the island of Leven that he might speak with S. Adamnan in person. Now S. Adamnan joyfully received the blessed man with honour, and thinking that he was seeking a place suitable for his religion, yielded that island to him as a gift with good will. Servanus therefore abode in it seven years, founded a monastery, and won many souls. Thence departing, he traversed and went round all the region of Fife, raising divers divine edifices to the Most High Creator.

CHAPTER VII.

ON a certain occasion S. Servanus was in the cave at Dysart, and a certain brother, a monk, who was with him and was sick, desired a drink of wine and could not get one. Then Blessed Servanus took water from the fountain which is there and blessed it and changed the water into wine, and the sick man was healed. Moreover in that cave when S. Servanus was lying upon his couch after matins, the devil came to him, tempting him and disputing with him. And he said to him,

"Art thou a wise cleric, Servanus?" "What wishest thou O most miserable of all creatures?" The devil said: "I wish to dispute with thee and to question thee a little?" S. Servanus said: "Begin thou miserable wretch, begin." Satan asked him: "Where was God before He created the heavens and the earth, and before all the creatures were made?" Blessed Servanus said to him: "In Himself: for He is not local, and is held by no place, neither is He divided, nor subject to the motions of time, but is whole everywhere." And the devil said: "Why did God create creatures?" The Saint said: "Because there cannot be a Creator without creatures." "Wherefore did He make them very good?" To this the Saint replied: "Because God did not wish to do evil, or lest He should seem envious by being unwilling that aught should be good except Himself." The devil said: "Where did God form Adam?" The Saint said: "In Hebron." Satan said: "Where was he afterwards cast out from Paradise?" The Saint said: "Where he was formed." Satan said: "How long was he in Paradise after he had sinned?" The Saint replied: "Only seven hours." Satan said: "Why did God permit Adam and Eve to sin in Paradise?" To this the Saint replied: "Because God foresaw what great thing would come thereof. For Christ had not been born according to the flesh, had not Adam and Eve sinned." Satan said: "Why could not Adam and Eve be set free of themselves?" Servanus to this replied: "Because they did not fall of themselves, but through another, that is through the Devil persuading them. Therefore by another, that is Christ, born of their own stock they were set free." "Why did not God make a new man and send him to deliver the human race?" The Saint said: "Because he would not have pertained to us unless he had been of the race of Adam." "Why are you men delivered by the Passion of Christ, and not we demons?" "Because we have not the origin of our fall in ourselves, but from you demons? But as for you demons, because you are not of a fragile nature nor desire to repent and have contracted the origin of sin in yourselves, the Passion of Christ does not avail for you." The Devil therefore seeing that he could do nothing against the true Saint, and being vanquished in the interrogation, said : "Thou art wise Servanus, and I can dispute no more with thee." Servanus responded : "Go thou wretched creature, go and quickly depart hence, and never more venture to appear in this place to any man." And that place in honour of the holy, holy, holy Servanus, has been sacred up to this present day.

CHAPTER VIII.

MOREOVER, on a certain occasion blessed Servanus was at Tuligbotuan (Tillicoultry), and an evil spirit entered into a certain miserable man so that he had such a desire to eat, that he could in no wise be satisfied. S. Servanus placed his thumb in his mouth, and the devil crying out terribly came out of him and left him. On another occasion Blessed Servanus was in the same place, and a certain poor little woman brought forth two dead sons there, and bore them to blessed Servanus, and with tears besought him to restore them to life for her. But the Saint prostrated himself on the ground, and entreated our Lord God to look upon this woman, and in love to restore to her her offspring alive. Accordingly, God hearkened unto the prayer of the holy man, and restored to the mother both her children alive. On another night the same Saint was at Alva, being entertained by a certain poor peasant who had no substance, except one pig, which he killed that night for the holy man, and when he rose on the morrow, he found it alive in his yard. At another time there was a man in Aitheren who had a sheep which he loved and nourished in his house. But a thief coming stealthily stole it away from him. Now the ram was sought through the whole parish, and was not found, and lo! when the thief was brought into the presence of the blessed man and interrogated by the Saint whether he was guilty of the crime laid to his charge, he affirmed on oath that he was not. And beginning again to swear by the staff of the holy man, the wether bleated in his bowels. And the wretch confessed his sin, and asked and received pardon from S. Servanus.

At the time when the Saint was in the cell at Dunning, it was told him that a dragon great and terrible and very loathesome, whose look no mortal could endure, had come into his city. The Saint went out to meet it, and taking his staff in his right hand, fought with the dragon in a certain valley and slew it. From that day that valley is called the Dragon's Den. After these things there came to Blessed Servanus from the Alps three blind men and three lame men and three deaf men, who had been told that if they came to Blessed Servanus in Scotland, they would be healed. Therefore when they came they addressed the holy man, saluting him, and revealed to him the reason of their great labour and journey, and earnestly besought him to cure them of their infirmities. But the holy man, fearing that they said these things for the purpose of tempting him, spoke to them saying: "Men, brethren, think you I am God, or do you tempt me beyond what you see in me when you ask this great thing from me that I should heal you?" But they, prostrating themselves at his feet and bursting into tears, said with an oath: "No, lord father, no; but we believe that thy prayers and petitions avail much with God, and that we can obtain health through thee from the great Creator." Blessed Servanus, therefore, hearing their faith, blessed a certain fountain, and made them wash in it three times. And they, coming out thence, were made sound through the merit of the holy man. And thus the most holy Servanus gave sight to the blind, the power of walking to the lame, and hearing to the deaf. To these and to many others suffering divers kinds of diseases, he, through the power of God, gave and furnished health. Afterwards this Saint, beloved brethren, was assailed by a grievous infirmity, and was held down by the virulence of fever, and called all his brethren and announced to them that the day of his dissolution was near. Then the brethren wept much, and continuing instant in prayer to God for him, responded: "Why dost thou desert us, O Father? or to whom wilt thou leave us desolate ones? For we would rather die with thee than live in the world without thee." But the holy man, after many miracles, after divers works, after founding many churches in Christ, when he had bestowed peace on the brethren, in the cell at Dunning, on the first day of the Kalends of July, gradually yielded up his spirit and commended it to the Great Creator. After his death his disciples and well nigh all the people of the whole province conveyed his corpse to Culross. And there, with psalms and hymns and chantings, they interred him honourably, where his merits and the virtues of his merits flourish unto this day, to the praise and honour of Almighty God, who in the perfect Trinity liveth and reigneth for ever and ever. Amen.

THE LIFE OF S. MARGARET,
QUEEN OF SCOTLAND.

THE LIFE OF S. MARGARET.

PROLOGUE.

To the honourable and excellent Matilda, Queen of the English, T[urgot], a servant of the servants of S. Cuthbert, sends the blessing of peace and health in this present life, and in the life which is to come the blessing of all good things.

FORASMUCH as you have requested, you have also commanded me, to present to you in writing the story of the life of your mother, whose memory is held in reverence, and of whose life, which was well pleasing to God, you have often heard by the concordant praise of many. You are wont to say that in this matter my testimony is especially trustworthy, since you have understood that by reason of her frequent and familiar intercourse with me I am acquainted with the most part of her secrets. These your commands and desires I willingly obey; obeying them I greatly venerate them, and venerating them I congratulate you, that, having been appointed by the King of the Angels, Queen of the English, you desire not only to hear about the life of the Queen, your mother, who ever longed for the Kingdom of the Angels, but also to look upon it in writing continually, so that, although you were but slightly acquainted with her face, you may at least obtain a more perfect knowledge of her virtues. My own wish, indeed, is to fulfil your commands, but I am wanting, I must own, in the ability; the materials for this undertaking being, in sooth, much greater than I am able either by speech or writing to set forth.

2. Thus I am in a strait between two, and am drawn hither and thither. On account of the greatness of the undertaking I fear to obey; and on account of the authority of you who

command, and the memory of her of whom I am to speak, I dare not refuse. But, though I am unable to treat so great a subject in the manner it deserves to be treated, I am nevertheless bound, as far as in me lies, to make it known. I owe this to the love I have for her and to the obedience which is due to your command. The grace of the Holy Spirit, which gave such efficacy to her virtues, will vouchsafe help to me, I trust, to narrate them. "The Lord shall give the word to them that preach good tidings with great power," and again, "Open thy mouth wide and I will fill it." For no man can fail in the Word who believes in the Word. "In the beginning was the Word, and the Word was God." In the first place, therefore, I desire that you, and that through you others, should know that if I were to attempt to relate all that could be told respecting her, I should be thought to be flattering you under cover of your mother's praises on account of the greatness of your queenly dignity. But far be it from my grey hairs to mingle the crime of falsehood with the virtues of such a woman, in setting forth which, I profess, God is my Witness and Judge, that I add nothing to the truth; but suppress many things lest they should seem incredible, and that I may not be said, as the orator has it, to be decking out a crow with the colours of a swan.

CHAPTER I.

Her noble descent and virtues as a Queen and as a Mother.

MANY, as we read, have derived the origin of their name from a quality of the mind, so that there is shewn in respect to them a correspondence between the word of their name and the grace they have received. Thus Peter was so named from "the Rock," that is Christ, on account of the firmness of his faith; so John, that is "the grace of God," because of his contemplation of the Divinity and his prerogative of the Divine love; and the sons of Zebedee were called Boanerges, that is, the Sons of Thunder, because they thundered forth the preaching of the Gospel. The same was true of this virtuous woman, in whom the fairness indicated by her name was surpassed by the exceeding beauty of her soul. She was called Margaret, *i.e.* a Pearl, and in the sight of God she was esteemed a goodly pearl by reason of her faith and good works. She was a pearl indeed to you, to me, to us all, yea even to Christ; and because she was Christ's, she is all the more ours, now that she has left us and is taken to the Lord. This pearl I say was taken from the dunghill of this world and now shines in her place among the jewels of the Eternal King. This I think no one will doubt, when he has read the following account of her life and death. When I recall the conversations I had with her, seasoned as they were with the salt of wisdom, when I think of the tears wrung from her by the compunction of her heart, when I consider the sobriety and staidness of her manners and remember her affability and prudence, I rejoice while I lament, and while lamenting I rejoice. I rejoice, because she has passed away to God after whom she longed; I lament, because I am not rejoicing with her in the heavenly places. I rejoice for her, I say, because she now sees in the land of the living the goodness of the Lord in which she believed; but for myself I mourn, because as long as I suffer the miseries of this mortal life in the land of the dead, I am daily compelled to cry, "O wretched man that I am, who shall deliver me from the body of this death?"

4. Since, then, I am to speak of that nobility of mind which she had in Christ, it is fitting that something should be first said of that nobility by which she was also distinguished according to this world. Her grandfather was King Edmund, who, because he was strong in battle and invincible by his enemies, derived his distinctive name from the excellence of his valour, for he was called in English Ironsides. His brother on his father's side, but not on his mother's, was the most religious and meek Edward, who proved himself the Father of his Country; and as another Solomon, that is, a lover of peace, protected his kingdom by peace rather than by arms. He had a mind that subdued anger, despised avarice, and was entirely

free from pride. And no wonder; for as he derived the glory of his kingly rank from his ancestors, so also he derived from them, as by hereditary right, the nobility of his life; being descended from Edgar, King of the English, and from Richard, Count of the Normans, his grandfathers on either side, men who were not only most illustrious, but also most religious. Of Edgar, in order to describe how great he was in this world and what he was in Christ, it may be briefly said that he was marked out beforehand both as a King and as a lover of justice and peace. For at his birth S. Dunstan heard the holy angels rejoicing in heaven and singing with great joy: "Let there be peace, let there be joy in the Church of the English, as long as this new-born boy shall hold the kingdom and Dunstan runs the course of this mortal life."

5. Richard, also, the father of Emma, the mother of this Edward, was an illustrious ancestor worthy of so noble a grandchild. He was a man of the greatest energy, and deserving of every praise. None of his forefathers ruled the earldom of Normandy with greater prosperity and honour, or were more fervent in their love of religion. Endowed with great riches, like a second David, he was poor in spirit; exalted to be lord over his people, he was a lowly servant of the servants of Christ. Among other things which he did as memorials of his love of religion, this devout worshipper of Christ built that noble monastery of Fecamp, in which he was often wont to reside with the monks, and where, in the habit of a secular but in heart a monk, he used to place the food of the brethren on the table when they were eating their silent meal, and serve them with drink; so that, according to the Scripture, "The greater he was the more he humbled himself in all things." If any one wishes to know more fully his works of magnificence and virtue, let him read the *Acts of the Normans*, which contains his history. From ancestors so renowned and illustrious, Edward, their grandchild, did in no wise degenerate. On the father's side only, as was before said, he was the brother of King Edmund, from whose son came Margaret, who by the splendour of her merits completes the glory of this illustrious family.

6. While therefore Margaret was still in the flower of her youth, she began to lead a life of great strictness, to love God above all things, to occupy herself with the study of the Holy Scriptures, and to exercise her mind therein with joy. Keen penetration of intellect was hers to understand any matter whatever it might be, tenacity of memory to retain many things, and a graceful facility of language to give expression to her thoughts. While therefore she meditated in the law of the Lord day and night, and, like another Mary, sitting at His feet, she delighted to hear His word, by the desire of her friends rather than by her own, yea, rather by the appointment of God, she was married to Malcolm, son of Duncan, the most powerful King of the Scots. But though compelled to do the things which are of the world, she deemed it beneath her to set her affections upon them ; for she delighted more in good works than in abundance of riches. With things temporal she procured for herself everlasting rewards ; for in heaven where her treasure was, there she had placed her heart. And because before all things she sought the kingdom of God and His righteousness, the abundant grace of the Almighty freely added to her honours and riches. All things which became the rule of a prudent Queen were done by her ; by her advice the laws of the kingdom were administered ; by her zeal the true religion was spread and the people rejoiced in the prosperity of their affairs. Nothing was more firm than her faith, more constant than her favour, more enduring than her patience, weightier than her counsel, more just than her decisions, or more pleasant than her conversation.

7. After she had attained this high dignity, she at once, in the place where her nuptials were celebrated, built an eternal monument of her name and devotion. For she erected the noble church there in honour of the Holy Trinity with a threefold purpose ; for the redemption of the King's soul, for the good of her own, and to obtain prosperity in this life and in the life that is to come for her children. This church she adorned with divers kinds of precious gifts, among which, as is well known, were vessels not a few of solid and pure gold for the holy service of the altar, of which I can speak with the

greater certainty, since by the Queen's commands, I myself for a long time had them all under my charge there. A cross, also, of incomparable value, having upon it an image of the Saviour which she had caused to be covered with a vestment of purest gold and silver studded with gems, she placed there, which proves to those who behold it even now the earnestness of her faith. To this the Church of St. Andrews bears witness, where is preserved, as is seen to this day, a most beautiful crucifix which she erected there. Without these things, those, I mean, which belong to the celebration of the divine service, her chamber was never found ; it seemed, so to say, to be the workshop of a heavenly artificer. There were always to be seen in it copes for the cantors, chasubles, stoles, altar-cloths, also other priestly vestments and church ornaments. Some were in course of preparation, others, already finished, were of admirable beauty.

8. With these works women of noble birth and approved gravity of conduct who were deemed worthy to be engaged in the Queen's service, were entrusted. No men were admitted among them, save such as she allowed to accompany her when she sometimes paid them a visit. There was no unseemly familiarity among them with the men, nor any pert frivolity. For the Queen united such strictness to her sweetness and such sweetness to her strictness that all who were in her service, men as well as women, while fearing loved her and while loving feared her. Wherefore in her presence no one ventured to do anything wrong, or even to utter an unseemly word. For repressing all evil in herself, there was great gravity in her joy and something noble in her anger. Her mirth was never expressed in immoderate laughter ; when angry she never gave way to fury. Always angry with her own faults, she sometimes reproved those of others with that commendable anger tempered with justice which the Psalmist enjoined, when he says : " Be angry and sin not." Her whole life, regulated with the utmost skill of discretion, was, as it were, a pattern of the virtues. Her conversation was seasoned with the salt of wisdom : her silence was filled with good thoughts. Her bearing so corresponded with the gravity of her character that

she might be believed to have been born simply to show what comeliness of life is. But to speak briefly, in whatever she was wont to say or do, she showed that her mind was dwelling on things divine.

9. Nor did she spend less pains upon her children than upon herself, that they might be brought up with the utmost care, and especially that they might be trained in virtue. Hence because she knew the Scripture: He that spareth the rod hateth his child, she instructed the governor of the nursery as often as the children fell into such faults as are common to their age, to curb them with threats and the rod. By reason of their mother's religious care they excelled many who were of greater age in their good behaviour. Among themselves they were always kindly and peaceable, and the younger everywhere paid respect to the elder. Hence, also, during the celebration of the Mass, when they went up after their parents to make their offerings, the younger never in any way presumed to precede the older, but the older were wont to go before the younger according to their age. She would often call them to her, and, as far as their age would allow, instruct them concerning Christ and the faith of Christ, and carefully endeavour to admonish them to always fear Him. "O my children," she would say, "fear the Lord; for they that fear Him shall not want anything that is good; and if you love Him, He will give you, my darlings, prosperity in this life and eternal felicity with all the saints." This was the mother's desire, her admonition, the prayer which she uttered day and night with tears for her little ones, that they might acknowledge their Maker in the faith that worketh by love, and acknowledging worship Him, and worshipping Him, love Him in all things and above all things, and loving Him attain to the glory of the heavenly kingdom.

CHAPTER II.

Her care for the honour of the Kingdom and discipline of the Church. Abuses corrected.

NOR need we wonder that the Queen ruled herself and her household wisely, since she was always guided by the most wise counsel of the Holy Scriptures. For what I used frequently to admire in her was that amid the distraction of lawsuits, and the countless affairs of the Kingdom, she gave herself with wonderful diligence to the reading of the Word of God, concerning which she used to ask profound questions of the learned men who were sitting near her. But as among them no one had a profounder intellect, so no one had the power of clearer expression. Thus it often happened that these teachers left her much more learned than when they came. She had a religious and earnest desire for the sacred volumes, and very often her affectionate familiarity with me urged me to exert myself to obtain them for her. Nor in these things was she anxious for her own salvation alone ; she sought also that of others. And first of all, with the help of God, she made the King himself most attentive to works of justice, mercy, almsgiving, and other virtues. From her also he learned to keep the vigils of the night in prayer : from her exhortation and example he learned to pray with groanings from the heart and abundance of tears. I confess I marvelled at this great miracle of the mercy of God when I saw such earnestness of devotion in the King, and such sorrow in the heart of a layman when engaged in prayer.

11. A Queen whose life was so venerable, he as it were feared to offend, since he clearly perceived that Christ was truly dwelling in her heart ; he hastened rather the more quickly to obey in all things her wishes and prudent counsels. What she refused he refused, and what she loved, he loved for the love of her love. Hence also the books which she used either in her devotions or for reading, he, though unable to read, used often to handle and examine, and when he heard

from her that one of them was dearer to her than the others, this he also regarded with kindlier affection, and would kiss and often fondle it. Sometimes also he would send for the goldsmith, and instruct him to adorn the volume with gold and precious stones, and when finished he would carry it to the Queen as a proof of his devotion. The Queen, on the other hand, herself the noblest gem of a royal race, made the splendour of her husband's royal magnificence much more splendid, and contributed much glory and honour to all the nobility of the kingdom and their retainers. For she brought it to pass that merchants who came by land and sea from divers lands, brought with them for sale many and precious kinds of merchandise which in Scotland were before unknown, among which, at the instigation of the Queen, the people bought garments of various colours, and different kinds of personal ornaments; so that from that time they went about clothed in new costumes of different fashions, from the elegance of which they might have been supposed to be a new race. She also appointed a higher class of servants for the King, that when he walked or rode abroad numerous bodies of them might accompany him in state; and this was carried out with such discipline that wherever they came none of them was permitted to take anything from anyone by force; nor did any of them dare to oppress or injure the country people or the poor in any way. Moreover, she increased the splendour of the royal palace, so that not only was it brightened by the different coloured uniforms worn in it, but the whole house was made resplendent with gold and silver; for the vessels in which the King and nobles of the kingdom were served with food and drink, were either of gold or silver, or with gold or silver plated.

12. And this the Queen did not because the honour of the world delighted her, but because she felt compelled to do what the royal dignity required of her. For when she walked in state clad in splendid apparel, as became a Queen, like another Esther, she in her heart trod all these trappings beneath her feet, and bore in mind that under the gems and gold there was nothing but dust and ashes. In a word, in the midst of her

exalted dignity she always took the greatest care to preserve her lowliness of mind. It was easy for her to repress all swellings of pride arising from worldly glory, inasmuch as the fleeting nature of this frail life never escaped from her thoughts. For she always remembered the text in which the miserable condition of human life is described: "Man that is born of woman, is of few days, and full of trouble. He cometh forth like a flower, and is cut down, and fleeth also as a shadow and continueth not." She meditated continually also on that passage of the Blessed Apostle James, in which he says: "What is your life? It is even a vapour that appeareth for a little time, and then vanisheth away." And because as the Scripture says, "Happy is the man that feareth alway," this venerable Queen made it the easier for her to avoid sin, as in fear and trembling she continually kept before her mind's eye the dreadful day of Judgment. Hence she frequently entreated me not to hesitate to point out and reprove in private anything which I saw amiss in her words or actions. Because I did this less frequently and sharply than she wished, she urged the duty on me and accused me of being asleep and, as it were, negligent towards her: "The just man," she said, "shall correct me in mercy, and shall reprove me; but let not the oil of the sinner, that is the flattery, fatten my head;" for "Better are the wounds of a friend than the deceitful kisses of an enemy." She would say this because she sought censure as helping her advancement in virtue, where another might have regarded it as a disgrace.

13. This religious and devout Queen, while she thus in mind and word and deed journeyed on to the heavenly country, also invited others to accompany her on the undefiled way, in order that they with her might attain true happiness. The wicked whom she saw, she admonished to become good; the good to be better, and the better to strive to be best. The zeal of God's house, which is the Church, consumed her so that, aglow with Apostolic faith, she laboured to root out entirely those unlawful things which had sprung up within it. For when she saw that many things were done among the Scottish people which were contrary to the rule of the right faith and the holy

custom of the universal Church, she appointed frequent councils to be held, in order that by some means or other she might, through the gift of Christ, bring back the wandering into the way of truth. Of these councils, the most important is that in which she alone, with a very few of her friends, for three days combatted the defenders of a perverse custom with the sword of the Spirit, that is, with the Word of God. You would have thought that another Helena was present; for just as she formerly overcame the Jews with the authority of the Scriptures, so now did this Queen those who were in error. At their discussion the King himself was present as an assessor and chief actor, fully prepared to say and do whatever she in this matter might direct. And as he knew the English language quite as well as his own, he was in this Council a most expert watchful interpreter for either side.

14. The Queen opened the proceedings by remarking that all who serve one God in one faith along with the Catholic Church ought not to vary from that Church by new or strange usages. She then pointed out in the first place that they were observing the fast of Lent in a way which was not lawful, inasmuch as they were in the habit of beginning it not with the Holy Catholic Church on the fourth day of the week at the beginning of Lent, but on the Monday of the week following. To this they answered: "The fast which we observe, we keep according to the authority of the Gospel, which states that Christ fasted six weeks." She replied by saying: "In this matter you differ widely from the Gospel, for we read there that the Lord fasted forty days, which you clearly do not do. For when during the six weeks, six Lord's days are deducted from the fast, it is plain that only thirty and six days remain for fasting. Plainly therefore the fast which you keep is not the forty days enjoined by the Gospel, but one of thirty and six days. It remains therefore for you, if you wish to observe an abstinence of forty days, after our Lord's example, to begin to fast with us four days before Quadragesima; otherwise you alone will be acting contrary to the authority of our Lord, and in opposition to the tradition of the entire Holy Church." Convinced by this clear demonstration of the truth, they

henceforth began the solemnities of the sacred fasts at the same time as Holy Church does everywhere.

15. The Queen also raised another point, and required them to explain for what reason they neglected to receive the Sacrament of the Body and Blood of Christ at Easter according to the custom of the Holy and Apostolic Church. They answered: "The Apostle speaking of those who celebrate the Lord's Supper says: 'He that eateth and drinketh unworthily, eateth and drinketh judgment to himself.' And hence because we acknowledge that we are sinners, we fear to approach that mystery lest we should eat and drink judgment to ourselves." "What!" said the Queen, "Shall all who are sinners not taste that holy mystery? No one therefore ought to receive it, for there is not one who is not stained with sin; not even the infant whose life is but one day on the earth. And if no one ought to receive it, why did the Lord when he proclaimed the Gospel say, 'Except ye shall eat the flesh of the Son of Man, and drink His blood, ye shall not have life in you.' But if you would understand the passage you have adduced from the Apostle in the same way as the Father, it is evident that you must take quite another view of it. For the Apostle does not say that all sinners are unworthy to receive the sacraments of salvation, for after saying, 'he eateth and drinketh judgment to himself,' he adds, 'Not discerning the Body of our Lord,' that is, not distinguishing it in faith from bodily foods, 'he eateth and drinketh judgment to himself.' But he who without confession and penance, and with the defilement of his sins presumes to draw near to the sacred mysteries—he it is, I say, who eats and drinks judgment to himself. But we who many days previously have made confession of our faults, are chastened with penance and fasts, and washed from the stains of our sins by almsgiving and tears—we on the day of the resurrection of the Lord, approaching His Table in the Catholic Faith, receive the Body and Blood of the Immaculate Lamb, Jesus Christ, not to judgment, but to the remission of sins and to the salutary preparation of our souls for the reception of eternal blessedness." To these arguments they could make no

reply, and understanding now the practices of the Church, observed them in the reception of the mystery of salvation.

16. Moreover, there were some in certain parts of Scotland who were wont to celebrate Masses according to I know not what barbarous rite, contrary to the custom of the whole Church. This the Queen, fired by zeal for God, sought to destroy and abolish, so that henceforth throughout the whole of Scotland there was no one who presumed to continue any such practice. It was their custom also to neglect the reverence due to the Lord's Day, and to follow their earthly occupation on that day as on others—a practice she showed them which was forbidden both by reason and authority. "Let us reverence the Lord's Day," she said, "because of the Lord's Resurrection, which took place upon it; let us no longer do servile works on the day on which we know that we were redeemed from the bondage of the devil. This also the Blessed Pope Gregory affirms, saying: 'On the Lord's Day we ought to abstain from earthly labour, and devote ourselves wholly to prayer, in order that if during the six days we have been negligent in anything, we may on the Lord's Day expiate it by prayers.' The same Father, Gregory, after condemning one with the greatest warmth for a certain piece of earthly work which he had done on the Lord's Day, decreed that those on whose advice he had done it should be excommunicated for two months." Unable to contradict these arguments of the wise Queen, they henceforward at her instance observed the Lord's Days with such reverence that no one dared to carry a burden on them, nor did any man venture to compel another to do so. Next she showed how utterly abominable, and to be shunned by the faithful as death itself, was the unlawful marriage of a man with his step-mother, or with the widow of his deceased brother; both of which customs had hitherto prevailed in the country. Many other abuses also which had grown up contrary to the rule of faith and the institutions and observances of the Church, she likewise in this Council succeeded in condemning and expelling from the Kingdom. For whatever she proposed, she so supported with the testimony of the Holy Scriptures and with citations from the holy Fathers, that no one on the

opposite side could say anything at all against it; nay, rather, laying aside their obstinacy and yielding to reason, they willingly undertook to adopt whatever she desired.

CHAPTER III.

Her charity towards the poor. Her manner of passing Lent. Her prayerfulness.

THUS the venerable Queen, who by the help of God had endeavoured to cleanse His house from defilements and errors, was found day by day as the Holy Spirit illuminated her heart, more and more meet to become His temple. And such I well know she truly was, for I both saw the works which she did outwardly, and knew her conscience, for she revealed it to me. She condescended to converse with me in the most familiar way, and to disclose to me her secret thoughts; not because there was anything good in me, but because she thought there was. When she conversed with me concerning the salvation of the soul and the sweetness of the life which is eternal, she uttered words so full of all grace that the Holy Spirit, which truly dwelt in her heart, evidently spoke by her lips. And so deeply was she moved while speaking, that it might have been thought that she would be wholly dissolved in tears, and at her compunction I also was moved to weeping. Beyond all whom I have ever known she devoted herself to prayer and fasting, and to works of mercy and almsgiving. Let me speak first of her prayerfulness. In a church no one was ever more silent or composed, and in prayer no one was ever more earnest. For while in the house of God she would never speak of worldly matters, nor do anything which savoured of the earth. It was her custom there only to pray, in prayer to pour forth her tears. In the body only was she here on earth; her soul was with God; for besides God and the things which are God's, in her pure supplications she sought nothing.

But what shall I say of her fasting? This only, that by her too great abstinence she brought upon herself a very serious infirmity.

18. To these two, that is, to prayer and fasting, she joined the gifts of mercy. For what could be more compassionate than her heart? What more gentle to the needy? Not only would she give her goods to the poor, but if she could, she would have freely given herself. She was poorer than any of her paupers, for they, having nothing, desired to have, but she was anxious to dispose what she had. When she walked or rode out in public, crowds of poor people, orphans and widows, flocked to her as they would to a most beloved mother, and none of them ever left her without being comforted. And when all she had brought with her for the use of the needy had been distributed, she used to receive from her attendants and the rich who accompanied her their garments and anything else they had with them at the time, to bestow upon the poor, so that no one might ever go away from her in distress. Nor did those who were with her take this ill; they rather strove among themselves to offer her what they had, since they knew for certain that she would pay them the double of what they had given. Now and then she took something or other, whatever it might be, from the King's private property to give to a poor person, and the King always took this pious plundering in good part and pleasantly. On Maundy Thursday and at High Mass he used to make an offering of gold coins, and some of these she would often piously steal and give away to the beggar who was importuning her for alms. Often indeed the King, who was quite aware of what she was doing, though he pretended not to know anything about it, was greatly amused at this kind of theft, and sometimes, when he caught her in the act with the coins in her hand, would jocularly threaten to have her arrested, tried, and condemned. Nor was it to the poor of her own people alone that she exhibited the abundance of her cheerful and open-handed charity, those also were sharers of her bounty whom the fame of her liberality drew towards her from almost every other nation. Of a truth,

to her may be applied the Scripture: "He hath dispersed; he hath given to the poor; his righteousness endureth for ever."

19. But who can tell the number of the English of all ranks carried away captive from their own country by the violence of war, and reduced to slavery, whom she restored to liberty by paying their ransom? She sent secret spies everywhere throughout the provinces of Scotland to ascertain who among the captives were oppressed with the more cruel bondage or were the more inhumanely treated, and to report privately to her where they were and by whom they were ill-treated; and, commiserating them from the bottom of her heart, she hastened to their assistance, paid their ransom, and restored them to freedom. At that time there were very many in different parts of the kingdom of Scotland who, shut up in separate cells, were leading lives of great strictness, in the flesh but not according to the flesh, for though on this earth, they were living the life of angels. In these the Queen venerated Christ and loved Him, and frequently occupied herself in visiting and conversing with them, and used to commend herself to their prayers. And since she could not prevail upon them to accept from her any earthly gift, she used to earnestly entreat them to honour her by prescribing for her some work of almsgiving or mercy; and forthwith this devout woman did whatever they desired, either by rescuing the poor out of their poverty or by relieving the afflicted from the miseries by which they were oppressed.

20. Since the church of St. Andrews was much frequented by the devout, who flocked to it from all sides, she erected dwellings on either shore of the sea which divides Lothian from Scotland, that, after the fatigues of their journey, pilgrims and the poor might take shelter and rest, and there find already prepared for them all they needed for the refreshment of the body; for she had appointed servants whose exclusive duty was always to have in readiness everything that these wayfarers might need, and to attend to them with the greatest care. She also provided ships for the transport of these pilgrims, both coming and going; nor was any toll ever levied from those who were ferried across.

21. As I have spoken of the daily manner of life of this

venerable Queen, and of her daily works of mercy, I will now attempt to give a brief account of how she used to spend the forty days before Christmas and the whole season of Lent. After she had rested a little at the beginning of the night, she went into the church, and there alone she completed first the Matins of the Holy Trinity, next the Matins of the Holy Cross, and then the Matins of Our Lady. When these were ended she began the Offices of the Dead, and after these the Psalter, nor did she cease until she had gone through it. While the priests were saying the Matins and Lauds at the fitting hour, she either finished the Psalter she had begun, or if she had finished it, began it a second time. When she had gone through the office of the Matins and Lauds, she returned to her chamber, and along with the King himself washed the feet of six poor persons, and used to give them something wherewith they might relieve their poverty. It was the Chamberlain's especial duty to bring these poor people in every night before the Queen's arrival, so that she might find them ready when she came to wait upon them. After she had waited upon them, she betook herself to rest and sleep.

22. When the day dawned she rose from bed, and continued for a long time in prayer and reading the Psalms, and whilst reading them performed this work of mercy—nine orphan little children, who were utterly destitute, she caused to be brought in to her at the first hour of the day in order that she might feed them. For she ordered soft food, such as little children delight in, to be prepared for them daily; and when the little ones were brought to her, she did not think it beneath her to take them on her knee and make little sups for them, and to place them in their mouths with the spoons she herself used. Thus the Queen, who was honoured by all the people, performed for Christ's sake the office of a most devoted servant and mother. To her the words of the Blessed Job might very fittingly be applied: "From my infancy mercy grew up with me, and it came out with me from my mother's womb." While this was going on, it was the custom to bring three hundred poor people into the royal hall, and when they had been seated round it in order, the King and Queen came in, and the doors

were shut by the servants, for with the exception of the chaplains, certain religious, and a few attendants, no one was permitted to witness their alms-givings. The King on the one side, and the Queen on the other, waited upon Christ in the person of His poor, and with great devotion served them with food and drink, which had been specially prepared for this purpose. When this was finished, the Queen used to go into the Church and there offer herself a sacrifice to God with many prayers, sighs, and tears. For besides the Hours of the Holy Trinity, the Holy Cross, and the Holy Mary, recited within the space of a day and a night, she would on these holy days repeat the Psalter twice or thrice, and before the celebration of the Public Mass cause five or six Masses to be sung privately in her presence.

23. By the time these things were finished, the time for eating was at hand, but before taking her own food she fed twenty-four poor people, whom she humbly waited upon herself. For besides the many alms-deeds I have spoken of already, she supported poor people to this number, that is, twenty-four, throughout the whole course of the year as long as she lived. These she desired to live near to wherever she herself was living, and to accompany her wherever she went. After she had devoutly waited upon Christ in these, she used to refresh her own feeble body. In this meal, since according to the Apostle we ought not to make provision for the lust of the flesh, she hardly allowed herself the necessaries of life, for she ate only to sustain life and not to please her palate. Her light and frugal meal excited rather than satisfied her hunger. She seemed to taste her food, not to take it. From this let it be considered, I beseech you, how great her abstinence was when she fasted, when such was her abstinence when she feasted. And though her whole life was one of great temperance, yet during these fasts, that is, during the forty days preceding Easter and Christmas, the abstinence with which she was in the habit of afflicting herself was incredible. Hence, on account of her excessive fasting, she suffered up to the end of her life from a very acute pain in the stomach. Nevertheless, her bodily infirmity did not impair

her virtue in good works. Assiduous in reading the sacred Scriptures, instant in prayer, and unceasing in alms-giving, she exercised herself continually and watchfully in all things pertaining to God. And because she knew the Scripture: "Whom the Lord loveth, he chasteneth, and scourgeth every son whom he receiveth," she accepted the pains of her body willingly, and with patience and thanksgiving, as the stripes of a most gracious Father.

24. Since therefore she was devoted to these and similar works, and struggled with her continual infirmities, God's strength, to use the words of the Apostle, was made perfect in her weakness, and going on from strength to strength, she was each day made better. Forsaking in her heart all earthly things, she longed with her whole soul for the things of heaven, yea, thirsted for them, crying out with her heart and voice with the Psalmist: "My soul thirsteth for God, for the living God; when shall I come and appear before God." Let others admire the tokens of miracles which they see in others, I, for my part, admire much more the works of mercy which I saw in Margaret. Miracles are common to the evil and to the good, but the works of true piety and charity belong to the good alone. The former sometimes indicate holiness, but the latter are holiness itself. Let us, I say, admire in Margaret the things which made her a saint, rather than the miracles, if she did any, which might only have indicated that she was one to men. Let us more worthily admire her as one in whom, because of her devotion to justice, piety, mercy, and love, we see rather the works of the ancient Fathers than their miracles. Nevertheless, it will not be out of place if I here narrate one incident which seems to me to indicate the holiness of her life.

25. She had a book of the Gospels beautifully adorned with jewels and gold, and ornamented with the figures of the four Evangelists, painted and gilt. The capital letters throughout the volume were also resplendent with gold. For this volume she had always a greater affection than she had for any others she was in the habit of reading. It happened that while the person who was carrying it was crossing a ford, he let the vol-

ume, which had been carelessly folded in a wrapper, fall into the middle of the stream, and, ignorant of what had occurred, he quietly continued his journey. But when he afterwards wished to produce the book, he, for the first time, became aware that he had lost it. It was sought for for a long time, but was not found. At length it was found at the bottom of the river, lying open, so that its leaves were kept in constant motion by the action of the water, and the little coverings of silk which protected the letters of gold from being injured by the contact of the leaves, were carried away by the force of the current. Who would imagine that the book would be worth anything after what had happened to it? Who would believe that even a single letter would have been visible in it? Yet of a truth it was taken up out of the middle of the river so perfect, uninjured, and free from damage, that it looked as though it had not even been touched by the water. For the whiteness of the leaves, and the form of the letters throughout the whole of the volume remained exactly as they were before it fell into the river, except that on the margin of the leaves, towards the edge, some trace of the water could with difficulty be detected. The book was conveyed to the Queen, and the miracle reported to her at the same time, and she having given thanks to Christ, esteemed the volume much more highly than she did before. Wherefore let others consider what they should think of this, but as for me I am of opinion that this miracle was wrought by our Lord because of His love for this venerable Queen.

CHAPTER IV.

The Queen's preparations for her end. Her sickness and happy death.

MEANTIME, while Almighty God was preparing everlasting rewards for her works of devotion, she was preparing herself, with more than her usual carefulness, for entering another life. For, as her own word a little after showed, it would appear that her own departure from this life and certain other events were known to her long before they occurred. Therefore summoning me to come to her privately, she began to recount to me in order the story of her life, and as she proceeded shed floods of tears. In short, so great was her compunction while she conversed with me, and out of her compunction there sprang such an abundance of tears, that, as it seemed to me, there was, beyond all doubt, nothing which she might not at that time have obtained from Christ. As she wept I also wept; thus for a time we wept and at times were silent, since by reason of our sobs we were unable to give utterance to our words. The flame, as it were, of the compunction which consumed her heart reached my own soul also, borne into it by the spiritual fervour of her words. And when I heard the words of the Holy Ghost speaking by her tongue and clearly perceived her conscience revealed by her words, I judged myself unworthy of the grace of so great a familiarity.

27. When she had ceased to speak of the things which it was needful for her to speak, she began to address me again, saying: "Farewell, I shall not remain long with you in this life; but you will survive me for a considerable time. Two things, therefore, I beg of you. One is, that as long as you live you will remember me in your prayers and at the Mass; the other is, that you will take some care of my sons and daughters, pour out your affection upon them, above all things teach them to fear and love God, and never cease from instructing them; and when you see any of them exalted to the height of earthly dignity, then at once, as a father or a teacher in the highest sense, go to him, warn, and when circumstances require it, censure him, lest, on account of a passing honour, he be puffed up with pride, or offend God with avarice, or through the prosperity of the world neglect the blessedness of life eternal. These are the things," she said, "which I ask you, as in the sight of God who is now present along with us two, to promise me that you will carefully do." At these words I again burst into tears and promised her that I would carefully perform what she had asked me; for I did not dare to oppose one whom I heard unhesitatingly predict what was to come to pass. The truth of her prediction has now been verified by the things

which now are ; since I live and she is dead and I see her offspring raised to dignity and honour. Thus having finished her conference with me and being about to return home I said farewell to the Queen for the last time ; for I saw her face no more.

28. Not long after this she was attacked by an illness more severe than usual, and was purified by the fire of a tedious sickness before the day on which she was called away. I will describe her death as I heard it narrated by her priest, whom, on account of his simplicity, innocence, and purity, she loved more intimately than the others, and who after her death gave himself to Christ in perpetual service for her soul, and having put on the monk's habit, offered himself as a sacrifice for her at the tomb of the incorrupt body of the most holy Father Cuthbert. Towards the end of the Queen's life he was continually with her, and with his prayers commended her soul to Christ as it was leaving the body. Of her decease as he saw it he more than once gave me a connected account, for I often asked him, and he was wont to do so with tears.

29. "For a little more than half a year," he said, "she was never able to sit on horseback, and seldom to rise from her bed. On the fourth day before her death, while the King was absent on an expedition, and at so great a distance that it was impossible for any messenger, however swift he might be, to bring her tidings of what was happening to him that day, she became sadder than usual, and said to me as I sat beside her: 'Perhaps so great a calamity is to-day befalling the realm of Scotland as has not overtaken it for many ages.' When I heard the words I did not pay much attention to them ; but a few days after a messenger came who informed us that the King had been slain on the very day the Queen had spoken about them. As if foreseeing the future, she had been very urgent with him not to go with the army, but it chanced, I know not from what cause, that he did not follow her advice.

30. "When the fourth day after the King's death approached, her weakness having abated a little, she went into her oratory to hear Mass, and there she took care to fortify herself beforehand for her departure, which was already at hand, with the holy

Viaticum of the Body and Blood of the Lord. Refreshed with this health-giving food, she went back to bed, for her former pains returned with greater severity. Towards the end her trouble increases and she was very sorely pressed. What can I do? Why do I delay? As if I were able to defer the death of my Queen, or lengthen her life—thus I fear to come to the end. But 'All flesh is grass, and all the glory thereof as the flower of the grass; the grass withereth and the flower falleth.' Her face had already grown pale with death when she directed that I and other ministers of the sacred Altar with me should stand beside her and commend her soul to Christ with our psalms. Moreover, she requested that a cross should be brought to her, called the Black Cross, which she had always held in the greatest veneration. But as the chest in which it was kept could not be quickly opened, the Queen said with a deep sigh: 'O unhappy that we are! O guilty that we are! Shall we not be permitted one last look of the Holy Cross!' When at length it was taken out of the chest and brought to her, she received it with reverence, and frequently tried to embrace it and kiss it, and to sign her eyes and face with it. Every part of her body was already growing cold, yet as long as the warmth of life throbbed in her breast she continued in prayer. She repeated the whole of the Fiftieth Psalm, and while so doing, placed the Cross before her eyes and held it there with both her hands.

31. 'It was whilst she was doing this that her son, who now after his father holds in this kingdom the helm of the State, arrived from the army and entered the Queen's chamber. What must then have been his distress? What his agony of soul? He stood there in a strait, with everything against him; whither to turn he knew not. He had come to announce to his mother that his father and brother had been slain, and he found his mother, whom he loved most dearly, at the point of death. Whom to lament first he knew not. Yet, the loss of his dearest mother, whom he saw lying almost dead before his eyes, pierced his heart with the sharpest pain. Besides all this, the condition of the kingdom was filling him with the deepest anxiety, for he well knew that disturbances would follow on

the death of his father. On every side he was met by sadness and trouble. The Queen when lying, as it seemed to those present, rapt in agony, suddenly collected her strength and addressed her son. She asked him concerning his father and his brother. He was unwilling to tell her the truth, lest if she heard of their death she herself would immediately die, and answered that they were well. But she, sighing deeply, said: 'I know it, my son; I know it. By this holy Cross, by the bond of our blood, I adjure thee to tell me the truth.' When he was thus pressed, he told her all as it had happened. What could she do, think you? Who would have believed that in the midst of so many adversities she would not murmur against God? At the same moment she had lost her husband and her son, and a disease had tormented her until she was on the point of death. But in all these things she sinned not with her lips, nor spoke foolishly against God, rather she raised her eyes and hands to heaven and broke forth into praise and thanksgiving, saying: 'Praise and thanks I give to Thee, Almighty God, that Thou hast been pleased that I should endure such great afflictions at my departing, and art pleased, as I trust, that, through enduring these afflictions, I should be cleansed from some stain of sin.'

32. "She now felt that death was close at hand, and at once began the prayer which is wont to be said by the priest after he receives the Body and Blood of our Lord, saying: 'Lord Jesus Christ, who, according to the will of the Father, through the co-operation of the Holy Ghost, hast by Thy death given life to the world, deliver me.' As she was saying the words 'Deliver me,' her soul was delivered from the chains of the body, and departed to Christ, the author of true liberty, whom she had always loved, and by whom she was made a partaker of the happiness of the saints, the example of whose virtues she had followed. With such tranquillity and such quietude was her departure, that there can be no doubt that her soul passed to the land of eternal rest and peace. It was remarkable that her face which, when she was dying, had exhibited the usual pallor of death, was afterwards suffused with red and white tints, so that it might have been believed that she was

not dead but sleeping. Her corpse was honourably shrouded as became a Queen, and we bore it to the Church of the Holy Trinity, which she herself had built; and there, as she had directed, we committed it to the grave opposite the Altar and the venerable sign of the Holy Cross which she had erected. And thus her body now rests in the place where she was wont to humble herself with vigils, prayers, shedding of tears, and prostrations."

THE LIFE OF S. MAGNUS.

THE LIFE OF S. MAGNUS.

PRAISE, glory, and honour with reverence be unto Almighty God, our Redeemer and Creator, for His manifold goodness and mercy which He has granted unto us, who dwell in the uttermost parts of the earth, and seem to the learned, as they have written in their books, as if we were utterly gone out from the world. Albeit, it has pleased God to show unto us His mercy; especially in this, that he has suffered us to come to the knowledge of His blessed name, and therewith given us strong pillars, most saintly fore-runners of Holy Christianity by whose holiness all the Northern world shines and beams near and far. These are: the King, S. Olaf, and the illustrious Halward, his kinsman, who adorn Norway with their sacred relics; the worthy Magnus, Earl of the Isles, who illumines the Orkneys with his holiness, and to whose honour this history following has been composed. With these are the blessed Bishops, John and Thorlak, who have shed, with holy splendour, their illustrious merits upon Iceland. Wherefore it may be seen that we are not far off from the mercy of God, although our dwellings be placed far from those of other nations; and therefore ought we to give thanks, honour, and reverence all the time of our life.

Master Robert, who has put together this history of the holy Earl Magnus and endited it in Latin, begins his prologue thus, as who will may hear:—

2. Such things as he is able each one brings to the tabernacle of God for help and mercy to himself: one gold, others silver, some precious stones, some goats' hair and red skins of he-goats; and such offerings are not despised; for of such is made the covering for the tabernacle of God, to shelter it and

protect it against moisture and the heat of the sun. These words may thus be glossed with a few words: Let every Christian man offer to God of the gifts and loans which he has granted him, the best he has: so that God's Christianity, which is the tabernacle, which Moses built for the service of God, signifies, that it may serve to defend and strengthen him against the assaults of his enemies. Gold signifies wisdom and knowledge; silver, chastity; precious stones, the miracles of the saints; goats' hair, the repentance of sin; the red skin of the he-goats, martyrdom. Now may the reader observe that all these offerings has S. Magnus offered to his Lord, as the story of his life bears witness. Now, although the praise of God may not be seemly in the mouth of sinful man, still it may be meet and helpful to others; for so we read that the whole house was filled with the sweetest perfume from the ointment and spices of the woman which was a sinner, who in penitence stooped down to wash and anoint the feet of the Lord. But after the wont of the men who till the fields of others but their own neglect and let lie dry, we begin this story of the life of the holy Earl Magnus with the greater confidence and love, and our labour spend upon so holy and noble a narrative, because we trust and fully expect his help to support and strengthen us to his own honour and glory. Now since he is a sharer in the kingdom of heaven and has entered into the kingdom of the Lord, he is able to obtain whatsoever he desires. But since we are sinful and may not, because of our wretched life, set of ourselves good examples to others, we show you the holy Magnus with his glorious life, whom all ought to follow, and take holy example from. Now that we may not be wearisome to the reader with this sermon (for the Lord made short sermons), we shall set forth this story in simple words and in pure speech as God gave us to perceive.

3. In the days of Harold Sigurd's son, King of Norway, there ruled over the Orkneys as Earls, two brothers, Paul and Erlend, the sons of Thorfinn, the most powerful of all the Earls of Orkney. He was son of Earl Sigurd whom King Olaf Tryggvi's son converted, along with all the people of the Orkneys, to the Christian Faith. This Sigurd fell at the

battle of Clontarf in Ireland. The mother of Erlend and
Paul was Ingibiorg, who was called Earlsmother, the daughter
of Earl Finn Arni's son. Harold Sigurd's son married Thora,
daughter of Thorberg Arni's son, and mother of Olaf the Quiet,
and therefore third cousins were King Olaf and the aforesaid
Earls. Earl Erlend married a woman called Thora, daughter
to Summarlid Ospak's son. Ospak's mother was Thordis,
daughter of Hall of Sida. Egill was the name of a son of the
aforenamed Hall; his daughter was Thorgerd, the mother of
S. John, bishop of Holar. The sons of Earl Erlend and Thora
were S. Magnus and Erling, and daughters, Gunnhild and
Cecilia. Gunnhild was married afterwards to Kol Kali's son,
a franklin in Norway. Their son was Rognvald Kali, who
afterwards was Earl in the Orkneys; he was a very holy man,
and sister's son to Earl Magnus the Saint. Earl Paul, Erlend's
brother, married a daughter of Earl Hakon, son of Ivar and
Ragnhild, daughter of King Magnus the Good, son of King
Olaf the Holy. Paul's son was called Hakon, who afterwards
comes into the story.

4. Earl S. Magnus was born in the Orkneys, the most noble
of race and illustrious of kindred. His father Erlend was
Earl of Orkney, a worthy lord and ruler, honoured for his
power and greatness, as is the wont of those who live magnificently in this world. His mother Thora was descended
from the most noble chiefs of this land. And though with
many greatness of birth is turned to pride and spoiling of
temper, yet was this blessed child already from the earliest
days of his childhood illuminated and instructed by the teaching of the Holy Spirit; for he held to and loved, honoured
and preserved the highest virtue of the mind, a kindly nature,
and becoming manners, and steadfastness in honourable
ways. This boy showed himself old in good manners, share-
less in childish life in his deeds, glad spoken aud blithe, gentle
in his loving words, yielding and reasonable in his ways and in
all his behaviour; well matured and staid, so that nothing was
found in his conduct to anger or offend men who beheld him.
At an early age he was sent to school, to learn the sacred
Scriptures and the other knowledge men then most studied to

know. Magnus was gentle and tractable, docile and obedient to his father and mother and teachers; kind and dear to all the people. He attached himself little to wickedness and pastimes as other young men, but conducted himself in a seemly way, though he was young in the number of his years; for there at once shone in him the manifest gift of the Holy Spirit, which guided him to all good things.

5. While the brothers, Erlend and Paul, held rule in the Orkneys, there came west from Norway King Harald Sigurd's son with a mighty army to the Orkneys, and left there Queen Elizabeth, and Mary and Ingigerd, his daughters. The earls resolved to accompany the King with a great army, and held them south to England: and in the battle they fought with King Harald Godwin's son, fell Harald Sigurd's son, the fifth night after S. Matthew's day, in the autumn. After this battle Olaf the Quiet, Harald's son, sailed with the earls that autumn back to the Orkneys. The same day and the same hour King Harald fell in England, died suddenly Mary, his daughter, in the Orkneys; and the saying is that they had but one life between them. Olaf the Quiet passed the winter in the Orkneys, and was the best of friends with the Earls, his kinsmen, for brother's daughters were Thora, Olaf's mother, and Ingibiorg, the mother of the Earls. Olaf went in the Spring east to Norway, and was there made King with Magnus, his brother.

6. These brothers, Paul and Erlend, ruled the Orkneys a long time, and long was their agreement good. But when their sons began to grow up, Hakon and Erling became very overbearing, but Magnus was the quietest and best mannered in every thing. All the kinsmen were men of large stature, strong, and highly accomplished in all things. Hakon, Paul's son, wished to be overman to Erlend's sons, because he thought he was of better birth than they; for he was daughter's son to Earl Hakon, Ivar's son, and Ragnhild, daughter of King Magnus the Good, as was before told, and he wished to have a greater share out of all their dealings. So it came about that they began not to agree; for many men inclined to Erlend's sons, and would not have them to be inferior to any in the islands, for they

were of all the people better liked and beloved of men. This was a cause of great offence to Hakon all his life. The sons of the Earls were never safe with each other. Their fathers tried to arrange matters for them, that they might be at peace among themselves. A meeting was called, and it was soon found that each Earl favoured his own sons, and they began not to agree. Then great quarrels arose between these brothers, and so they parted. Next went men between them to make peace, and a meeting was called between them in Hrossey. At this meeting they were reconciled on this condition, that the Islands should be divided into two equal parts; and so things stood for a while. Hakon, Paul's son, greatly molested the men who served Erlend and his sons, so much so that it seemed to them that they could not endure it; and so they began to quarrel, and marched against each other with many men. Havard, Gunni's son, and other chiefs and friends of the Earls then tried to make peace between them, but Erlend and his sons would come to no agreement if Hakon was to remain in the Islands. But as it seemed to their friends that there would be great danger if they were not reconciled to each other, Hakon left the islands at once; and then an agreement was come to between those brothers on the advice of good men. Hakon first went east to Norway to see King Olaf the Quiet; it was towards the end of his days; he dwelt there a short time. Thence went he east to Sweden to see King Ingi, Steinkel's son, and was with him for some time well received. Christianity was then young in Sweden: many men were there who practised the old magic, and thought to become acquainted by it with many things which were not yet come to pass. King Ingi was a good Christian, and took great pains to root out the evils which had long attended heathenism.

7. When Hakon, Paul's son, was in Sweden, he heard tell that there was in the land a man who dealt in divination and spaecraft, whether it was by witchcraft or other means. Hakon was very anxious to meet this man, and to see what he could learn about his fate. He went in search of him and found him in a certain forest country, where he used to go about from feast to feast, and tell the franklins of the seasons and

other matters about which they were curious. When Hakon found this man he inquired of him how it would go with him for power or other fortune. The soothsayer asked him who he was. He tells him his name and family, that he was daughter's son to Earl Hakon, son of Ivar. Then answers the soothsayer: "Why wilt thou have knowledge or soothsaying of me? Knowest thou not that thy former kinsmen have had little faith in the kind of men that I am? And it may serve thy turn to try and learn thy fate from Olaf the Stout, thy kinsman in Norway, in whom all your faith is placed. But I suspect he will not stoop to tell thee that about which thou art curious, or else he is not so powerful as you call him." Hakon replied: "I will not speak ill of him: I think rather I am not worthy to get knowledge from him than that he should not be able to make me wise, if he would. But I have come to thee because it has come into my mind that neither of us will have need to look down upon the other because of virtue or religion." The man answers: "It likes me well to find that thou thinkest not to have all thy trust in that in which thy former friends had faith. It is strange also that the men who seek such things should keep fast and vigil, and think that thereby it will be given them to know the things about which they are curious. But though you apply yourselves to such, it turns out that you know less about them as your curiosity is greater and it is of the greater importance for you to know them; but we put ourselves to no pains, and yet we are able to ascertain the things which it is important for our friends to know. Now it shall be thus between us two, thou shalt have this service from me as I see that thou thinkest thyself better able to get the truth from me than from King Ingi's priests, in whom it seems to him all his trust ought to be placed. Thou shalt come to me on the third night, we two shall then see whether I am able to tell thee some of the things thou art anxious to learn." After this they parted, and Hakon remained there in the district. And after three nights he came again to the soothsayer. He was then in a certain house alone, and breathed heavily when Hakon went in, and wiped his forehead, and said that he had had to struggle hard before he became wise in the things he wanted to foreknow. Hakon replied he would like to know what he had to tell. He said then: "If thou wouldst know thy fate and about thy life, it is long to tell : for from thy faring west to Orkney very great events will come to pass when all the things to which they lead are fulfilled. And I have a presentiment that thou wilt become sole ruler of the Orkneys at last, though it may be that to thee it will seem long to wait. I also think that thy descendants will remain there. Thou wilt also in thy days cause a crime to be done for which thou mayest, or mayest not, get forgiveness from the God in whom thou trustest. But thy steps lie further out into the world than I can see, yet I think that thou wilt bring back thy bones to these northern parts. Now have I told thee the things which at this time I am permitted, but thou wilt decide how thou wilt be content with thy lot or errand." Hakon answered : " Great things thou tellest me, if they be true ; but I think it will go better with me, as it may well be that thou hast not seen these things in their verity." The spaeman bade him believe what he liked of it. And on this they parted.

And when Hakon had been a little while with King Ingi, he fared thence to Norway to see King Magnus Bareleg, his kinsman ; there he heard tidings from the Orkneys that Earl Erlend and his sons ruled there most, and were in favour with all the people, and that Earl Paul, his father, was caring little about the government. It seemed to him also on inquiry, that the Orkneymen were longing very little for his own return home ; they had then good peace, and thought, if Hakon returned, discord and strife would arise. Also it seemed to Hakon not unlikely that his own kinsmen would keep him out of the government. He took counsel, therefore, to seek help from his kinsman, King Magnus, to place him in the government of the Orkneys. Hakon egged on King Magnus greatly to go a hosting to Scotland and Ireland and then to England to avenge there King Harald, Sigurd's son. The King answers: "Thou must bethink, thee, Hakon, if I did this at thy word, and fared west with an army across the sea, whether it would not take thee by surprise, if I put forward a strong claim to those kingdoms beyond the sea, and did it without regarding the claim of any man." And when Hakon heard this, he grew cold and was little pleased, but King Magnus ordered a levy of men and ships over all Norway.

8. Now shall we next turn to the man about whom this history was written, the holy Magnus ; for a little before you have heard how he was well-behaved in all his conduct and unlike to other young men in his growing up. But as it is the way with many to shape their conduct after that of those with whom they live, and he who touches pitch is defiled by it, so when Magnus had almost reached the fulness of his growth, placed in the midst of fierce and wicked men, who were ill-disposed towards good morals, infirm in faith, opposed to just laws, stiff-necked in learning, complaisant in evil ways, quarrelsome and disobedient towards the commandments of God, he seemed, for some winters, to be like wicked men, and as a viking with robbers or soldiers, he lived by rapine and spoil, and stood by with others at murders ; and it is credible that he did this more from the wickedness and egging on of evil men than from his own badness. It seems likest to men that Magnus did this at the time when his kinsmen, Hakon and Erling, were all together in the Orkneys, for later no time can be found for it. Of this conduct, thus speaks Master Robert, who endited this history :—

"Ah ! I marvel," he says, " how unspeakable is the depth of the riches of the divine wisdom and of the knowledge of God ; how unsearchable are his judgments, and his ways past finding out by human kind. Why permitted Almighty God this His servant to lust after robbery and murder, and to be defiled with such manifold sins and misdeeds ? Why tholed the divine clemency His knight and martyr to let himself fall so fearfully, who, from his birth, chose gloriously to crown him in heaven ? With gladness and joy God enriched him, and turned his dust into heavenly glory, and gave him eternal joy after this world's sorrow, a garment of beauty and praise after the smitings of the heart. What is this? unless it be what we daily as openly as gloriously see, that God raises up and makes sons to Abraham from stones, just from unjust, honourable from sinners, glorious from mortal, smooth and polished, and four-cornered, with four main virtues, that they may be made to fit into the heavenly structure, strong and steadfast corner-stones in our chief corner-stone, Jesus Christ, they being of one heart and one mind with Him in the eternal charity and in the bond of infinite love. For the Lord Jesus is the son of the great Builder, who made the earth and all things which are therein, and creates and rules by His own power, and fashions vessels of His wrath into vessels of mercy, polishing them with the file of the Holy Spirit, and He receives sinful men into the widest bosom of His clemency and mercy, all who leave off their foolishness and turn to Him with their whole heart. For it belongs to the great glory and mercy of the Lord to let the abundance of His mercy appear there, where before the burden of our wretchedness was in the way, and he cures and heals the more mightily when the sickness already more fiercely assails the sick man, and makes whole all, and helps those who look to Him for help. See at last how the holy Magnus, though he was entangled in such sins, came to leave off these works and followed his father and brother and the landed men in Orkney."

9. At the time to which we have now come in the story, came west from Norway King Magnus Bareleg with countless ships and many troops. Him followed many of his vassals, Vidkunn Jonsson, Serk of Sogn, Kali of Agde, Saebjörn's son, and Kol, his son, and many other chiefs. The king intended, in this hosting, to subdue and harry the Western lands, England and Ireland, as was before said. When King Magnus came to Orkney, he took the Earls, Erlend and Paul, and drave them out of the islands and sent them East to Norway, and set Sigurd his son over Orkney, and gave him councillors, as he was not older than nine winters. Magnus and Erling, Erlend's sons, and Hakon, Paul's son, he ordered to go with him on the hosting. Magnus, Erlend's son, was tall in stature, bold and fleet and of great strength, of a goodly countenance, fair of complexion, and well shapen in limb, noble in bearing, and most courteous in all his demeanour. Him King Magnus made his table-swain, and he served continually at the King's table. King Magnus fared out of the Orkneys to the Hebrides and subdued in this

expedition all the Hebrides to his rule, and took prisoner Lawman, Gudrod's son, the king of the Hebrides. Thence fared he South to Wales and had there a great fight in the Menai Straits with two Welsh Earls, Hugh the Stout, and Hugh the Brave. But when men picked up their weapons, and got them ready for the fight, Magnus, Erlend's son, sat down in the forepart of the ship, where he was used to sit, and did not arm himself. The king inquired why he did so. S. Magnus answers: "Here I have nothing against any man, and therefore will I not fight." "Go, then," says the king, "below, and lie not here under men's feet, if thou dare not fight, for I do not think thou doest this because of thy religion." Magnus, the Earl's son, sat in the same place, and took a psalter and sang during the battle, but did not shelter himself. The battle was both hard and long. At last fell Hugh the Brave and the Welsh fled; and King Magnus got the victory, and had lost many good men, and many others were wounded. Kali, Saebjörn's son, received many and great wounds. Magnus, Erlend's son, was not wounded in the fight, though he did not shelter himself. And it might be seen of all, that it was the clearest miracle, that in so thick a flight of arrows, and so heavy a meeting of weapons, he should not be wounded, while on all sides around him fell armed men. And this need not now be wondered at, since God was preserving him for a greater crown and victory than to fall there. King Magnus was not pleased with this, and laid on Magnus, the Earl's son, great feud and dislike on account of it. And when the holy Magnus saw that it would not be for his honour or salvation to remain longer with King Magnus, he took another counsel with himself to do what God taught him.

10. It was one night, when King Magnus lay off Scotland, that Magnus, Erlend's son, stole away from the King's ship, and so arranged his bed, that it seemed as though a man lay there. In the morning, when the King was dressed, he inquired if Magnus, Erlend's son, were sick. He was then inquired for and was missed. The King then let search be made for him, but he was not found. Then the King caused the spoor-hounds to be let loose on the land. Magnus, the Earl's son, had hurt his

foot when he leapt ashore, and the spoor-hounds at once found the scent. Magnus had made for the woods and climbed up into a tree. The hounds came to the oak and climbed up into it. Magnus then struck one of them with a staff he held, and they immediately took to flight, laid their tails between their legs, and ran for the ships. Magnus, Erlend's son, hid himself in the wood while the King's men searched for him. He then fared up the country and came to the court of Malcolm, King of the Scots, and dwelt there for a while; but for some time he was in Wales with a certain bishop. The same autumn King Magnus fared back to the Hebrides, and was there through the winter. That winter died Kali, Saebjörn's son, of his wounds. Early in spring King Magnus fared to the Orkneys. There he heard from Norway of the death of the Earls; Erlend had died at Nidross and was buried there; and Paul at Bergen. Then King Magnus gave Gunnhilda, Earl Erlend's daughter, the sister of S. Magnus, in marriage to Kol, Kali's son, as an atonement for the life of his father, with many farms in Orkney. Kol was then made one of the King's vassals. Their son was Rognvald Kali. Some say that Erling, Erlend's son, and brother to S. Magnus, fell in the Menai Straits; but Snorri Sturlason says he fell in Ulster with King Magnus. For when King Magnus had ruled nine winters in Norway, he fared west to Ireland with a great army, and during the following summer fell in Ulster on Bartholomew's day. And Sigurd, his son fared at once out of the Orkneys east to Norway, and was there made king along with his brothers Eystein and Olaf.

11. You have already heard in a former chapter how Almighty God is ready to show mercy, whose singular goodness is always to spare, and to turn hindrances into helps, and how He preserved this His chosen champion from the turmoils and dangers of the world, that he might reveal to him and show how great things it behoved him to suffer for His name's sake; and he who had often stood among great manslayers should at length become an offering of the Holy Spirit, and give to God his own blood with his life and body. Therefore came he out from the power of the greedy king, as was before read.

When the holy Magnus was in Scotland, he heard of the death of Earl Erlend, his father, and the other tidings which were before written. And when he had tarried as long in the Scots King's court as pleased him, honoured with the King's gifts and a noble retinue, he fared to Caithness, and there was well received, honoured and esteemed of all, and at once chosen and ennobled with the title of "Earl," beloved and honoured of all the friends of God.

12. Thereafter, without delay, the holy Earl Magnus was made Paul out of Saul, a preacher from a manslayer, and he avenged on himself that which he had lived ill. He began to bewail himself dead in sin with daily moanings and steadfast repentance ; and he now took fitting revenge in manifold inflictions on the sinful lusts of the wretched flesh. He then showed himself a new man, as one who is inclined to that in which God is honoured and whom He has changed into another man, into good from evil, into seemly from sinful, into holy from defiled, into blessed and pure from polluted. This is the conversion of Thy right hand, O Almighty God ! Thou art strong to strengthen, gracious to help, ready to restore, mighty to preserve ! In this way was Magnus changed into a holy man. He began to ear the soil of his heart with the strong ploughshare of confession. Then slew he his man of misfortune and hid him under the sand. Then buried he the graven images of Laban under the roots of the trees. He tore out his sins and pollutions and adorned himself with illustrious virtues in good deeds after a godly manner with manlike steadfastness. He began then to flourish as an olive tree, and to be exalted in all good things and gracious works. Even as a cyprus excels other trees, so S. Magnus grew that he might be truly *magnus* ; i.e., "great" in divine things as he was in name, increasing in prosperity and holiness.

13. A winter or two after King Magnus Bareleg fell, fared from the west over the sea to Norway, Hakon Paul's son, and the kings gave him the title of Earl, and such possessions as stood to him by birth. Fared he then west over the sea and took to himself all the government of the Orkneys, and with such great and aggressive greed that he slew without cause the

steward of the King of Norway, who held and governed that part of the Islands which the holy Magnus inherited, and in that way took possession of all the Orkneys by sheer force; for half of the Islands belonged to S. Magnus as his patrimony. Now when the holy Magnus heard with what violence Hakon, his cousin, had, with manifest injustice, seized his hereditary lands, he took counsel with his men as to what he should do. It was agreed among them that he should wait a while, in order that the anger and greed of Hakon, his kinsman, might abate, and that it might not appear that he sought his inheritance by arms, but as a friend and dear lover of law and justice.

14. Now when the time was come that the holy Magnus wished to visit his patrimony, he fares with a noble company from Caithness to Orkney, and his kinsmen and friends were fain of him. He asked to take possession of his patrimony. This was well pleasing to the franklins; for he was well loved; and he had many kinsmen and connections who were anxious to help him to hold his dominions. Thora, his mother, was then married to a man named Sigurd; they owned a large farm in Paplay. When Earl Hakon heard that Magnus was come into the Islands, he gathered troops around him, and wished not to give up the government, but to defend it. Fared then the friends of both between them, and tried to make peace. So it came to pass, through the counsel of good men, that they were reconciled on the condition that Earl Hakon should give up half the kingdom if it were so decided by the King of Norway. Magnus, Erlend's son, fared at once east to Norway to seek King Eystein; for King Sigurd had then fared out to Jerusalem. King Eystein received the young lord Magnus exceeding well, and gave up to him his patrimony, the half of Orkney, and therewith he received the title of Earl in the Orkneys from the Kings, along with very handsome presents. And after this fared the lord Earl Magnus west over the sea to his dominions, and his friends and kinsmen were glad and with them all the people. Then there was much good fellowship between him and Earl Hakon for many winters, which their friends brought about. There was then plenty and peace in the Orkneys while their friendship held. The kinsmen,

lord Earl Magnus and Hakon, had both the land defence together for a while, so that they were well agreed. So it was said in the songs, which were made on them, that they fought with the viking called Dufnial, who attacked their kingdom. He was a man one degree further off than first cousin to the Earls, and he fell before them. A man named Thorbjorn, rich and powerful by descent, but poor in good works, they, for sufficient reasons, put to death at Borgarfiord in Shetland. Many other things are also told in songs which they did together, though we cannot here minutely narrate them. The holy Magnus had these things done, not as a viking or robber, but as a just ruler of a province and a guardian of the laws, and a lover of peace, to chastise ill doing and to punish wrong, to make peace and quietness for his subjects and his kingdom against the violence and agression of wicked men, who were always on the watch to break the peace.

15. Lord Magnus was a man the most renowned in his rule and authority, dignified and upright, a steadfast friend and brave, skilled in feats of arms and blessed with victory in battle, gentle in peace, yet a strong ruler, condescending in speech, and clement, prudent in counsel, and had every man's praise. He was open-handed with his money, and generous among chieftains. Every day he gave great help to poor men for the love of God. He punished much harrying and theft, and caused vikings and ill doers, rich as well as poor, to be slain. No respecter of persons was he in his judgments; he respected God's law more than differences of estate among them. In all things he observed strictly the commandments of God, and was unsparing towards himself. Many were the excellent virtues which he manifested before God, but hid from men.

But since the holy Earl Magnus had rule and government over worldly folk, he desired to be like the great ones of the earth in the customs of life; he took and betrothed himself to a high-born princess, and the fairest maiden of the most noble house of the chiefs of Scotland, and brought her home with him and married her. This did the blessed Magnus, as experience proved, with the deep laid counsel of the divine mercy, to impose upon the enticing temptations of this world, rather than to fulfil the lusts of the flesh, for he was helped by divine protection and heavenly power. He dwelt ten years with this virgin, pure and unstained of all the pollutions of sin. And when he felt within himself the temptation to fleshly lust, he plunged into cold water and sought help from God.

16. Behold this strong athlete of God in his daily wrestlings, how wonderfully he lived with this maiden so long a time. For although he lawfully might have enjoyed her, he preferred, sustained by the mercy of the Holy Ghost, to chose the better part, to live inviolate, than to do what is permitted in wedlock, for they suffer the burning of the flesh who do such things. Because better and safer is it to preserve the flowers whole than to restore them after they are bruised; for no wound ever becomes so well as the flesh which has remained whole. But to live in the body without carnal lusts comes not of the power of man, but of the Divine gift. But what temptation and chastening he endured from the lust of the flesh, what heavy blows of forbidden motives, and how hard a struggle he conquered, and calmed the strong lusts of the burning flesh, those know who have experienced them, but the inexperienced believe not. Behold my dearest! This is the great sight which Moses beheld when he saw the bush burning and not consumed; that is to say, this young man was tempted but not overcome. But, as says the Apostle Paul, no one is crowned except he who strives lawfully and works manfully for it, so this prince and wrestling knight preferred Thy courts, to endure the daily conflict and constant battle of the burning flesh. And he fought valiantly and triumphed happily, for it seemed to him that he would be much too easy a knight, who would have glory before he had done works of virtue; for virtue is the way to glory, and glory comes from virtue. Treacherous is the glory, and vain is the beauty which is not begotten by holy virtue. And I marvel, says the Scripture, how fair and winsome is the immaculate conception with its purity and love. This the glorious knight of God, girt with his girdle of chastity, was careful with all mindfulness to do and fulfil all manner of charity to the glory of his Lord. But what of the things of this world would

he deny his God, who expended his very life and body, and poured out his own blood for the sake of God?

17. Now since no one can be an Abel unless he suffer and experience the ill-will and malice of Cain, and the holy Ezekiel dwelt among men full of the poison of adders, and just Lot was oppressed by unjust men, the enemy of all mankind stirred up temptations and hot persecutions on every side against this knight of God, sowing discord and hatred among brethren and kinsmen and dear friends, all to hinder him, and to bring to naught his good deeds, which then began to increase with him; but the branch of the good vine might be moved, but not cut off. For as wood swims in water and is turned over by the winds and waves, but not sunk, and as the Wain turns round in the heavens, and sinks not, as gold is purified in the furnace and is not consumed, and as a strong house is beaten upon by the storms and falls not; so in the same way was the mind and heart of this noble martyr strong and steadfast, undaunted and undismayed amid the fierce trials and onsets of manifold temptations, in the midst of storms and great breakers both of secret envy and treachery, as well as of open ill-will and spite, against the shafts of the tempting foe. It must next be set down how this discord was made between the Earls.

18. When the kinsmen, S. Magnus and Earl Hakon, had for some winters ruled their lands in peace and good agreement, it came to pass, as it often does, that evil disposed men began to destroy their brotherly concord. Earl Hakon then drew towards those evil men, for the kinsmen were very unlike in temper. Lord Earl Magnus was benevolent and faithful in his promises; he wished to retain the kingdom which God had given to him, and desired nothing more. For in what way could he be proved to desire other men's kingdoms or possessions, who was so free with his own flesh, that he did not spare his life for the love of God? He reformed his subjects and accustomed them to right living, so that after he had delivered and given peace to his kingdom from the aggressions of wicked vikings, he did not allow any of his men to go a hosting, and punished severely all lawlessness and wickedness. But Earl

Hakon was hard-hearted and cruel, greedy both of wealth and power, and more prone to egg on his men to go a hosting than to prevent them, and punished little wickedness and ill-doing. He was very jealous of the liberality and popular favour of the holy Magnus, and would willingly with the greed of his evil counsellors overcome the honour of Earl Magnus, and subdue his kingdom to himself with pillage and injustice, and began to plot with his men against his life with treacherous cunning.

19. Now when the blessed Magnus has become thoroughly aware of this through much experience, which he thinks cannot be passed over in silence, that Hakon was attempting to deprive him of his life and kingdom, he took counsel with his counsellors, and it seemed to them that he ought to give way for a little to the malice and fury of Hakon. Chose he then out of his people those who were the most suitable and best of his followers to accompany him, and sailed to England and sought a meeting with King Henry, son of William the Bastard, who was then sole king over England. When the holy Magnus was come to this King, he made known to him the occasion and object of his coming. And the King received him with great honour; and into so great a friendship did he rise with the King, that he maintained him and all his people at his own cost for twelve months magnificently, as it was fitting for a King to treat a famous leader. But this holy martyr held himself and his retinue so wisely, that he shunned and was wary of all fellowship with wicked men. And when the lord King learned from his prudence, how Earl Magnus was a doer of good works and of seemly manners, and that the Holy Spirit dwelt in him, he earnestly gave heed to his counsel, and followed his advice in his conduct, for he was sound and wholesome in counsel and in making of plans, of gentle disposition and patient as Chusa, gladsome and loving as Jonathan, just and zealous for the law as Phinehas. Hence he was dear to all and beloved, pleasant, and acceptable, so that there were many who said: "Blessed are they that saw thee, and that won thy friendship." He was pleasant and kind to the rich, open-handed and gentle with the poor, good

natured, benevolent, and condescending to all the people. And although he dwelt at the Court with the princes of this world, he took care and avoided all kinds of vice which corrupt the manners of courtiers. And that he might not for the future stain his chastity by consenting to other men's sins, he made ready his home-going as soon as the twelve months were passed, which he had spent with King Henry. It may be that God had made known to him that he should finish his labours within a short time, and offer to God as well the bright flowers of his purity as the victorious death of his martyrdom; for to be loosed from the body, and to live with Christ, is much more glorious than to abide here in this polluted world.

20. After that S. Magnus had taken leave of King Henry, honoured with rich and manifold gifts, and esteemed and glorified by the Lord King, they parted with the greatest love and friendship. He visited first all the holy places which were near, and then fared home to his own land. But while the holy Magnus was abroad, Earl Hakon with great greed and harrying had subdued not only all the Orkneys, but all Caithness as well, with great robbery and violence; and so it came to pass, that Hakon sat at that time in Caithness, when the holy Earl Magnus landed in the Orkneys with five ships well manned with valiant and well armed men, ettling to get back his kingdom, though with no false passion of this world's ambition, nor greed of unlawful possession, especially when he had already so long desired God, and was with the joy of his whole heart wholly taken up out of the lusts of mortal things into the desire for eternal joy, for he came now to end his long life into a brief space all the more gloriously the more quickly he departed. The tidings of his return home were at once told on all sides. Earl Hakon, immediately awaking as a fierce she-bear robbed of her whelps, summoned and gathered together to him the sons of Belial, cruel ill-doers, and sons of the wretched Dohet, who always and everywhere wrought evil from their birth from their mother's womb. Hakon meant then to come unawares upon the holy Magnus, and to work and complete in that way the malice and treachery which he had long before had in mind and prepared for. But

the Supreme Heavenly King, who from eternity had ordained that He would keep His glorious chosen vessel in His treasuries, saw in this man of His own election some rust still of worldly behaviour which required to be purified. Therefore God would that he should be made most pure and fair in a few days with the fire of suffering and insult, and with the files of temptation and of many adversities, though there was no deadly sin in him to wash away. God wished to increase his merit, if in anything it was lacking, that according as his temptation and wrestling were greater and harder, the higher and more splendid should be the glory and joy of the victor. Thus it came to pass that the Earls sent between themselves with messages for peace and reconciliation their most prudent counsellors, who truly bear the marks of Chusa and Ahitophel, who brought about the reconciliation between King David and his son Absolom, when they were at variance. It came then at last in this matter, through the intervention of good men, that a reconciliation was made between the kinsmen in this way, that the earldom of Orkney, Caithness, and Shetland should be divided into halves between the Earls Magnus and Hakon, and that neither should assail the other's kingdom with any greed. When this agreement had been made and confirmed with oaths and handsellings, the Earls met with the kiss of peace. But that which the holy Earl Magnus intended for peace, Hakon turned to deceit and cunning. And the longer he retained the poison of evil, the more wickedly did he spew it up, for his wickedness and villainy increased so much as time went on, that he could no longer hide it. In the same way as a cancer on the face of a man works the more harm the longer it remains, so fares every kind of evil; thus, the longer it is hid in the mind and heart, the fiercer it becomes for working mischief.

21. The holy Earl Magnus then began again to rule his kingdom with peace and joy for a time. And it is known best in the sight of God how holily he lived in this biding of his death; how he adorned himself with holy virtues and the exercise of every kind of grace, in prayer, and in shedding of tears, and searchings of heart, in purity and nobleness, in alms-giving, and in

all gentleness towards his people, in afflictions and manifold sufferings, which he endured in his body, and in many other virtues more than sinful man can call to mind. As every holy man of God does, in the same way prepared Earl Magnus for his martyrdom; the story of which we shall now with God's help begin.

22. When the above mentioned reconciliation and peace had lasted between the Earls some winters, Hakon showed himself traitorous by pouring out from his breast the great wickedness, which he had for a time held back. Hear how true is that saying of the ancient skald, which says:

> "Nulla fides regni sociis, omnisque potestas,
> Inpatiens consortis erit, totum sitit illa."

That is to say: Never can fellowship in this world's power be true, for no ruler can endure a rival, and would have all to himself alone. From this thou mayest learn what fruit treason begets and what springs up from greed. All sins are done of lust, and every unhallowed desire starts from greed. This is proved by Ahab, that most iniquitous king, who persecuted Elijah the prophet. It is shown by the most wicked Judas, who sold our Lord for money. This same, the traitor, Earl Hakon, showed, both by examples and proofs in the treachery with which he betrayed his kinsman, Earl Magnus, under the show of friendship, though in various ways happened the things which led to their dealings and quarrel.

23. Two men were with Earl Hakon who are mentioned as by far the worst in going between the kinsmen; the one was called Sigurd; the other Sigvat Sokki. Sigurd had a brother, called Thorstein, who was the most faithful follower of Earl Magnus. Many others there were who had an evil hand in this matter, and these were all with Hakon, for S. Magnus would keep no slanderer among his followers. These slanderings went so far that the Earls gathered their troops together, and each fared against the other with a great following. They both held their way to the island of Hrossey, for there was the Thingstead of the Orkneys. And when they were come there, each of them drew up his troops in battle array and prepared

to fight. There had come all the men of rank with the Earls, and many were friends of both, who did everything to reconcile them, and went between them with courage and good-will. This meeting was in Lent. And because many well disposed men were anxious to prevent strife between them, and wished to help neither to do harm to the other, they bound themselves to keep the peace by oaths and handsellings at the witness of the best men. It was settled they should meet in the spring in Egilsey after Easter. At this meeting each Earl was to have two ships and an equal number of men. Both Earls took oaths to have and hold the agreement which the best men should settle at that meeting to declare between them. And after this was done each fared to his own home. With this conditional reconciliation and agreement the holy Magnus was well pleased, as he was thoroughly whole hearted and of good conscience, without all distrust. But Earl Hakon had at this meeting glosed over his treachery and hid it with a cloud of hypocrisy; for this agreement he had made with deceit and treachery and complete fraud, as was afterwards proved; for at the time Hakon, who is rightly called a treasury of hidden evil, and his wicked servants conspired together in the counsel of their wickedness for the slaughter and death of the holy Magnus. For strong and very dear is all evil amid the fellowship of the scornful; therefore settled they among themselves that this crime should no longer be delayed, and that now will they fully slake their cruel thirst with the shedding of sackless blood. But the Highest Lord of all power watched over his beloved friend and chosen martyr, that being at this time ready for the kingdom of heaven, he might be taken out of this life under the heavy storm of a violent death; as grapes under the winepress, trodden upon and crushed, give off the clearest wine in their time with much fragrance and sweet taste, so gave this the glorious martyr of God, by his death, to all the friends of God and his own, the heavenly sweetness of divine mercy, from that glory and joy which he has inherited in the unending gladness of eternal life with God and his saints.

24. As soon as the holy Easter time was passed, each of the two made ready for this meeting in different ways. The holy

Magnus called to him all the men whom he knew had the most good-will to make things better between the kinsmen. He had two longships manned with the bravest men, as many as were agreed upon. And when he was ready he held to the island of Egilsey. But as they were rowing on a calm sea and in still weather, there rose a wave of the sea beside the ship in which Earl Magnus was, and broke over the place where the Earl was sitting. The chief men in Earl Magnus's ship were called : Thorstein, who was mentioned before, Arnkell, Grim, and Gilli, and many other doughty men. They marvelled greatly at this circumstance, that the wave fell on them in a calm sea, where no man knew that a wave had fallen before, and where the water under was deep. Then the holy Earl Magnus said : " It is not strange though you wonder at this. But my thought is, that this is a foreboding of the end of my life. Maybe that will happen here, which was before spaed, that Earl Paul's son will perpetrate the greatest crime : maybe Hakon is plotting treachery against us at this meeting." Earl Magnus's men were much distressed at this speech when he spoke of so speedy expectation of his death, and prayed him to take care of himself and guard his life, and risk nothing to the faith of Earl Hakon. Earl S. Magnus replies : " I shall certainly go to this meeting, as was agreed upon, and make no breach of my promise for the sake of a mere foreboding. And let all be as God wills about our voyage. But if there be any choice, then would I much rather suffer wrong than do it to another. So may God let Hakon, my kinsman, get forgiveness, though he do me wrong."

Now it is to be told of Earl Hakon, that he called to him a great army. He had seven or eight warships, all of great size, manned with troops; all the men were well armed as if they were going to battle. But when the force came together, then did Earl Hakon make it clear before his men, that at this meeting it should be so settled with Magnus, that they should not both rule from that time forth. Many of the Earl's men, who might verily be called children of the devil, expressed delight at this purpose, and added many abominable words; but Sigurd and Sigvat Sokki were still giving the worst advice ; they were ever egging on to wickedness. The men then began to row fast, and went furiously and with great speed. Havard Gunni's son, who was spoken of before, was with Earl Hakon; he was a close friend of both Earls. Hakon had hid from him this bad counsel. But as soon as he was aware of it, he leapt overboard from the Earl's ship and swam to an uninhabited island; for he would be in no treachery with Hakon against the holy Magnus. That man was with Earl Magnus, who was called Holdbodi, a trustworthy franklin from the Hebrides; he was Earl Magnus's most dear follower. He was near by all that happened, and has since most clearly related the dealings and all the discourse of Earls Hakon and Magnus, which may here be heard next after this.

25. The holy Earl Magnus came sooner to Egilsey with his men than Hakon. And when they saw Hakon's eight warships, Earl Magnus thought he knew that treachery was being prepared, and all the men, who had any insight saw well that such a multitude of armed men was not wanted for a peaceful purpose. When the holy Earl Magnus saw that the treachery of Hakon was about to show itself, he went with his men up into the island to a church to pray, and was there through the night, not because of fear or dread, but rather to commit all his care to God. His men offered to defend him, and fight against Hakon. But he answered: "I will not place your lives in danger for me. And if peace cannot be made between us two kinsmen, then let it be as God wills; for rather will I suffer evil and treachery than do it to others." For this noble martyr, when saying this, knew that all guile and deceit is returned to him who does it. Now thought his men most true that which he had before said to them about the treachery of Hakon. But as Earl Magnus knew before of his death, whether it were of his foresight or of divine revelation, he wished neither to fly nor to go far from the meeting of his enemies, and he went for no other reason to the holy church than for religion. Earl Magnus watched long in prayer during the night and meditated on his salvation, and prayed earnestly; he committed all his cause and himself into the hands of God. In the morning he let Mass be sung, and received in that Mass the *Corpus Domini*. And this his deed

was necessary for the highest reason, that in that place he should become an offering to God, as was offered the redeeming sacrifice of the Body and Blood of our Lord Jesus Christ for the salvation of the whole world. But Earl Hakon, who at that time was void of all piety and affection, violating the privileges of the Church, feared not to go into the holy sanctuary, so breaking its peace and immunity, that he might show his wickedness the more fiercely, the more sacred the place he perpetrated it in. For sin is ever increased by ill-doing, and evil by outrage ; and sinful man, when he falls into the depths of sin, abandons all fear of God ; and the more he is acquainted with sin the more he dares, and the less he cares what ill he does ; for he thinks it is nothing worth, however great his misdeeds be. The same morning that Earl Hakon had come up on to the island with his ill-doers, he sent four of his men, the worst of his servants, who were the fiercest and most eager to work ill, to seize Earl Magnus wherever he was. These four, who, from their ferocity, may rather be called the wildest wolves than rational men, always thirsting for bloodshed, leapt into the church just as Mass was ending. Snatched they at once the holy Earl Magnus with great violence, uproar, and clamour, out of the peace and bosom of Holy Church, as the gentlest sheep of the fold.*
The Saint was holden of the thralls of sin, the righteous was bound, dragged unjustly by the unjust, and then led away before the greedy judge, Earl Hakon. But this strong champion had such great steadfastness in all these wrestlings, that neither his body shook from fear, nor his mind from dread or grief, for he forsook this thorny world with all its fruitless flowers. He hoped that God would recompense his patience

---

* The Shorter Saga gives a different account. "Next morning he went out of the Church with two men out on the island down to the shore to a certain hiding-place, and prayed there before God. Some men say that Earl Magnus caused mass to be said for him before he went out from the Church and that he took the *Corpus Domini*. Earl Hakon and his men ran up on the island in the morning, and first to the church, and sought for Earl Magnus, and did not find him there. Then they searched for him about the island. But when Earl Magnus saw where they were, he called to them and said "Here I am." And when Hakon saw that, they ran thither. Cc. 11, 12.

with an ineffable crown ; but their cruelty and fury with everlasting torture in the hot fire of hell, because of their inhuman wickedness and monstrous greed. He was as glad and cheerful when they took him, as if he had been bidden to a banquet, and had so settled a heart and mind that he spoke to his enemies with no bitterness, anger, or tremor in his voice.

26. When the holy Earl Magnus was come before Earl Hakon, he said to Hakon with great calmness : " Not well doest thou, kinsman, when thou kept not thy oath, and it is much to be looked for that thou didst this more from the malice and egging on of others than from thine own ill-will. Now I will make to thee three offers, that thou mayest take one of them rather than that thou shouldst break thy oath, and let me thy kinsman be slain, sackless as some will say." Earl Hakon said: " I will first hear what thou offerest." S. Magnus said : " This is the first offer, that I shall fare abroad to Rome or all out to Jerusalem, to seek the holy places, and so make atonement for both of us ; I will take two ships out of the land furnished with good men and the equipment needful to have. I will swear never to come to Orkney again." This offer was quickly refused by Hakon and his men. Then said Earl Magnus : " Now since our life is in your power, and I know that in many things I have offended against Almighty God, and have need thereof to make amends, send me up to Scotland to the friends of us both, and let me there be in ward with two men with me for amusement ; and see thou so to it that I may never come forth of that wardship without thy leave." This they at once rejected and found many reasons why it could not be. Then spake this doughty knight : " Now is my choice very limited, says he. Now is there but one choice left, which I will offer thee, and God knows that I am more concerned for thy salvation here, than for the life of my body ; for, after all, it beseems thee little to take my life. Let me be maimed in my limbs, or let my eyes be put out, and set me so in a dark dungeon, whence I may never come out." Then said Earl Hakon : " This offer take I, and no more do I ask." Then leapt up Earl Hakon's men and said : " In this finding we do not agree, to torture Earl Magnus : but one or the other of

you two we will slay; and from this day you shall not both of
you reign over these lands." Then says Earl Hakon: "Rather
will I rule the lands than die at once, if ye are so strict in this
matter." So tells Holdbodi of their parley.—After this S.
Magnus fell to prayers and bowed his face into his hands and
shed many tears before God, giving his cause, his life, and himself, into the power of the Lord.

27. Next to this, when the holy friend of God, Earl Magnus,
was condemned and doomed to death, Earl Hakon bade Ofeig,
his standard-bearer, slay Earl Magnus; but he refused with
greatest anger. Then compelled Earl Hakon his cook, who
was called Lifolf, to smite Earl Magnus, but he began to weep
aloud. Then said Earl S. Magnus to him : " Weep not; for
there is fame to thee in doing the like. Be thou of steadfast
mind, for thou shalt have my clothes as is the wont and law
of the men of old. Thou shalt not be afraid, for thou doest
this by force, and he that forces thee to it has more sin
than thou." And when he had said this, he took off his
kirtle and gave it to Lifolf. Then begged the blessed Earl
Magnus leave to pray first, and it was granted him. He fell
then to the ground and gave himself into the power of God,
offering himself to Him in sacrifice. Not alone for himself prayed
he, but rather for his enemies and murderers as well; and
forgave he them all with his whole heart that which they were
misdoing against him; and confessed he all his sins to God,
and prayed that they might all be washed away by the shedding of his blood; and he commended his spirit into the hands
of God, praying God's angels to come to meet it, and bear
it to the rest of Paradise. Then when this noble martyr
of God had ended his prayer, he said to Lifolf: " Stand before
me and hew me on the head a great wound ; for it beseems
not to behead chiefs like thieves. Be strong, man, and weep not,
for I have prayed God to pardon thee." After this Earl Magnus
crossed himself, and bowed him to the stroke. Lifolf struck
him on the head a great blow with an axe. Then said Earl
Hakon : " Strike again." Then struck Lifolf into the same
wound. Then fell the holy Earl Magnus on his knees, and
fared with this martyrdom from the miseries of this world to the

everlasting joys of the kingdom of heaven. And him whom the murderer took out of the earth, Almighty God let reign with Him in heaven. His body fell to the earth, but his spirit was gloriously taken up into the heavenly glory of the angels. The spot where the holy Earl Magnus was slain was stony and mossy. But a little after his merits before God were made manifest, so that since then there is there a green field, fair and smooth, and God showed by this token, that Earl Magnus was slain for righteousness sake, and gained the fairness and greenness of Paradise in the land of the living.—The death-day of the holy Earl Magnus is two nights after the feast of Tiburtius and Valerianus ; it was on the second day of the week, that the worthy Earl Magnus was slain, the third week after Lady Day in Lent. He had then been twelve winters Earl with Hakon. Then were Kings in Norway Sigurd the Crusader, and his brothers Eystein and Olaf. Then had passed from the death of the holy Olaf, Harald's son, seventy-four years [eighty-six]. It was in the days of Pope Paschal, the second of that name, and of S. John Bishop of Holar in Iceland.—In honour of the holy Earl Magnus thus speaks Master Robert who in Latin this history endited :

28. "To-day shines upon us, dearest brethren, the day of the death of the blessed Earl Magnus the Martyr, the day of his rest and of his eternal joy. Let us be glad and rejoice on this glorious day ; for he requires of us solemn devotion and especial thanksgiving, who live beside his holy relics and under his protection and keeping, and have hope in his merits. For it was on account of his noble example and holy life that first flourished in the coasts of the kingdom of the Orkneys the seemly ordinances of pure devotion, and the most holy laws of this most glorious martyr brought forth manifold fruit in good living. He drave abroad the lordly throne of Satan out from the northern regions of the world and set in its place the tabernacle of Almighty God. He laid waste and uprooted all the tares by his preaching, and let spring up the fairest flowers and the sweetest harvest of most life-giving fruit. He turned all the bitterness of the Orkneys into praise and sweetness of holy living. On this day he overcame the

world and the princes of the world, and he went up, a radiant conqueror over the world, receiving from his holy Master, our Lord Jesus Christ, a crown of glory. On this day he was set free from all bondage of fleshly corruption, entering into heaven; and he went into joy, made like the saints in all glory. On this day he laid aside the earthly garments of this changeful life, and went up higher than human weakness may reckon; and on him therefore is bestowed greatness in heaven, honour and blessedness in the presence of all the saints. He ascended radiant according to his merits, rich in the fulness of blessing, glorious in noble victories. This glorious martyr of God, the blessed Earl Magnus, adorned with the crown of his own blood, suffered after the incarnation of our Lord Jesus Christ, one thousand one hundred and four [sixteen] years, on Monday the sixteenth of the kalends of May. Now it remains, my dearest brethren, that we lay aside fleshly lusts and beware of loving unlawful things, vanquishing and overcoming the assaults of sin, and follow the footsteps and life of this glorious martyr with all the strength of our mind as far as our weakness will allow. Let us follow the way of his life; let us hold to the example of his works. Let us strive to make our lives like his, though it daily appeareth and is shown forth—by those wonderful tokens and glorious works which Almighty God doth grant unto the North both by sea and land for the sake of his excellent prayers and famous merits—that his life and holy righteousness are things more meet for us to honour and wonder at than to be imitated by our weakness. He appeared on earth, that he might become our protector and ask help and grace for us from Almighty God. Therefore it behoves us, who are pressed down under the great load of our sins, honour always to do to him with the especial goodness of bounden obedience and honour, that this glorious martyr, Earl Magnus, may vouchsafe to obtain for us, by means of his merits and prayers, that we may win to become sharers of his victorious crown and eternal glory, which he won on the day of his passion. This grant us the Lord Jesus Christ, who is the honour and blessing, the help and salvation, the gladness and glory of all His holy and righteous men;

who with the Father and Holy Ghost liveth and reigneth, One God in Three Persons, world without end. Amen."

Master Robert wrote this history in Latin to the worship and honour of the holy Magnus, Earl of the Isles, when twenty years were gone from his passion.

29. Now must we take up the story again, and tell of the things which were done after the death of the holy Earl Magnus. So great was the fierceness and cruelty of Earl Hakon, and so great his anger and fury at the blessed Magnus, that he bore not less malice to Earl Magnus dead than living. And though the anger and fury of most men can be abated after the doing of their ill deed, the ill will and malice in the heart of Hakon took no rest and abated not; for he forbade Earl Magnus to be buried at the Church as Christian men, but ordered that he should be hidden there in the ground where he was slain.

30. It had been agreed at the first meeting of the Earls in Hrossey, that when their reconciliation had been fully made and confirmed as the best men determined, as they had bound themselves by oaths, that both Earls, when they fared from the meeting, which was fixed to be held in Egilsey, should go to a feast in Paplay at Thora's, the mother of Earl Magnus. But now, after the slaying and death of the Earl, went Earl Hakon to the banquet with his men. The feast was of the best. Now when drink took hold on Earl Hakon, then went Thora to him and spake thus: "Now art thou come here alone, lord; but I expected both of you, thee and Earl Magnus my son. Now be thou so to my prayer as thou wilt that Almighty God shall be to thee at doomsday; that thou grant to me that my son may be buried at church." Earl Hakon looked on her, and shed tears, and said: "Bury thy son, woman, where it likes thee." Earl S. Magnus was then borne to the church, and buried in Birsay, at Christ's Kirk, which Earl Thorfinn, his grandfather, let be built. Immediately a heavenly light was often seen to shine over his grave. Then men began to call upon the holy Earl Magnus, when they were placed in danger, and he met their need as they prayed. Always was a heavenly odour perceived at his grave, and there sick men obtained health,

Next, sick men made journeys from Orkney and Shetland, who were hopeless of cure, and watched before his tomb, and were cured of all their diseases, but still men did not dare to make known the miracles of Earl Magnus while Earl Hakon lived. So it is told, that the men who had been worst between the Earls and most in treachery towards Earl Magnus, came most of them to speedy ends and short life, and died a shameful death.

After the death of Magnus, Hakon, Paul's son, took possession of all the Earldom of the Orkneys. He compelled all men to swear oath and fealty to himself, as well those who before had served Earl Magnus. He became great, and laid heavy burdens on the friends of Earl Magnus, whom he thought had been most against himself in their negotiations. Some winters after, Hakon made ready to go abroad. He went south to Rome, and on that journey went all the way to Jerusalem, as was then the custom for palmers. He sought the holy places, and bathed in the river Jordan. After that he returned to his own land and took up the government in the Orkneys. He became then a good ruler, and established good peace in his kingdom. He made new laws, which the franklins liked much better than those which had been before. By such things he began to increase his popularity. So it came to pass that the people of the Orkneys would have no other than Earl Hakon and his offspring to hold rule among them. And here is the end of what is to be said about Hakon in this book.

31. The most merciful God, our Lord Jesus Christ, who invites and leads His friends to everlasting joy, from all the bondage of this world, . . . the same who redeems all who humble themselves to His mercy, with their whole heart, from all the sins and pollutions of this sorrowful world, and makes of the ignorant the wisest, of the lowly and despised the most famous, of the poor the richest, of the ignoble the noblest rulers, not only of the kingdoms of this world, but also of the kingdom of heaven, and of eternal glory, as He did aforetime with the patriarch Joseph, who was led out of a dark dungeon and at once made prince and ruler over all the land of Egypt : the

same who made of the shepherd boy, David, the greatest king over all the tribes of Israel, and led Judas Maccabæus out of the famine of the desert, that he might obtain honour and the renown of victory, and so great a fame that in many things he is thought to far excel others, and Alexander, the son of Philip, who was called the Macedonian, because of the hard mastership of Aristotle *

15. At this time William was bishop in the Orkneys. Then was the bishop's seat at Christ's Kirk in Birsay where the holy Earl Magnus was buried; he doubted long about his holiness and kept down this new thing [*i.e.*, the miraculous virtue experienced at the grave of S. Magnus, c. 30.]

16. Bergfinn, Starri's son was the name of a franklin north in Shetland. He was sightless, and fared south to the Orkneys and watched at the tomb of the Earl S. Magnus. With him watched two men, one was named Sigurd and the other Thorbjorn; they were both cripples. Earl S. Magnus appeared to them all and made them quite cured. Again twenty-four men watched at the tomb of Earl Magnus and all got healing for their hurts.

Many men told this before Bishop William and urged him to speak about it with Paul, Hakon's son, who then ruled over the Isles after his father, and ask him to give leave that the sacred relics of Earl Magnus might be taken up out of the ground, but the bishop took that heavily. Often was he reminded in dreams that he should make up his mind about the Earl's holiness, and yet he would not believe in it. Afterwards it so came about that he was beaten with divine scourges that he might honour the tokens and holiness of Earl Magnus.

17. One summer Bishop William sailed East to Norway on some pressing business, and immediately turned homewards in the autumn, and came in the beginning of winter to Shetland. There he was laid up by contrary winds and storms. But when for a long time during the winter there was no fair

---

* The following paragraphs are taken from the Lesser Saga in order to fill up the gap which occurs here in the Greater Saga.

wind for the isles, the Bishop despaired of being able to reach his see before spring. The captain asked him if he would agree to the holiness of Earl Magnus if he should sing mass the next Lord's Day at home. The bishop, so to say, gave his consent to this, but more from necessity than of free promise. But when this was agreed, there was calm weather and soon a fair wind. And afterwards they sailed for Orkney; and he came home also before the next Lord's Day; and all praised God and also his holy martyr Earl Magnus. Some men say this, that Bishop William did not agree to take out of the ground the sacred relics of Earl Magnus before it happened there at home one day at a time that he could not get out of the church. For he had become blind and could not find the door, till he repented of his unbelief, and wept bitterly, and besought God that he might light upon the tomb of Earl Magnus. And when he came there, he fell all his length on the ground, and promised to at once take out of the earth his sacred relics, when he received his sight. And when he had ended his prayer, he received his sight there at the tomb.

18. Afterwards he summoned the wisest and the best men in Orkney, and there came a great multitude to Christ's Kirk at Birsay. Then were taken out of the ground the sacred relics of Earl Magnus, and then the bones were almost come up out of the ground. He then let wash the bones, and the joint of the finger to be taken and tested in the consecrated fire thrice. But it burnt not, rather it became like burned silver. Some men said it ran into the form of a cross. Then there were many miracles done by the holy relics. After that took learned men the holy relics and laid them in a shrine, and set them over the altar. That was on Lucy's day [December 13] before Yule; and then there had passed twenty years since the slaying of Earl Magnus. The day of his death is holden in spring, the sixteenth of the kalends of May [April 16]. Bishop William directed the festival to be held on either of the two days over all his bishopric; and he was afterwards in great love with the holy Earl Magnus. William was the first bishop in Orkney, and ruled sixty-six years.

* . . and prepared in every respect as becomingly as possible. Then enshrined the lord Bishop the holy relics of the blessed Earl Magnus with honour and reverence and the hymns of all the people, and there were healed all who were lacking health, and in need of pity, who at that time had thither sought his sacred relics. Earl S. Magnus was enshrined on the Feast of the Virgin Lucy, before Yule in the winter. And that day is widely held in veneration both for the holy Magnus and God's blessed Virgin Lucy, but in Spring is his home-faring day to the kingdom of heaven.

32. Now was before told, though less fitly than briefly, about the uptaking, probation, and enshrinement of the sacred relics of the blessed Earl Magnus, and not less of the fixing of his festival. And it is to be remembered and recorded that with sundry privileges does the Lord God honour his beloved friends because of their righteousness, some here immediately in this life, but others after life. Yet seem those dignities among the saints, somewhat special and surpassing, which belong to God's martyr Magnus. That is to say, that when his bone was proved at home in the Orkneys, it turned into the most beautiful cross in the eyes of the men who were present. Of this same is another example, that this same bone-cross was afterwards turned into the most brilliant gold colour even before the Lord Pope himself at Rome. Wherefore he receives this purple martyr into the Catalogue of Saints; but that has been granted to few others in these Northern lands, that he himself [the Pope] has done this. Therefore may we behold and wonder, though none may conceive it as it is, how abundant is God Almighty in His riches and in the depths of His mercy: for He grants these gifts of love to some of His friends, which He grants not to others, and divides them among them as He wills; and He fails none, though He gives the gifts of the Holy Spirit to each of them. Therefore be His name ever praised and blessed throughout the ages. Amen.

33. From that time were spread abroad and celebrated the miracles of the holy Earl Magnus over all the western and

---

* The narrative of the Greater Saga is here resumed.

northern parts of the world, and men fared from neighbouring lands, burghs and towns, castles and districts, with great hearts and offering hands, to seek his holy relics, and some sent presents to his sacred shrine, to his honour but for their own healing and salvation, both in this world and in the next. Therefore shall here be told some miracles, though but a few, from the countless number which God granted because of his merits :—

34. When Bergfinn, the franklin north in Shetland, who was named before in this history, heard the joyful tidings of the translation of the holy Earl Magnus, he fared a second time south from Shetland with his leprous son, named Halfdan, to Kirkwall; and watched, both father and son, at the sacred relics of Earl Magnus. And the holy man of God appeared to Halfdan and passed his hands over his body and at once fell from him all his leprosy. Then he rose up healed. Earl S. Magnus also appeared to the franklin Bergfinn in a dream and said to him : " Now shalt thou receive clear sight, for hither hast thou now come with a true faith and didst not distrust my sanctity, and didst offer to me fair vows, both in prayers and offerings." Then he made the sign of the Cross over Bergfinn's eyes ; and he awaked seeing as well as when he had been sharpest sighted. And father and son both fared home healed, praising God and the holy Earl Magnus.

A man, hight Thorkell, who dwelt in the Orkneys, fell off his barley-rick and was maimed all over one side when he came to the ground. He was borne to the holy Earl Magnus and received there the speedy healing of his hurt, so that his broken bones grew together again and his body was made strong. He thanked God and the holy Earl Magnus for his healing gift.

A man, called Amundi, son of Illugi, a franklin north in Shetland, was a leper and very sick. He fared to the holy Earl Magnus and watched at his shrine and prayed for mercy and healing. As he slept Magnus Earl of the Isles appeared to him and passed his hands over his body and gave him so speedy a cure that he awoke quite whole ; and gave he to God thanks for his healing and to the gracious Magnus.

A man, hight Sigurd, Tandri's son, dwelt in Shetland at the farm called Dale. He became mad, so that he was sewn up in hide. This man was carried to the holy Earl Magnus and got there his senses and complete health, and fared thence sound and whole, praising God and the holy Earl Magnus.

Another man, also hight Sigurd, north in Shetland, had his hands so twisted that all the fingers lay in the palm. He sought the sacred relics of the holy Earl Magnus and received there healing, with straightness and suppleness of his fingers for all his needs. Thanked he God for the mercy which He had granted him for the merits of Earl Magnus.

A man called Thorbiorn Olaf's son, north in Shetland, was witless and possessed of a devil. He was taken to the place of the holy Earl Magnus, and was there at once made whole, and fared back to his house rejoicing and praising God and this blessed martyr.

Thord, who was surnamed Dreka-Skolptr (Dragon-Snout), was hireling to the aforenamed franklin Bergfinn. He was threshing corn in the barley barn on the day before the mass-day of the holy Earl Magnus. But about 3 o'clock in the afternoon Bergfinn bade him leave off work. "It is very seldom," said Thord, "that it seems to thee that too much has been done." Bergfinn said: "The festival which falls tomorrow ought to be kept with all the honour we may and can." Bergfinn then went away, but Thord worked on as before. When a little while was passed, Bergfinn went out again and said to Thord in great anger: "It is the greatest offence to me that thou workest at holy times. Leave off at once on the spot." The franklin went away very wroth, but Thord went on working as before. But when men had nearly done eating, in came Thord in his working clothes and began at once to drink greedily. When he had drunk one horn of ale, he became mad, so that the men had at once to bind him with bonds and that continued for six days. Then the franklin Bergfinn promised for him to give half a mark of silver at the shrine of the holy Earl Magnus, and to let Thord watch there three nights if he might be made whole. Thord was at once healed the next night after the promise had been made for him. And all praised the Highest King of Heaven and his beloved friend the holy Earl Magnus.

It is also said that two men broke gold off from the shrine of the holy Earl Magnus ; one was a Caithness man, the other an Orkneyman. He of Caithness was lost and drowned in the Pentland Firth, and was hight Gilli. The Orkneyman went mad and told in his ravings what they had done. Then was a promise made for him of a pilgrimage to Rome if he were made whole. Afterwards he was taken to the holy Earl Magnus, and a vow was made to him for his recovery, and he became whole at once, and praised God and the holy Earl Magnus.

There was a man called Asmund. On his head fell a great tree and broke all his skull, but the oft-named franklin Bergfinn made a vow for him ; and lots were cast whether there should be promised for him a pilgrimage to Rome or an offering to the Church of Magnus. And the lot came up that he should visit the sacred relics of the holy Earl Magnus. He obtained at once the use of his tongue which he had before lost. He fared then after that to the holy Earl Magnus and watched there and obtained a complete cure of all his hurts. And the franklin Bergfinn gave to Earl Magnus half a mark of silver weighed as he had promised.

There was a woman called Sigrid ; she was the daughter of Sigurd of Sand north in Shetland. She was blind from tender babyhood until she was twenty. Her father took her south to Orkney and let her watch at the shrine of Earl S. Magnus. He offered there a great present. Sigrid received then clear sight in both eyes, and they fared thence, father and daughter, rejoicing and praising God and the holy Earl Magnus.

There was another woman also called Sigrid, daughter of Arnfrid, from the farmstead called Unst north in Shetland. Her leg was broken in twain, and she was taken to the holy Earl Magnus ; and was quickly cured, and thanked God and the holy Earl Magnus.

A third woman also called Sigrid from Unst north in Shetland, was working with the franklin hight Thorlak who lived at Bollastede (Batlasta). Sigrid was sewing in the evening before the mass-day of the holy Earl Magnus after others were keeping the festival. Thorlak enquired why she worked so long, and she answered she would stop. The franklin went out, but she sewed as before. Then came Thorlak again to her and said: "Why doest thou so wrongly at so holy a time? Now go away and work no longer in my house." She made light of the offence, and then went on sewing as before till it was dark night. But when the men were getting ready to eat, Sigrid became mad so that she had at once to be put in bonds and was grievously possessed, till Thorlak made a promise for her and lots were cast, whether she should fare to Rome or give goods to Earl Magnus. And the lot was thrown that she should go to Kirkwall to the sacred relics of the holy Earl Magnus. Afterwards she was taken thither and got there a wonderful gift of healing of her madness; and she praised God and his exalted knight Earl Magnus, nevertheless she afterwards fared to Rome for her salvation.

A woman called Groa, from Hrossey, was possessed by an evil spirit and fared to Kirkwall to the holy Earl Magnus, and got there a good cure, and praised God and the holy Earl Magnus.

There was a woman named Ragnhild; she became a cripple when she was four winters old and all up till she was twenty, then watched she three nights at the holy relics of the Earl S. Magnus. On the third night there appeared to her in her sleep a man bright and glorious, and splendidly clad, and said to her: "Long and often hast thou lain here, great is thy need, rise up now and be made whole and take this staff in thine hand." After that he vanished from her. But she wakened; she was then holding on to the lock that was on the aumbry on the other side of the Magnus choir. Rose she then up at once completely healed, as if she had never been crippled, with sound bones and sinews, praising God and the holy Earl Magnus. She was with the bishop many winters.

Asa was the name of a woman who had all her days been a cripple. She obtained so excellent a cure from the blessed

Earl Magnus, that she went to Rome that same summer she was healed.

Gudrun was the name of a woman; she was a cripple for a long time. She obtained a speedy cure of her maimness and a complete cure through the merit and intercession of the holy Earl Magnus, and praised God and his beloved Earl Magnus.

There was a man called Sigurd. He was alms-man at Knot-Sand. He was so very decrepit that he crept on his knees and could not stand upright. He was cured at the shrine of Earl Magnus. He praised God and the holy Magnus.

Two Southerners cast dice for money—one lost a hundred marks. Then was lost all his wealth, except one cog he had left. He then staked the cog against every thing he had lost. Then he who won before, threw two sixes. But for his help the other made a vow to the holy Earl Magnus, that he might get back the rest of his property. After that he threw, and turned up six on one dice, but the other sprang asunder in two parts, and there were seven spots on the two together and thirteen on the three; and so he won back all his wealth.

35. It happened in Norway, in the days of Harold Gilli, that some rich men and distinguished gave out that two brothers intended to beguile their kinswomen. But the accusation was not true. All the same, the two rich men attacked them, and took them captive, carrying them away from others into a wood, and slew the one of whom they had the greater suspicion. Afterwards they took the other and gave him many and hard tortures with much cruelty, insomuch that they brake in sunder both his legs and as well his arms. After this these cruel men put out both his eyes, therewith cutting his tongue away out of his head, and in such inhuman wise leaving him, they went away; but he lay there half dead. As soon as they were away, leapt out from the woods many wolves, riving and tearing the flesh from the bones of him who was slain, faring after back into the wood. But of him who was wounded it is to be told that though he could not pray with his tongue for pity, he continually bethought him that Almighty God would grant him some help. Especially did his mind turn there where the holy Earl Magnus was, for at that time

was flourishing most of all his miracle-working. And when he had made a vow, he became aware that a man was come to him who was stroking his broken arms and legs. Therewith he takes the short part of his tongue and brings it to its place at last; he then lays his hand on the sockets of his eyes. And with this handling came a wonderful change; the eyes took their places with clear vision, the tongue immediately becomes framed for all kinds of speech, the broken limbs were healed, and all his former health restored. He sees standing by him a man of fair countenance, with whom he spake, saying: "What is thy name, noble lord?" The resplendent man answers: "Here is Earl Magnus, but take good heed to perform that which thou hast promised to the Lord." At this he became joyful, and spake thus to him again: "Since, exalted friend of God, thou hast granted to me a great gift of healing, I beseech also of thy clemency to intercede with God for my brother's life." After he had thus spoken, the holy Magnus vanished away from his sight without answering to his prayer. But he fell down and thanked God for the mercy vouchsafed to himself, intending to bide in that place two nights in steadfast prayer for the help of his brother. And as the time wore on he looks round, and sees a great pack of wolves run from the wood to where the corpse lay, and spew up there all they had eaten of his flesh and bones, and turn again to the wood. And when a little time was passed, he sees S. Magnus come, and bless with his right hand all the wolves' vomit and the bones; then next to this the body becomes all sound. S. Magnus blesses again his lifeless body, wherefore he rises up whole and living who before was slain, and goes to his brother. Greeted then each of them the other, giving thanks to God and the holy Magnus for so marvellous a mercy as had been granted them. So also let all hearing such miracles, give manifold praise to the true God, who grants such wonderful things to sinful men because of the prayers and merits of his own best beloved friends.

19.* There was a trusty franklin in Westray, called Gunni. He dreamt that the holy Earl Magnus came to him and said:

---

* This and the following chapters are from the Lesser Saga.

"This shalt thou say to Bishop William, that I would fare out of Birsay east to Kirkwall, and I trust that God will there grant me of His mercy that those who seek me there with a true faith may be healed of their pains. Thou shalt tell thy dream boldly." But when he awoke, he did not dare to tell the dream, because he feared the wrath of Earl Paul. The following night Earl Magnus appeared to him and bade him tell the dream when many were by : " But if thou dost not do so, thou shalt suffer punishment in this world and more in the next." And when he awoke he was filled with fear and fared to Hrossey to see the bishop, and tells the dream at the bishop's mass in a great crowd of men. Earl Paul was there, and all the people prayed the bishop to bear the sacred relics to Kirkwall as Earl Magnus had shown. But Earl Paul stood by silent, and turned blood red. After that fared Bishop William east to Kirkwall with a noble retinue and bore thither the sacred relics of Earl Magnus. The shrine was set over the altar in the Church which is there. There was then at Kirkwall but a trading village with few houses, but it has since greatly increased. Many men have since fared thither and watched there in the Church at the holy relics and have been healed if they vowed to Earl Magnus with true faith.

20. When Earl Rognvald Kali, sister's son to Earl S. Magnus, had come to rule in the Orkneys, and was quietly seated, he caused the ground-plan of the Magnus Church in Kirkwall to be marked out, and got workmen for it, and the work went on well and swiftly ; and it is a noble work and well finished. Afterwards were the sacred relics of Earl Magnus flitted thither, and many signs were wrought there at his holy relics. There is now also a bishop's see which was before at Christ's Kirk in Birsay.

A man, called Eldjarn, the son of Vardi, had a wife and many children, and lived north in Kelduhverf. But during a bad season he became poor and sick, so that he could not help himself, and so little strength had he that he was unable to walk and was driven about among the homesteads. It fell after Easter in spring that he had been driven about on Thursday, Friday, and Saturday, and had had no food. He came at nones on Saturday to where the priest lived and was there through the night. In the morning when men fared to matins, he prayed that he might be taken to the Church; and it was done. After the matins men fared indoors between the services. But he lay out of doors there where his bed was made: he was so feeble that he thought he was about to die. It came also into his mind how he had been before his poverty when he had his property all together, and his prayer which he prayed, touched him so much that he was greatly moved. Then he took and promised a six days' fast, if God would give him some relief: this fast he vowed both before S. Olaf's and S. Magnus' day. When he had uttered his vow, men came to the service and the priest sang mass. When the Epistle was read he fell asleep, but those who were beside him thought he was about to die. In his sleep a vision passed before him, in which he thought he saw a great light within the choir, and that it came out to him. He saw with the light a beautiful man, and he said to him: "Eldjarn! hast thou little strength now?" He thought he answered: "So methinks, though perhaps it may not be so. But who art thou?" He answers: "I am Earl S. Magnus, Erlend's son. Wilt thou be made whole?" He answers: "I will." He replied: "King S. Olaf also has heard thy prayer and the vow which thou hast made to us two for thy healing. But he sent me hither to give thee healing: for a woman made a vow to him west in the Firths, and he has fared thither to make her whole." Then began Earl Magnus to pass his hands over him, but he woke up when the Gospel was begun. He asked the men who stood nearest him to lift him up. But they answered: "Why should we lift thee up, when thou hast no strength?" He replies: "I think I am now cured." They took him and raised him on to his feet, and he stood all through the Gospel and so on to the end of the mass. After mass he went in to the priest and tells the miracle, how God had given him healing. And all praised God for the mercy which He had granted to him for the merit of Earl S. Magnus. May he obtain for us mercy and pardon for our sins from our Lord Jesus Christ, who, with the Father and the Holy Spirit, liveth and reigneth God for ever and ever. Amen.

INDEX.

INDEX.

	PAGE
Ached-bou,	108
Aethne, mother of S. Columba,	53
Aid the Black,	83
Aid, son of Ainmurech,	94
Aid, King,	66, 67
Aidan, King,	33, 65, 149
Aid Slane,	68
Aidan, son of Fergno,	76
Ailbine, Delvine,	100
Ainmire, son of Setna, King,	64
Airtheara, Kings of,	89
Airthrago, island of,	143
Ait-Chambas Art-Muirchol,	115
Alva,	291
Aporic Lake, the,	128
Artbranan,	81
Ard Ceannachte,	101
Ardnamurchan,	67
Artur, son of Aidan,	65, 66
Baitan, of Lathreginden,	72
Bede, the Venerable, his statements as to SS. Ninian and Columba,	5
Berach,	71
Berchan, surnamed Mesloen,	162
Boend, river,	104
Bos, river,	88
Brecan, whirlpool of,	107
Breg, plain of,	86
Brenden Mocualti,	76
Brito, a monk,	150
Broichan, the Druid,	124, 125
Brude, King,	55, 124, 126
Brude, King, son of Dagart,	289
Cailtan,	79
Campulus Bovis,	108
Candida Casa,	11
Catlon, King, defeated and slain by Oswald,	57
Cellrois, monastery of,	89
Cethirn, fortress and well of,	94
Christ's Kirk, Birsay, burial of S. Magnus, 353; enshrinement of his relics,	356, 357
Clochur,	102
Clonifinchoil, monastery of,	169
Cnoc Angel,	158

	PAGE
Cogreth, lake,	92
Coire Salchain,	92
Colga, son of Aid Draigniche,	70
Colga, son of Cellach,	82, 103, 157
Colonsay, island of,	87, 115
Colman, the Hound,	89
Columb, a blacksmith,	153
Cooldrevny, battle of,	53, 64
Congal, abbot,	94
Conall, bishop of Coleraine,	95
Connal, King,	64
Cronan, bishop,	90
Cronan, the poet,	88
Culross,	187, 289
Cuuleilne, in Iona,	84
Daire Calgaich,	134
Dairmaig (Durrow),	61, 95, 99
Deathrib, great cell of,	96
Deisuit, her sight restored by S. Ninian,	27
Delvin, the river,	101
Dermit, King (Aid Slane),	68
Diormit, King,	82
Diormit, S. Columba's servant,	42, 44, 65, 67, 74, 76, 78, 81, 96, 121, 122, 166
Diuni, a monk,	79
Domingart, son of Aidan,	65, 66
Domnall, son of Aid,	66
Domnall, son of Mac Erca,	65
Druids,	55, 106, 124
Druim Ceatt,	66, 103
Drumalban,	81
Drumpelder, hill of,	184
Dunning,	292
Dysart,	289
Echoid, Bude,	66
Echoid Find, son of Aidan,	65, 66
Echoid Laib,	65
Edgar, King,	300
Edmund, King,	298
Eigg, island of,	160
Eilean-na-naiomh,	33, 37, 91, 117, 149, 159, 160
Elgu, the river,	229
Elne plain of,	95
Emchath,	156

368   INDEX.

	PAGE		PAGE
Erco Mocudruidi, a thief,	87	Holdbodi,	347
Erland, Earl in the Orkneys, 326; his sons quarrel with Hakon, Earl Paul's son, 328; driven from the Orkneys to Norway by Magnus Bareleg, 333; dies at Nidross,	335	Hynba (Eilean-na-Naoimh), 33, 37, 73, 91, 112, 117, 159,	160, 170
		Ictean Sea,	288
		Inchkeith, island of,	288
		Indairthir, Anterii,	151
Ernan,	69	Iogenan,	105
Ernan, uncle of S. Columba,	91	Iona, island of, 69, 71, 72, 87, 120, 131, 155, 157, 163,	
Ernene, son of Crasen,	61		171, 264
Failbhe, Abbot of Iona,	57	Islay, isle of,	116
Farres Last,	18	Jocelin, Bishop of Glasgow,	177
Fechna, a penitent,	78	John, son of Conall,	115
Fedilmith, father of S. Columba,	53	Kinel,	288
Feradach,	116	Kernach (Carnoch),	199
Field of the Two Streams, monastery of,	128	Lairran Mocumoie, the gardener,	71
Finten, son of Aid,	122	Laisran, son of Feradach,	67, 78
Forcus, son of Mac Erea,	65	Laloecen,	279
Ford Clied, Dublin,	101	Lam-deas,	117
Gallan, son of Fachtna,	82	Langueth, Queen,	256
Gemman,	118	Lea, district of	74
Germanus, Bishop,	126	Ledon, the river,	199
Glasderc,	69	Libran of the Rush-ground,	131
Gore, son of Aidan,	92	Lifolf,	350
Hakon, Earl, son of Earl Paul, 327; his pride, 328; molests the sons of Earl Erlend, 329; goes to Norway, ibid.; consults a spaeman, ibid.; visits Magnus Bareleg, 331; receives his patrimony from the Kings of Norway and the title of Earl, 336; seizes the whole Earldom of the Orkneys and slays the King's steward, ibid.; on the arrival of Magnus comes to an agreement with him, 337; a quarrel fomented between him and Magnus, 340; seizes the whole Earldom and Caithness, 342; agreement with Magnus, 343; another quarrel fomented between him and Magnus, 344; they meet at Hrossey, ibid., and agree to meet at Egilsey after Easter, 345; their meeting there, 349; the slaying of Magnus, 350; goes to the house of Thora, who begs of him the body of Magnus, her son, 353; rules the Earldom, 354; makes a pilgrimage to the Rome, Jerusalem and the Jordan, in which he bathes, ibid.; his rule,	ibid.	Lothwerverd,	270
		Lough Key,	88, 112
		Lugaid, surnamed Laitir,	130
		Lugbe Mocumiu, messenger of S. Columba, 69, 75, 77, 87, 119	
		Lugne, a pilot,	137
		Lugne Mocublai,	157
		Lugne Mocumin,	119
		Lugucencalad,	106
		Lugud Clodus,	86
		Lunge, plain of,	88, 109
		Magnus Bareleg, is visited by Hakon, 331; visits the Orkneys with a fleet, compels Earls Paul and Erlend to go to Norway and their sons to accompany him on his expedition south, 333; subdues the Hebrides and overcomes Hugh the Stout and Hugh the Brave, 334; returns to the Orkneys and Norway, 335; his death,	ibid.
		Malcolm, son of Duncan, King,	301
		Mallena, the river,	197
		Manus Dexters,	117
		Maugina, daughter of Daimen,	102
		Maugdorn, district of,	89
		Mayonius, Bishop of Alexandria,	284
		Melconde Galganu,	231
		Meldan,	69
		Mellindenor, Molindenar,	265
		Miathi, battle of,	65
		Monglas,	288
Harald, Sigurd's son,	328	Morken, King of Cambria, 221, 223, 225	

INDEX. 369

	PAGE
Morthec,	279
Muirbolc Paradisi,	67
Mull, island of,	87
Munbu (S. Kentigern),	194
Munitio Magna,	100
Neman, son of Gruthrich,	86
Ness, the river,	119
Nigra Dea, river of,	129
Oingus, son of Aid Comman,	68
Oissene, son of Ernan,	61
Ommon, island of,	83
Ondemone, battle of,	64
Oswald, King, his vision, 46, 56; made Bretwalda,	57
Paul, Earl, in the Orkneys, 326; his sons quarrel with those of Earl Erlend, 328; is compelled to leave the Orkneys for Norway by Magnus Bareleg, 333; dies at Bergen,	335
Pertnech, Patrick,	279
Picts, Northern,	55
Picts, Southern, converted by S. Ninian,	15
Pilu, a Saxon,	163
Pons Servani,	197
Plague, the,	144
Rechrea, island of,	137
Rederech, 244, 247, 250, 256, 260,	278
Roderc, son of Tothal, King of Alcluith, 69. *See* Rederech.	
Robert, Master, 325, 351,	353
Rognvald Kali, 335; founds the Magnus Church at Kirkwall,	304
Ronan, son of Aid,	89
S. Adamnan, his reasons for writing the life of S. Columba, 51; meets Servanus, 288; is visited by him,	289
S. Ailred complains of the manners of his age,	19
S. Asaph,	232, 246
S. Baithene, Abbot of Iona, 59, 72, 74, 84, 109, 152,	160
S. Brendan, of Birr, his death revealed to S. Columba, 34, 154; sees an angel accompanying him,	147
S. Cainnech, Abbot of Achedbou,	63, 108
S. Ceran of Clonmacnoise,	61
S. Colman, in danger in the whirlpool of Brecan,	63
S. Columba, his Life by Cuimene the Fair, 31-47; his nativity, 31, 147*; a globe of fire appears over his face, 32, 147; he has an angel for his companion, *ibid.*, 148; turns water into wine, *ibid.*; is shown the glass book of the ordination of Kings, consecrates Aidan king, and foretells future things concerning his son, 33, 149; sees a monk received up into heaven, 34, 150; has the death of S. Brendan revealed to him, also the death of S. Columban, 35, 155; he fights with demons, *ibid.*, 152; by means of an angel renders help to a monk in Ireland though himself in Iona, 36, 157; he converses with angels, 37, 157; a ball of fire is seen to rise from his head, *ibid.*, 159; enjoys celestial visions during three days, 38, 160; relieves a poor man, *ibid.*; is suffused with heavenly light, 39, 161, 162; his life is prolonged, 40, 164; he predicts his own death, 41, 164; sees an angel, *ibid.*, 165; indicates the hour of his death, 42, 166; his occupation just before his death, *ibid.*, 168; his last words, 43, 168; dies in the Church, *ibid.*, 169; burial, 44; the storm during his obsequies, 45, 171; various miracles, *ibid.*; a miracle wrought by his tunic, 47, 147; a prediction concerning Ernene, son of Crasen, ... *ibid.*	
Life by S. Adamnan, 51-174; meaning of his name, 52; his birth predicted by Maucta, *ibid.*; his parentage and childhood, 53; his miracles, 55; a prophecy he uttered concerning S. Fintan, son of Tailchan, 60; Ernene, son of Crasen, 61; the speedy arrival of S. Cainnech, 63; prays for the safety of bishop Colman, *ibid.*; prophesies concerning Cormac, 64; foretells the issue of the battle between King Ainmire and the two sons of Mac Erca, Domnel and Forcus, *ibid.*; also of the battle of the Miathi, 65; prophecies	

---

* The second numbers refer to the same incidents in S. Adamnan's Life.

concerning the sons of Aidan, *ibid.;* Domnal, son of Aid, 66; Scandlan, son of Colman, *ibid.;* Baitan and Echoid, 67; Oingus, 68; Aid Slane, *ibid.;* King Roderc, 69; two boys, *ibid.;* Colga, son of Aid Draigniche, 70; Laisran, the gardener, *ibid.;* a great whale, 71; a certain Baitan, 72; one Neman, 73; one guilty of incest, *ibid.;* the vowel I, 75; a book, *ibid.;* his inkhorn, *ibid.;* the arrival of a guest, 76; a man calling out from the other side of the Straits, *ibid.;* a Roman city, 77; a vision concerning Laisran, son of Feradach, 78; prophecies concerning a penitent, *ibid.;* his monk Cailtan, 79; two brothers, 80; Artbranan, 81; a fire, *ibid.;* Gallan, son of Fachtna, 82; Findchan, 82; the consolation he sent to his wearied monks, 83; his voice, 85; he chants evensong before the gates of King Brade, *ibid.;* prophecies concerning Lugud Clodus, 86; Neman, son of Gruthrich, *ibid.;* a priest in Trioit, 87; the thief Erco Mocudruidi, *ibid.;* the poet Cronan, 88; two noblemen, 89; he recognises in a visitor a bishop, 90; prophecies concerning Ernan, the priest, 91; a peasant, 92; Gore, son of Aidan, *ibid.;* a crane, 93; the fortress of the Cethirn and its well, 94; certain presents, 96; he turns water into wine, 98; makes the bitter fruit of a tree sweet, 99; causes corn sown after midsummer to be reaped in August, *ibid.;* by blessing water cures many, 100; water into which a box he had blessed was dipped heals Maugina, 102; the cure of divers diseases at the Ridge of Ceatt, 103; salt blessed by the Saint cannot be consumed by fire, *ibid.;* a book written by him is not destroyed by water, 104; a similar miracle, *ibid.;* water caused to flow from a hard rock, 105; a prophecy concerning Lugucencalad, 106; the water of another fountain sweetened, *ibid.;* he stills a tempest, 107; his prayers rescue Cainnech, *ibid.;* the miracle of Cainnech's staff, 108; he gives prosperous winds to Baithene and Columban though sailing in different directions, 109; drives a demon out of a milk-pail, 110; he discovers and brings to naught the works of a sorcerer, 111; heals Lugne Mocumin, 112; miracle of the salmon, *ibid.;* he indicates where two fish will be found, *ibid.;* increases the herd of Nesan, and prophesies the minishing of Uigene's, 113; multiplies the number of Columban's cows, 114; prophesies the death of John, son of Conall, who had despised him, 115; also of Feradach, 116; of Manus Dextra, 117; of another oppressor of the innocent, 118; slays a wild boar with his word, 119; drives back an aquatic monster in the river Ness, *ibid.;* drives poisonous reptiles out of Iona, 120; blesses a knife so that it will hurt neither man nor beast, 121; cures Diormit, 122; Finten, son of Aid, *ibid.;* raises a dead boy to life, 123; causes the Druid Broichan to be seized with sickness, and a captive maiden to be set free, 124; he overcomes Broichan, 126; causes the gates of King Brude's fortress to open, 127; also the doors of a church, *ibid.;* provides for a poor peasant by blessing a stake, 128; predicts that the flowing tide will bring back a milk-skin which the ebb had taken away, 130; his prophecy concerning Libran, 131; his prayer brings help to a woman in child-birth, 139; he reconciles Tutida and his wife, 137; his prophecy respecting Cormac,

INDEX. 371

grandson of Lethan, 139; his prayers change the directions of the winds, 142; and protect against the plague, 144; the apparition of angels which S. Brendan saw about him, 147; he sees angels carrying the soul of the blacksmith Columb to heaven, 153; the soul of a woman, *ibid.*; sees angels meet the soul of S. Brenden of Birr, 154; also the soul of S. Comgell, *ibid.*; and the soul of Emchath, 156; he sees angels coming to meet his own soul, 163; a white pack horse places its head in his bosom and seems to bemoan the Saint's approaching end, 167; his death revealed to Lugud, son of Tailchan, 169; to Ernene, 170; his twelve companions, 173; his parents and relatives, ... *ibid.*
S. Columba visits Kentigern,.. 264
S. Columban, death revealed, ... 35
S. Comgel, ... 95
S. Cormac, grandson of Lethan, 64, 138
S. David, ... 226, 229, 235
S. Fernaus sees S. Columba surrounded with heavenly light, 39
S. Findchan, founder of Artchain, Tiree,.................... 82
S. Findbarr (Vinnian), bishop, a teacher of S. Columba,...... 98
S. Finnian sees an angel accompanying S. Columba, 32; celebrates Mass when water drawn by S. Columba is turned into wine,.............. *ibid.*
S. Finnio, a teacher of S. Columba, sees an angel accompanying him,.................... 148
S. Fintan, Abbot, son of Tailchan, S. Columba's prophecy concerning him,................ 58
S. Kentigern, conception, 179; birth, 184; education, 187; is falsely accused and restores a bird to life, 189; kindles fire by breathing upon a hazel bough, 191; raises the dead cook to life, 194; leaves S. Serf, 196; visits Fregus at Carnoch, 199; blesses Anguen, 201; the punishment of Telleyr, 202; election and consecration as bishop at Glasgow, 203; his example and doctrine, 206; his dress, 207; couch, vigils and bath, *ibid.*; his mode of speaking, 209; is adorned while celebrating Mass, *ibid.*; how he spent Lent, 211; the brightness of his countenance, and his opinion of hypocrites, 214; he converts and edifies the people, 216; yokes a stag and a wolf together in a plough, and, sowing sand, reaps wheat, 218; uses the force of the Clyde to confute Morken, 221; is struck by Morken, 223; withdraws to Wales, 226; meets S. David, 227, and Cathwallain, 228; led by a white boar to the spot he builds a monastery on the banks of the Elgu, 229; is opposed by Melconde Galganu, 231; number of brethren in the monastery, 233; sees S. David crowned in heaven, 235; his prediction concerning Britain, 236; visits to Rome, 237; Pope Gregory confirms his election, 240; the character of two clerics revealed to him, *ibid.*; divine vengeance overtakes his adversaries, 242; is invited back to Strathclyde by King Rederech, 244; leaves S. Asaph to govern the monastery and sets out for Cambria, 246; his reception and and works, 248; is honoured by King Rederech, 250; his zeal, success and miracles, 252; the miraculous protection of his clothes, 254; he restores to the Queen her ring, which had been thrown into the Clyde, 256; he provides fresh mulberries after Christmas, 260; milk turned into cheese when spilled into the river, 263; is visited by S. Columba, 264; he relieves and converts certain thieves who had killed one of his sheep, the head of which stuck to the hands of him who had seized it, and had been turned to stone, 267; he erects crosses

in various places, 268; he prepares for death, 271; his disciples desire to die with him, 273; the manner of his death, 275; his burial, ... 279

S. Margaret, her descent and virtues, 298; marriage, 301; builds the Church of the Holy Trinity at Dumfermline, *ibid.*; presents a magnificent cross to the Church at St. Andrews, 302; her chamber like the workshop of a heavenly artificer, *ibid.*; the women she employed, *ibid.*; her care for her children, 303; for the honour of the kingdom, 304; the King's devotion to her, and her influence over him, *ibid.*; encourages trade, 305; her influence over the Court, *ibid.*; reforms the Church, 306; her charity, manner of passing Lent, and prayerfulness, 310; redeems captives, 312; places vessels for the conveyance of pilgrims across the Forth, *ibid.*; her copy of the Gospels is miraculously preserved, 315; her preparations for death, 316; her last illness and death, 318; her burial, ... 321

S. Martin of Tours visited by S. Ninian, ... 10

S. Maucta, prediction concerning S. Columba, ... 51

S. Ninian, his birth, 6; parentage, baptism and education, 7; his arrival at Rome, 8; his studies there, 9; is sent by the Pope to Britain, *ibid.*; visits S. Martin of Tours, 10; desires masons of him, *ibid.*; builds the Church of S. Martin at Whithorn, 11; heals and converts King Tudvallus, *ibid.*; vindicates an innocent presbyter, 13; undertakes the conversion of the Southern Picts, 15; his miracle among the leeks, 16; he protects certain cattle, 17; restores a thief to life, 18; is protected when reading against the rain, 20; why on one occasion he was not, 20; a miracle wrought by his staff, *ibid.*; the miracles wrought by his relics, ... 25-28

S. Servanus (Serf), ... 178, 191

S. Servanus, his conception, 283; baptism and education, 284; ordination, *ibid.*; elected bishop of the Canaanites, *ibid.*; patriarch of Jerusalem, 285; resides at Constantinople, 286; visits the island of Salvatoria, *ibid.*; elected to the Chair of S. Peter at Rome, *ibid.*; leaves Rome, *ibid.*; ascends the Alps, 287; he and his company are assailed in the Valley of Beasts, *ibid.*; crosses the Ictean Sea, 288; meets S. Adamnan, *ibid.*; arrives at Kinel, *ibid.*; takes up his abode at Culross, 289; is opposed by Brude, son of Dagart, *ibid.*; builds a church, *ibid.*; visits Adamnan in the island of Leven, *ibid.*; restores a brother in the cave at Dysart, *ibid.*; his controversy with the Devil in the same cave, 290; cures a man of an evil spirit at Tillicoultry, 291; a miracle performed at Alva, *ibid.*; slays the dragon in the Dragon's Den at Dunning, 292; is visited by three men from the Alps whom he heals, *ibid.*; his death and burial at Culross, ... 295

Salvatoria, island of, ... 286
Saxonia, ... 66
Scandlan, son of Colman, ... 66
Seghine, Abbot of Iona, ... 57, 62
Sigurd, one of Hakon's retainers, 344
Sigvat Sokki, one of Hakon's retainers, ... 344
Silnan, a monk, ... 87, 100
Skye, isle of, ... 81, 119
Snam-luthir, monastery of, ... 141
Snorri Sturlason, ... 335
Suibne, son of Columban, ... 68

S. Magnus, his parentage, 326; early virtues, 327; youth and conduct, 332; is compelled to accompany Magnus Bareleg, and is made his table swain, 333; his conduct during the battle in the Menai Straits, 334; he escapes from Magnus Bareleg, *ibid.*; visits the Court of Malcolm Canmore, 335, and a certain bis-

INDEX.

hop in Wales, *ibid.;* goes to Caithness and receives the title of Earl, 336 ; his austerities, *ibid.;* goes to the Orkneys and comes to an agreement with Hakon, 337 ; the agreement confirmed by the King of Norway, *ibid.;* his character as a ruler, 338; a quarrel fomented between him and Hakon, 340 ; he visits the English Court, 341 ; his return to the North, 342 ; reconciliation of Hakon, 343; another quarrel fomented between him and Hakon, 344 ; they meet at Hrossey, *ibid.*, and agree to meet at Egilsey after Easter, 345; their meeting there, 346; his death, 350; his burial in Christ's Kirk, Birsay, 353; sick men healed at his grave, *ibid.;* enshrinement of his relics, 356, 357 ; canonisation, 357 ; his miracles, 355, 358, *et seq.;* translation of his relics to Kirkwall, ... 364

Taneu, mother of S. Kentigern, 179, 188
Tarain, ... 116
Tauri Vestigium, ... 18
Tillicoultry, ... 291
Tiree, island of, ... 71, 72, 109
Tomma, Ridge of, ... 170
Trena, a monk, ... 70
Triot, monastery of, ... 87
Tudvallus, his conversion by S. Ninian, ... 11
Valley of Beasts, ... 287
Virgnous, Abbot, ... 161
William, Bishop of the Orkneys, refuses to believe in the miracles wrought at the grave of S. Magnus, and how he is brought to honour him, ... 355, 356

www.ingramcontent.com/pod-product-compliance
Lightning Source LLC
Chambersburg PA
CBHW020836020526
44114CB00040B/950